THE TOURISM SYSTEM

An Introductory Text

Robert Christie Mill

School of Hotel and Restaurant Management
University of Denver

Alastair M. Morrison

The Economic Planning Group of Canada
Ontario

PRENTICE-HALL, INC., Englewood Cliffs, New Jersey 07632

Library of Congress Cataloging in Publication Data

Mill, Robert Christie.
  The tourism system.

  Includes bibliographies and indexes.
  1. Tourist trade. I. Morrison, Alastair M.
II. Title.
G155.A1M5   1984   380.1'459104   84–18289
ISBN 0-13-925645-8

Editorial/production supervision
  and interior design by Margaret Rizzi
Cover design: Lundgren Graphics, Ltd.
Manufacturing buyer: Ed O'Dougherty

Printed in the United States of America

10 9 8 7 6 5 4 3 2 1

ISBN 0-13-925645-8   01

Prentice-Hall International, Inc., *London*
Prentice-Hall of Australia Pty. Limited, *Sydney*
Editora Prentice-Hall do Brasil, Ltda., *Rio de Janeiro*
Prentice-Hall Canada Inc., *Toronto*
Prentice-Hall of India Private Limited, *New Delhi*
Prentice-Hall of Japan, Inc., *Tokyo*
Prentice-Hall of Southeast Asia Pte. Ltd., *Singapore*
Whitehall Books Limited, *Wellington, New Zealand*

To

Patty Mill

Calum and *Jessie Morrison*

Market 1,2,3,4.

Travel 5,6,7

Destination 8,9,10,11,12,13.

CONTENTS

Marketing 14,15,16

Part One

Market ↓

4
TRAVEL PURCHASE:
The Traveler's Buying Process   *69*

5
PURPOSES OF TRAVEL:
The Characteristics of Traveler Segments   *98*

6

GEOGRAPHY OF TRAVEL:
The Characteristics of Traveler Flows   *118*

7

MODES OF TRAVEL:
People-Mover Alternatives   *146*

Summary p. 173

Part three:
Destinations

Summary P. 344

FOREWORD

When I was asked by the authors to write the foreword to this book, I was suddenly aware that I knew little about North American tourism, other than as a tourist to that vast and spectacular continent, or as one who likes to be on the receiving end of as many North America's citizens as the transatlantic carriers care to send on vacation to Scotland.

Therein, perhaps, lies the first reason why *The Tourism System* is such a welcome addition to the body of tourism literature. In both domestic and international terms, tourism is a major industry in Canada and the United States, yet little has been written on this industry from a North American standpoint. Here is a text written specifically for students familiar with that environment and which can be related to immediate experiences. However, it is also valuable to those of us operating in the tourism industry outwith North America, who, in dealing with U.S. and Canadian visitors, can better do so through a closer understanding of their domestic tourism industry.

Any introductory text should provide an easier understanding of the temporary mass migratory movements of people throughout the world, movements that are done in the name of leisure and tourism. *The Tourism System* provides such an understanding. Although the roots of tourism can be traced to Europe in the late eighteenth and nineteenth centuries—a period in which the North American nations were forging their own national identities and prosperity—it is the industrial and technological advances of the twentieth century that have spawned the mushroomlike growth of tourism. It is a service industry that has its component parts in many other industries; it is seen by many to produce employment and prosperity; it is seen by others to cause environmental problems and create social problems. In this light, it differs little from the many other major forms of industrial activity that create economic wealth for nations; yet somehow it continues to have to prove itself as a legitimate, respectable "industry" in many countries.

In order to progress in understanding the tourism system, it is, however, essential to understand not only the component parts and applications of different skills, but also the linkages and relationships between these components that in their entirety create *The Tourism System.*

Thus, while the text contains the anticipated and familiar elements of an introductory volume on tourism—marketing, transportation, planning, legislation, and so on—it is the added dimension of examining the linkages between the segments of the system that enhances the value of this book to the student. The authors have consciously and rightly identified the important, but often forgotten, linkages in the tourism system as being fundamental to its comprehension.

I believe that *The Tourism System* is an innovative new introductory text for tourism students. Tourism is a multimillion dollar international industry. Alongside microtechnology and bioengineering it offers extensive potential for the future. It is essential, therefore, that it attracts the best professional minds to work in the industry—not simply advertising experts, hotel entrepreneurs, and operators or airline directors, but professionals who understand the entire scope of tourism, not simply one enclave of the industry.

The Tourism System gives the opportunity to students setting out on this road to start with a sound understanding of the industry that will be their future.

David A. Pattison, *Chief Executive*
Scottish Tourist Board

PREFACE

In writing this book we set out to do two things: describe how tourism works and indicate how people who are part of tourism can utilize this knowledge to make tourism work for them and their particular business or destination.

Tourism is a difficult phenomenon to describe. We have trouble in thinking of tourism as an industry. The idea of a "tourism industry" would give some unity to the idea of tourism, and from an image and a political viewpoint it sounds attractive. From an image viewpoint, tourism is presently thought of in ambiguous terms. No definitions of tourism are universally accepted. There is a link between tourism, travel, recreation, and leisure, yet the link is fuzzy. All tourism involves travel, yet not all travel is tourism. All tourism involves recreation, yet not all recreation is tourism. All tourism occurs during leisure time, but not all leisure time is given to tourist pursuits. The definition of tourism as an industry with clearly defined limits would aid both those within and outside of tourism in getting a clear picture of what tourism is all about. With a clear image would come a better understanding.

The idea of a "tourism industry" is also attractive politically. One of tourism's strengths is the fact that its effect is felt by many businesses, organizations, and people. The tourist dollar finds its way into many pockets. At first glance this might seem ideal as a means of gathering political support for the development, management, and marketing of tourism. However, this apparent strength is a basic weakness for those interested in tourism. Because tourism touches so many people in major or minor ways, the overall effect is difficult to totally measure or appreciate.

THE TOURISM SYSTEM

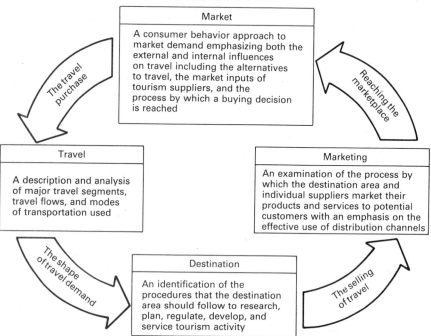

Market

A consumer behavior approach to market demand emphasizing both the external and internal influences on travel including the alternatives to travel, the market inputs of tourism suppliers, and the process by which a buying decision is reached

The travel purchase

Reaching the marketplace

Travel

A description and analysis of major travel segments, travel flows, and modes of transportation used

Marketing

An examination of the process by which the destination area and individual suppliers market their products and services to potential customers with an emphasis on the effective use of distribution channels

The shape of travel demand

Destination

An identification of the procedures that the destination area should follow to research, plan, regulate, develop, and service tourism activity

The selling of travel

There is no standard industrial classification number for "tourism." Also, many people whose lives or businesses are touched by tourism are primarily engaged in other activities serving other markets. The storekeeper sells to tourists and local people. The museum serves visitors and residents. We may know that tourism affects us. It is often difficult to evaluate the extent of our involvement. Thus, from a political viewpoint, the idea of a tightly defined "tourism industry" would allow us to demonstrate to everyone's satisfaction the impact and importance of tourism. Political support matched with economic assistance would more readily be forthcoming.

Yet, tourism is not an industry. Tourism is an activity. It is an activity that takes place when, in international terms, people cross a border for leisure or business and stay at least twenty-four hours, but less than one year. Those who stay less than twenty-four hours are defined by the World Tourism Organization as "excursionists." Domestically, the United States has emphasized distance traveled from home. The present definition of a "trip" is a person traveling to a place at least 100 miles from home. The purpose may be for business or pleasure.

The study of tourism is the study of this phenomenon and its effects. The business of tourism is the business of encouraging this kind of activity and taking care of the needs of people while engaged in this kind of activity.

We chose to describe tourism as a system. It is important to see tourism as consisting of interrelated parts. Because of reasons mentioned earlier, businesses and organizations that have been, to some degree, affected by tourism, often do not consider themselves part of tourism. Many people within the hotel industry or the restaurant industry do not feel part of tourism. Their business begins when the customer walks in the front door. This myopic view has meant that those in the industry have ended up *reacting* to changes that have occurred outside their front door, rather than *acting* in anticipation of upcoming changes. The system is like a spider's web—touch one part of it and reverberations will be felt throughout. By showing where the hotelier is linked to the tourist and by further examining the factors that influence the decision to become a tourist, the hotelier can watch for changes in those factors and can anticipate changes in the number and characteristics of tourists to the destination that may be induced to stay at his or her hotel.

The Tourism System consists of four parts—Market; Travel; Destination; Marketing. The decision to travel or become a tourist can be understood by an examination of the market segment of the system. The decision to travel is made if the individual has learned in the past that travel satisfies felt needs, if the individual perceives that future travel will satisfy felt needs and within the external constraints of that individual's environment. A consumer behavior model is the mechanism by which these processes are examined. Changes in any of these three processes will affect the individual's travel purchase behavior.

Once a person decides to travel, decisions must then be made as to where, when, and how to go. The second segment of *The Tourism System* describes and analyzes these choices. Trends in the various travel segments are outlined. An examination of tourist flows both internationally and domestically is the first step in understanding present movements; it will also help to predict future travel movements. In conjunction with this, the modes of travel are discussed to determine recent trends and future prospects. The shape of travel, then, is the combination of who is traveling, and where, when, and how she or he is traveling.

The destination is the third major part of the system. The destination mix consists of the attractions and services used by the traveler. If one examines the parts of the mix, it becomes clear that each part is dependent upon the others for success in attracting, servicing, and satisfying the tourist. In order to sell travel, the destination must be aware of the benefits to be gained from tourism and the pitfalls to be avoided. An overall policy towards tourism can then be formulated and development plans drawn up within the context of the regulatory framework affecting tourism.

The destination area reaches people in the market and encourages them to travel through the process of marketing, the fourth part of the system. The development of a marketing plan, the selection of an appropriate marketing mix, and the choice of a distribution channel will spell success or failure for the destination's attempt to encourage tourist travel.

At the conclusion of each section a reading is presented that summarizes the overall theme of the preceding section.

In describing the various parts of the system and their interactions, those who operate within the system can see who they and their businesses or destinations affect and are affected by other participants in the system.

The text goes beyond a description of tourism to outline principles to influence tourism. In describing the process by which tourists decide to travel, insight is shared into how that process can be influenced. The segment on travel leads readers to an understanding of how to benefit from existing movements and future changes. The destination chapters give specifics on how those who are part of a destination's attractions and services can optimize tourism's contribution to the destination. The section on marketing lays out ways and means to develop a marketing plan and work through the appropriate channel to reach the target market.

This book will be of assistance to students and practitioners alike in understanding how tourism works and how it can be made to work for them, their business, and their destination.

1

TO TRAVEL OR NOT TO TRAVEL
Travel
as a Need/Want
Satisfier

The reasons people give for taking vacations are insufficient to explain their travel motivations. In order to market to potential tourists and to serve them at their destinations it is essential to understand the underlying needs that tourists wish to satisfy when considering a vacation.

This chapter explores tourism as a satisfier of needs and wants. The relationship between lists in travel literature showing reasons for pleasure travel and Maslow's hierarchy of needs is developed.

Some people hypothesize that tourists travel if they have learned that travel for a particular reason will help satisfy various needs and wants considered important to them, and if they perceive that their needs and wants will be satisfied within the constraints of such things as time, money, and social pressure.

THE TOURISM SYSTEM

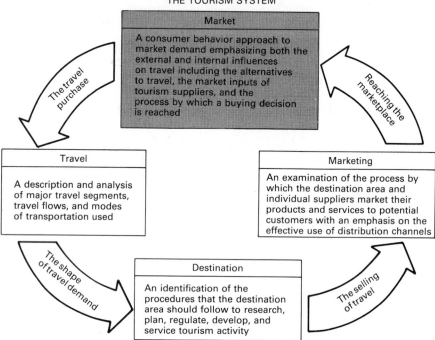

Market

A consumer behavior approach to market demand emphasizing both the external and internal influences on travel including the alternatives to travel, the market inputs of tourism suppliers, and the process by which a buying decision is reached

The travel purchase

Reaching the marketplace

Travel

A description and analysis of major travel segments, travel flows, and modes of transportation used

Marketing

An examination of the process by which the destination area and individual suppliers market their products and services to potential customers with an emphasis on the effective use of distribution channels

The shape of travel demand

Destination

An identification of the procedures that the destination area should follow to research, plan, regulate, develop, and service tourism activity

The selling of travel

IMPORTANCE OF MOTIVATION

Why do people take vacations? To date, studies of tourist motivations have concentrated on developing lists of the reasons people say they travel. A variety of studies report that tourists travel, for example, to view scenery, to learn about other cultures, or to visit friends and relatives. This approach to understanding tourist motivation is insufficient for two reasons. First, the tourists themselves may be unaware of the true reasons behind their travel behavior. Individuals are often unaware of the real reasons for doing certain things. A person leaving for a tennis vacation may see the trip as simply a reason "to play tennis." When questioned however, the traveler may reveal that a concern for his or her health prompted the trip. Also, the tourist may not wish to divulge the *real* reason or motivation behind a trip. For instance, much of the tourism literature mentions "status" as a tourist motivator, yet many tourists will not feel comfortable admitting that a major reason for taking a vacation is that they will be able to impress their friends upon their return home. A second reason that such lists are insufficient for explaining consumer motivations is that they concentrate on selling the product rather than on satisfying the needs of the market. But the development of such lists is a necessary first step toward establishing a classification system that

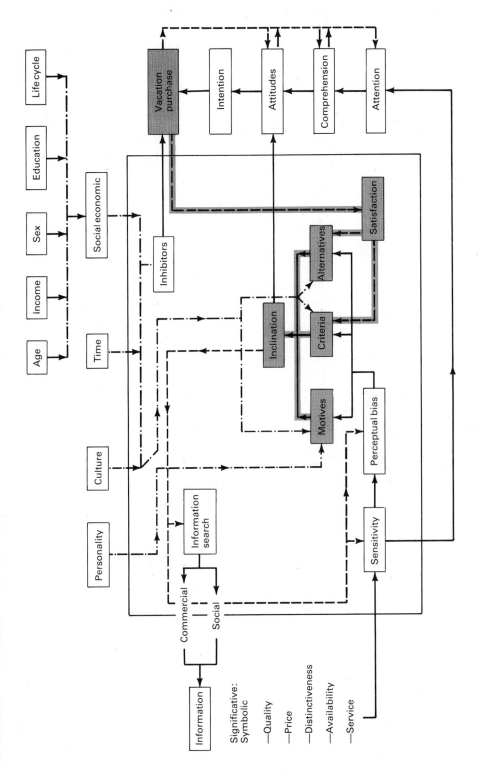

will enable us to understand and ultimately predict the tourist's decision-making process.

TRAVEL AS A NEED/WANT SATISFIER

The key to understanding tourist motivation is to see vacation travel as a satisfier of needs and wants. Tourists do not take vacations just to relax and have fun, to experience another culture, or to educate themselves and their children. They take vacations in the hope and belief that these vacations will satisfy, either wholly or partially, various needs and wants. This view of tourist motivations, while seemingly a partial one, is critical. It is the difference between seeing a destination as a collection of palm trees and hotel rooms for the tourist and seeing it as a means for satisfying the needs and wants of tourists. It is the difference between those travel agents who see themselves as sellers of airline seats and those who view themselves as dealers in dreams.

Needs, Wants, and Motives

A description of the process begins with a consideration of the needs of an individual. When an individual takes a trip, buys a cruise, or rents a cabin, the action is done in hopes of satisfying some need of which he or she may be only partially aware. We could provide a better service if we could only be aware of which need or needs the individual is attempting to satisfy.

A business is not interested so much in a person's needs as in how that person seeks to satisfy those needs. The difference between a need and a want is one of awareness. It is the task of the people in marketing to transform needs into wants by making the individual aware of his or her need deficiencies.

A person needs affection, but wants to visit friends and relatives; *needs* esteem from others, but *wants* a Mediterranean cruise. In these and other situations people can be made aware, through advertisements, for example, that the purchase of an airline ticket to visit parents will result in feelings of love and affection for them, thereby helping satisfy that need.

Although a person may want satisfaction for a need or needs, no action will be taken until that person is motivated.

Motivation occurs when an individual wants to satisfy a need. A motive implies action; an individual is moved to *do* something. Motivation theories indicate that an individual constantly strives to achieve a state of stability—a homeostasis. An individual's homeostasis is disrupted when she or he is made aware of a need deficiency. This awareness creates wants. For the individual to be motivated to satisfy a need, an objective must be present. The individual must be aware of a product or

FIGURE 1.1 Needs, Wants, and Motives

service and must perceive the purchase of that product or service as having a positive effect on satisfying the need of which she or he is now aware. Then, and only then, will the individual be motivated to buy. Again, it is the role of marketing to suggest objectives—cruises, flights, or vacations—to satisfy needs, an awareness of which has already been created. (This process is outlined in Figure 1.1.) For example, several years ago an advertisement ran in the Scottish papers showing two little girls with one saying, "Guess what? Next month Grandma and Grandpa are visiting us—from *Scotland.*" The advertisement was promoting flights from Scotland to Canada. It managed to say (between the lines), "We know you love your grandchildren [a need]. By showing you this picture we have made you aware of that [a want]. By visiting them [an objective] you will satisfy that need for love." In such a way grandparents are motivated to fly to Canada.

Behavior is influenced by a number of things, with motives being only one. We cannot even specify that an individual is motivated at any one time by only one motive. It is important, as we discuss needs and motives individually, to bear in mind that behavior results from the interaction of various motives, one of which may be dominant at any one time as well as interacting with various other socioeconomic and psychographic factors.

Motives may be specific or general. A general motive would be the end objective, and a specific motive would be a means to reach that end objective. For example, a person may be motivated to take a spa vacation. This, however, may be no more than an indicator of a more general motive, that of good health. Viewed in this way, it can be seen that good health can be achieved by means other than taking a vacation. We are in competition not only with the next destination, but also with other activities for the consumer's time and money. Although a vacation represents a break from routine for many, that same feeling can also be obtained from decorating the house or laying out a garden. The marketing task is to convince an individual that the purchase of whatever we are selling is the best, if not the only way of satisfying that need. To the extent that we are successful in accomplishing this, an individual will be motivated to buy.

MASLOW'S NEED THEORY AND TRAVEL MOTIVATIONS A study of the travel literature indicates that travel motivations can fit into Maslow's hierarchy of needs model. Maslow proposed the following listing of needs arranged in a hierarchy:

1. Physiological—hunger, thirst, rest, activity
2. Safety—security, freedom from fear and anxiety
3. Belonging and love—affection, giving and receiving love
4. Esteem—self esteem and esteem from others
5. Self-actualization—personal self-fulfillment

This hierarchy suggests that lower needs demand more immediate attention and satisfaction before a person turns to the satisfaction of higher-level needs.

Although the first need listed is physical, the other four are psychological. To this original list two intellectual needs were added:

To know and understand—acquiring knowledge
Aesthetics—appreciation of beauty

The relationship between the physical, psychological, and intellectual needs is unclear. It is thought that the intellectual needs exist independently of the others.

The relationship between needs, motives, and references from the tourism literature is shown in Table 1.1. Those who say they travel "to escape" or "to relieve tension" can be seen as seeking to satisfy the basic physiological need. Such motivation may be for physical or mental relaxation. Vacationers often return from a trip physically exhausted but mentally refreshed. Although there seems to be a difference between those people who take an active vacation and those who opt for a passive vacation, both are motivated by a need for tension reduction. Passive vacationers are seen as achieving tension relief by giving in or submitting to the surrounding environment. From this submission comes the very relief of tension that will result in their returning refreshed and renewed. The active vacationer achieves tension reduction through physical activity. (The activity can also be seen as being related to achievement and mastery of the environment and, as such, being related to the need for self-esteem. This illustrates the point made earlier that, at any one time, one may be motivated to satisfy more than one need).

Traveling for reasons of health can be interpreted as a way of attempting to satisfy one's safety needs. By taking care of the body and/or mind, we are "protecting" ourselves and helping assure our own longevity. Several references specifically link recreation and health, implying a relationship between the two.

TABLE 1.1   Maslow's Needs and Motivations Listed in Travel Literature

Need	Motive	Tourism Literature References
Physiological	Relaxation	Escape
		Relaxation
		Relief of tension
		Sunlust
		Physical
		Mental relaxation of tension
Safety	Security	Health
		Recreation
		Keep oneself active and healthy for the future
Belonging	Love	Family togetherness
		Enhancement of kinship relationships
		Companionship
		Facilitation of social interaction
		Maintenance of personal ties
		Interpersonal relations
		Roots
		Ethnic
		Show one's affection for family members
		Maintain social contacts
Esteem	Achievement	Convince oneself of one's achievements
	Status	Show one's importance to others
		Prestige
		Social recognition
		Ego-enhancement
		Professional/business
		Personal development
		Status and prestige
Self-actualization	Be true to one's own nature	Exploration and evaluation of self
		Self-discovery
		Satisfaction of inner desires
To know and understand	Knowledge	Cultural
		Education
		Wanderlust
		Interest in foreign areas
Aesthetics	Appreciation of beauty	Environmental
		Scenery

The need for belonging and love relates to the desire for affection, for both giving and receiving love. The organized tour is often mentioned as a method of encouraging and satisfying this need for companionship and social interaction.

This motivation is frequently referred to as the "VFR" market—"visit friends and relatives." Part of this is the ethnic or roots market—the desire to revisit the homeland or previous residence of oneself or one's ancestors. This segment of the market tends to fall into two groups. First, there are those who were born somewhere else and desire to return to their own homeland. Second, there are those in later generations who wish to experience the land of their ancestors. For the people in the first segment of the market, the desire is to see people and things and to relive experiences as they are remembered. This desire to recapture previous experiences means that these tourists are willing to adjust to the conditions of the destination visited. They are there, after all, to again enjoy what they remembered from their past. Inconveniences of the homeland can be tolerated. At the same time, however, people in this market segment may have little economic impact on the destination because of the tendency to stay with friends and relatives. Later generations will have the slightly different desire to experience vicariously the land of one's ancestors; however, because the personal experience of one's roots are missing and have been replaced by standards of living learned in one's country of birth, it is these accustomed standards of living that are taken on the journey for one's roots. Therefore, living standards are expected to be comparable to those experienced at home. At the same time, however, this segment of the market tends to have a greater impact on the economy if lodging and meals are taken in hotels instead of with family.

Maslow's concept of the need for esteem breaks down into two components—that of self-esteem and that of esteem from others. The idea of self-esteem is embodied in such ideas as the need to exhibit strength, achievement, mastery, competence, and independence. Esteem from others is explained by such concepts as reputation, prestige, status, and recognition. Travel can certainly boost one's ego, both at the destination and upon one's return. It may be that as people grow older, their status in society declines. Travel is one way to enhance that status.

Self-actualization can, in fact, be considered the end or goal of leisure. Leisure is the state of being free from the urgent demands of lower-level needs. Vacations offer an opportunity to reevaluate and discover more about the self, to act out one's self-image as a way of modifying or correcting it.

The need to know and understand can be viewed in light of the desire for knowledge. Many people travel to learn of others' cultures. It is also true that contact with people of another culture offers an opportunity to discover one's own culture. This same concept has also been expressed as a motivation for education, wanderlust, and interest in foreign parts.

The need for aesthetics is seen in those who travel for environmental reasons—to view the scenery.

The traveler, then, is better understood and better appealed to if she is recognized as a person consuming products and services. Seeing the traveler in this manner will result in a change of attitude on the part of the observer and enable the marketer to provide a better product or service to the traveler. A second more tangible benefit to be gained from this approach relates to the idea of prepotency. If one accepts Maslow's idea of prepotency—that lower-level needs should be satisfied to some extent before the satisfaction of higher-level needs becomes a concern—we would expect that products and services, including vacations, which are targeted towards the satisfaction of lower-level needs, would be regarded as more of a necessity than a luxury and would, as such, be more resilient to external pressures of time and money.

WHY TRAVEL?

We have said that an individual's needs—for safety, for belonging, and so on—can be satisfied by setting different objectives or by taking certain actions. What determines how an individual will seek to satisfy a need? It is proposed that an individual is motivated to satisfy a particular need in a particular way (by taking a vacation, for example) based upon three factors. First, an objective will be set if the individual perceives that the objective will satisfy her need: If she feels that taking a cruise will result in her returning relaxed and refreshed and if it is important to her that she do something to relax and refresh herself, then she is more likely to take that cruise. (The process by which an individual perceives is covered in Chapter Two.) Second, a particular action will be taken if the individual has learned that that action will satisfy that need: If she has taken a cruise that has resulted in her returning home refreshed, she will be more inclined to take it again. (The learning process is explored in the remainder of this chapter.) Third, the decision as to what action to take in order to satisfy a need must be taken within the limitations of the individual's external environment: She may perceive that a cruise will satisfy her need, she may have learned that a cruise will satisfy her need, but if she does not have sufficient time or money or if there are strong social or cultural factors that inhibit this option, she may not be able to take the cruise. The effect of the external environment on the individual's decision-making process is considered in Chapter Three.

Tourist's Learning Process

An individual will purchase a specific vacation package or trip if he has learned that the purchase will help satisfy an important need. This process is illustrated in Figure 1.2. The tourist weighs various alternatives against a list of criteria important to him to determine which alternatives are most likely to satisfy a particular motive. The inclination that results will have an effect upon the decision to purchase. This influence may be positive or negative, depending upon the "fit" between motives and alternatives—how well it is felt a chosen alternative will meet the motivation. Travelers have a low upper limit on the number of destinations that they perceive they may visit within a specified time period. Most travelers have identified seven or fewer destinations that they list as

FIGURE 1.2   Tourist's Learning Process

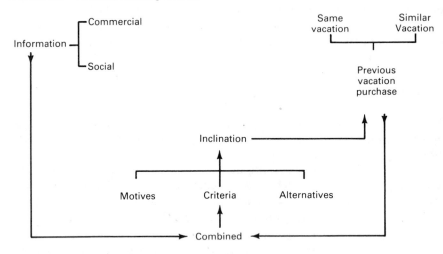

Adapted from: John A. Howard and Jagdish N. Sheth, *The Theory of Buyer Behavior* (New York, John Wiley & Sons, Inc., 1969).

alternatives. The number of alternatives will vary relative to the characteristics of the travelers. Travelers who have previously visited foreign destinations have a larger number of alternatives to choose from than do those who haven't. It may be that travel broadens the number of destinations likely to be visited. Whether or not a destination will be included as an alternative depends in great part upon whether or not that destination has previously satisfied the individual. The level of satisfaction is a function of one's expectations of a situation and one's perception of the actual situation. If the level of expectation is higher than the actual experience, the individual will be dissatisfied. For an individual to be satisfied with a product, service, or situation, the level of actual experience must be equal to or greater than the level of expectation. Tourists can attempt to reduce the psychological risk involved in a purchase by expecting less from the vacation. This, however, is not a popular strategy, especially in travel.

We would expect that, as the amount of satisfaction increases, the number of alternatives considered next time decreases. The more an individual is pleased with a vacation choice, the higher that choice will be placed on the list of alternatives and the fewer will be the other alternatives considered. This places great importance on the level of service given the vacationer to assure a quality experience and a level of satisfaction that will bring the traveler back. The one exception to this might be the vacationer with a high need to know and understand. If this is very important, it may not matter how satisfied he or she is with, for example, a trip to Paris. Having visited that spot, the individual, making the most of limited resources of time and money, may never return to that city.

Serving as a bridge between the motives of an individual and the perceived alternatives are the criteria used for making a decision among those alternatives. A choice is made that the individual believes will produce maximum satisfaction of a need or needs. The criteria used to distinguish between alternatives are learned. These criteria are developed as a result of past experience and from information taken in from either the commercial or the social environment. The effect of information on learning will be considered in the following chapter when we look at the process of perception and image formation.

An individual's learning input, based on past experience, can come from having experienced the same thing that is being contemplated or having experienced something similar. If you stayed in a particular town on vacation and were very satisfied, you learn that visiting that particular town is liable to satisfy you again. Those factors that accounted for your satisfaction—good weather, friendly service—are the criteria by which you determine where to take your next vacation.

On the other hand, by staying at one property of a chain and having a poor experience, you may infer that you would have a similarly poor experience at all properties of that chain and behave accordingly when faced with a choice of places to stay. This process of generalization (which, by the way, may not be an accurate representation of what would have happened at another property in the chain) is known as the psychology of simplification. To make the decision-making process easier, the potential tourist generalizes from what he or she perceives to be similar situations. The more experiences you have, the more firmly established your decision criteria and the easier it is for you to generalize.

The individual moves from what is termed an extensive problem-solving process through a limited problem-solving process to a routine problem-solving process. In the process known as extensive problem solving, the tourist has little in the way of information or experiences from which to make a decision. The need and, consequently the search for information is high, and few decision criteria have been established. We may know what criteria are important to us, but we may be unaware of whether or not they can be satisfied by the various alternatives available. Additionally, as we experience certain destinations or vacations, we may find that the criteria that were important to us previously have become less significant.

Thus, our decision criteria are developed or modified (that is, learned) in great part by our actual experiences. As we become more confident in our decision criteria, decision making is easier for us. Our experiences, and the resultant generalization from them, are weighed more heavily than any information received. This is due, in part, to the fact that, as our decision criteria are strengthened, our need for information is weakened. Additionally, we have a tendency to filter incoming information so that it will support and reinforce our decisions. This is explored further in the next chapter. This progression leads to a routine problem-solving process whereby little or no information is sought and the decision is made rather quickly in reference to the decision criteria that have been established.

Consistency vs. Complexity

The movement described above—from extensive problem solving to routine problem solving—suggests that people seek to maintain consistency in their lives. Indeed, many psychologists adhere to this philosophy. Their theory is that inconsistency leads to psychological tension, which we constantly seek to avoid. Other psychologists argue the opposite. They feel that individuals find change and uncertainty extremely satisfying. This is referred to as the need for complexity.

The aforementioned two concepts are balanced by Edward J. Mayo and Lance Jarvis in *The Psychology of Leisure Travel*.[1] It is their feeling that individuals vary in the amount of psychological tension they can handle. Too much repetition or consistency can result in boredom for an individual and a corresponding amount of psychological tension greater than the optimum for him. He will attempt to introduce some complexity in his life, thereby reducing the tension to an optimum level. Should this level be exceeded by an overly complex situation, the tension level will be greater than the optimum for him. This explains why someone, who for years has driven to a particular vacation spot, will change either the destination or the method of reaching that spot.

Similarly, too much complexity can result in more tension than an individual can handle. She will introduce consistency into the experience to reduce the tension level. An American tourist in Europe may find the different language and culture (complexity) need to be balanced by staying in a hotel chain with which she is familiar (consistency). This model may also help explain a person's choice of vacation. The individual who experiences a great deal of consistency in everyday life may compensate by seeking vacations which offer variety. The reverse is also true.

Summary

People are motivated to satisfy needs that may be innate or learned. Part of marketing's task is to make people aware of their needs and present them with an objective, the purchase or attainment of which will help satisfy that need. Vacations or trips are ways of satisfying various needs.

---

[1]Edward J. Mayo and Lance P. Jarvis, *The Psychology of Leisure Travel* (Boston, C.B.I. Publishing Company, Inc., 1981), p. 172.

There are, however, ways other than taking vacations to satisfy those same needs. An individual will purchase a vacation to satisfy a need or needs if he perceives that the vacation will satisfy those needs, or if he has learned that a vacation will satisfy those needs under the constraints of external factors such as time, money, and social pressure.

An individual learns of the alternative ways of satisfying her needs from personal experience, from the same or similar experiences, and from information gained from the commercial or social environment. The alternatives considered are linked to the person's motives by a set of decision criteria—guidelines used by the individual to select among alternatives. These guidelines are also learned from the sources described. If an individual has learned that a particular purchase results in satisfaction, strong decision criteria favoring that purchase will have been built up as the number of alternatives considered will have been reduced. There is a great likelihood that a specific motive under the conditions described above will result in a tendency to purchase a particular product, service, or experience.

REFERENCES

CRISSY, W., R. BOEWADT, AND D. LAUDADIO, *Marketing of Hospitality Services-Food, Lodging, Travel* (East Lansing, MI, Educational Institute of the American Hotel and Motel Association, 1975).

CROMPTON, JOHN, "A Systems Model of the Tourist's Destination Selection Process with Particular Reference to the Roles of Image and Perceived Constraints" (Ph.D. dissertation, Texas A&M University, 1977), pp. 34, 316, 345.

DANN, GRAHAM M. S., "Tourist Satisfaction: A Highly Complex Variable," *Annals of Tourism Research*, vol. 5, no. 4, October/December, 1978, pp. 440–43.

FARINA, J., "Toward a Philosophy of Leisure," in *Concepts of Leisure*, J. F. Murphy, ed. (Englewood Cliffs, NJ, Prentice-Hall, Inc., 1974).

HOWARD, JOHN A., AND J. N. SHETH, *The Theory of Buyer Behavior* (New York, John Wiley & Sons, Inc., 1969).

IBRAHIM H., AND R. CRANDALL, *Leisure: A Psychological Approach* (Los Alamitos, CA, Hwong Publishing Company, 1979), p. 161.

LANSING, JOHN B., AND DWIGHT M. BLOOD, *The Changing Travel Market* (Ann Arbor, MI, University of Michigan, 1964), p. 6.

LUNDBERG, DONALD E., *The Tourist Business* (Boston, MA, C.B.I. Publishing Company, Inc., 1974).

MASLOW, A. H., "A Theory of Human Motivation," *Psychological Review*, vol. 50, 1943, pp. 370–396.

MAYO, EDWARD J., AND LANCE P. JARVIS, *The Psychology of Leisure Travel* (Boston, C.B.I. Publishing Company, Inc., 1981), pp. 82, 156, 172.

MCINTOSH, ROBERT W., AND SASHIKANT GUPTA, *Tourism: Principles, Practices and Philosophies* (Columbus, OH, Grid Inc., 1980), p. 65.

ROBINSON, H., *A Geography of Tourism* (London, Macdonald and Evans, 1976), p. 36.

"Vacations," *Psychology Today*, May 1980, pp. 62–76.

VOGT, JAY, "Wandering: Youth and Travel Behavior," *Annals of Tourism Research*, vol. 4, no. 1, September/October 1976, pp. 25–41.

WALTERS, C. GLENN, *Consumer Behavior: Theory and Practice* (Homewood, IL, Richard D. Irwin, Inc., 1978), p. 197.

WHEELER, MACEL MARTEWA, "Spatial Analysis of the Distribution of Visitors Among State Operated Recreational Sites in Kentucky" (Ph.D. dissertation, University of Kentucky, 1978).

WOODSIDE, ARCH G., TEKKA RONKAINEN, AND DAVID M. REID, "Measurement and Utilization of the Evoked Set as a Travel Marketing Variable" (paper presented to The Travel Research Association, 1978).

2

SELECTING
A TRAVEL DESTINATION:
Information Sources
and Perceptual Biases

A travel destination is chosen in part based upon our perception of its ability to satisfy our felt needs.

This chapter examines the process by which we receive information about a destination and how our perception of that information influences the travel decision.

Information is received from both the commercial and social environments. The factors that influence from where the information is sought and how much is taken in are examined. The process by which the information taken in is distorted by our perceptual biases is explored.

Implications for the marketer seeking to develop a specific image for a destination or to change an unsatisfactory image are pointed out.

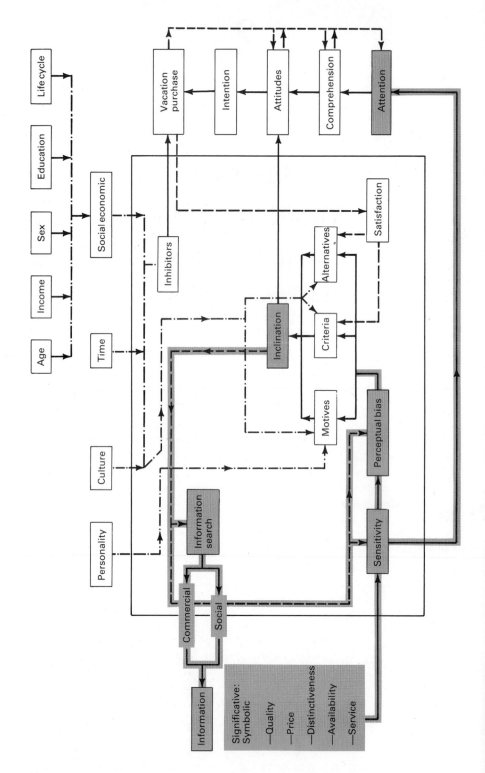

THE PROCESS OF PERCEPTION

In the previous chapter it was suggested that, in part, a travel purchase is made based on the extent that an individual perceives that the purchase will satisfy his or her needs. The key word is "perceive," for we buy based not so much upon what information is actually presented to us, but on how we perceive that information. This distinction will be explored in greater detail later.

It will be recalled that our inclination towards a particular product is derived from the linking of our motives with the alternatives available to us through a series of learned decision criteria (see Figure 2.1). The

FIGURE 2.1   Information Sources and Perceptual Biases

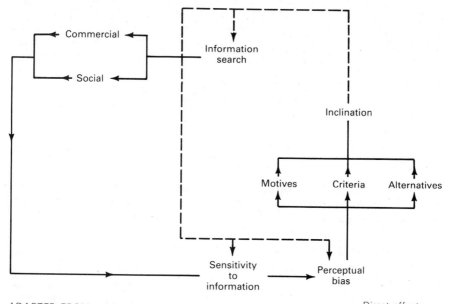

ADAPTED FROM: John A. Howard and Jagdish N. Sheth, *The Theory of Buyer Behavior* (New York, John Wiley & Sons, Inc., 1969).

——— Direct effects
— — — Feedback effects

strength of our preference has an effect on how new alternatives are perceived and even if any new alternatives are considered. For example, if an individual is well traveled and consequently knows which destinations please and which do not, a strong set of decision criteria will have been developed—"There must be a sunny climate"; "The culture must be significantly different from my own"; and so on. This, in turn, leads to a strong inclination towards certain destinations. The results are:

1. The tourist is less inclined to seek out information about new places.
2. The tourist is less sensitive to any information about vacation spots; the preferred destination is "protected" by a reluctance to allow in any information about other destinations.

3. Because a strong preference for a particular destination has been developed, any information seen about that destination is filtered to emphasize the positives while any negatives are rationalized or otherwise downplayed. The reverse is also true. In a study of perceptions regarding first-class and coach airline seating, those who preferred first-class travel perceived a lesser difference in ticket price but a greater difference in the positive aspects of choosing first class, such as more luggage allowance, better meal selection, and so on.[1]

Information will come from two major sources—the commercial environment and the social environment. The commercial environment refers to information coming from companies, destinations, countries, or tourist businesses. These are businesses or organizations that have a vested interest in persuading the tourist to buy—those that would profit by such a purchase. The social environment, characterized by friends, relatives, and reference groups, presumably would have nothing materially to gain from the tourist's decision to buy. As such, it is presumed that their information or advice is more objective and worthy of trust. Although friends, relatives, and those in our reference groups may not benefit financially from the decision to buy a particular vacation, they may have their egos stroked if their advice is accepted and a decision made based upon their input.

INFORMATION SOURCES

What sources of information are sought when planning a vacation? Much evidence suggests that the social environment—the influence of friends and family—is instrumental in selecting a travel destination. The role of the retail travel agent in this process has been documented in a series of reports by Louis Harris & Associates since 1971.[2] These reports indicate that, over the past ten years, between 30 and 40 percent of those who visit travel agencies have only a vague idea of where they want to go and thus rely, to some extent, on the agent's advice in selecting a destination. However, not everyone uses a retail travel agent. There is an increased tendency to use travel agents as the distance being traveled increases and if the tourist uses air transportation. This tendency is displayed in Table 2.1, which includes some of the results of a study by the United States Travel Service (USTS). A steady increase can be seen in the use of travel agents as distance traveled by passengers increases. For example, while only 3 percent of Ontario residents used travel agents for travel within Ontario, 19 percent used their services when vacationing

---

[1] J. C. Makens and R. A. Marquardt, "Consumer Perceptions Regarding First Class and Coach Airline Seating," *Journal of Travel Research*, vol. 16, no. 1, 1977, pp. 19–22.

[2] Louis Harris and Associates, "The Character and Volume of the U.S. Travel Agency Market," 1971, 1973, 1976, 1979, 1981.

TABLE 2.1   Use of Travel Agents by Canadian Travelers

Residents Of	*TRAVELING TO*			
	Own Province	Other Provinces	U.S. Mainland	Offshore
British Columbia	3%	16%	22%	66%
Ontario	3	19	36	78
Quebec	3	3	18	64

SOURCE: United States Travel Service, "Vacation Travel by Canadians in the U.S.," 1977.

in other provinces. This increased to 36 percent for those Ontario residents traveling within the U.S. mainland and 78 percent for those vacationing offshore. The same pattern was demonstrated in a USTS study of Mexican tourists.[3] While 14 percent of Mexican tourists taking a domestic vacation used a travel agent, 38 percent of U.S.-bound and over 50 percent of non-U.S. international tourists did so.

Thus, it appears that the social environment of friends, relatives, and reference groups is a prime source of information concerning vacations. Because the role of a retail travel agent increases in importance as the use of air transportation and the distance traveled increases, it might thus be better to view the important sources of information for the auto traveler separately from those used by the air traveler.

Travel to the United States

Many informative reports have been issued by the United States Travel Service. Table 2.2 summarizes information from four different reports relative to the sources of travel information on the United States. These four sources were chosen because they represent nonauto travel. It is clear that, for most travelers from these countries, most travel information on the United States comes from word of mouth and travel agents. Travelers from France and Sweden show a decided preference for information from personal sources; in Venezuela both travel agents and personal sources are equally used; in Japan, more people get information from travel agencies than from personal sources. It is also interesting to note the relatively high use of transportation carriers and newspapers and magazines in both Venezuela and France as a source of U.S. travel information. Based upon these studies we can conclude that word of mouth is an important source of travel information for air travelers to the United States. The travel agent is also a prime source of travel information. It is also evident that travelers of different countries have different ways and priorities for obtaining information for travel purposes. Newspapers and magazines are relied upon more heavily in some countries than in

---

[3]United States Travel Service, "A Mexico: A Study of the International Travel Market," 1977.

TABLE 2.2   Sources of U.S. Travel Information

	France[1]	Sweden[2]	Venezuela[3]	Japan[4]
Word of mouth	79%	58%	87%	56%[x]
Travel agency	54	44	86	68
Business associates	–	35	48	–
Transportation carrier	43	24	79	23
Newspapers, magazines	66	38	68	38
Embassies	40	15	–	4
Paid advertising	41	26	42	26
Tour operators	34	19	48	20
USTS	43	–	–	10

NOTE: Multiple responses—percentages may add to more than 100 percent.
[x]Friends and relatives.

SOURCES: [1]USTS "France: A Study of the International Travel Market," 1978.
[2]USTS "Sweden: A Study of the International Travel Market," 1978.
[3]USTS "Venezuela: A Study of the International Travel Market," 1977.
[4]USTS "Japan: A Study of the International Travel Market," 1978.

others. Thus, while the importance of personal sources and retail travel agents can be noted, the travel marketer must be aware of the fact that information to different travelers in different countries must be communicated through different channels to reach the intended audience.

Automobile Travel

A number of studies have been completed on the tourist's use of travel information sources when traveling by automobile. These studies indicate the importance of information from the social environment. Information from family or friends and from personal knowledge is regarded as more significant than that from commercial sources. The non-media-preferred commercial sources are billboards and signs. It appears that as motorist travelers become more familiar with the location of establishments in a geographic area they rely more on previous experience than on physical appearance and on credit-card directories rather than on commercial billboards.

A link between the social and commercial environment is suggested by a consideration of the role of opinion leaders. There is evidence to indicate that the flow of communications is a two-step flow process. The tendency is for influence to flow from the mass media to opinion leaders who are receptive to the idea presented, and from these opinion leaders to the general public. Opinion leaders act as channels of information. They tend to be demographically indistinguishable except for higher income and occupational levels, tend to read more media about related consumer issues, are more knowledgeable about new product developments, and participate more often in related consumer activities. A study by Troncalli and Thompson of travel opinion leaders found that they were active seekers of information but did not see either personal or media sources of information as being significantly important sources for them.[4] It appears that travel opinion leaders may be better able to determine the credibility of various source materials and are not as easily swayed by the advice of friends and relatives as are the general population. Others, after all, look to them for advice—they do not look so much to others.

SENSITIVITY TO INFORMATION

Thus far we have considered the sources to which potential tourists turn to determine vacation patterns. The personal sources—those from the social environment—have been shown to exert considerable pressure compared with those from the commercial environment. All information from both the commercial and social environments reaches us if we are sensitive to the incoming information. Our sensitivity to receiving incoming information is first a function of how inclined we are to that information. If, for example, we feel strongly inclined towards taking a vacation, we will readily be open to information regarding vacations. If we have a strong preference for a Bahamas vacation, any information about the Bahamas—about travel packages, the weather, the political situation—is liable to receive attention. On the other hand, if we have definitely decided against a European vacation, our preference to go to Europe will be low, as will our sensitivity to information about Europe. Consequently, we will probably ignore any information that would affect those taking a European vacation. Our sensitivity to information is also a function of the ambiguity of the message. If the information received is familiar to us already, it may be too simple and straightforward and thus be ignored. On the other hand, if the information presented—an advertisement, a travelogue, a personal opinion—is too complicated for us to absorb, the high level of ambiguity may lead us to put up a shield to "defend" ourselves, and the information will not get our attention. This process may be thought of as controlling the quantity of information received. In order to gain tourists' attention, the information presented should be aimed at their capacity to absorb it. Its chances of being taken in will be enhanced if the tourists have a preference for the destination or package being mentioned.

PERCEPTUAL BIAS

The information-receiving process, described above, controls the quantity of information taken in. The quantity of information received, however, is distorted by how that information is perceived. Two people presented

---

[4]Michael T. Troncalli and John R. Thompson, "Relative Importance of Information Sources Used by Travel Opinion Leaders," *Journal of Travel Research*, vol. 15, no. 4, Summer 1976, pp. 11-14.

with the same travel advertisement may perceive it differently. One person may view the advertisement positively, the other negatively. Feedback from our motives, the alternatives considered, and the decision criteria used will affect our image of information received. Various studies have shown, in fact, that visiting a destination or staying at a particular lodging chain causes a positive change in the image of that destination or chain. If we are strongly motivated to seek a historical, cultural vacation, one which could readily be satisfied by a trip to the province of Quebec, and if it is important (decision criteria) that we avoid crowds, then an advertisement showing throngs of people at an art festival in Quebec will be perceived negatively. Similarly, an advertisement that stresses the magnificent scenery of the province will not be perceived positively because that image runs counter to that which motivates us.

Although information from both the commercial and social environments is distorted, information received from personal sources is less subject to perceptual bias. This is because information from the social environment is regarded more favorably by the individual receiving the information. It should be remembered, however, that before a friend or relative gives us information, he or she has already distorted it to meet his or her value system. A recommendation of a "wonderful" place to visit, stay, or eat will only be given in those terms if it has met with what our friend determines is a wonderful place to visit, stay, or eat. This, of course, depends upon whether or not our friend perceives that his or her experience satisfied unmet needs. There is also liable to be less distortion when information is actively sought. When the tourist is unsure of which vacation will result in a more satisfying experience—when preference for any particular vacation is low—there will be less bias in the way information is perceived. In addition, there will be greater reliance upon the social environment for information if the tourist is unsure of the satisfactions from various alternatives and if the purchase is important. To the extent that we are influenced by the social group of which we are a part, our motives will be influenced by the (subjectively weighted) information from our social environment. Similarly, the social environment will affect the alternatives a buyer considers, particularly where experience is lacking. Also, information received will be fed into the buyer's decision criteria and will influence those criteria in the direction in which the information is perceived. A tourist, for example, may have a criterion of looking for the lowest priced hotel. If information is received that suggests that paying a little more will actually be a better value, and if the tourist perceives this to be true, the decision criterion of "lowest cost" may change.

A link has been established between perception and behavior. We behave—buy, travel, stay at home, and so on—based in part upon our perception of information received. But how do we perceive products or services?

HOW WE PERCEIVE

It is generally felt that we perceive products and services as consisting of a bundle of benefits or attributes. A vacation package consists of a variety of parts—for example, in a ski vacation, excellent snow conditions, few lift lines, après-ski entertainment, saunas, continental cuisine, and so on. A significant association between overall preference for a particular brand and preference based on the attributes of that brand has been demonstrated in the choice of an airline, a destination, and a tourist attraction. Thus, we buy a bundle of benefits. The decision to purchase the overall brand or package will be based upon two factors. First, the skier, for example, must believe that the attributes of the package will help satisfy his or her felt needs. Second, the satisfaction of those felt needs must be important to the skier. The former contributes more to determining an individual's attitude towards a product or service. The implication is that, if we wish to sell a particular vacation, we should sell that vacation as consisting of a number of benefits that will contribute towards the satisfaction of the buyer's needs. As we saw earlier, an individual may be seeking to satisfy several needs at the same time. Our package, therefore, should contain many elements that will aim at satisfying different needs. The provision of American-type meals and English-speaking guides may satisfy primary physiological and safety needs during a trip to Europe, while the inclusion of side trips to certain "name" resorts may help in satisfying the need for status.

Consumers have a tendency to buy things that have attributes consistent with their own perceived image. An individual's total image is made up of several parts. First, the real self is the objective person—what the individual is deep down. In reality, few of us know ourselves this well. Yet this true self governs our purchase and travel behavior, even if we are unaware of what it is that moves us in a particular way. Second, there is the ideal self. The ideal self is what we would like to be. This aspect of the individual is easier to discover for two reasons that are important to marketers: consumers are more readily willing to discuss to what they aspire than what they believe *really* motivates them; and by simple observation of purchase behavior much can be learned about what a consumer is striving for. Last, the self-image is how consumers see themselves. It is a combination of the real and the ideal self. Consumers make purchases that will maintain or improve their self-image, as they perceive it. According to Walters, consumers attempt to preserve the self-image in several ways.[5] They

---

[5]C. Glenn Walters, "Consumer Behavior: Theory and Practice" (Homewood, Il, Richard D. Irwin, Inc., 1978), pp. 182–86.

Buy products consistent with the self-image
Avoid products inconsistent with the self-image
Trade up to products that relate to an improved self-image
Purchase products that relate favorably to group norms of behavior
Avoid products that show a radical departure from accepted group norms

These three aspects of the self—the real, ideal, and self-image—are totally concerned with the individual. There are two other aspects of the self concerned with external facets. The apparent self—in essence a combination of the real self, ideal self, and self-image—represents how the consumer is seen by outsiders. The impressions that outsiders have of an individual will determine whether or not any commonality of interests or desires is perceived and whether or not any friendship will develop. This affects purchases because we tend to copy the purchases of those we admire. Thus, the picture of myself that I give to others—made up of my real and ideal selves and my self-image—will tell others if they and I seem to be the same "type" of people. If we are, my buying patterns, for a vacation for example, may influence others to purchase that type of vacation. The reference-group self is how we believe others see us. What is believed, however, is more important than what is real, for behavior is predicted on what we *believe* others want us to do. The important influence of reference groups will be explored further in the following chapter. This self, then, is a combination of all of these aspects.

BENEFIT SEGMENTATION

So far the link between purchase of a product, attitudes towards that product, and perceptions of that product has been stressed. We have said that individuals perceive of products and services in terms of bundles of benefits or attributes. Their likelihood of buying a product is determined by the extent to which they perceive the product to contain sufficient benefits to satisfy their felt needs and also to the extent that the satisfaction of those felt needs are important to them. Also, consumers buy products that are consistent with their existing self-image or that they feel will allow them to improve their self-image. This is done within the boundaries of what kinds of purchases are sanctioned by their own reference groups. To make an effective marketing application of this process, it would be possible to divide up the tourist potential into segments and develop different vacation alternatives for the different segments based upon the various benefit bundles being sought by each segment. For example in the skiing market people look for different things from the ski experience. To some, the quality of the slopes is of prime importance; to others, the *après*-ski entertainment is paramount. Each segment looks for different attributes. To the first segment a campaign stressing the quality of the slopes and the short lift lines would work. This campaign would not particularly interest the "entertainment" skiers. A brochure showing people sipping hot buttered rum round a blazing fire would be more effective.

There has been some question as to the individuality of specific destinations in providing unique benefit bundles. Does each destination contain those elements that will satisfy particular felt needs? It has been suggested that sociopsychological motives are unrelated to destination attributes. The emphasis may shift from the destination itself to its function as a medium through which sociopsychological needs can be satisfied. Later we will see that a large percentage of tourists who use travel agents enter with a vague idea or with little or no idea about which particular destination they wish to visit. This suggests the difficulty, from a marketing viewpoint, of establishing a destination as the unique place offering various unique benefits to satisfy particular needs.

Perception/Technical Factors

If the decision to travel to a particular destination is linked to our perception of that destination, then an examination of the perception process may help us understand if and how we can change an individual's perception of a destination in order to increase the likelihood of that individual's visiting the destination. Any information from either the social or commercial environment is molded into an image through our perceptual processes. The resultant image is less a function of the promotional message of a destination than of our individual perception of that message. There are many factors that affect consumer sensitivity and perception. Although these elements are working at the same time and although the effect of one often contradicts the effect of another, they are discussed individually. The first of these factors can be referred to as technical ones. Technical factors refer to the object, product, or service as it actually exists. The various elements of a particular product or service, such as price, quality, service, availability, and distinctiveness, can be communicated through the product or service itself. These inputs are termed significative stimuli. The elements may also be communicated in a symbolic way through the use of words and/or pictures. There are several factors that are termed technical. *Size* is an important consideration. To many, size is equated with quality. The larger the company, the airplane, or the hotel, the better the service is perceived to be. Generally speaking, larger advertisements will receive greater attention. A travel company might use a big advertisement or emphasize the largeness of its operation to gain more attention and give the impression of quality to the reader. *Color* also attracts more attention than black and white. Color advertisements are 50 percent more effective than are black and white ones. The *intensity* of a stimulus also affects the perception of it. The greater the intensity, the more the attention. Intensity can refer to the brightness of colors, the use of certain "strong" words, or the importance of a present or past purchase or experience. Stressing the importance of a decision to buy will increase the attention given a message. *Moving* objects attract more attention than stationary objects. This accounts for much of the success of advertising on television. Point-of-purchase displays with moving parts—in a travel agency, for example—can also be used to good effect. The *position* of a piece of information can affect whether or not the information will attract attention. In a brochure rack, pamphlets at shoulder height will attract the most attention. When placing advertisements in a newspaper, it is important to consider that the upper part of the page attracts more attention. *Contrast* is another element that affects the attention given a stimulus. By varying the thought, color, size, pattern, or intensity of a stimulus, enough discontinuity may be created between what is expected and what is actually perceived in order to attract attention. If competing messages are bright, colorful, and somewhat gaudy, a very simple, dignified message may be noticed because of the contrast. The final technical factor is that of *isolation*. Advertisers are fond of putting a border, called "white space," around their messages to isolate them from other messages on a page. As noted earlier, these elements interact often in contradictory ways. The greatest impact comes when several factors combine to give a more significant effect. This is illustrated in Figure 2.2.

FIGURE 2.2   Getting Attention

The task is to communicate these elements:	using these means:	to gain:
Quality	Size	Attention
Price	Color	
Distinctiveness	Intensity	
Availability	Movement	
Service	Position	
	Contrast	
	Isolation	

Image Shaping Forces

Technical factors are concerned with getting information through to the potential traveler. However, the information and impressions that do get through are distorted by a number of forces into an image. First let us consider an individual's *state of readiness*. Part of this is a tendency on our part to *stabilize our perception* even after the original basis for the perception has changed. A traveler may continue to stay at an old favorite hotel where the level of service has declined because the perception remains in the past. An image, whether positive or negative, may continue long after the factors causing that original image have been changed. This illustrates the difficulty involved in changing an image. Linked with this very closely is that, as a creature of habit, a traveler will perceive in a certain *habitual way* until forced to think differently. Stress here is placed on the need for marketers to break through the traveler's "habit barrier" by means of various stimuli mentioned above. A third shaping force relates to the extent to which individuals have a tendency to be *confident or cautious*. The confident individual takes in a complex situation more quickly, can more readily see positive elements in a situation, and can assimilate more detail. Decisions are made faster by confident persons, although those who are cautious make slower decisions and hence their perceptions tend to be more accurate. This factor points to the need to communicate different messages to different segments of an intended market. This, of course, will work only if marketers are able to determine that the more-confident traveler reads different newspapers or magazines or watches different television programs than the more-cautious traveler. The amount of information that can be perceived is limited by the fact that we have a *limited span of attention*. This refers to the number of stimuli that can be taken in at the same time. Experiments have shown this number to be approximately eight. This infers that messages should not consist of too many elements for fear that an important element may be missed or that the message may be disregarded because it is too confusing. The tendency to react to a given stimulus in a certain way is referred to as an *individual's mental set*. This suggests a learned response. It may be possible, for example, to suggest in a campaign, "Whenever you think of hotels, think of Hilton." If the campaign has the desired effect, an individual will think of Hilton (the response) whenever she or he thinks of hotels (the stimulus). Parts of this mental set are the *expectations* we bring to a situation. People tend to perceive what they expect to perceive. There is a tendency to round out a particular image in our minds by adding pieces that we do not have *based upon what we expect to be there*. For example, a highway traveler may see a sign for a motel that advertises an indoor pool. The traveler may expect that if a motel has an indoor pool, it will also have a certain high quality of service in other facilities. Because there is a pool the expectation is that other high-quality facilities will be present. In another example,[6] patrons of several restaurants were questioned about their dining experience after they left the restaurant. They were asked, among other things, to describe the clothing of the waiter and waitress. Although most could describe in great detail the waiter's clothing, few could do so for the waitress. The

---

[6]David B. Kronenfeld, John Kronenfeld, and Jerrold E. Kronenfeld, "Toward a Science of Design for Successful Foodservice," *Institutions/Volume Feeding*, June 1, 1972, pp. 40–48.

interesting fact is that none of the restaurants had waiters. Similarly, where there was no music people could describe the music in greater detail than they could when there actually was music. The point is that these customers noticed several elements from the restaurants and from that developed an image of all the elements they expected to be present in that type of an operation. Because certain elements were present, this "should" be a restaurant with waiters. This is known as bringing "closure" to a situation. Another part of our state of readiness is the degree of *familiarity* we have with incoming stimuli. To the extent that we are familiar with the stimulus we will have some idea of how to respond to it. This effect of past experience manifests itself in several ways. First, if we have visited Germany, then information about Germany will be perceived by us, in part, based upon our experience there. If we experienced negatives we will perceive new information about Germany negatively because it evokes memories of a negative experience. The reverse is also true. In addition, if we perceive new information to be *similar* to an experience with which we are familiar, we will tend to act upon that new information in a way similar to our behavior in our previous experience. For example, assume we perceive Austria and Germany to be similar as vacation destinations, yet we have visited only Germany and were pleased with the experience. Information received about Austria will be perceived positively in light of our German experience. This, of course, can work to encourage or discourage purchase behavior. If we know positive feelings exist for a product or service, we may wish to stress the connection when advertising a new product from the same company. A major selling point in a chain operation is the uniformity of quality standards. The message is that if you stayed at one Holiday Inn and were pleased, you will be pleased when you stay at another Holiday Inn. This also can work in reverse. An unpleasant experience at one chain operation will be generalized into a perception about the entire chain. There are times when an advertiser will have to work hard against this tendency. Some tourists will have a tendency to perceive all "sun 'n fun" destinations as being similar. The task for any one such destination is to show that it is different from the others. A further complicating factor is that stimuli in close proximity to each other tend to be perceived as being similar. Despite the fact that islands in the Caribbean have unique identities because of different historical and cultural influences, the fact that they are relativey close together means they will be perceived as being similar. Again the marketing task is to differentiate one from another. Another related part of this perceptual process relates to *context*. A stimulus will be perceived relative to the context in which it is viewed. A resort will be judged, in part, by the perceptions of the media in which the resort is advertised. Advertising in a magazine viewed as exclusive will bring a certain perception of exclusivity to the resort.

TABLE 2.3   Places of Interest in Singapore: Degree of Appeal to Different Visitors

Places of Interest	RANK			
	U.S.A.	Canada	U.K.	Japan
Botanic Gardens	1	1	2	1
Change Alley/Raffles Place	3	4	1	8
Orchard Road Shopping Centre	5	11	3	2
House of Jade	2	2	10	6
Mount Faber	7	3	5	3
Singapore River	4	5	9	21
Chinatown and Sago Lane	6	7	6	21
Chinese Emporiums	12	12	4	9
Haw Par Villa	9	9	8	9
Esplanade	8	8	7	7

SOURCE: Tourist Promotion Board Annual Report, Singapore, 1972.

How consumers perceive a situation is also affected by various *social and cultural factors*. A Mediterranean cruise, for example, will be perceived differently by individuals from different social classes. Males and females will perceive the same advertisement differently. This point is illustrated in Table 2.3. The table consists of a ranking of various attractions in Singapore by tourists from different countries. The table clearly shows that tourists from different countries and cultures have different perceptions as to favorite attractions. Although there are several similarities in the responses of U.S. and Canadian visitors, differences emerge. The Orchard Lake Shopping Centre is ranked fifth by U.S. tourists and eleventh by Canadian visitors. The House of Jade was ranked second as a place of interest by both Americans and Canadians, yet placed tenth by the British and sixth by the Japanese. It is clear that the relative merits of attractions at a particular destination are perceived differently by those from different cultures. The difference in perception necessitates different marketing themes for those different market segments. Even within the same country a destination will be perceived in different terms by those in different social or cultural groups.

AN IDEAL IMAGE

What images do particular destinations, services, and facilities actually have? Although we have noted that different people perceive the same situation differently, is it possible to generalize about the image of perceptions of particular places? A major study by the International Travel Research Institute uncovered some interesting findings. A study of upper socioeconomic males who were frequent travelers sought to identify image characteristics associated with destinations that travelers would be inclined to revisit. The characteristics that appeared to cause people to repeat their visit were:[7]

1. Advanced, developed country
2. Many scenic attractions
3. Good facilities for visitors
4. Warm, friendly people
5. Good potential for business
6. Good food
7. Good shopping

This research effort is particularly interesting because it deals with an ideal destination to revisit rather than the image of a particular destination.

Perception of Distance

The subject of distance in general and perceptions of it in particular is very important in relation to the study of tourism. The reason for this is that much of tourist travel revolves around differences. People may travel to a different climate, from snow to sun; to see different scenery, from plains to mountains; or to experience a different culture, from modern to traditional. By its very nature, then, tourist travel to experience differences implies covering some distance. The distance to be traveled may act as a barrier depending upon how it is perceived.

The perception of a particular distance is not a constant. Rather the perception of a particular distance seems to vary relative to various socioeconomic factors as well as to the activity to be undertaken. It appears that travelers in higher levels of occupation and income are inclined to travel farther. This may, of course, be partially explained by the fact that they can afford to travel farther. However, those who favored active vacations over inactive vacations are inclined to travel long distances. Some researchers feel that occupation is the key, while others link personality variables to the propensity to travel. Although all of the answers are not known, it does seem that distance can be viewed either positively or negatively in terms of its effect on travel. Certainly the greater the distance, the greater the financial cost. As such, distance is a limiting factor. It may also be that great distances represent a psychological barrier because of the tediousness involved in traveling or the fear of being far from home. At the same time, a destination may increase in attractiveness because of the distance that must be traveled to get there. It has been demonstrated that, for some tourists, beyond a certain distance the friction of

---

[7]"Intramar: A Study of Some of the World's Great Airlines, Hotels and Destinations," International Travel Research Institute, 1980, p. 20.

distance becomes reversed—the farther they go, the farther they want to go. Especially on unplanned trips there may be a tendency to view closer-to-home destinations and attractions as stepping stones to stopping points farther away rather than as competition for the farther destination.

Marketing Implications

The topic of perception has very real marketing implications. Effective marketing strategies can be determined only after determining the extent to which potential visitors perceive that our destination contains those attributes that they consider important. This involves a three-step process:

1. What do you, the potential visitor, consider important?
2. Do you *perceive* that we have this?
3. Do we *actually* have this?

In a survey of potential tourists (see Table 2.4) individuals were asked what attributes they considered very important in planning a foreign trip and the extent to which they perceived that Britain did the best job of satisfying these same attributes. By comparing these responses, various strategies are suggested. The model for this process is contained in Figure 2.3.

The first consideration is "what does the market consider important or unimportant?" The market is particularly interested in physical safety, scenic beauty, historical attractions, climate, and hospitality. Because it is important to the market, it is important to us. The people in the market are not particularly interested in gambling, the country's political position, good nightlife, or American-style comforts. These latter elements should be ignored by us. To include them in any marketing effort would overload the consumer and may result in the potential visitors, "protecting" themselves by ignoring the entire message.

We now know what is important to the visitors. Will they be satisfied with our destination if they visit it? The answer depends upon a comparison of their image of the destination compared to our knowledge of what actually exists on the attributes they consider important. Several outcomes are possible. First, the visitors' perception or image may be negative when we know that it should be positive. For example, climate is important (ranked 4), but Britain rates poorly (ranked 8). There are, however, times of the year when the British climate is good. In this case the image must be changed before visitors will feel positive. A campaign may stress the amount of sunshine or lack of rain in certain months. Some destinations in the Bahamas offer rain insurance. If you get more than a certain amount of rain during your vacation your hotel room is free.

TABLE 2.4 Comparison of Important Attributes and Perception of Britain*

	A Rank	B Rank
Safety from physical harm	1	5
Real scenic beauty	2	6
Seeing things of historical interest	3	2
Good weather and climate	4	18
Having people make you feel welcome	5	7
Getting really good food	6	16
Cost of trip fits regular income without special saving	7	11
Famous cities	8	3
Visit more than one country easily	9	8
Easy language communication	10	1
Being sympathetic to people and their achievements	11	12
Famous art museums	12	4
Finding everything different from the United States	13	17
Good beaches, swimming, water sports	14	21
Shopping for things you'd like to buy	15	9
Religious pilgrimage, seeing shrines	16	19
Being familiar with country and area	17	14
American-style comfort, convenience	18	10
Good nightlife	19	13
Sympathy with political position of country's and area's government	20	15
Being able to gamble at casinos	21	20

A: Attributes considered very important when planning a foreign trip

B: Attributes that travelers perceive Britain as doing the best job of satisfying

  Based on 1513 people interviewed at 200 locations throughout the U.S.

SOURCE: Michael Perry, "Comparison of Tourist Destination Image as Perceived by Travelers and Travel Agents," in New Perspectives and Policies Proceedings of the International Tourism Congress, Turkey, 1978.

to consider the factors that influence image formation. According to Gunn[8] an image evolves at two levels. An organic image is formed as a result of general exposure to newspaper reports, magazine articles, television reports, and other specifically nontourist information. Thus, even the individual who has never visited a particular country nor even sought out information on that country will have some kind of image, perhaps incomplete, of that country. At this point, as mentioned earlier, other pieces of the image picture will be added that the individual perceives *should* be there to match the pieces already known, in order to make a complete picture. The second level is that of an induced image. This refers to an image brought about by tourist-directed information, such as advertisements and travel posters. The organic image tends to develop first and, as such, may be regarded as a stronger influence than the induced one in overall image formation. There is little that can be done to influence

---

[8]Clare A. Gunn, "Vacationscape: Designing Tourist Regions" (University of Texas, 1972), pp. 110–13.

FIGURE 2.3   Perception—Marketing Implications

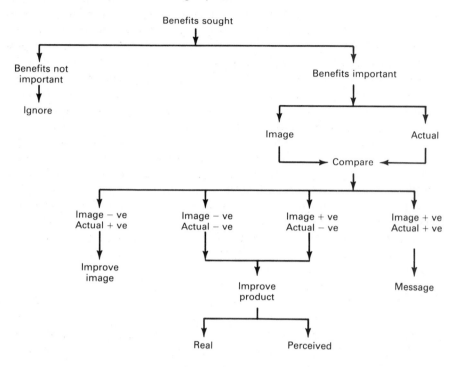

the formation of an organic image. Filmmakers may be persuaded to shoot a movie such as *The Sound of Music* which, although not a travel film, influences people in their image of Austria. In general, however, little can be done. Marketers do seek, obviously, to induce an image through the production of films, posters, and advertisements. If the organic image is set in an individual's mind, an induced image may be disregarded in favor of the previously held organic image.

An image *can* change over time. Research has indicated that, although consumers have stable perceptions about frequently bought products, their image of an infrequently bought product changes over time. Although an image can change over time, can that image *be changed* over time? There is some literature that suggests that an image cannot be changed, but it appears that the task, though difficult, costly, and time consuming, is not impossible.

What if the image is negative and the actual is negative also? Britain's climate is rated poorly, and there certainly are some very wet months there. The solution is to change the product. If we score low on a factor important to the market we have to get our own house in order before we can attract them. This may mean a real or perceived change. For example, to attract tourists during those wet months it may be necessary to develop more indoor facilities where activities can take place irrespective of the weather. The product change may, on the other hand, be perceptual. There is a segment of skiers who place high priority on short lift lines. If a ski area is perceived as having long lift lines, it will be necessary to change the product if, in fact, the lines are long. How can a lift line be shortened? A real change would be to open up more hill capacity. This, however, is expensive. A perceived change would be to make the wait *appear* shorter. Some Michigan ski areas provide entertainers or musicians to those in line to make the time spent in line seem short.

The same strategy is appropriate if the image is positive but the actual situation negative. In such a situation we may attract visitors because they think they will be made to feel welcome. If we know that our employees do not have enough training to give this expected level of service, dissatisfaction will result unless the product (employee hospitality) is changed.

Last, what if the image is positive and the actual is positive? This becomes the thrust of our message. In this example, we would sell Britain on a combination of history and hospitality.

REFERENCES

ABBEY, JAMES, "The Relevance of Life Style and Demographic Information to Designing Package Travel Tours" (Ph.D. dissertation, Utah State University, 1978).

CHASE, DAVID R., AND NEIL H. CHEEK, "Activity Preferences and Participation: Conclusions from a Factor Analytic Study," *Journal of Leisure Research*, vol. 11, no. 2, 1979, pp. 92–101.

CORY, LAWRENCE G., "People Who Claim to be Opinion Leaders: Identifying Their Characteristics by Self Report," *Journal of Marketing*, vol. 35, no. 4, October 1977, pp. 48–53.

CROMPTON, JOHN, "A Systems Model of the Tourist's Destination Selection Process with Particular Reference to the Roles of Image and Perceived Constraints" (Ph.D. dissertation, Texas A&M University, 1977).

CROMPTON, JOHN L., "An Assessment of the Image of Mexico as a Vacation Destination and the Influence of Geographical Location Upon That Image," *Journal of Travel Research*, vol. 17, no. 4, 1979, pp. 18–23.

DARDEN, WILLIAM R., AND WILLIAM D. PERRAULT, JR., "A Multivariate Analysis of Media Exposure and Vacation Behavior with Life Style Covariates," *Journal of Consumer Research*, vol. 2, no. 2, September 1975, p. 100.

GOODRICH, JONATHAN, "The Relationship Between Preferences for and Perceptions of Vacation Destinations: Application of a Choice Model," *Journal of Travel Research*, vol. 17, no. 2, 1978, pp. 8–13.

GOODRICH, JONATHAN, "An Investigation of Consumer Perceptions of, and Preferences for, Selected Tourist Destinations: A Multidimensional Scaling

Approach" (Ph.D. dissertation, State University of New York at Buffalo, 1977).

HOROWITZ, I. A., AND R. S. KAYE, "Perception and Advertising," *Journal of Advertising Research*, vol. 15, no. 2, September 1975, pp. 15-21.

"How Hotels/Motels Register With Their Guests," *Time Marketing Research Report 1955*, Time Inc., 1976.

HUNT, JOHN, "Image as a Factor in Tourism Development," *Journal of Travel Research*, vol. 13, no. 3, Winter 1975, pp. 1-7.

International Travel Research Institute, "Intramar: A Study of Some of the World's Great Airlines, Hotels and Destinations," 1980.

KAUFFMAN, PHILLIP, "The Effect of a Study-Tour to the People's Republic of China Upon Participants' Personality and Attitudes" (Ph.D dissertation, The Ohio State University, 1976).

MATEJKA, J. KENNETH, "Vacation Behavior: An Investigation of Experience, Adequacy Importance and Perceived Risk" (Ph.D dissertation, University of Arkansas, 1976).

MAYO, EDWARD J., AND LANCE P. JARVIS, *Psychology of Leisure Travel* (Boston, C.B.I. Publishing Company, Inc., 1981), pp. 43-48; 60-62.

MERCER, DAVID, "The Role of Perception in the Recreation Experience: A Review and Discussion," *Journal of Leisure Research*, vol. 3, no. 4, Fall 1971, pp. 261-277.

MYERS, PAUL B., "Decision Making and Travel Behavior: A Midwestern Study" (Ph.D. dissertation, Michigan State University, 1974).

NARAYNA, C. L., "The Stability of Perceptions," *Journal of Advertising Research*, vol. 16, no. 2, April 1976, pp. 45-49.

NOLAN, SIDNEY D., JR., "Tourists' Use and Evaluation of Travel Information Sources" (Ph.D. dissertation, Texas A&M University, 1974).

O'BRIEN, T. V., H. DE GENNARO, AND G. W. SUMMERS, "Customer Perception of Product Attributes in the Airline Industry," *Journal of Travel Research*, vol. 15, no. 3, Winter 1977, pp. 9-13.

PERRY, MICHAEL, "Comparison of Tourist Destination Image as Perceived by Travelers and Travel Agents," in *New Perspectives and Policies* (Proceedings of the International Tourism Congress, Turkey, 1978).

REIBSTEIN, DAVID J., CHRISTOPHER H. LOVELOCK, AND RICARDO DE P. DOBSON, "The Direction of Causality Between Perceptions, Affect and Behavior: An Application to Travel Behavior," *Journal of Consumer Research*, vol. 6, no. 4, March 1980, pp. 370-76.

SCHMOLL, G. A., *Tourism Promotion*, Tourism International Press, London, England, 1977, p. 59.

SCOTT, DOUGLAS R., C. D. SCHEWE, AND D. G. GREDERICK, "A Multi-Brand/Multi-Attribute Model of Tourist State Choice," *Journal of Travel Research*, vol. 17, no. 1, Summer 1978, pp. 23-29.

SETH, JAGDISH, AND W. WAYNE TALARZYK, "Perceived Instrumentality and Value Importance as Determinants of Attitudes," *Journal of Marketing Research*, vol. 9, no. 1, February, 1972, pp. 6–9.

STERN, B. L., R. F. BUSH, AND J. F. HAIR, JR., "The Self-Image/Store Image Marching Process," *Journal of Business*, vol. 50, no. 1, January 1977, pp. 63–69.

STUMPF ROBERT V., "Perceptions and Preferences of Tourist Attractions: A Nonmetric Multidimensional Scaling Approach" (Ph.D. dissertation, Claremont Graduate School, 1976).

TREAS, CHARLES E., "Selected Ordinal Measures of Travel Related Information Cues and Choices Affecting Automobile Motorist Travel Behavior: A Case Study" (Ph.D. dissertation, University of Alabama, 1966).

WALTER, C. K., AND HSIN-MIN TONG, "A Local Study of Consumer Vacation Decisions," *Journal of Travel Research*, vol. 15, no. 4, Spring 1977, pp. 30–34.

WALTERS, C. GLENN, *Consumer Behavior: Theory and Practice* (Homewood, Il, Richard D. Irwin, Inc., 1978), pp. 327; 249–55.

WHEELER, MACEL MARTEWA, "Spatial Analysis of the Distribution of Visitors Among State Operated Recreational Sites in Kentucky" (Ph.D. dissertation, University of Kentucky, 1978).

WOODSIDE, ARCH G., AND ILLKA A. RONKAINEN, "Vacation Travel Planning Segments: Self-Planning vs. Users of Motor Club and Travel Agents," *Annals of Tourism Research*, vol. 7, no. 3, Winter 1980, pp. 385–94.

3

EXTERNALS:
The Environment for Tourism

The vacation decision is influenced, if not shaped, by various "forces" external to the individual. This chapter examines these forces.

The culture of which we are a part serves as a barometer of general trends within a country, and it exerts social pressure to conform to the broad cultural values represented by the majority of individuals making up that culture.

The amount and type of time available also helps determine if and where we can vacation.

Marketers have long segmented the travel market along the socioeconomic criteria of age, income, sex, and education. It is therefore appropriate to determine whether tourism demand differs on these criteria.

The characteristic patterns of demand at various stages in the family life cycle are examined, with particular reference to the effect of children on the family's demand, the demand pattern of the empty nester, and the various barriers to leisure enjoyment at different life-cycle stages.

Finally, the role of personality in shaping demand is explored. It has been felt that a link between personality and vacation behavior exists. Do certain types of people take certain kinds of vacations because of their personality characteristics? From a marketing viewpoint the segmentation of a target market by life-style provides a better picture of the characteristics, likes, and dislikes of the potential tourist.

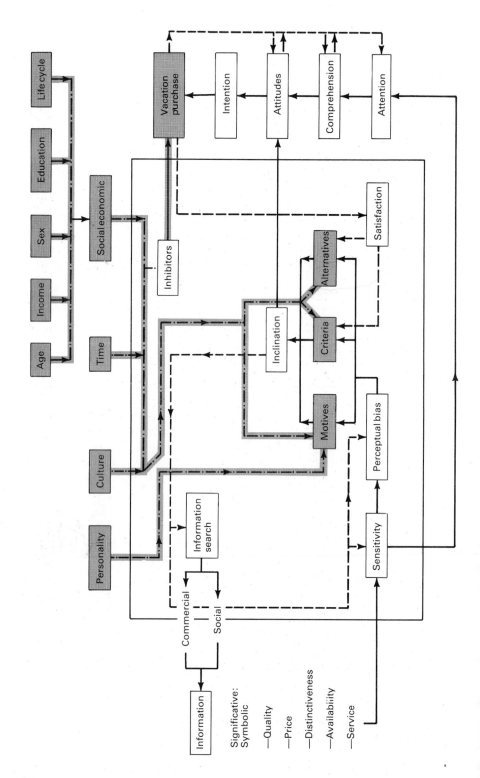

Life cycle

Education

Sex

Income

Age

Social economic

Time

Culture

Personality

Inhibitors

Vacation
purchase

Intention

Attitudes

Comprehension

Attention

Satisfaction

Alternatives

Criteria

Inclination

Motives

Perceptual bias

Sensitivity

Information
search

Commercial

Social

Information

Significative:
Symbolic

—Quality

—Price

—Distinctiveness

—Availability

—Service

38

Many factors external to the individual act as inhibiting factors on travel-purchase behavior. In this chapter the effect of these variables will be examined. Although these factors will be explored separately, it should be noted that their effect is often a compound one.

THE EFFECTS OF CULTURE ON TRAVEL

While an individual acts to satisfy certain internal needs and wants, the way in which these wants are satisfied is heavily influenced by forces external to the individual. As individuals we are part of larger social groups by which we are influenced. These groups themselves are part of and influenced by the surrounding culture. A knowledge of the culture of a country or subunit within that country is important to an understanding of how individuals within that country or subunit will behave.

Culture can be defined as a "set of beliefs, values, attitudes, habits and forms of behavior that are shared by a society and are transmitted from generation to generation."[1]

Culture and Society

Culture affects society in four ways. First, the overall values of the culture determine which goals and behavior will gain social approval or disapproval. To the extent that people are concerned about how others think of them, they will be influenced to seek gratification of their needs and wants in ways acceptable to society. This means that in order to induce those individuals to buy various products and services, it will be necessary to state the appeals and benefits of those products and services in terms acceptable to society. The many advertisements that advertise the hedonistic vacation life-style can only work because society is increasingly condoning this value. Several decades ago, such an appeal would not have worked because it was not socially acceptable to be self-indulgent, even on vacation.

The many social institutions of a society are also reflective of its culture. In the United States, for example, the ideas of individual initiative and equal opportunity for all (part of the culture) influence the way in which the educational system is organized to provide for mass education with a somewhat liberal child-rearing philosophy. Yet this expresses itself in different ways throughout society. Although lower-middle-class parents in the United States tend to be child-dominated and concerned with satisfying their children, upper-class parents are more interested in seeking ways to help their children seek status achievement. This suggests

---

[1]Peter D. Bennett and Harold J. Kassarjian, *Consumer Behavior* (Englewood Cliffs, NJ, Prentice-Hall, Inc., 1972), p. 123.

that upper-class parents can more readily be sold a travel vacation if that vacation is perceived by them as being something that will advance their child's progress in society.

The third way in which culture affects the social backdrop is in the established conventions and practices of society. Society adopts various practices relative to such things as which foods can be eaten, how to entertain, and which gifts are or are not appropriate. It is acceptable, for example, for horsemeat to be eaten in France but not in the United States; it is appropriate for a U.S. dinner guest to bring the host a bottle of wine, but in France this would be an insult. When attracting or servicing a market from a culture different from our own, it is necessary to know the established practices to avoid inadvertent behavior.

Last, culture's effect on society is felt in the language people use to communicate with one another. It is important to consider not only words but also gestures, expressions, and other body movements. A smile in Western culture is a warm signal to further a relationship, but in Oriental culture it may be used to cover embarrassment and shame.

Culture and Social Groups

Social groups have roles or standards of behavior peculiar to each group. These group norms differ from one culture to another. Groups can be classified either as primary (family or friends) or secondary (unions, fraternities, church, and so on). An individual will belong to more than one group, and consequently he or she will adopt a role for each social group. These roles may overlap. The surrounding culture will help define for each group the appropriate objects people use to show their membership in the group as well as the relevant status symbols.

Is there a distinct "vacation role"? One of the attractive features of taking a vacation is that it allows the freedom to be someone other than who we are in everyday life. Traveling to places where we are not known, meeting people who do not know us allows us to choose how we will behave.

The social role that an individual takes is learned through socialization—the process of social learning by which cultural role expectations are handed down from one generation to another. The link between participation in recreational activities as a child and subsequent participation as an adult has been repeatedly demonstrated. If we also accept that travel is a learned experience, the importance of encouraging travel participation at an early age can be demonstrated. The norms of behavior for a group change by virtue of both internal and external sources. Within a group there are those people (innovators) who are more willing than others to try new things. Usually these group members are better educated, have high income, and are more achievement-oriented than others. The innovators also tend to be opinion leaders and, as such, highly sought-after by marketers. A common saying in explaining destination development is "mass follows class." This phrase suggests that a destination first attracts a relatively small number of high-status individuals whose actions are eventually copied by a larger number of less-innovative others.

Culture patterns also change by virtue of external forces. As a result of contact with other environments, previous attitudes and behaviors may change. A visit to a foreign country may result in a change in attitude towards the people of that country as well as a stimulation of a desire for cuisine from that country. Travel may also stimulate the sale of other products from the destination visited. A vacation in Germany might improve the chance of purchasing a German car upon one's return home.

Culture and the Individual

The effect of culture is felt by the individual in three ways. First, culture affects the daily life patterns of individuals in society. An afternoon siesta is common in certain countries in Southern Europe to cope with high midday temperatures. In the United States, the physical separation of work and residence leads to an uninterrupted workday and consequently a smaller lunch compared to those in Southern Europe. Concepts of time vary from culture to culture. In the United States, time is money; in other cultures time is of less consequence. Second, culture affects the way emotions are expressed. In the Latin culture there is much touching—people feel comfortable at distances from one other that would make an American or Briton uncomfortable—and emotions are expressed in a spontaneous and enthusiastic manner. Last, there is every indication that certain cultures have a predominance of certain personality types. The German national character exhibits a predominance of authoritarian personality traits. In this culture, we would expect that a decision as important as an annual vacation would be made primarily by the male in a family.

It can readily be seen that in order to truly understand a consumer it is necessary to understand the surrounding culture of that consumer. A knowledge of how the culture affects the individual, the social groups to which that individual belongs, and society as a whole will better enable the marketer to sell a travel product. Insight will be gained as to what to say, to whom to say it, and how the message should be phrased. As hosts, we will be better able to understand why visitors act the way they do and be in a better position to anticipate and satisfy their needs and wants.

Analyzing a Culture

Louden[2] has developed a checklist of factors to be considered in analyzing a culture. The analysis would be particularly appropriate before developing a marketing approach to people from different cultures.

1. *Determine relevant motivations in the culture*: Which needs do people seek to fulfill?
2. *Determine characteristic behavior patterns*: How often are vacations purchased?
3. *Determine what broad cultural values are relevant to this product*: Are vacations, leisure, and recreation thought of in positive terms?
4. *Determine characteristic forms of decision making*: Who makes the vacation purchase decision? When is it made? What information sources and criteria are used in making the decision?
5. *Evaluate promotion methods appropriate to the culture*: What kinds of promotional techniques, words, and pictures are acceptable or not acceptable to the people of this culture?
6. *Determine appropriate institutions for this product in the minds of consumers*: Do people tend to purchase vacations directly from suppliers, or are retail travel agents used? What alternatives, acceptable to the consumer, are available for distributing the product?

The U.S. Culture

Within the culture of a country various subcultures can be found. Nevertheless the following characteristics are those that are generally found in the dominant culture of the United States.

Evaluative and moralistic. The dominant culture in the United States is one that is evaluative and moralistic in its judgment of objects, people, and behavior. The judgments that people make are usually quite simple and concise, that is, something or someone is either right or wrong, good or bad, or moral or immoral.

Humanistic and egalitarian. Americans as a whole believe in equal rights for all and that people are created equal. If possible, these people are generous to charitable causes.

Human mastery over nature and human perfectability. This attribute is portrayed by corporations and individuals continuously devising new technology and ideas that will be of benefit to their economic goals and to the goals of people to become knowledgeable and well-educated.

Materialism and progress. People place values on the amount of possessions one has and the necessity to be progressive both materially and educationally.

Individualism and achievement. The U.S. dominant culture places a great deal of emphasis on a high level of achievement motivation, which

---

[2]David L. Louden and Albert J. Della Bitta, *Consumer Behavior: Concepts and Applications* (New York, McGraw-Hill Book Co., 1979), pp. 135–39.

distinguishes it tremendously from certain subcultures and cultures of other countries. We achieve goals and become individualistic through intense competition.

Time orientation. Time is important to many because it is equated with money. Many things are organized and run by the clock.

Youthfulness. Many people turn to youth activities and procedures for renewed inspiration. Advertising, promotion, and products are all geared toward youthfulness.

Activity. Americans value hard work and also hard play. This stems from the Puritan ethic that idleness is evil.

Efficiency and practicality. People in the United States are continually searching for better ways of doing things, whether it is with a new product, service, or procedure. A product or service that is not quite "in" will be set aside and the new product or service will be implemented, even if the old product or service had not become obsolete.

Religious and moral orientation. A large percentage of Americans are religious. Many in the culture believe that the U.S. culture and way of life is the best and feel that it is their duty to bring others around to this country's way of thinking and acting.

Social interaction and conformity. Even though many in the United States value individualism, marketers promote products of all kinds that incorporate the theme of how beneficial these products are in achieving pleasurable social interaction.

Subcultures

The point was made earlier that, not only do countries have unique cultures, but within a country subcultures exist. Within the United States there are, to name a few, Spanish, black, and Jewish subcultures. Each subculture is different in several ways to the national culture. In the Spanish subculture, family ties are very strong, with the husband having strong authority over buying decisions. The upper-class Spanish-American has been almost totally assimilated into American culture. Because Spanish-Americans are respected for this, they are regarded as opinion leaders and are a useful group to reach to penetrate the market.

In the black subculture, women have a great influence on the attitudes and behavior of black children and on purchase behavior in general. It is dangerous to generalize even when talking about the characteristics of a subculture. It appears, however, that blacks tend to spend their income on personal consumption items with which they feel they get value. Although some blacks base their purchase behavior on the whites they may seek to match, others go in the opposite direction.

The Jewish subculture is strongly family oriented, with joint decision making more common than in the subcultures of the previous examples. A strong emphasis is placed on education, and there is a willingness to buy new items, try new places.

Regional differences are also apparent. Southerners are regarded as being more conservative, westerners as being more liberal and tolerant of others, and easterners as being more self-reliant than those in the rest of the country. Thus, it can be seen that it is necessary to understand not only the national culture but the regional, racial, and religious subcultures in order to effectively understand and market to the travel consumer.

Cultural Changes

The culture within which the travel consumer exists does change. It is difficult to determine when a movement becomes a trend and when a trend becomes part of the culture. Yankelovich, Shelley and White is a very successful marketing and social research organization that specializes in identifying and tracking social trends. Many trends or tendencies in the United States have been developed, all of which have significance for the marketer of travel and tourism.[3,4]

PSYCHOLOGY OF AFFLUENCE

Trend toward physical self-enhancement: Spending more time, effort, and money on improving one's physical appearance; the things people do to enhance their looks.

Trend toward personalization: Expressing one's individuality through products, possessions, and new life-styles; the need to be "a little bit different" from other people.

Trend toward physical health and well-being: The level of concern with one's health, diet, and things to do to take better care of oneself.

Trend toward new forms of materialism: The new status symbols and the extent of deemphasis on money and material possessions.

Trend toward social and cultural self-expression: The cultural explosion and what it means to various segments of the population.

Trend toward personal creativity: The growing conviction that being "creative" is not confined to the artist. Everyone can be creative in her or his own way, as expressed through a wide variety of activities, hobbies, and new uses of leisure time.

Trend toward meaningful work: The spread of the demand for work that is challenging and meaningful more than just being well paying.

Implications: Greater demand for spa vacations; physically and mentally active vacations; allowing tourists more options on packages to let them personalize their trip; themes that say "This one's for *you*."

---

[3]Philip N. Robertson "The Search for Identity," *Cornell H.R.A. Quarterly*, February 1971, pp. 13–18.

[4]Florence R. Skelly "Outline of the Changing Consumers," in *The 80s, Its Impact on Travel and Tourism Marketing* (The Travel Research Association Eighth Annual Conference Proceedings, 1977), pp. 201–204.

ANTIFUNCTIONAL TRENDS

Trend toward the "new romanticism": The desire to restore romance, mystery, and adventure to modern life.

Trend toward novelty and change: The search for constant change, novelty, new experience, reaction against sameness, and habit.

Trend toward adding beauty to one's daily surroundings: The stress on beauty in the home and the things people do and buy to achieve it.

Trend toward sensuousness: Placing greater emphasis on a total sensory experience—touching, feeling, smelling, and psychedelic phenomena; a moving away from the purely linear, logical, and visual.

Trend toward mysticism: The search for new modes of spiritual experience and beliefs, as typified by the growing interest in astrology.

Trend toward introspection: An enhanced need for self-understanding and life experiences in contrast to automatic conformity to external pressures and expectations.

Implications: Greater demand for packages (that simplify vacation planning); "get away from it all" appeals; finding one's roots; deemphasizing large size of airline, destination, and so on; selling personal attention; regions rather than countries.

REACTION AGAINST COMPLEXITY TRENDS

Trend toward life simplification: The turning away from complicated products, services, and ways of life.

Trend toward return to nature: Rejection of the artificial, the "chemical," the man-made improvements on nature; the adoption of more "natural" ways of dressing, eating, and living.

Trend toward increased ethnicity: Finding new satisfactions and identifications in foods, dress, customs, and life-styles of various ethnic groups such as black, Italian, Irish, Polish, or German.

Trend toward increased community involvement: Increased affiliation with local, community, and neighborhood activities; greater involvement in local groups.

Trend away from bigness: The departure from the belief that "big" necessarily means "good," beginning to manifest itself with respect to "big" brands, "big" stores.

Implications: Greater demand for packages (that simplify vacation planning); "get away from it all" appeals; finding one's roots; deemphasizing of large size of airline, destination, and so on; selling of personal attention; regions rather than countries.

TRENDS THAT MOVE AWAY FROM PURITAN VALUES

Trend toward pleasure for its own sake: Putting pleasure before duty; focus on self.

Trend toward blurring of the sexes: Moving away from traditional distinctions between men and women and the role each should play in marriage, work, and other walks of life.

Trend toward living in the present: Straying from traditional beliefs in planning, saving, and living for the future.

Trend toward more liberal sexual attitudes: The relaxation of sexual prohibitions and the devaluation of "virtue" in the traditional sense among women.

Trend toward acceptance of stimulants and drugs: Greater acceptance of artificial agents (legal and illegal) for mood change, stimulation, and relaxation as opposed to the view that these should be accomplished by strength of character alone.

Trend toward relaxation of self-improvement standards: The inclination to stop working as hard at self-improvement, letting yourself be whatever you are.

Trend toward individual religions: Rejection of institutionalized religions and the substitution of more personalized forms of religious sects and cults.

Implications: Greater demand for "do it now," "you deserve to have fun" type of appeals; greater acceptance of sexual innuendo in advertising.

TRENDS RELATED TO CHILD-CENTEREDNESS

Trend toward greater tolerance of chaos and disorder: Less need for schedules, routines, plans, regular shopping, and purchasing; tolerance of less order and cleanliness in the home, less regular eating and entertaining patterns.

Trend toward challenge to authority: Less automatic acceptance of the authority and "correctness" of public figures, institutions, and established brands.

Trend toward the rejection of hypocrisy: Less acceptance of sham, exaggeration, indirection, and misleading language.

Trend toward female careerism: Belief that homemaking is not sufficient as the sole source of fulfillment and that more challenging and productive work for the woman is needed.

Trend toward familism: Renewed faith in the belief that the essential life satisfactions stem from activities centering on the immediate family unit rather than on "outside" sources such as work or community affairs. Restructuring of the way the family operates, from self-sacrifice on behalf of other family members to wanting a family setup in which each member can focus on self without guilt.

Implications: Greater demand for vacations off-peak and of shorter duration to fit into "two career" schedules; increased consumerism, including questioning of advertising claims; accent on "*you* deserve to have fun."

THE EFFECT OF TIME ON TRAVEL

Time, or rather the availability of time, acts as a major inhibiting factor to tourist travel. The amount of available time and the form in which it is available is, in fact, a major shaper of the destinations that can be visited, the modes of travel that can be used, and the activities that can be engaged in at the destination or enroute. The desire to travel and the financial ability to travel are insufficient if one does not have the time to travel. All three factors must be present for travel and tourism to take place.

Our time can be spent in one of three ways:

FIGURE 3.1   Time Divisions

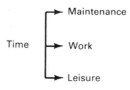

Spending Time

Time is spent in many maintenance activities. Maintenance activities can be thought of as activities that involve a certain degree of obligation and that are necessary to sustain and maintain life. Included in this definition are such activities as eating, sleeping, maintaining the house, and caring for the lawn. Time can also be spent at work. For most of us this involves a degree of obligation greater than that spent in maintenance activities. Leisure can be defined, although some people may feel it is a rather simplified definition, as the time remaining after work and maintenance activities have been completed. By its very definition leisure implies that the individual has a level of discretion over how to spend time that is not present in the other two categories. Leisure is often contrasted with the economic activity of work, and it is connected with pleasure and a feeling of freedom with a minimum of obligation. Leisure is also seen as inner directed rather than other directed. It is the time for one's self. Although leisure time offers opportunities for creativity and personal growth, the accent must be on freedom of choice. Traditionally, researchers have talked about leisure as time spent in productive pursuits. Yet this imposes a value system upon the individual's discretionary time. "Productive" is a term defined by the researcher. The crucial point is that leisure-time activities are those that are undertaken freely by individuals within their discretionary time.

By seeing time broken down into these three categories, it is easy to demonstrate a relationship between all three. Because time is absolute—there are twenty-four hours in a day, seven days in a week, fifty-two weeks in a year—any change in one of the three parts will automatically affect the others. As the workweek declines, more time is freed for maintenance and/or leisure activities. This is important because in the study of tourism we are concerned with the use of leisure time, and a recognition that leisure time is bound to the other two concepts will help us to be concerned with changes in those concepts as they might affect leisure time.

How is time actually spent? In a "typical" week most time is spent on maintenance activities. This is true for both females and males. The significant differences between the sexes is that females spend more time on housework, necessary home maintenance, lawn care, and playing with or helping the children than do males. Leisure-time activities take up between 20 to 25 percent of the average workweek. This amounts to approximately thirty-nine hours per week. There are no major differences between the sexes as to how leisure time is spent. Most leisure time is spent watching television.

We might expect that the above distribution would change relative to changes in the family life cycle. This relationship is demonstrated in Figure 3.2. In the young and single phase, people are characterized by great physical capacity, disposable time, and few demands on their in-

FIGURE 3.2   Time Phases in the Family Life Cycle

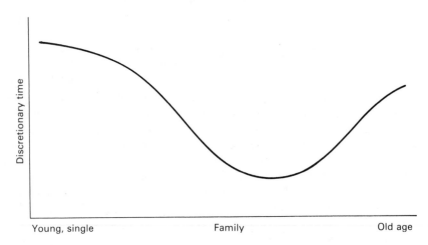

come. In the family phase, discretionary income and time decrease, and the physical capacity of the family is limited by that of its weakest member. The third phase is characterized by an excess of discretionary time and a decrease in physical capacity.

Historical Development of Leisure Time

The distribution of time between the three categories mentioned has changed over the years. In 1850 the average workweek was close to seventy hours; today it is approximately forty hours. The reasons for the long workweek in the nineteenth century have been traced to the industrial revolution. Prior to the industrial revolution in Britain, most people were connected with the farm. Hours of work and leisure were dictated by the farming seasons. People worked long hours when the harvest had to be brought in, but in winter, because of the lesser number of daylight hours, hours of work were less. The industrial revolution brought a movement of a rural population which had work hours conditioned by nature to an increasingly urban population which had work hours increased by employers who sought to have output on a continuous basis year round. In addition, many of the leisure-time pursuits of the working class were rough and violent. In order to better control their workers, owners adopted various strategies. Wages were kept low so that saving money was difficult and people had to continue working rather than take time off in order to live. In addition, the Sabbath was strictly enforced. As a complement to this, the idea of work was made the most important part of life. The idea of spending time at work was praised almost to the point of sanctification, but the idea of spending time at leisure was derided. Religious movements developed this thought into an ethic—the Protestant ethic. Leisure time was first given to celebrate various religious festivals. These holy days were the forerunner of our holidays, as the idea of associating a break from work with religion has gradually diminished.

Although the workweek has undoubtedly decreased, other factors have prevented more people from seeing an increase in their leisure time. As affluence has increased the incidence of material possessions, much of the reduced work time has manifested itself in increased maintenance time to take care of the new possessions, such as the car and the house. In addition, as cities have grown as a result of the country becoming more urbanized, commuting time to work has increased. A related factor is that, for many, the stress of big-city living means that more time is required before individuals are mentally ready for leisure pursuits. A third factor is that, as the economy moves from primary and manufacturing industries to a service economy, the distinction between work and nonwork becomes increasingly blurred. It is easier for the steel worker to punch out at the end of a shift and forget about work problems than it is for the manager of a business. In addition, the growing number of part-time workers has hidden the fact that over the past twenty-five years the average non-student workweek has remained steady at about forty-three hours.

Attempts have been made to show a relationship between the type of work and the type of leisure activities engaged in. Leisure has been seen as a compensation for work in that leisure activity is quite different from work activity. A passive job, for example, may result in active leisure-time activities. A second view is that the development of certain skills and life-styles learned at work will spill over into a demand for similar kinds of leisure-time activities. The problem, of course, is that any leisure-time behavior can be explained by reference to whichever theory is more appropriate to one's purpose. The link between type of work and leisure activities has not been demonstrated. In fact, several studies have demonstrated that there are no significant differences in leisure activity between workers who are doing what they consider boring jobs and those who are doing more interesting and enjoyable jobs. It does seem clear, however, that the place of leisure in a person's life is becoming more important relative to that of work.

More important than the absolute amount of leisure time available, however, is the way in which it is spent. An individual who finishes dinner at seven o'clock and plans to go to bed at midnight has five hours of leisure time. The amount of time available limits what activities can be done and where they can be pursued. Leisure time may be thought of as being divided into three categories.

FIGURE 3.3 Leisure Time Divisions

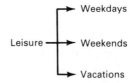

Leisure occurs on weekdays, weekends, and on vacations. The importance of this distinction can be illustrated by means of an example. If the workweek were to be reduced by 20 percent, the opportunities for tourism activities would be affected by the way in which the reduction was taken: the workday could be shortened to six-and-a-half hours from eight; the workweek from five to four days; one week's paid vacation could be granted in each of three quarters of the year, with one month's vacation in the fourth quarter, with six months vacation every five years. All three alternatives represent a cut of 20 percent in the workweek, yet the form in which it is taken affects the opportunities to participate in various activities and to visit various destinations.

It is clear that, although the absolute amount of leisure time may have increased little over the past several decades, the form in which it is being taken is changing. Although most of the gains in leisure in the past century have been taken in the form of a shorter workweek, since 1950 added leisure time has increasingly been taken in blocks of extended periods away from work. Yet the vast majority of full-time U.S. workers still are engaged in a five-day workweek.

The concepts of work, leisure, and money are intertwined as far as tourism is concerned. Individuals need both leisure and money to travel. Usually this money is earned by working. Thus, it is necessary to work in order to earn money to engage in leisure-time pursuits. The more one works, the more money is earned (and, therefore, available for leisure activities), but the less time one has to spend and enjoy it. Consumers can thus be thought of as having both a time budget and a money budget, and some make rational decisions in allocating one over the other. The auto worker who takes Friday off to lengthen the weekend for a fishing trip chooses time over money; the college professor who chooses not to teach during the summer, but to travel cross-country chooses time over money. This idea has been expressed as the *principle of resource value inversion*. As consumers' incomes rise, time becomes increasingly precious to them compared to money. Money, after all, can be saved; time cannot. Combined with this is a perception on the part of many that "time is now." To what extent are people increasingly unwilling to put off gratification? Are people choosing more time over more money? Several generalizations can be made. First, although Americans desire both more income and free time, it appears that three units of income are preferred for every unit of free time worth one unit of income. Second, this preference gap seems to be closing as free time gradually is increasing in importance relative to more income. In times of economic slowdown, this statement does not hold true. Third, the income-free time choice is made within the context of other factors and values associated with an individual's perception of the quality of life. Fourth, the choice between income and free time may be affected by the way in which the free-time options are offered. Some options were demonstrated above with the example of the 20 percent workweek reduction. It appears that most workers prefer free time in the form of extended time away from work.

Much has been made of the effect of a four-day workweek on pleasure travel. People representing a nationwide sample were asked to indicate what activities would be undertaken if every week included a three-day weekend. The activities chosen by more than half of either male or female respondents are indicated in Table 3.1.

The major response given indicated that a significant proportion of both male and female respondents would take weekend trips. However, studies of workers engaged in a four-day, forty-hour workweek have indicated that, because of fatigue from the workweek, most people tended to be more favorably inclined to home-centered relaxation. Another study compared the leisure participation of four-day-a-week and five-day-a-week workers. It found that both sets of workers devoted approximately equal

TABLE 3.1   Activities Respondents Would Engage in With A Three-Day Weekend Every Week

Activity	Females (%)	Males (%)
Take weekend trips, visit places I've always wanted to see	70	63
Socialize, visit friends	56	45
Spend time with family, play with children	53	50
Drive around, go sightseeing	52	48
Spend time on outdoor hobbies	45	52

SOURCE;   Douglas K. Hawes, "Time Budgets and Consumer-Time Behavior," in *Advances in Consumer Research*, vol. 4, p. 228.

amounts of time to participation in leisure activities. The only difference was that those who worked only four days a week pursued, on average, a greater number of different activities than the five-day-a-week worker. It may be that the extra day offers an opportunity to experiment with new activities, spending less time on each of more activities. This is rather interesting because, if this can be generalized, an extra day of nonwork actually places more time pressure on leisure activities.

What will be the effect of these time trends on travel products? We can conclude the following:

1. A growing importance for goods and services that economize on the consumers' use of time.
2. A growing importance of goods and services that require spending leisure time in blocks.
3. A decline in the effectiveness of monetary incentives relative to leisure-time incentives.

These trends can already be seen in the development of shorter cruises, thus capitalizing on those who can afford the trip but not the traditional three weeks, which was a previously common cruise time. As these trends continue, we would expect an increasing demand for time-intensive activities such as golf, water skiing, and eating out, as well as for two- and three-day holiday weekends.

SOCIOECONOMIC VARIABLES AND THEIR EFFECT ON TOURISM DEMAND

Age

The relationship between tourism and age has two components—the amount of leisure time available relative to age and the type and extent of activities undertaken at various age levels. The amount of leisure time available changes curvilinearly, with the younger and older age groups having proportionately more leisure time.

Yet the amount of available time is, by itself, insufficient to explain age as a factor in tourism behavior. It is safe to conclude that the rates of participation in the overwhelming majority of leisure activities declines with age. The decline in participation varies relative to the type of activity. There is a greater decline for active recreational activities than for the more passive forms of recreation. Preferred activities among the elderly are the more passive ones such as visiting friends and relatives, sightseeing, fishing, and playing golf. Yet for many retirees, although the number of activities participated in may drop upon retirement, the amount of time spent on each remaining one in terms of participation often increases.

There appears to be several differences between patterns of travel based on age. Older people tend to have a smaller share of tourists in proportion to their numbers than do younger people. This may also be influenced by other socioeconomic factors, such as income. Although younger people tend to select more adventurous destinations than do older people, older tourists tend to travel to farther destinations. The older tourists tend to dominate ship travel, spend less than middle-age tourists but more than younger tourists, and, while preferring to travel in the summer (in common with younger travelers), tend to travel more in the spring than do younger tourists.

In summary, leisure time decreases with age until children leave the nest; then the amount of leisure time increases. This increase continues with retirement. Though participation in physical activities declines with age (together with a corresponding rise in participation in the gentler forms of recreation) interest levels in activities previously participated in remains high. Opportunities may exist for tapping these interests by developing nonparticipatory means of expressing that interest. A skier, for example, may be unable to ski for reasons of age, but may be interested in other related activities such as watching skiers or sharing experiences.

Income

Income is obviously an important inhibiting factor in shaping the demand for travel. Not only does travel itself entail a certain cost, but the traveler must pay for services rendered at the destination as well as have money to engage in various activities during the trip. In addition, expenditures may be required in the form of specialized equipment to engage in various recreational activities while at the destination or enroute. It is difficult, however, to determine the relative importance of income per se, because this variable is interrelated with other socioeconomic variables. Generally speaking, higher income is associated with higher education, with certain jobs, and with certain age groups. Total family income has risen steadily as more wives have entered the labor force. The fact that family income has risen will have an effect upon tourism demand. Yet the fact that more families have two spouses in the labor force will also affect the shape of tourism demand. Different types of vacations and recreational activities may be demanded because of the time pressures involved in having two working spouses. The difficulty arises in determining the effect of these two interrelated variables on the demand for new tourism and recreation products.

It is important to see that the income spent on travel is spent at the expense of something else. (See Figure 3.4.) Travel expenditures are in competition with other expenditures, some of which are discretionary.

FIGURE 3.4   Personal Income Distribution

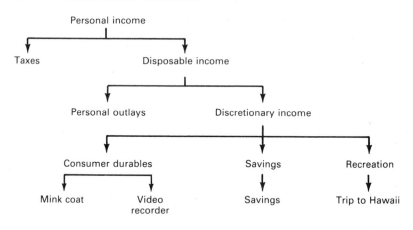

An individual's personal disposable income is the amount of income left after taxes have been paid. After various necessary personal outlays to maintain basic living needs have been spent, an individual has discretion to do with the remainder whatever is desired. A mink coat may be purchased, money may be saved, or a trip taken to Hawaii. It is important to look at income in this way to realize that the trip to Hawaii is in competition not only with a trip to the Bahamas, but also with various other recreational activities and other uses of that discretionary income. As the level of personal income increases, so does the amount of discretionary income.

Many studies have attempted to determine the percentage of income spent on recreation as a whole. It appears that at the lower levels of income and education approximately 2 percent of income is spent on recreation. As income increases the proportion spent on recreation increases to between 5 and 6 percent for all education levels. The highest recreational expenditures, 7 percent, are reported by respondents who are heads of households, under forty years of age, and without children. Other studies have indicated a positive correlation between income and recreation expenditures. In fact, it appears that increases in income result in a proportionately greater increase in recreation expenditures. As might be expected, higher-income tourists stay longer and spend more per day than do those with lower incomes. The type of recreational activities participated in differs based upon income. Higher-income people tend to participate in activities such as reading, bridge, fencing, squash, and chess; and middle-income people tend to engage in bowling, golf, and dancing. Lower-income families are identified with television viewing, dominoes, and bingo. The implication of these activities is clear to companies who wish to put together travel packages with specific activities involved aimed at particular market segments. A package, for example, aimed at a high-income segment of the market might be built around a recreational activity in which that segment tends to participate.

In addition to the relationship between income and recreation expenditure, some work has been done on the amount of participation in recreation and income. It has been shown that participation in most recreational activities increases as income increases up to a certain point ($10,000 in 1972 dollars), but declines slightly at incomes higher than this.

The only significant demographic difference between U.S. domestic and foreign travelers is that of income. A greater percentage of foreign travelers had incomes of $25,000 or more, and a smaller percentage had incomes of $10,000 to $20,000.

Sex

There are more similarities than differences between the sexes in terms of leisure participation rates. Overall, participation rates in leisure activities do not differ between men and women, although many engage in slightly fewer activities than do men. As might be expected, nonworking women have slightly higher participation rates than do employed women, except for such things as going out to dinner and either taking part in active sports or watching sports. There is a clear difference between the sexes in terms of preferred activities. Women are more involved in cultural activities, and men lead in outdoor recreation and playing and watching sports.

Education

The strong correlation between education, as it relates to income, has been well-established. Independent of income, however, the level of education that an individual has tends to influence the type of leisure and travel pursuits chosen. The amount of education obtained most likely will determine the nature of both work and leisure-time activities. By widening one's horizons of interest and enjoyment, education influences the type of activities undertaken. Education itself can serve as the primary reason for travel.

Researchers have found that participation in outdoor recreation tends to increase as the amount of education increases. There is also some evidence to suggest that the more educated prefer those activities that require the development of interpretive and expressive skills. Such activities include attending plays, concerts, and art museums, playing tennis and golf, skiing, reading books, attending adult education classes, and undergoing a wilderness experience.

In summary, it appears that the more education people have the broader their horizons and the more options they can consider. The more-educated travelers also tend to be more sophisticated in their tastes. They may not, however, be bigger spenders. A study of visitors to Hawaii found that visitors with less education spent more per day while on vacation in Hawaii. The authors suggested that the less-educated visitor may equate having fun with spending money.

LIFE-CYCLE STAGES

Families evolve through a certain life cycle. The characteristics of the family at the various stages of its life cycle offer certain opportunities or exert various pressures that affect purchase behavior.

Single-people take part in a much wider variety of activities outside the home than do married people. Married life brings about certain changes in leisure habits. Activities that were previously done alone or with friends are participated in less for reasons intrinsic to the activity itself.

Presence of Children

The narrowing of the types of activities participated in is intensified by the presence of children. When a married couple has children, there is a shift from activities engaged in primarily for intrinsic satisfaction

TABLE 3.2 Family Life Cycle

Life-cycle Stage	Title	Characteristics
First stage	Bachelor	Single persons below age 34
Second stage	Newly married	Young couples, no children, below age 34
Third stage	Full nest I	Young couples, young children, below age 34
Fourth stage	Full nest II	Older couples, older children, age 34-54
Fifth stage	Empty nest	Older couples, no children, over 54
Sixth stage	Solitary survivor	Single persons, over 54

SOURCE: William D. Wells and George Guber, "Life Cycle Concepts in Marketing Research," *Journal of Marketing Research*, vol. 3, November 1966, pp. 355-63.

to activities that are role-related, such as "family" activities. Before children come on the scene, the spouse was the chief leisure companion. This companionship is diluted by the presence of children. The presence of children seems to be crucial. Travel is curtailed, more leisure time is spent at home, and few new leisure interests are acquired. In at least one case, that of camping, the onset of parenthood has varied effects. Although the addition of young children in a camping family may produce a curtailment of camping activity, the shift to the empty-nest stage produces either an increase or a decrease in the activity. For those couples who enjoy camping, the situation of children leaving the nest may actually increase their participation. For others, who saw camping primarily as a family activity, the departure of children from the home may result in less camping.

Basic attitudes and behavior patterns of family life established in the early years of the family life cycle affect the future activities of both husbands and wives throughout the marriage. For the young child, leisure pursuits are restricted by the dictates of parents and the limitations of money. As children enter school, leisure activities outside the home increase. As children grow older their leisure habits and attitudes are more heavily influenced by their peers. Because of the high rate of social interaction among young people, leisure fads are easily spread. There is also at this stage an attempt to duplicate the behavior and attitudes of older age groups. Particularly important in this respect are college students, who tend to be leaders, often being the first to try new products and services.

Empty Nesters

As children leave the home, more time and money tend to be available for leisure. The empty nesters left behind have been the subject of a focus group study conducted by Plog Research.[5] A focus group consists of a small group of people, usually ten to twelve, getting together for a two-hour discussion. The groups are made up of individuals who have already been screened through questionnaires and interviews to arrive at a group that has members similar to one another in background. The discussion is led by a psychologist who attempts to develop a picture of the needs, interests, and personal psychologies of the group. The findings of the study are quite revealing. The typical empty nester doesn't think of extended trips by air, especially to foreign destinations. Their thinking is geared to the kinds of trips taken with their children, trips which have typically involved travel by car and visits to friends and relatives. There appears to be a strong desire for travel experiences as a means of self-actualization. Several barriers present themselves. The surface barriers of lack of time and money are true up to a point. For couples who

---

[5]"Increasing Your Sales to New and Existing Markets," Plog Research, Inc., undated.

work, scheduling may be a problem, and there is a reluctance towards using all of one's vacation time at once. Financially, although more discretionary income may be available, many empty nesters feel uncomfortable in spending their money on an intangible, such as travel. In addition, they tend to believe that the cost of a trip is more expensive than it really is, estimating the cost at twice the actual one. More than anything however, they express fear as a barrier to traveling. They are afraid of not knowing how to act in a new environment, of being taken advantage of. In a more subtle way, they feel that travel may be a way for them to learn how to be a couple again. Combined with this, however, is the fear that they may discover that they really do not like each other.

It is necessary to understand the particular inhibiting factors felt by each of these market segments at each stage of the family life cycle in order to be able to offer a product or service that will overcome the barriers and induce purchase behavior. For the empty nesters, for example, a tour would be very appropriate. A package tour relieves the participants of making decisions they may well feel inadequate to make. The regular tour may have a negative connotation for them, however. Empty nesters usually want to spend more time in fewer places than many tours offer. Popular kinds of destinations are those that help the empty nesters find their roots. This appeals to the need to find some meaning to their lives. The tour also helps alleviate some of the fears of being a couple again with no children around. The fact that there are other people around means that the empty nesters do not have to totally rely upon each other for companionship and support during the trip.

Barriers to Leisure Enjoyment

The barriers to leisure enjoyment have been the subject of a study by Witt and Goodale.[6] They identified the relationship between various barriers to the enjoyment of leisure and stages in the family life cycle. Understanding these barriers is a crucial step towards knowing what to say, do, and offer to lower those barriers. It was found that different patterns of change developed over the family life cycle relative to the barriers under discussion. Figure 3.5 illustrates the fact that various barriers (see Table 3.3) showed an approximately U-shaped pattern, with the barriers having the least effect when the youngest child was between six and eighteen years of age. These barriers refer to difficulties in knowing with which activities to get involved and with whom to share participation. This suggests that as children reach school age, parents have more knowledge of what is available and how to utilize those opportunities. It may

---

[6]Peter A. Witt and Thomas L. Goodale, "The Relationship Between Barriers to Leisure Enjoyment and Family Stages," *Leisure Sciences*, vol. 4, no. 1, 1981, pp. 29–49.

FIGURE 3.5 Barriers to Leisure Enjoyment at Different Family Stages (U-Shaped Pattern)

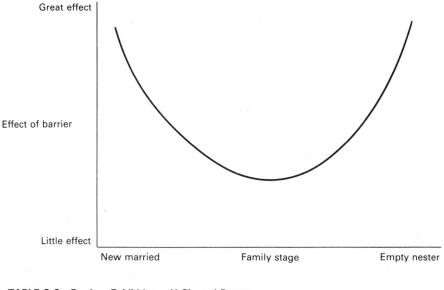

Great effect

Effect of barrier

Little effect

New married   Family stage   Empty nester

TABLE 3.3 Barriers Exhibiting a U-Shaped Pattern

Not being sure what activities to be involved in
Not knowing what's going on or what's available
Not being sure how to use available resources
Difficulty in planning and making decisions
Not having anyone to do things with
Not being at ease in social situations
Difficulty in carrying out plans

also be, as mentioned earlier, that their leisure activities are more closely defined for them by the expectation of their role as parents of school-age children. The time when the youngest child leaves home appears to be a critical passage relative to these barriers, a point made in the earlier discussion of the empty nesters.

A second group of barriers exhibit an inverted U-shaped pattern when expressed over the life cycle of the family. (See Figure 3.6.) During the child-rearing period, family obligations increase significantly for women and, to a similar but lesser degree, for men. This fact and the fact that neither parent feels there is enough free time represent the barriers felt; they increase until children leave the home, and then their effect drops off sharply.

The effect of various barriers has been found to increase as the family goes through various life-cycle stages. (See Figure 3.7.) The expecta-

FIGURE 3.6   Barriers to Leisure Enjoyment at Different Family Stages (Inverted U-
Shaped Pattern)

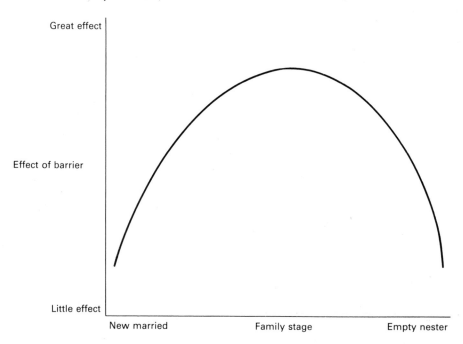

tions of family and friends increase for women, but for men they are more
constant and less of a limitation over the family life cycle. The feelings
of daily stress increase for both sexes as time goes on, while often the
feeling of not doing anything stays somewhat constant during the
child-rearing stage and increases dramatically when children leave the
home. Two other barriers have been analyzed for males only. It has been
found that there is an increased effect by males who don't feel fit enough
or don't have the physical skills for certain activities. This is reflected
in the effect of a falling off in physical skills and fitness levels with age.

    Certain points are worthy of note. First, it appears that stages in
the family life cycle can help explain and help predict leisure-time behavior.
Care must be taken, however, in the use of correlation or regression techniques for projecting or forecasting leisure activities because of the non-
linear pattern of many of these barriers. Second, it is noted that the family
life-cycle stage can only very partially explain leisure behavior. Third, it
is determined that noting which barriers are predominant at various life-
cycle stages will enable product, packages, and messages to be targeted
to reflect an understanding of these barriers and potential objections of
the many market segments.

FIGURE 3.7. Barriers to Leisure Enjoyment at Different Family Stages (Direct Effect Pattern)

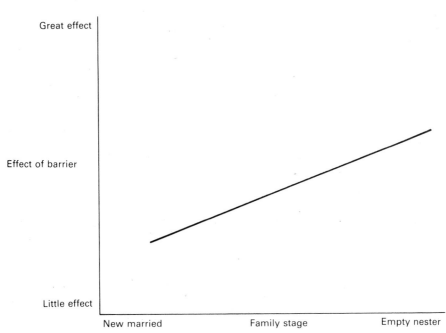

PERSONALITY

An individual's personality has an effect on the purchase behavior described in Chapter One. It has been suggested that most people view their vacation as an extension of their personality. Howard and Sheth have postulated that the effect of personality is felt on two areas—nonspecific motives and the alternatives considered for purchase. They have proposed that the more authoritarian a person is, for example, the fewer alternatives that will have to be considered in arriving at a purchase decision. The relationship between personality and nonspecific motives has been explored by various researchers in an attempt to better understand existing behavior and better predict future behavior.

The personality of an individual can be described as "the summation of the characteristics that make the person what he or she is and [that] distinguish each individual from every other individual."[7] It is logical that there is a link between the type of person one is and the type of purchases

[7]C. Glenn Walters, *Consumer Behaviors: Theory and Practice* (Homewood, IL, Richard D. Irwin, Inc., 1978), p. 296.

one makes. A "conservative" person will tend to make "conservative" purchases. But which influences which? Is a person called conservative because conservative purchases have been made, or is the fact that many conservative purchases have been made a sufficient reason to label someone "conservative"?

Personality Traits

Personality can be thought of as consisting of a variety of traits. Individuals who participate in recreational and tourist activities can be typed in terms of their personality traits in an attempt to determine whether such participants exhibit markedly different personality traits than do nonparticipants. The purpose of such analysis is to determine whether or not personality can be used as a variable for segmenting the market. If it is found that certain personality traits are dominant in winter vacations, marketers will know better the kind of tourist to appeal to and will gain valuable information as to what to say to appeal to this potential vacationer. To date, the research evidence is inconclusive as to whether or not personality is a significant variable in explaining purchase behavior. Although several studies indicate a strong relationship between personality and consumer behavior and a few indicate no relationship, the great majority indicate that existing correlations are weak.

The relationship between personality and participation in recreational activities is also of interest. As we have seen, recreational activities can serve as a major reason or motivation for vacation travel. If a relationship between certain activities and certain personality traits can be established, an appropriate marketing strategy can be developed.

Figure 3.8 indicates that hikers, river tourers, and women golfers are all seen as leaders and people who talk about their personal achievements. Hikers see themselves as people who are able to come and go as they desire, and both they and river tourers have scored high on the traits of doing new and different things and doing one's best or accomplishing something. River tourers are also viewed as people who have attacked contrary points of view or who have gotten revenge. Hikers and women golfers both are seen as people who have analyzed their motives and feelings.

The desire for social contact within an outdoor setting seems to be the primary motivating factor for individuals who participate in nature/pleasure activities, social sports, and water-oriented activities. Lack of structure and competitiveness characterizes both nature/pleasure activities and uses. Although competition is more of a factor in social sports, socializing is still important. Participants in predator sports are more dominant and aggressive. The relationship between personality traits and those who participate in the conquering nature/riding horses and bike-

FIGURE 3.8   **Recreation Behavior and Personality Characteristics**

Recreation Behavior	Personality Characteristics of Participants
Hiking	Come and go as desired; talk about personal achievements; are leaders; do new and different things; analyze motives and feelings; accomplish things
River touring	Accomplish things; talk about personal achievements; are leaders; do new and different things; attack contrary points of view
Golfing (women)	Talk about personal achievements; analyze motives and feelings; are leaders

SOURCE: Constance A. O'Conner, "A Study of Personality Needs in the Selection of Specific Leisure Interest Groups" (Ph.D. Dissertation, University of Southern California, 1970).

Nature/pleasure (e.g., sightseeing, jogging, nature walks)	Associate with other people
Social sports (e.g., golf, tennis)	Provide help and care to others
Water oriented sports (e.g., swimming, waterskiing, sunbathing)	Do new and different things
Predator sports (e.g., fishing, hunting)	Accomplish things; are leaders; have endurance; analyze motives and feelings; like order
Conquering nature/riding horses (e.g., primitive camping, horseback riding)	(Those with characteristics related to nature/pleasure did not participate in these activities)
Bike-riding/concert-going (e.g., bicycling, attending outdoor concerts)	

SOURCE: Hardeep S. Bhullar, Alan R. Everson, and Scout L. Gunn, "Social-Psychological Implications for Recreation Resource Planning" (paper presented at the *Outdoor Recreation Trends Symposium,* Durham, New Hampshire, April 1980).

riding/concert-going is less evident, but is suggested, as expressed in the above figure.

Personality Types

Often a person is described as having a certain type of personality. Personality types consist of characteristics that, when taken together, form a certain kind of person. One way of typing people is to the extent that they are perceived as being introverted or extroverted. Introverts look into themselves and tend to be shy and reserved. Extroverts are other-oriented, looking outside the self, and tending to be objective rather than subjective in outlook. Participants in vigorous physical activity in general tend to be extroverts. In fact, outdoor recreational activities in general are not participated in by introverted personality types. The following relationships between recreational participants and personality types have been made:

Recreational Participant	Personality Type
Sedentary, culturally broadening person	Indulgent
Passive participant in recreational activities	Of a higher social class
Participant in less-vigorous activities	Fragile
Skier	Carefree, with a solitary life-style
Water-related sports enthusiast	Easygoing
Physical fitness expert	Innovative, nimble

SOURCE: Kent L. Grazin and Robert H. Williams, "Patterns of Behavioral Characteristics as Indicants of Recreation Peferences: A Canonical Analysis," *Research Quarterly*, 49(2), 1979, pp. 135-145.

Travel trailer owners/truck camper owners	Conservative, traditionalist
Camping trailer owners	Youthful, family-oriented, with a strong leisure ethic
Non-R.V. owners	Upper middle class, urban, living graciously, with a strong work ethic

SOURCE: Douglas K. Hawes, "Empirically Profiling Four Recreational Vehicle Market Segments," *Journal of Travel Research*, vol. 16, no. 4, 1978, pp. 13-20.

Campers vs. noncampers	More traditional
Hunters vs. nonhunters	More traditional
(Level of intelligence correlated negatively with traditionalism)	
Group campers vs. nongroup campers	More dogmatic
Hunters vs. nonhunters	More dogmatic
Family campers vs. nonparticipants	More rigid

SOURCE: William T. Moss, Lois Shackelford, and G. L. Stokes, "Recreation and Personality," *Journal of Forestry*, 67, 1969, pp. 182-84.

Psychographics and Life-Style

The application of studies of personality to the business world has been hampered because the terminology of personality has come from clinical sources. Psychographics has developed as a way of describing consumer behavior in terms of a distinctive way of living in order to determine whether or not people with distinctive life-styles have distinctive travel behaviors. Psychographics is the development of psychological profiles of consumers and psychologically based measures of types of distinctive modes of living or life-styles. There are three recognized dimensions of life-style—attitudes, interests, and opinions. These three categories can be described as follows:

Activities	Interests	Opinions
Work	Family	Themselves
Hobbies	Home	Social issues
Social events	Job	Politics
Vacation	Community	Business
Entertainment	Recreation	Economics
Club membership	Fashion	Education
Community activities	Food	Products
Shopping	Media	Future
Sports	Achievements	Culture

SOURCE: Carl McDaniel, *Marketing: An Integrated Approach* (New York, Harper & Row, 1979), p. 67.

Is it, in fact, possible to identify different segments of the market based upon life-style? It appears that an individual's life-style is influenced by participation in various social groups and is a social rather than a unique behavior. Further, a person's life-style spills over to other aspects of behavior. These life-style differences are patterned rather than random. Knowing how an individual behaves in one aspect of his or her life may enable us to predict how the individual will act in others. Some feel, however, that one of the problems in using life-style variables is that often general variables are used rather than those that are product specific. They argue that to understand vacation intentions it is necessary to determine attitudes and opinions about and interest in vacations and vacation destinations rather than information about general life-style. This division of the market into psychographic segments would be of no practical value unless these segments could be identified and reached. It has been shown that life-styles vary according to different socioeconomic variables. Although it may be beneficial to initially segment a market on the basis of life-style dimensions for marketing purposes, it is necessary to identify the socioeconomic characteristics of these segments in order to effectively reach the target markets.

REFERENCES

BEST, FRED, PHILIP BOSSEMAN, AND BARRY STEM, "Income-Free Time/Trade-Off Preferences of U.S. Workers: A Review of Literature and Indicators," *Leisure Sciences*, vol. 2, no. 2, 1979, pp. 122, 133.

BISHOP, DOYLE W., "Stability of the Factor Structure of Leisure Behavior: Analysis of Four Communities," *Journal of Leisure Research*, vol. 2, no. 3, Summer 1970, pp. 160–168.

BOLLMAN, STEPHAN R., VIRGINIA M. MOXLEY, AND NANCY C. ELLIOT, "Family and Community Activities of Rural Nonfarm Families with Children," *Journal of Leisure Research*, vol. 6, no. 2, Spring 1974, p. 101.

BRUNNER, B. C., "Personality and Motivating Factors Influencing Adult Participation in Vigorous Physical Activity," *Research Quarterly*, 40(3), 1969, pp. 464–69.

WOOD, BULTENA, AND VIVIAN WOOD, "Leisure Orientation and Recreational Activities of Retirement Community Residents," *Journal of Leisure Research*, vol. 2, no. 1, Winter 1970, p. 3.

CONNER, KAREN A., AND GORDEN L. BRELTENA, "The Four-Day Workweek: An Assessment of Its Effects on Leisure Participation," *Leisure Sciences*, vol. 2, no. 1, 1979, pp. 55–69.

DOUGLAS, SUSAN, AND BERNARD DUBOIS, "Culture and Consumer Behavior: Time for a Fresh Look?" *Marketing Science Institute, Report No. 77–106*, July 1977, pp. 7, 15.

DOYLE, WILLIAM S., JOSEPH PERRIC, AND MARTIN STERN, "Some Technical Aspects of a Recent Study of Tourism in New York State," in *The 80's: Its Impact on Travel and Tourism Marketing* (The Travel Research Association, Eighth Annual Conference Proceedings, 1977), p. 109–21.

DUMAZEDIER, JOFFRE, *Sociology of Leisure* (Elsevier Scientific Publishing Company, 1974), ch. 3.

FRECHTLING, DOUGLAS, C., "Travel in the 1980's: The Demographic and Economic Climate," in *The 80's: Its Impact on Travel and Tourism Marketing* (The Travel Research Association, Proceedings of the Eighth Annual Conference, 1977), pp. 12–15.

GUNN, JANET SCOUT L., "A Comparative Study of Selected Personality Traits in College Students and Their Participation in Selected Outdoor Recreational Activities" (Ph.D. dissertation, University of Georgia, 1972).

GRAHAM, JOHN E. J., AND GEOFFREY WALL, "American Visitors to Canada: A Study in Market Segmentation," *Journal of Travel Research*, vol. 16, no. 3, 1978, pp. 21–24.

HARRY, JOSEPH, "Socioeconomic Patterns of Outdoor Recreation Use Near Urban Areas: A Comment," *Journal of Leisure Research*, vol. 4, no. 3, Summer 1972, pp. 21–32.

HAWES, DOUGLAS K., "Time Budgets and Consumer Leisure-Time Behavior," in *Advances in Consumer Research*, vol. 4, William D. Perrault, Jr., ed., *Proceedings of the Seventh Annual Conference of the Association for Consumer Research*, pp. 224–228.

"How's Business," *The Travel Agent*, February 20, 1978, p. 54.

JACKSON, REINER, "Children's Conceptualization of Leisure: Education For Leisure Through Time-Skills," *Recreation Research Review*, June 1979.

KASSARJIAN, H. H., "Personality and Consumer Behavior: A Review," *Journal of Marketing Research*, vol. 8, no. 4, 1971, pp. 409-18.

KELLY, JOHN R., "Socialization Toward Leisure: A Developmental Approach," *Journal of Leisure Research*, vol. 6, no. 3, Summer 1974, p. 181.

KELLY, JOHN R., "Family Leisure in Three Communities," *Journal of Leisure Research*, vol. 10, no. 1, Winter 1978, p. 47.

LINDSAY, JOHN T., AND RICHARD A. OGLE, "Socio-economic Patterns of Outdoor Recreation Use Near Urban Areas," *Journal of Leisure Research*, vol. 4, no. 1, Winter 1972, p. 19.

LOUDEN, DAVID L., AND ALBERT J. DELLA BITTA, *Consumer Behavior: Concepts and Applications* (New York, McGraw-Hill Book Co., 1979), pp. 125-29.

LUNDBERG, DONALD E., "Why Tourists Travel," *Cornell H.R.A. Quarterly*, 1972, 12(4) pp. 64-70.

MAK, JAMES, JAMES MONCUR, AND DAVE YONAMINE, "Determinants of Visitor Expenditures and Visitor Lengths of Stay: A Cross-Section Analysis of U.S. Visitors in Hawaii," *Journal of Travel Research*, vol. 15, no. 3, Winter 1977, p. 5.

MAYO, EDWARD J., AND LANCE P. JARVIS, *The Psychology of Leisure Travel* (Boston, MA, C.B.I. Publishing Co., Inc., 1981), p. 234.

MCAVOY, LEO H., "The Leisure Preference Problems and Needs of the Elderly," *Journal of Leisure Research*, vol. 1, no. 1, Winter 1979, p. 40.

MCDANIELS, CARL JR., *Marketing: An Integrated Approach* (New York, Harper & Row, 1979), p. 66.

MORGAN, ANN, AND JEOFFREY GOODBEY, "The Effect of Entering an Age-Segregated Environment Upon the Leisure Activity Patterns of Older Adults," *Journal of Leisure Research*, vol. 10, no. 3, Summer 1978, p. 177.

MORRIS, GLENN, RICHARD PASEWORK, AND JOHN SHULT, "Occupational Level and Participation in Public Recreation in a Rural Community," *Journal of Leisure Research*, vol. 4, no. 1, Winter 1982, p. 25.

MYERS, JAMES, AND WILLIAM H. REYNOLDS, *Consumer Behavior and Marketing Management* (Boston, Houghton Mifflin Company, 1967), ch. 8.

NEULINGER, JOHN, *The Psychology of Leisure* (Springfield, Ill.; Charles C. Thomas, 1974).

PARKER, STANLEY, "The Sociology of Leisure" (London, Allen & Unwin Ltd., 1976), ch. 4.

PEARSON, LYNN R. "Non-Working Time: A Review of the Literature," *Research Memorandum 65*, University of Brimingham, 1978, p. 11.

PERREAULT, WILLIAM D., DONNA K. DARDEN, AND WILLIAM R. DARDEN, "A Psychographic Classification of Vacation Life Styles," *Journal of Leisure Research*, vol. 9, no. 3, Summer 1977, pp. 208-24.

RITCHIE, J. R. BRENT, AND MICHAEL ZINS, "An Empirical Evaluation of the Role of Culture and its Components as Determinants of the Attractiveness of a Tourism Region," *Annals of Tourism Research*, vol. 5, no. 2, April/June 1978, pp. 252-67.

RODGERS, BRIAN, "Leisure and Recreation," *Urban Studies*, vol. 6, no. 3, November 1969, pp. 368-384.

RUNYON, KENNETH E., *Consumer Behavior and the Practice of Marketing* (Columbus, OH, Charles E. Merrill Publishing Co., 1977), pp. 80-83.

SCHEWE, CHARLES D., AND ROGER J. CATALONE, "Psychographic Segmentation of Tourists," *Journal of Travel Research*, vol. 16, no. 3, Winter 1978, pp. 14-20.

SELZER, JOSEPH, AND JAMES A. WILSON, "Leisure Patterns Among Four Day Workers," *Journal of Leisure Research*, vol. 12, no. 2, Spring 1980, pp. 116-27.

THOMPSON, C. STASSEN, AND A. W. TINSLEY, "Income Expenditure Elasticities for Recreation: Their Estimation and Relationship to Demand for Recreation," *Journal of Leisure Research*, vol. 10, no. 4, Fall 1978, p. 265.

VOSS, JUSTIN, AND ROGER D. BLACKWELL, "Markets for Leisure Time," paper presented at the Association for Consumer Research, 1974, pp. 7-8.

WALTERS, C. GLENN, *Consumer Behavior: Theory and Practice* (Homewood, IL, Richard D. Irwin, Inc., 1979), pp. 334-35, 464-70.

WEISS, CAROLINE, "Tourist Statistics Reexamining the Older Traveler as a Case in Point," *Journal of Travel Research*, vol. 13, no. 1, Summer 1974, p. 1.

ZUZANEK, "Social Differences in Leisure Behavior: Measurement and Interpretation," *Leisure Sciences*, vol. 1, no. 3, 1978, pp. 271-93.

4

TRAVEL PURCHASE:
The Traveler's Buying Process

When travelers are made aware of a vacation opportunity they go through a series of stages before committing to a purchase decision. This chapter explores these stages.

There is general agreement in the travel literature that the buying process consists of a series of steps through which individuals must move before making a purchase. The characteristics of each of these steps are examined.

The communications strategy of the marketer will vary depending upon where the target market is in the buying process. Appropriate strategies for each stage in the buying process are outlined.

The decision to take a vacation is, in fact, a series of subdecisions — where to go, when to go, how long to stay, how to travel, and so on. The order in which these decisions are made, as well as the influence of children on the various subdecisions is examined.

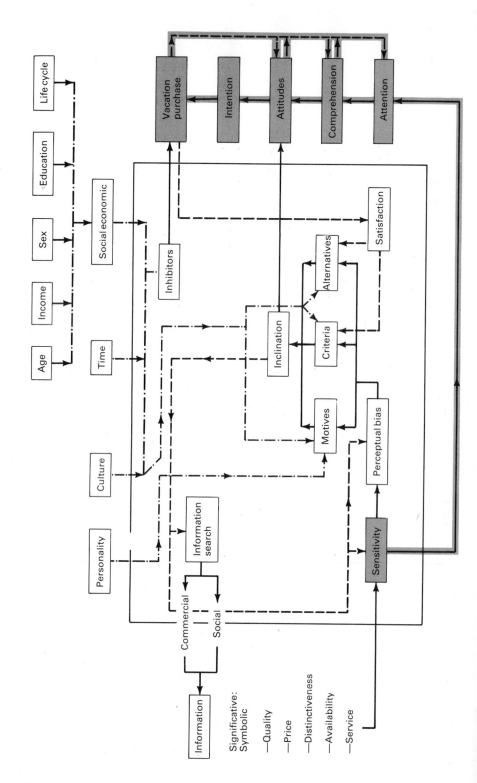

TRAVEL PURCHASE: THE TRAVELER'S BUYING PROCESS

Attention/Awareness

When making a travel purchase a consumer moves through several stages. The wise marketing manager realizes that different communication strategies are appropriate for different stages of the buying process. Fig. 4-1 illustrates the various stages as defined by several authors. When deciding whether or not to visit a previously unknown destination, for example, an individual may at first be unaware of the destination. The destination has, first of all, to be brought to the awareness or attention of the potential traveler. A prime function in communicating to the consumer is to gain attention. Advertising is very influential at this point.

Knowledge/Comprehension

The task in the next stage of the buying process is to make the customer goal directed. If the potential traveler's attention has been successfully stimulated, she or he will seek out more information on the destination. The attempt is to become more knowledgeable about what the destination has to offer, to comprehend what it is all about. The emphasis will be on information, and the task of the communicator will be to provide sufficient information to direct the potential traveler toward purchase. Advertising is again important at this stage. The choice of media is crucial. Media should be chosen that can convey a great deal of information. Brochures or folders can do this, as can magazine and newspaper

FIGURE 4.1   The Traveler's Buying Process

Howard/Sheth	McDaniel/Crissy	McDaniel	AIDA	IUOTO
				Unawareness
Attention	Awareness	Awareness	Attention	Awareness
Compre-		Knowledge		Compre-
hension				hension
Attitudes	Interest	Liking	Interest	
	Evaluation	Preference	Desire	
		Conviction		
Intention				Conviction
Purchase	Trial	Purchase	Action	Action
	Adoption			

SOURCES: John Howard and Jagdish N. Sheth, *Theory of Buyer Behavior* (New York, John Wiley & Sons, Inc., 1969).

W. J. E. Crissy, Robert J. Boewadt, and Dante M. Laudadio, *Marketing of Hospitality Services: Food, Lodging, Travel* (East Lansing, MI, The Educational Institute of the American Hotel and Motel Association, 1975) pp. 94-95.

Carl McDaniel, Jr., *Marketing: An Integrated Approach* (New York, Harper & Row, 1979), pp. 170, 343-54.

IUOTO, *Study and Analysis of the Long-Term Effectiveness of Promotional Campaigns and Other Tourist Publicity and Advertising Activities*, undated.

advertisements with a great deal of copy or words. Radio and television cannot provide the large amounts of information needed at this stage. It is important to talk about the destination in terms of the benefits offered. It will be remembered that destinations are perceived in terms of their benefits to the individual. To the extent that we understand a message, we will be more inclined to pay attention to it.

Attitudes/Interest/Liking

The potential traveler next moves to developing a liking, interest, or attitude about the destination. The promotion objectives at this stage are to create or reinforce existing positive attitudes or images or to correct negative attitudes or images. A positive attitude is, in part, influenced by the individual's tendency or predisposition to visit that particular destination. (See Chapter One.) It is also a function of how well we have gained the traveler's attention and provided sufficient information for him to determine whether or not the benefits of the destination match his needs and wants. Attitudes are difficult to change in part because, as a new attitude is developed, new incoming information is often screened to conform to an old attitude. (See Chapter Two.) It has been demonstrated that awareness or attention must exist before an attitude can change. The interest in a particular destination will influence how much effort is put into the comprehension of a particular message.

Evaluation/Preference/Desire

After evaluating various alternatives the consumer will develop a preference or desire for a destination. At this stage, there is heavy reliance on the opinions of other people and their experiences with what is being marketed. The importance of advertising is somewhat less at this stage. The most effective types of messages are testimonial ads and comparison ads. In a testimonial advertisement a person, usually a well-known public figure, praises what is being sold. The hope is that if the viewer or reader respects the person in the message their opinion on the product or service being sold will be respected. The same effect can be gained by "testimony" from someone who has already visited the destination being advertised. It is crucial that the spokesperson be believable. It is also important, for maximum impact, that the person chosen to be in the advertisement have some connection with what is being sold. A good example would be James Mitchener advertising Hawaii. Because he is the author of the best-seller entitled *Hawaii*, Mitchener is a well-respected personality with an obvious link to what is being advertised. Karl Malden, one of the detectives in *The Streets of San Francisco*, also makes a good spokesman for the security gained from American Express Traveler's Cheques. A form of testimonial is the rating found in various guidebooks. To the extent that the rating system is respected, advertising the rating of a particular facility will gain the respect of the readers.

In a comparison advertisement one destination or facility is mentioned in a promotional message in comparison with another. The destinations are compared on particular attributes. For this kind of message to work it is necessary to select for the basis of comparison attributes that the customer thinks are important. It is, obviously, crucial that the destination being advertised be stronger on those attributes than the competition.

Intention/Conviction

At this stage in the buying process, the potential travelers are convinced that the benefits of the destination will meet their needs and wants and are almost at the point of purchase. Studies have shown that the intention to purchase precedes the actual purchase. One international study of travel attitudes and desires brought to light the fact that tourists differ in their travel intentions.[1]

Respondents were asked if, given the time, money, and opportunity, they would like to travel to other nations of the world. The figures in Table 4.1 indicate the percentage of respondents who answered in the affirmative. These figures give some indication of the overall place in the buying process of international tourism of these countries. It would appear that in countries such as Australia, France, and Scandinavia, a majority of the people are rather close to making a purchase decision, based on their strong desire to go. If one could determine the remaining barriers to travel in those countries, travel offerings could be advertised assuming that many of the earlier stages in the buying process had been reached. At the other end of the scale only 17 percent of the population of India (a sizeable number in absolute terms) has reached the point of desiring foreign travel. Because the economic situation has to be considered even though the survey asked respondents not to use this as a barrier (people who do not have sufficient income to travel may be unable to envision a situation without that constraint), the people of India as a whole will need a much longer informative marketing campaign to get them to purchase foreign travel.

This research project also sought to determine which countries the respondents would most like to visit. The United Kingdom, with 13 percent of the respondents, was the most favorite choice of U.S. respondents, followed by Italy, which was chosen by 10 percent of the respondents. The United States was the first choice of Europeans, capturing 19 percent of the first-place votes. The United States was listed the top choice of all but those in the Benelux countries (Belgium, the Netherlands, and

---

[1]American Express V.P. Delineates Profile of the International Traveler," *Travel Weekly*, April 27, 1978, pp. 65–66.

TABLE 4.1   Desire to Travel to Other Nations of the World

Home Country	Percent desiring to Travel
Australia France Scandinavia	84%
Canada	79%
Mexico United Kingdom	74%
West Germany	67%
United States	68%
Brazil	60%
Africa (sub-Sahara)	57%
Japan	42%
India	17%

SOURCE: Travel Weekly, April 27, 1978, pp. 65-66.

Luxembourg) who chose Spain ahead of the United States. People in the Latin American countries also chose the United States as the most popular destination. The only country in which the respondents did not place the United States as a top choice was Brazil; citizens there slightly preferred France and Italy. Sub-Sahara Africans placed the United Kingdom in first position (22 percent of the responses) and the United States next (11 percent of the responses). In Japan the United States was ranked first, chosen by 13 percent of the respondents, followed by Switzerland with 7 percent. The Far East as a whole identified the United States the first choice by 13 percent of the respondents and Japan the second choice at 5 percent.

Studies such as the one described give an indication as to how many people in a potential market have, at the least, a positive attitude about foreign travel. By identifying to which potential receiving country these people would like to travel can determine the size of the potential market and the appropriate communications strategy to use.

Purchase/Trial/Action

If the potential traveler has reached the conviction stage of the buying process, the barrier to travel is likely to be a physical one. It may be lack of time or money. It is clear, however, that the motivation is present. The marketing task is to identify the barrier and develop a product to breach it. If the problem is lack of money, a tour package may be successful. Lodging in smaller, cheaper hotels can be suggested. Research by Plog Research of several underdeveloped market segments indicated that people in all three segments estimated the true cost of a trip at twice the actual cost.[2] If the problem is one of time, it may be possible to offer

---

[2]Plog Research, Inc., "Increasing Tour Sales to New and Existing Markets," undated report.

a package that capitalizes on the time available. One of the reasons that fly/cruise packages have been developed is to respond to a market that has the money and the motivation, but not the time. Previously, when ships cruised out of New York much time was lost because two days of bad weather often had to be experienced before the ships reached sunny climates. The solution has been to fly travelers to Florida, sail out of a southern port, and give more sun for the time available.

Adoption

The final stage of the buying process is the adoption stage. At this point, the traveler has become a repeat purchaser. To achieve this end, it is necessary to provide a quality experience to the first-time traveler. However, advertising also has a role to play. The necessity for some form of communication to the purchaser arises because of cognitive dissonance. Cognitive dissonance arises after a choice between two or more alternatives has been made. It is a feeling of anxiety, a feeling that perhaps the choice made was not the best one. The amount of dissonance felt is influenced by the type of decision made. The anxiety is stronger if:

The rejected alternative is attractive.

The decision is important.

The purchaser becomes aware of negative characteristics in the alternative chosen.

The number of rejected alternatives increases.

The alternatives are perceived as being similar.

The decision made goes against a strongly held belief.

The decision is a recent one.

Because vacation travel represents an important decision, it has the potential for creating a great deal of anxiety after the purchase has been made. The potential is even greater if the traveler has chosen between a large number of attractive alternate destinations. The key is to indicate to the traveler as soon as possible after the decision has been made that the decision has been a good one. A note to the purchaser of a package tour or cruise may be sufficient to avoid second thoughts and cancellations. For advertisers, the key is to provide in their advertisements information that purchasers can use to justify to themselves the purchase made as well as the messages to convince people to buy.

BUYING-COMMUNICATION PROCESSES INTERACTION

We have noted that there is an appropriate and different communications strategy for each stage in the traveler's buying process. This realization is particularly important because it helps in determining why a communications campaign failed. It is fairly easy to determine that a campaign did not work. For example, the promotion to induce travel to a particular destination can be assumed a failure if there has been no increase in visitors to the destination after the campaign. A more interesting question is not so much *did* the promotion fail, but *why* did it fail? Were enough people exposed to the message? Was the message memorable? Did it result in a change of attitudes? The only way that campaign managers can determine why the campaign failed is to break the process into its various stages and measure the results of each stage.

The information presented in Figure 4.2 refers to this process. At the first stage in the buying process, the objective is to expose the message to a certain number of people. The number of readers or viewers exposed to the message serve as a measure of whether or not the campaign reached this objective. At the next level, the objective is to transfer information to those exposed to the message. To determine the effectiveness it is possible to measure the extent to which people exposed to the message have recalled the essential parts of it.

To measure a change in attitude it is necessary to survey attitudes both before and after a campaign. A similar strategy is necessary to measure whether preferences have been developed. The extent to which a message initiates action can be measured by the percentage of those who send in a response to a particular advertisement or the number who take an advertisement into a travel agent. Lastly repeat purchases, signifying the adoption of a product or service, can be measured by the percentage of visitors who are repeat purchasers.

FIGURE 4.2 Interaction Between the Buying and Communications Processes

Buying Process	Communication Objective	Communication Measurement
Awareness/attention	Exposure	Number of readers/viewers exposed to message.
Knowledge/comprehension	Transmission of information	Percentage of readers/viewers who remembered essential parts of the message.
Attitudes/interest/liking	Attitude change	Attitude surveys before and after message to determine degree of change.
Evaluation/preference/ desire	Creation of preferences	Preference surveys before and after message to determine preference.
Intention/conviction	Initiation of action	Number of actions taken (e.g., travel agent contact, tours booked, responses received) in response to a particular message.
Purchase/trial/action	Purchase	Number of bookings made, etc.
Adoption	Repeat purchase	Percentage of visitors who are repeat purchasers.

By being aware of these different stages, communication objectives, and ways to measure their accomplishment, it is possible to determine where things went wrong. It may be, for example, that we reached a sufficiently large number of the right kind of people, a large percentage of whom remembered our message. It may be, however, that the message was not sufficiently strong to result in a change in attitude about the destination being promoted. The promotion manager knows that the media used were on target in terms of reaching the right numbers of prospects. The program has to be strengthened to result in an attitude change. A strategy offering cheap package tours, on the other hand, will be totally ineffective because the necessary prerequisite steps have not been taken in the minds of the readers.

Buying Process Feedback

Although each step in the buying process is a prerequisite for the next, there are also feedback effects. The adoption of a particular destination affects and reinforces the purchase of it. The purchase itself has an effect on future intentions, either a positive or a negative one. Each higher stage thus tends to reinforce the lower stages. Study abroad, for example, has been shown to result in a change in attitude about foreigners. It is, therefore, easier to induce a repeat purchase if a good job has been done of satisfying the traveler the first time than to get that first purchase.

VACATION SUBDECISIONS

Although the vacation buying process has been treated as a series of stages culminating in a buying decision, the vacation purchase is actually comprised of a series of subdecisions. From a marketer's viewpoint, it is important to know the order in which decisions are made and who makes the particular decisions. In this way, a marketing campaign can be developed that is aimed at the decision maker.

What the order of decisions is and who the decision maker is varies by which stage in the life cycle the family is in. At the stage in which the couple has been married for less than fourteen years and in which the couple is at most in their mid-thirties and may have young children at home, the decision to vacation tends to be a joint one. Although discretionary income is low, the first subdecision is "where to go," followed by "whether to go." This seems to reflect a more hedonistic attitude, which indicates an expectation to take a vacation despite income constraints. Decisions are next made concerning the amount to spend, the length of time to stay, and the accommodations to be use. In the next stage, in which the couple has been married for fourteen to twenty years, has a mid-forties age median, and has children eighteen years old or more, the husband tends to slightly dominate the decision making. This is due primarily to the vacation being designed around the husband's work schedule. At this stage, the question of whether or not to go is most important, followed by decisions on destinations, amounts to spend, length of stay, and place to stay. When the spouses are in their mid-fifties and have been married twenty to thirty years, the process is largely wife-dominated. This coincides with vacation purchases at a peak and disposable income close to a peak. The wife-dominated decision making continues until the husband is close to retirement; then he exerts a slight dominance, due perhaps to anxiety about financial matters. For couples married for over forty years, when the couple is retired, the wife once again takes over the decision making.

Other researchers have studied vacation decision making and have suggested that more joint decision making rather than individually dominated decision making occurs. Obviously more research is necessary to determine whether or not the decision focus changes with stages in the family life cycle.

The research to date on family vacation decision making indicates that the dominance of either spouse depends upon the particular subdecision to be made. External factors also come to bear on the decision. Vacation dates, for example, are probably determined by job and school dates, and hence decisions on these are husband dominated, with heavy influence by the children. There is some indication that the number of joint decisions is greater in middle-class families than in lower-class ones, but less than in the highest class ones.

A review of Table 4.2 will indicate that most vacation subdecisions are joint decisions. The husband tends to dominate in decisions regarding the length of stay, the dates of the vacation, the amount to spend, and the route to take. Although some studies indicate that husbands tend to dominate the vacation destination decision, most studies indicate this to be a joint decision.

Influence of Children

Studies by Jenkins and Ritchie (cited above) indicate that children influence some vacation subdecisions. The children's effect is felt on the decision of whether to go on vacation, what dates and destinations to choose, what type of lodging is preferred, and which activities to undertake while on vacation.

A knowledge of who influences the various vacation subdecisions will aid marketing managers in selling their products and services. Facilities and messages can be more clearly geared to the decision maker in an attempt to increase the attention given the message, the comprehension of the message and ultimately, the final purchase behavior.

TABLE 4.2   Family Vacation Decision Making

Subdecision	Standish[1]	Jenkins[2]	Myers[3]	Ritchie[4]	Omura[5]	3M[6]	Newsweek[7]
Whether to go							
Whether to take the children		♀					
How long to stay		♂		♀			
How much to spend	♀	♂		♂			
Vacation dates		♂		♂			
Vacation destinations	♀	♀	♀	♀	♀	♂	♂
Mode of transportation	♀	♀					♂
Route		♂	♂				
Lodging	♀	♀	♀				
Activities							

Key: ♂   male dominated decision
         ♀   joint decision

SOURCES: [1]Theodore C. Standish, "How the Computer Views the Family Vacation Travel Market," in "Using Travel Research for Planning and Profits," *The Travel Research Association Ninth Annual Conference Proceedings*, Ottawa, Canada, 1978.
[2]Roger L. Jenkins, "Family Vacation Decision-Making," *Journal of Travel Research*, vol. 16, no. 4, 1978.
[3]Paul B. Myers and L. W. Moncrief, "Differential Leisure Travel Decision-Making Between Spouses," *Annals of Tourism Research*, vol. 5, no. 1, 1978.
[4]J. R. Brent Ritchie and P. Filiatrault, "Family Vacation Decision-Making — A Replication and Extension," *Journal of Travel Research*, vol. 18, no. 4, 1980.
[5]Glynn S. Omura, Mary Lou Roberts, and W. Wayne Talavzyk, "An Exploratory Study of Women's Travel Attitudes and Behavior: Directions for Research," *Advances in Consumer Research,* vol. 7, (*Proceedings of the Association for Consumer Research Tenth Annual Conference*, October 1979).
[6]3M National Advertising Company, "Psychographics of the Automobile Traveler," 1972.
[7]"1970 Travel Study," *Newsweek Magazine*, 1970.

REFERENCES

CRISSY, W. J. E., ROBERT J. BOEWADT, AND DANTE M. LAUDADIO, *Marketing of Hospitality Services: Food, Lodging, Travel* (East Lansing, MI, The Educational Institute of the American Hotel & Motel Association, 1975), p. 95.

"How's Business," *The Travel Agent*, February 8, 1982, p. 20.

KAUFFMAN, PHILLIP D.,   "The Effect of a Study Tour to the People's Republic of China Upon Participant's Personality and Attitudes" (Ph.D. dissertation, The Ohio State University, 1976).

McDaniel, Carl, Jr., *Marketing: A Integrated Approach* (New York, Harper & Row, 1979), pp. 354, 351.

Myers, Paul B., and L. W. Moncrief, "Differential Leisure Travel Decision Making Between Spouses," *Annals of Tourism Research*, vol. 5, no. 1, 1978, p. 23.

The first section of *The Tourism System*—Chapters one through four—has explained the factors that influence the decision of an individual, any individual, to purchase travel. Individuals decide to purchase travel because they have *learned* that it satisfies various needs and wants they consider important (Chapter one), and because they *perceive* that it will satisfy various needs and wants that they consider important (Chapter two), yet within various external constraints (Chapter three). In actually making the purchase, travelers go through a series of steps in their own mind (Chapter four). The "end product" of this process will be, hopefully, a decision to "buy travel." Individuals decide in this way that they will "move round the tourism system" to their chosen destination.

It is impossible to describe the travel characteristics of each and every individual. Travel movements of the major *segments* can, however, be described. This is the task of the second part of the text—to describe *who* is traveling, to *where* they are traveling, and *how* this is being done.

Travel is done for either business or pleasure/personal reasons (Chapter five). People in these market segments choose destinations that are international, regional, or domestic (Chapter six) and travel by a variety of means to reach their destinations (Chapter seven). The shape of travel demand at the destination is a result of the interaction between who is traveling, when they are traveling, when, where they are going, and how they are going to go.

READINGS

This reading is an excellent example of a tourism-related corporation putting into practice many of the concepts discussed in the first section of this book.

The paper was originally presented to members of the Travel and Tourism Research Association and was published in *The Impact of Tourism*, the Sixth Annual Proceedings of the Travel and Tourism Association. The authors wish to express their appreciation to the Association for permission to reprint this paper.

Designing Products
for the Leisure Travel Market from Market Definition
to Product Information, 1975

Annabelle Bennetts, Manager,
Marketing Research — Canada of Air Canada
Paul Burak, Vice President,
Market Facts of Canada Ltd.

PART I—PAUL BURAK

Traditionally, airlines have marketed a product that was considered to be a seat from origin A to destination B and back again. Competitive products were differentiated by such things as departure and arrival times, destination points, and by such travel-related amenities as in-flight entertainment, meals, and friendly or attractive attendants.

This marketing approach is consistent with the definition of an airline as a transportation company, a means by which people get to their desired place at a desired time and in as comfortable a manner as possible. Although different kinds of advertisements may have been produced, the same basic product has been sold to the person who was travelling on business, or going to visit friends or relatives, or to the person who was trying to decide where to go or what to do on his vacation.

About four to five years ago, market planners at Air Canada decided that the time had come to market products that were fundamentally different for each type of traveller. For example, a major distinction was drawn between the traveller who had to travel to a particular destination, whether it be for business or personal reasons, and the potential traveller who might want to find a place to go.

For the non-discretionary traveller who is committed to getting to a particular destination, the airline simply has to convince him that flying is the best way of getting there and back and, specifically, that their particular airline is the best way to do it.

As for the leisure traveller, the market task is much less clearly defined. This person is usually not committed to a particular destination place nor even necessarily to long distance travel. In fact, the choice of a particular destination place, if any, for his leisure time may be an integral part of his decision on how to spend his vacation. Certainly, the choice of an airline flight is only one element in the planning of a vacation.

From this emerged the concept that marketing to potential leisure travellers was not a matter of selling specific destinations but rather a matter of selling the right kinds of vacation experiences. Places such as London, Paris, Bermuda and other well-known vacation spots in the world today are clearly associated with the expectation of having special kinds of experiences. Moreover, it is the anticipation of having these kinds of experiences which people find appealing and which sell airline tickets.

As a result of this marketing concept, a large-scale market research program was launched in conjunction with Market Facts to analyze the leisure time market for Canadians. The objectives of this research program were:

1. To analyze the demand structure in the leisure travel market
2. To identify possible new marketing opportunities
3. To develop a framework for the design of travel packages which would reflect the needs and desires of specific target groups among the population of potential leisure air travellers.

The first step in the market study consisted of in-depth group discussions. These were undertaken in order to develop an understanding of the range of attitudes toward leisure activities and vacation interests that might be found among different types of people; and to develop hypotheses about what underlying factors contribute toward vacation needs, influence the kinds of experiences that different people look for in an ideal vacation, and which may constrain the realization of these vacations.

This approach to the market study allowed us to formulate a conceptual model on which to base the following market analysis. (See Exhibit A.)

Our first hypothesis was that a person's general attitudes, interests and outlook toward life are related to his or her attitudes toward different kinds of vacation experiences and to the kinds of things that he or she would want to do or encounter on a vacation. This hypothesis, if borne out, would influence the ways in which one should communicate to different kinds of potential customers.

The questionnaire that was designed included some 370 general life-style statements such as the following:

"I would rather live in a big city than in a small town."

"I have more stylish clothes than most of my friends."

"I don't like to take chances."

EXHIBIT A   Research Model for the Leisure Travel Market

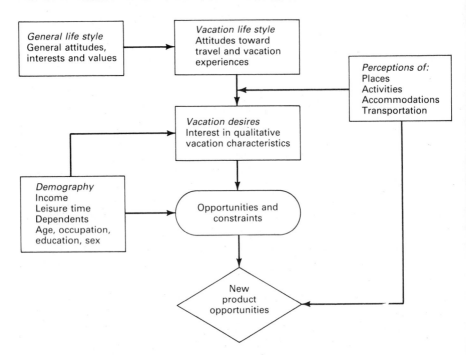

"My life is pretty dull."

"Spending money for an expensive vacation is a little like throwing money away."

"Memories make a vacation worth what it costs."

"I am interested in the cultures of other countries."

In addition, the questionnaire included some 440 statements about different things that people might like to do when on a vacation. These included such statements as:

"Visit an historical place."

"Watch a sunset."

"Lie on a beach."

"Visit friends or relatives."

"Go shopping in out-of-the-way places."

"Paint the house."

Another set of statements described the kinds of things that people might encounter on a vacation:

"Pretty girls"

"Neon lights"

"Fine wine"

"Educational experiences"

"People who speak a foreign language"

Our second hypothesis was that the kinds of vacation experiences that people wanted are related to the kinds of vacation packages that would appeal to them. Moreover, it was hypothesized that the relationship between the desired kinds of vacation experiences and the vacation packages which people find appealing is influenced by their perceptions of different places, activities, accommodations, etc. Socio-demographic considerations, such as household income, age, number of dependents, etc., may be thought of as either opportunities or as constraints to people's ability to realize their preferred vacations.

In order to develop such vacation types, the survey respondents were asked to imagine that they had a specific amount of time and money available to them. Sixteen combinations of time and money were used, depending on each person's own demographic characteristics.

Two such scenarios involving different combinations of time and money were presented to each respondent. In each case, he or she was free to choose to go away somewhere or to stay at home and use the money in some way other than travel. If the respondent chose to use the time and money to go away somewhere, he or she was asked to describe the kind of place they would go to from a long list of descriptions. Some of these descriptions included the following phrases:

"A place where it is warm and sunny."

"A familiar place."

"A resort hotel."

"A foreign place with a different culture."

"A foreign place where nature is unspoiled."

Respondents were then asked to describe the kind of place where they would want to go, the activities they would like to take part in, and the kind of facilities or accommodations they would prefer to stay at using different sets of descriptive adjectives and statements. They were also asked to identify some specific places, activities and types of accommodation that came closest to matching the description that they had selected as their ideal.

Other information collected included: the number and types of the people who would go along; whether they would prefer an all-inclusive package or not; the mode of transportation they would use to get to their vacation destination, as well as the type of transportation they would use while there; the time of year when they would probably go on this kind of trip; and their reasons for taking this kind of vacation. Those who thought it was unlikely that they would actually take such a vacation as they had described were asked for reasons why.

In order to determine the extent to which people's vacation desires are already being realized, respondents were asked about any vacations they had taken in the past two years. Additional information necessary to evaluate market opportunities for new vacation packages included at-home leisure activities and interests plus ownership of recreational equipment.

The data base for the market analysis was a survey of about 3,000 people representing the adult population of Canada.

The major elements in the analysis of the market demand structure were two cluster analyses which were conducted on the same respondent base. One cluster analysis was conducted on the general lifestyle data and the attitudes toward different kinds of vacation experiences. Four different groups of people were found:

Lifestyle Group	% of Total Adult Pop.
1. *Extravagant Consumers*—Are predominantly female, tend to have higher than medium household incomes, and include all age groups. An appealing vacation would emphasize luxury, service, pampering and clothes in places like Europe, Hawaii and the Caribbean.	18
2. *Nature People*—Tend to be young, unmarried, and well-educated. They want to go to new and different places to avoid schedules and routines, and to experience the universe generally without the usual concern about the usual comforts.	20
3. *Playsters*—Are primarily young males involved in the active pursuit of sensual pleasure. A vacation for them would need to be relatively inexpensive, but swinging, modern, and active, featuring no social values other than fun.	23
4. *Cautious Homebodies*—Tend to be older, less affluent, less well-educated, and less concentrated in urban areas. They want safety, security and a perfectly predictable environment on their vacation without any new experiences.	39

A second cluster analysis was carried out, using the same respondents, on the adjectives that people used to describe their ideal vacation. This analysis produced six distinct groupings of ideal vacation types:

Ideal Vacation Type	% of Total Adult Pop.
1. *Peace and Quiet*—Peaceful, quiet, and relaxing in a country setting; appeals to people in middle age and to those with less than average discretionary income.	20
2. *Aesthetic Appreciation*—A broadening, cultural, educational experience at historic places; appeals mostly to well-educated people and those in professional or managerial occupations.	22
3. *Hot Winter*—A vacation in a hot climate to get away from winters, lie on a beach and be pampered; appeals both to luxury and to fun seekers.	19
4. *Grand Hotel*—The luxury vacation providing entertainment, good food, and excitement; appeals both to luxury and fun seekers who have higher incomes.	19
5. *Inexpensively Active*—The low cost, active fun vacation good for meeting people; appeals most to males and young people.	9
6. *Relatives and Friends*—The family-centered vacation, full of familiar, friendly and inexpensive experiences; appeals most to older people who are not well-educated and have modest incomes.	12

Of course, not all of these people are equally likely to take vacations away from home, especially a vacation that involves travel by air. We therefore began to develop a set of probabilities for people that were based on:

1. Their responses to a short series of attitudinal statements about air travel;
2. Their reported likelihood of actually taking the kind of vacation that they described as being ideal;
3. Whether their ideal vacation involved air travel or not; and
4. Their actual vacation behavior over the past two years, taking into account any anticipated changes in their demographic circumstances.

When all of these factors were taken into account, the expected market potential for a vacation trip by air in any one year was found to be no higher than 35 percent of adult Canadians. Regionally across Canada we found some differences in this travel potential:

Maritimes	31 percent
Quebec English-speaking	35 percent
Quebec French-speaking	31 percent
Ontario	36 percent
Prairies	39 percent
British Columbia	37 percent

In the planning stages of this study, we had hypothesized that there is some relationship between the experiences that people want on a vacation and the type of vacation packages that they find appealing. If we cross-tabulate the lifestyle groups with the vacation types we get a 24-cell matrix. (See Exhibit B.)

The 35 percent potential air vacation travellers are distributed throughout all the cells of this matrix. However, if we compare the actual distribution with the distribution that would be expected to occur by pure chance, then we can find some significant relationships between lifestyle and ideal vacation types. (See Exhibit C.)

From a marketer's point of view, however, the major interest in this distribution is the market size in each cell. Their relative size and potential provides some sort of rank order for market development opportunities.

Each cell in the matrix can be thought of as a distinct marketing opportunity, representing different target consumer groups. The six vacation types can be thought of as distinct groupings of vacation packages, while the four lifestyle groups indicate different kinds of experiences that can be offered to target groups of people and represent different communications approaches to be used in advertising.

At this stage of the market research program, we had been able to identify specific target groups within the leisure travel market for Air Canada and to provide sufficient analytical information for the development of new vacation packages and communication strategies.

PART II—ANNABELLE BENNETTS

When we first began the research, as was mentioned earlier, it was intended to carry it right through to the testing of holidays designed from it. The identification of the consumer segments had involved such a large scale survey, however, that by the time it was completed, we had almost lost sight of the fact that it was only the beginning.

The communication and interpretation of this first phase of the work took some months to complete. All of Air Canada's product development and communications people were involved, and each, because of his route responsibilities, was interested in a different mix of lifestyle and vacation type segments.

While the communication of the research was being done, plans were underway for the next two stages, those of vacation testing and forecasting.

It was planned that the study be useable over a period of at least five years. We wanted it to be the basis of both product design and of product testing. But having completed the first phase, we still had to develop a methodology for testing the travel concepts we were yet to de-

EXHIBIT B Total Canada 24-Cell Market Demand Matrix

	Total	Peace and Quiet	Aesthetic Appreciation	Hot Winter	Grand Hotel	Inexpensively Active	Relatives and Friends
Extravagant consumers	7.5	0.8	1.8	1.9	1.2	0.5	1.3
Nature people	7.7	1.3	3.0	1.2	0.8	0.8	0.6
Playsters	7.3	0.8	1.1	2.1	1.1	0.9	1.3
Cautious homebodies	12.3	1.3	3.3	2.3	2.3	0.5	2.6
Total	34.8	4.2	9.2	7.5	5.4	2.7	5.8

And where: Total Population is 100 percent (about 14,000,000)
Adjusted for: *Potential Leisure Travel by Air*
Likelihood of Taking Ideal Vacation
Propensity for Air Mode
Past Vacation Behaviour

EXHIBIT C Lifestyle vs. Vacation Clusters/Actual vs. Chance Index

	Peace Quiet	Aesthetic Appreciation	Hot Winter	Grand Hotel	Inexpensively Active	Relatives and Friends
Extravagant consumers	− 11.2		+ 12.3		− 13.3	
Nature people	+ 41.9	+ 47.8	− 28.1	− 33.0	+ 35.1	− 53.2
Playsters		− 42.9	+ 32.7		+ 60.1	
Cautious homebodies	− 11.3		− 12.5	+ 20.5	− 47.3	+ 26.9

And where: Total Population is 100 percent (about 14,000,000)
Adjusted for: *Potential Leisure Travel by Air*
                  Likelihood of Taking Ideal Vacation
                  Propensity for Air Mode
                  Past Vacation Behaviour

sign. We felt we knew how many groups of people and vacation types there were and what the make-up of each was. The next problems then were how to design vacations to suit these types, how to find out whether the designs were all accepted by people, and most difficult, how to predict how many people would buy each one.

The job of designing the vacations to suit the various segments was done by Air Canada's product development group, having ascertained which lifestyle groups and which vacation types went together. What went toward the makeup of each holiday type (e.g., accommodations, destination, activities), was used to design new holidays around specific Air Canada destinations. The desire among extravagant consumers for a holiday in the sun with the luxuries of high class hotels and good service became one of Air Canada's "Sun Living" vacations. It included a one or two-week stay in Montego Bay, Ocho Rios and Kingston, accommodations in first class hotels, entertainment, sightseeing, beach parties, etc. The desire of the cautious homebodies to be led around and made to feel secure as opposed to being on a wild solo fling, was recognized and turned into a guided coach tour of England. In total, 20 vacation concepts were designed based on profile and need information from the study.

As the vacation packages were being designed, a methodology for testing them was worked out. It was planned to type a large body of people according to their lifestyles and preferred vacation types and to keep this group of people in reserve for testing purposes. Economics of time and money prevented us from trying to recontact the original sample of people to whom the first questionnaire had been administered. Instead, a methodology was worked out whereby an individual could easily and reliably type himself. A number of approaches were tried and the one which was found to be the most successful was, as is often the case, the simplest.

It was found that each of the four lifestyles and the six vacation types could be described with about nine statements. The nine statements for each of the four lifestyles were listed vertically and boxed off separately so that the four descriptions were side by side on a single page. The same was done for the six vacation types. The respondent had merely to check off one of the four lifestyles and one of the six vacation summaries which he felt to be most like him. The statements used were those that best discriminated each group from all of the others. Thus, while a statement such as "I would like to absorb the culture of a different place," might have received a positive reaction from a cross-section of people, it was believed in much more strongly by the "Aesthetic Appreciation" group than by any other. The boxes of statements were not, of course, labelled by the terms we now use to identify the requirements. It is unlikely that anyone would have recognized himself too readily with a title such as Cautious Homebody or Extravagant Consumer.

A test was done to check people's ability to classify themselves as one of the types described. The check involved having a sample of people answer a scaled questionnaire similar to the one used in the original study. At a later date, after we had categorized them, they were sent a self-classification questionnaire. The results compared favourably and it was decided that the simplified test would be used to categorize a large body of people to be used as future respondents for the concept testing.

The descriptions were sent to Market Facts mail panel members and the yield was about 6,500 people classified by lifestyle and vacation type. Information was also obtained on the sample's past and present vacation habits and demography. Having set up the data bank of people, we were then ready for the first series of concept testing. About half of the already classified panel was sent a questionnaire for this phase of the study. The rest of the panel will be used for further testing in 1976.

While the mail panel was being divided into lifestyle/vacation groups, the Market Development department was designing vacation packages based on the data from the first phase of the study. Air Canada is divided into four route areas (Canada, U.S.A., South America, Europe) and five concepts were formed for each of them. Each of the 20 concepts was laid out in the pattern as shown here. Each concept was presented on a single page containing seven columns of information (see below). The destination, what was included in the trip and paid for, the time of year the vacation was offered, special features such as golf, watersports, sightseeing tours, the length of stay and the cost were each dealt with separately.

Included in the list of 20 concepts was one which had already been on the market for a few years. It was called Skifari and it had been attracting steadily increasing numbers of travellers from one year to the next. Accurate counts of the number of people who had bought Skifari and some estimates of the number who were likely to buy it in the next couple of years were available from industry sources. It was also felt that

Skifari would appeal to only a small and well defined group of people and that this group was, in all probability, not found in more than one or two lifestyle/vacation groups of people. This concept was tested with the sole purposes in mind of checking how well it was targeted and how accurate our market forecasts for the other 19 concepts might be. It was felt that if the forecast model, yet to be developed, could accurately predict roles for Skifari, we could be fairly confident that the forecasts for the other concepts were not too far off the beam.

The model was designed from values assigned to respondents for their answers to various questions on both the self-classification and the concept testing questionnaires. Approximately 35 percent of adult Canadians had been judged to be potential travellers and this group became the base for concept projections. Included in the concept test itself had been a question on the likelihood of the respondent actually taking his chosen vacation. The answers to this question and others were included in the model for market projections. One interesting part of the formula was a factor derived from questioning the respondent as to whether his or her chosen vacation or that of the spouse would be most likely to be taken first. Thus, the impact of the influence of each household member on the decision to take a certain type of vacation was taken into account.

The forecast model which was developed was experimented with somewhat before a final format was established and the results of the ensuing forecasts were quite fascinating. We were able to predict sales for Skifari which were so close to what are actually expected for the coming season that they almost seemed a little suspicious. It remains to be seen whether the other concepts will be bought by Canadians in approximately the same numbers as we have forecast. The terms of the sale of some for these vacations are not as strictly "package" as are those for Skifari. Thus, someone may buy a touring trip of Europe very similar to one of the tested concepts but not actually be purchasing the exact holiday called "City Roamer" being sold by Air Canada. The job of counting all the "City Roamer"-type tours will be more difficult than that of counting well-defined Skifari-takers. It may be found that checking our forecast model's accuracy will be just as difficult a task as developing it was in the first place.

A number of reports were written on the concept test at various stages of its completion. It was, however, the generation of the actual forecasts for the concepts that elicited the most interest from the users. Since it was really our first attempt at cranking out these numbers from research data, the test will be closely monitored for its success or failure over the next couple of years. Undoubtedly, refinements will have to be made before we come up with something in which we are totally confident, but the first try shows signs of being a pretty reasonable start.

We were able to direct and design the communication of a concept

VACATION PACKAGE DESIGN

Destination	Includes	When	Special Features	Length of Stay	Cost (For each of two people sharing a room)
Jamaica Montego Bay and Ochos Rios and Kingston	Return air fare Toronto to Jamaica 4-5 day stay in each of the places Accommodations in first class hotels Transportation from airport to hotel Motor coach transfers from hotel to hotel Night entertainment Sighseeing	All year	Sightseeing in each place Entertainment and tours in each of three places Tours to places of interest Rafting Visits to waterfalls Beach parties Picnics	Summer 9 days 14 days Winter 9 days 14 days	$470 $650 $549 $799

Self-Classification of Lifestyle and Vacation Type

I *agree* that—	I *agree* that—
I'd rather live in or near a big city than in or near a small town	I enjoy going through antique stores
I enjoy looking through fashion magazines	I'd rather save up and spend a longer time in a foreign country
I feel attractive to the opposite sex	I am interested in spices and seasonings
Dressing well is an important part of my life	I think the women's liberation movement is a good thing
Eye make-up is as important as lipstick	My greatest achievements are ahead of me
I would like to have a maid do the housework	I'd rather spend money on travel than on a new automobile
I *disagree* that—	I *disagree* that—
I am a girl watcher	I admire a successful business man more than a successful artist or writer
I enjoy watching sports on T.V.	In a foreign country I'd rather stay at a Holiday Inn than at a native hotel
I'd rather spend a quiet evening at home than go out to a party	Canada would be better off if there were no hippies

I *agree* that—	I *agree* that—
I will probably have more money to spend next year than I have now	I stay home most evenings
I am a girl watcher	I am in favour of very strict enforcement of all laws
I enjoy watching sports on T.V.	All men should be clean shaven every day
I like sports cars	I am a homebody
I like science fiction	I'd rather spend a quiet evening at home than go out to a party
I like to think I'm a bit of a swinger	Young people have too many privileges
I *disagree* that—	I *disagree* that—
I would rather write stories than run a business	I am active in sports
The kitchen is my favourite room	I am an impulsive buyer
I usually wear perfume	I like sports cars

Self-Classification of Lifestyle and Vacation Type (*cont.*)

I would *like* to—	I would *like* to—	I would *like* to—
See places I've always wanted to see	Visit relatives/friends	Be active
Absorb culture of a different place	Feel as comfortable as at home	Spend not too much money
Visit historic places	Spend not too much money	Meet young people
Go to an art gallery	Eat same kinds of food that I'm used to	Do something unique/ different
Go to a classical concert	Go somewhere that's familiar	Listen to rock music
Live with a foreign family	Watch T.V.	Ride a horse, a motorcycle, or a surfboard
I would *not like* to—	**I would *not like* to—**	**I would *not like* to—**
Do nothing	Absorb the culture of a different place	Do nothing
Lie on a beach	Do something unique and different	Stay in a fancy hotel
Have a frivolous vacation	Meet new kinds of people	Watch T.V.

I would *like* to—	I would *like* to—	I would *like* to—
Stay in a modern hotel with great entertainment, air conditioning, and good food	Have peace and quiet	Get away from snow and ice
Go to a night club	Cook over an open fire	Lie on a bench
Shop for new clothes	Get away from hustle and bustle	Be pampered
Get away from everyday routine	Drink from a mountain stream	Have breakfast in bed
Go to a luau	Spend summer at a cottage	Get into warm weather
Get a sun tan	Ignore the clock	Sit in the sun
I would *not like* to—	**I would *not like* to—**	**I would *not like* to—**
Be in a very quiet place	Go to a night club	Visit relatives/friends
Do it 'on the cheap'	Absorb culture of a different	Visit historic places
	Have an 'educational' vacation	Have an 'educational' vacation

to specific audiences based on the information we collected much more accurately than had been the case previously. We were able to check the rightness or wrongness of offering a specific vacation to a certain group of people and to make changes to the holidays based on their suggestions. Information gathered included which vacations were the most preferred, additions or deletions the respondents would like made to the vacations, perceived monetary value of the vacations, reasons for choosing a particular concept and the likelihood of actually going on the vacation chosen. The final task was one of having the respondent create his or her own ideal vacation within certain parameters of time, money and mode of travel.

When the concepts were designed, it was the intent to structure them for specific target audiences such as Extravagant Consumers on Hot Winter holidays. Ideally, we should have been testing only among the groups for whom the vacations had been intended. However, it was felt that the buyers of some of the holidays might overlap among a few groups, and with this in mind, the research was structured to identify the groups for whom each vacation was ideally suited as well as to refine the structure of each of the holidays. Thus, while it had been the original intent to send only Cautious Homebody concepts to Cautious Homebodies, for example, all concepts were sent to a mix of everyone, regardless of lifestyle or vacation type.

The methodology proved to be the right one on the whole. Some of the concepts, most notably Skifari, were found to be perfectly targeted at only one or two groups of people. Others, however, unexpectedly found followers in a number of groups. Of all those who chose and were likely to go on Skifari, 84 percent were either Playsters or Nature People and 74 percent preferred a Grand Hotel or Peace and Quiet Vacation. One of the Southern concepts, on the other side of the coin, appealed to all groups in almost the same proportions as are actually found in the general population. Hopefully, by the next round of product testing, our ability to understand the needs of the various groups will be somewhat more advanced and we will come closer to being able to target a vacation as precisely as was the case for Skifari. It is clear that only by contacting people over and over will we be able to fully appreciate the differences among the segments originally defined in the study.

It is planned to conduct a second series of concept tests in 1976. Of all the original people who were classified according to lifestyle and vacation type, we have so far interviewed only about half. We still, therefore, have a large group of respondents who can be quickly and easily contacted for the next round.

Some of the concepts which were tested in the first phase are now on the market, a full three years after the fieldwork for the Leisure Market study was begun and at least four years after the work was authorized.

In any study of this magnitude, there are bound to be mistakes made and areas found in which changes could improve the work, and this study was no exception to the rule. We were given the opportunity recently to try our hand again in the European markets and were successful in anticipating most of the major problems which surfaced in the Canadian study. This work is about to go into the concept testing phase also. The methodology used will be similar to that used for the Canadian test and it is planned to use the experience gained in Europe to further refine the second stage of testing in Canada in 1976. It remains to be seen how well we teach ourselves. Our success in correctly targeting well designed and accepted concepts in the next series of tests will be the test of our expertise.

5

PURPOSES OF TRAVEL:

The Characteristics

of Traveler Segments

The two major classifications of travel purpose are business travel and pleasure/personal travel. The patterns and needs of people in both segments are the topic of this chapter.

Business travel is the "bread and butter" market for many tourism-related businesses. Business travel is broken down into regular travel, business travel related to meetings, conventions, and congresses, and incentive travel, which is somewhat of a hybrid as the people on the trip are traveling for pleasure although the purchasers of the trip are businesses. The characteristics of those in these market segments are explored in detail.

The pleasure/personal travel market is examined from the viewpoint of traditional segments, such as resort travelers and family pleasure travelers, and other major growth segments, such as the elderly, singles, and black travelers.

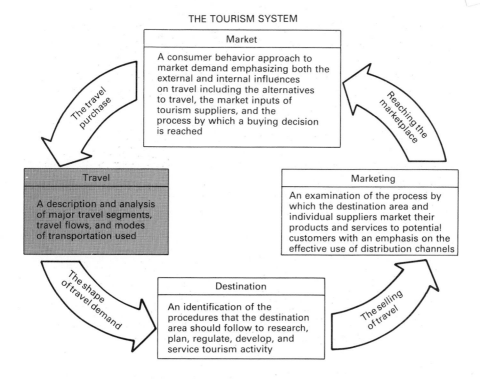

THE TOURISM SYSTEM

Market

A consumer behavior approach to market demand emphasizing both the external and internal influences on travel including the alternatives to travel, the market inputs of tourism suppliers, and the process by which a buying decision is reached

Reaching the marketplace

The travel purchase

Travel

A description and analysis of major travel segments, travel flows, and modes of transportation used

Marketing

An examination of the process by which the destination area and individual suppliers market their products and services to potential customers with an emphasis on the effective use of distribution channels

The shape of travel demand

Destination

An identification of the procedures that the destination area should follow to research, plan, regulate, develop, and service tourism activity

The selling of travel

Chapters one to four have examined how an individual—any individual—makes a travel decision. In order to describe the larger picture of travel flows, it is necessary to describe not individuals but segments of the total travel market. Those travelers relevent to tourism are either tourists, if they are in a destination for more than a day but less than a year, or excursionists, if they arrive and depart the same day. In either case their travel may be for reasons of business or pleasure (Fig. 5.1).

THE BUSINESS TRAVEL MARKET

In most developed countries, business travel is the "bread and butter" market for the tourism industry for much of the year. This is certainly the case in the United States, Canada, and the United Kingdom. Just as it is inadequate to use the "jumbo jet" approach to analyzing pleasure/personal travel markets, it is equally wrong to view the business travel market as an amorphous mass that cannot be further segmented. In fact, this first major travel market has many component segments, and the number of segments appears to grow from year to year. The business-related travel market segments can be broadly categorized as follows:

FIGURE 5.1   Segments of the Travel Market

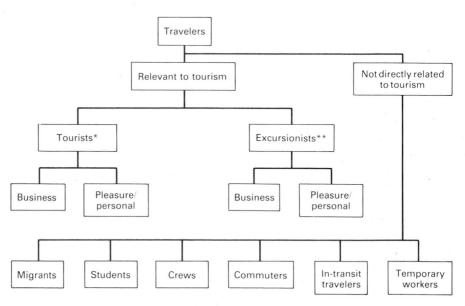

**One or more nights stay
**Arrive and depart same day

1. Regular business travel
2. Business travel related to meetings, conventions, and congresses
3. Incentive travel

The third category of incentive travel is really a "hybrid" segment since it is a type of pleasure travel that has been financed for business reasons. Thus, the persons on the incentive trips are pleasure travelers and the purchasers are businesses.

Regular Business Travel

Just under 20 percent of all trips in Canada and the United States are taken for business reasons. (Note: A trip in the United States is defined as one of over 100 miles from home; in Canada it is defined as one of over fifty miles from home). In addition to these levels of domestic business travel by United States and Canadian residents, there is also significant cross-border travel and travel from the two countries to other foreign nations.

Many surveys have been carried out that have attempted to profile the characteristics of the business travel market. It is clear from these surveys that the bulk of business-related travel in North America involves the use of airlines. Thus, by reviewing surveys of business travelers on airlines we can get a fairly accurate profile of the business travel market.

Table 5.1 shows the result of one such survey carried out by *Time* magazine at airports in New York and Chicago.[1] The key conclusions of this particular survey are that business travelers are well educated, affluent, have high-level jobs, and tend to fly often. More recent surveys have shown that the ratio of women business travelers to men has grown rapidly from that shown in Table 5.1. Depending upon the source you consult, it appears that women account for 15 to 25 percent of the business travel market. This growing segment is discussed in more detail later in this chapter.

The business executive travel market is proving to be more "segmentable" today, with many airlines and hotels making specific efforts to cater to these higher echelon persons. Airlines have been offering first-class seat service and first-class passenger lounges in airport terminals to these travelers for many years. More recent innovations include special check-in arrangements, bigger seats, and sleeper seats. Many hotel chains have begun to allocate whole floors or wings of their buildings for those business travelers seeking greater luxury in their accommodations. The rooms or suites are more spacious, contain more personal "giveaways," and they provide their guests with complimentary drinks and express check-in, check-out service. Normally the airline and hotel companies add a surcharge to their regular prices for the extra comforts and convenience provided to executive travelers; they have achieved considerable marketing successes in so doing. The airlines, particularly in the United States, have begun to search out and reward frequent fliers by logging their air miles in airline computers. The types of rewards offered include discounts on future trips and sometimes even free trips.

As we have highlighted in several places earlier, the businesswomen travel market segment is another growth area in tourism. Some tourism suppliers, like United Airlines, have gone on record as stating that it is their single fastest-growing or one of their fastest-growing market segments. Surveys of businesswomen travelers show that their needs and the appeals to them are in many ways different from those of male business travelers.

Some of the major differences between male and female business travelers and their preferences that have been noted are listed below:

Women business travelers are slightly younger.
They tend to stay longer at their destinations.
They are more apt to be unmarried than males.
They are more likely to be attending a meeting or convention.

---

[1]"Business Travelers: The Airline Experience," *Time Magazine*, Time Marketing Services, AA#2268, undated, pp. 4–5.

TABLE 5.1   A Profile of Business Travelers on Airlines

	All Business Fliers	Frequent Domestic[1] Fliers	Frequent International[2] Fliers
Sex			
Male	90%	94%	95%
Female	10	6	5
Age			
25-34	23%	21%	14%
35-49	44	47	53
50-54	10	9	11
Median age	43 years	44 years	45 years
Marital status			
Married	80%	84%	80%
Education			
College educated	94%	95%	96%
Graduated from college	76	79	84
Post-graduate degree	31	31	41
Household income			
Under $25,000	9%	4%	4%
$25,000-$34,999	16	12	7
$35,000-$49,999	28	29	20
$50,000-$74,999	26	29	32
$75,000-$99,999	10	13	14
$100,000 and over	11	13	23
Median income	$48,300	$54,500	$64,400
Job title			
Top Management	36%	32%	56%
All managers/administrators	72	69	80
Other	28	31	20

[1]Passengers who have taken twenty or more domestic flights in the past year for business reasons.
[2]Passengers who have taken ten or more international flights in the past year for business reasons.

SOURCE: "Business Travelers: The Airline Experience," *Time Magazine*, Time Marketing Services AA#2268, undated, pp. 4-5.

They are more likely to book through a travel agent.

They have a greater preference for downtown accommodation facilities closer to work.

They are more concerned with security aspects of accommodation facilities.

Meetings, Conventions, Congresses

A major segment of the business travel market is concerned with travel for the purpose of attending meetings, conventions, congresses, trade shows, and expositions. Travel Pulse surveys indicate that about 20 percent of all business travel trips are for the purpose of attending corporate meetings or conventions. Although it is true that some of the attendees have personal motivations for traveling to these gatherings, most of them have a business or at least a career orientation. The major division that can be made in these types of public and private gatherings is into the institutional and the corporate/government markets. Here the word "institutional" refers to associations and other groups that share a broad affinity; "corporate/government segments" refer to organizations that deal with specific corporate or government business matters and that are private in nature. Several subdivisions can usefully be made within the institutional group. Normally the terms "conventions," "conferences," "congresses," and "assemblies" are used for institutional gatherings. Lawson[2] has put forward the following definitions for these types of gatherings:

A congress, convention, or conference is a regular formalized meeting of an association or body, or a meeting sponsored by an association or body on a regular or ad hoc basis. Depending on the objectives of a particular survey, this may be qualified by a minimum size (e.g., 12 or 25 attendees), by the use of premises, by a minimum time or/and by having a fixed agenda or program.

Congresses are usually general sessions, mostly information giving and the commonly accepted traditional form of full-membership meeting. Meetings are usually large and formal and the word 'congress' carries a connotation of a serious working purpose. Congress halls are designed to accommodate large numbers of delegates, usually in close-seated auditorium or theater-style arrangements.

Assemblies are mainly policy-making or legislatory meetings attended by large numbers of representatives or representative groups who may formally speak and vote on the subjects of the agenda. Assembly layouts may require double banks of seats and tables for the principles and their advisors.

Convention is a term widely used in North America and the Pacific region to describe major or total-membership meetings. Over 80% of American associations hold a major annual convention for their total membership, and many companies provide similar opportunities for their staff to meet, formally as well as socially, in attractive surroundings.

Conferences are usually general sessions and face-to-face groups with a high participation, primarily concerned with planning, obtaining facts and information, or solving organizational and operational problems. Conferences are mainly confined to members of the same company, association, or profession. Meetings are less formally organized but encourage collective participation in reaching stated objectives or goals. Numbers of delegates attending a conference may range up to 150 or more but 30–50 is more typical.

---

[2]Fred R. Lawson, "Congresses, Conventions and Conferences: Facility Supply and Demand," *International Journal of Tourism Management*, September, 1980, p. 188.

Although Lawson uses the term "conferences" to include corporate groups, the most common North American interpretation of the word is that it refers to institutional and not corporate gatherings.

CONVENTION MARKET

1. International associations

2. Continental associations

3. National associations

4. Regional associations

The institutional or association convention market can be segmented geographically into four parts, namely international, continental, national, and regional conventions. International conventions usually involve members and nonmembers from more than two foreign countries, and they take place in different countries each year. They are nongovernmental events, and it has been forecast that the numbers of delegates attending these will double in the twenty-year span from 1973 to 1993. The groups or associations are generally of the nonprofit variety and attract persons with common fields of interest.

Continental conventions have attendees drawn primarily from a continents such as North America. The annual Travel and Tourism Research Association (TTRA) Conference is an appropriate example of a continental convention, being held in either the United States or Canada. It has members and draws conference delegates primarily from these two countries.

National conventions are limited by their by-laws or traditions to holding their gatherings within the countries in which they are located. Generally, their attendees are residents of that country. The Tourism Industry Association of Canada (TIAC) is an example of such a body which rotates its annual convention between Canadian cities.

Regional conventions are those meetings organized by associations at the state, provincial, or another regional level. Normally these organizations hold their conventions within their own regions.

The most comprehensive survey of this segment of the business travel market in North America is carried out once every two years by *Meetings & Conventions* magazine. The 1981 survey estimated that just under 850,000 conventions and meetings were held that year by the magazine's subscribers.[3] (These subscribers are based primarily in the United States). Approximately 82.4 percent, or 700,000 of these events were corporate meetings. There were 10,500 major association conventions, and the balance, or 125,000 meetings, were also staged by associations. It should be noted that all 850,000 conventions and meetings were "off-premises," meaning that they were held outside of the plants and offices of the corporations and associations. Quite obviously there are a large number of other "on-premises" meetings that generate business travel between corporate and association offices. Additionally, it should be noted that the *Meetings & Conventions* magazine survey includes incentive travel trips in the corporate meetings grouping. According to the Meetings and Convention Survey, the total and average attendance figures for these conventions and meetings were as follows in 1981:

Corporate meetings	−42 million participants
	−60 participants on average
Major association conventions	−9,475,000 delegates
	−900 delegates on average
Other association meetings	−13 million participants
	−100 participants on average

These three types of off-premises meetings and conventions generated close to 64.5 million business travel trips in 1981, the vast majority of which had U.S. destinations. Only 22,400, or 3 percent of the corporate "off-premises" meetings were held at destinations outside of the United States, approximately 4,250 being held in Canada and 3,135 in Mexico. Just 4 percent of the major association conventions had non-U.S. destinations.

The *Meetings & Conventions* magazine survey divided the corporate meetings market into nine distinctive subgroups based upon the overall purpose of the meetings. In order of their frequencies the subgroups were management meetings, regional sales meetings, new product introductions, national sales meetings, training seminars, incentive travel trips, professional/technical meetings, stockholder meetings, and other meetings. In the 1979 survey, it was estimated that some 3.8-million spouses accompanied the 39.2-million employees attending 614,000 corporate meetings that year. This would seem to suggest that about one out of ten corporate meeting attendees brings his or her spouse along on the trip.

---

[3]Hotel & Travel Index, *The U.S. Resort Travel Market: A Perspective on Trends and Forecasts for U.S. Resort Travel, 1982-83* (New York, Ziff-Davis Publishing Company, October, 1982), p. 72.

Prior to leaving the subject of conventions and meetings, we should note one barrier to this travel in recent times in North America that was imposed by the U.S. government in 1976. Section 620 of the Tax Reform Act of 1976 permitted U.S. corporations to hold only two tax-deductible meetings a year outside of the United States and required detailed record-keeping on the part of convention and meeting organizers and attendees. Individuals attending conventions were allowed to deduct their expenses from only two foreign conventions per year. This was the law in the United States for a four-year period between January 1, 1977 and December 31, 1980. It proved extremely unpopular with meeting/convention organizers, delegates, and with host cities outside of the United States, particularly those in Canada and Mexico. A new law is now in effect that allows U.S. residents and corporations to deduct all qualifying expenses incurred from every convention and meeting taking place in the "North American zone," which includes the United States, Canada, and Mexico. It should be realized that the incentive travel market was not affected by this temporary legislation.

Incentive Travel

Travel is the answer to a dream—a dream of luxury, prestige, in exotic places. It is the ultimate escape from daily routine[,] . . . and travel which is earned through effort salves not only the ego, but the conscience as well.

The above statement is indicative of the lure of travel trips as work incentives for employees and the reason why the incentive travel market segment has been booming in popularity among corporations in the United States and Canada.

It is estimated that the average incentive travel trip lasts five days—the longest duration of the nine corporate meeting subgroups—and involves an average of 174 people. The most popular destination areas for the incentive travelers are Mexico, the Caribbean, Bermuda, and Europe. Within the United States itself, Hawaii, Las Vegas, Miami, Disney World, San Francisco, San Diego, and New Orleans are popular incentive travel destinations.

The mushrooming popularity of incentive travel has given rise to the creation of a number of companies specializing in the organization of these trips. Many of their members belong to an association known as SITE (Society of Incentive Travel Executives).

Corporations usually have one or more of the following objectives in mind when purchasing incentive travel trips:

Increasing overall sales volumes
Selling new accounts
Improving morale and good will

Selling full-line or slow items
Introducing new products
Offsetting competitive promotions
Bolstering slow seasons
Helping in sales training
Obtaining more store displays and support consumer promotions.

The costs of incentive travel trips depend on the rates the incentive travel organizations can negotiate with suppliers such as hotels, airlines, and so on. In this way they act as a specialized type of tour wholesaler. To their prices they add a markup for their own services and costs in packaging the incentive travel trip, typically in the 15 percent to 20 percent range.

Heavy users of incentive travel trips are companies involved in insurance sales, electronics/radio/television manufacturing, automobile and truck manufacturing, farm-equipment manufacturing, auto parts/accessories/tires, heating/air-conditioning, electrical appliances manufacturing, office equipment manufacturing, and toiletries/building materials manufacturing.

Prior to beginning the discussion of the pleasure/personal travel market, the "hybrid" travel trip must be clearly identified. The hybrid trip is one in which the traveler mixes business and pleasure, be it on a regular business travel junket or in conjunction with a convention or a corporate meeting. Travel promoters at every travel destination should realize that having a business traveler really provides a three-part opportunity. First, the business traveler visits to carry out his or her work-related activities. Second, he or she, and perhaps his or her spouse, may be convinced to spend pleasure travel time before or after the meeting, convention, or other business activity. Third, he or she may be attracted to return to the destination in the future on a pleasure or a business travel trip.

The hybrid travel trip market is significant in North America. A question added to the Opinion Research Corporation's Travel Caravan Study in July, 1982 indicated that 10 percent of all employed U.S. adults were planning to tack on vacation days to one or more future business trips.[4] This figure rose to approximately 20 percent for those in professional and managerial positions, which covers more than seven out of ten business travelers. The same study also found the third marketing opportunity—business travelers considering return trips to resorts where they had attended business-related meetings or conventions—to be very significant. It indicated that one-third of these persons had actually revisited on a vacation resort sites where meetings or conventions had taken place, and

---

[4]Hotel & Travel Index, *The U.S. Resort Travel Market*, p. 83.

36 percent of these people had plans to visit such sites on future vacation trips. With the rise of two-income households in the North American work force, there is a higher incidence of situations in which both spouses travel. In situations in which their business travel plans match, or come close to coinciding, as to destinations and dates, this provides another incentive for hybrid travel trips by both partners.

In summation, the business travel market is a major component of tourism. It has several segments within it, and as with pleasure travel, more new, viable segments appear to emerge as time progresses. Businesswomen, executives, attenders of corporate meetings and conventions, incentive travelers, and hybrid travelers are some of the most readily identifiable of these segments.

THE PLEASURE/PERSONAL TRAVEL MARKET

Because there have as yet been no truly comprehensive pleasure-travel segmentation exercises for the entire North American continent our evaluation of the pleasure/personal travel market has had to revert back to the traditional approach that is better supported by available research and literature. We can begin by trying to pinpoint the approximate total scale of the pleasure-travel market. Recent surveys have provided the following estimates of domestic, intranational, and international travel volumes for the United States and Canada:

U.S.A.

79 million *American adults* took 180 million domestic and international pleasure-travel trips during 1981. These figures from the Travel Pulse 34 survey define a trip as involving a *round trip* of *200 miles* or more, and as involving the use of paid accommodations *or* the use of commercial airlines, ships, or trains. The survey therefore excludes trips in automobiles or other vehicles in which the travelers do not pay for their accommodations.

144 million of the trips were for personal/vacation purposes; 126 million of these were domestic, and 18 million were international. An additional 36 million trips were for other personally oriented reasons.

CANADA

90.9 million person-trips were taken by *Canadians* to domestic destinations in 1980. These figures are from the Canadian Travel Survey that defines a trip as one involving a *round trip* of *100 miles* or more. Trips include those involving the use of paid *and* unpaid accommodation and *all* travel modes.

10.52 million person-trips by Canadians involving a stay of one or more nights in the United States were made in 1979. These included business travelers as well as pleasure/personal travelers.

1.76 million person-trips by Canadians were made to foreign countries other than the United States in 1979. These included business travelers as well as pleasure-personal travelers.

When reviewing these statistics one important point should be clear. Pleasure/personal travel encompasses trips in which persons visit their friends and relatives (commonly referred to as VFR's) and trips in which they do not. For example, some 36 million of the domestic, pleasure/personal person trips in 1980 by Canadians involved visits to friends and relatives. This was 32.4 percent of all domestic travel trips and almost 40 percent of all pleasure/personal person trips. These travel flows are reviewed in greater detail in Chapter six.

Resort-Traveler

One of the segments of the pleasure travel market that has been researched in the United States involves the resort traveler. Figure 5.2 provides a profile of the U.S. resort traveler based upon an 1982 survey.[5] The profile given in Figure 5.2 is for U.S. pleasure/vacation travelers and does not include those using resorts for business purposes. The key conclusions of this survey have been that U.S. pleasure/vacation travelers utilizing resorts tend to be more "upscale" than the general public. They are better educated, have higher household incomes, and are more likely to have professional and managerial positions. It is also notable that 56 percent of the resort travelers have families with children.

On this latter point it is important to define what is and what is not the family pleasure-travel segment. We used to think of families as "nuclear" (husband, wife, and children), with the family pleasure-travel market consisting of trips "involving a husband and wife and at least one of their children." This definition therefore excludes married couples traveling without children, single parent families traveling with children, unmarried couples traveling with children, unmarried couples traveling alone, groups traveling without children, and "singles" traveling alone. As the earlier part of this chapter highlighted, these other travel party types are now growing more rapidly than the nuclear family units. Overall, however, the family pleasure travel market still remains the largest type of pleasure travel "unit" in North America.

Family Pleasure Travel

The family pleasure-travel market can be segmented into three groups, namely mature families, mid-range families, and junior families. These are defined according to the husband and wife's ages and the educational stages of their children as follows:

---

[5] Hotel & Market Index, *The U.S. Resort Travel Market*, p. 33.

FIGURE 5.2 Profile of the U.S. Resort Vacation/Pleasure Traveler, 1982

	Total Public	Total Travelers*	Resort Travelers*
Sex			
Male	50%	53%	55%
Female	50	47	45
Age			
18–24	18	16	17
25–34	29	27	28
35–44	19	20	20
45–64	23	27	25
65+	11	9	10
Education			
High school	14	9	11
High school graduate	40	35	32
Some college	20	23	24
College graduate	26	32	33
Household Income			
$15,000	27	21	14
$15,000–$24,999	25	25	24
$25,000–$34,999	27	26	30
$35,000+	22	28	32
Status			
Married	66	68	72
Not married	34	32	28
Household Size			
1–2 people	42	43	44
3–4	39	41	40
5+ people	19	16	16
Children			
No children	53	54	53
Children 12 and under	35	34	34
Children 12–17	21	22	22
Employment			
Professional/managerial	41	41	50
Sales/clerical	21	22	17
Blue collar	38	37	33
Geographic Area			
Northeast	22	22	19
North central	26	27	24
South	33	33	37
West	19	19	20

* Based on questions included in the Opinion Research Corporation's Travel Caravan Study that were commissioned by Hotel & Travel Index.

SOURCE: Hotel & Travel Index, *The U.S. Resort Travel Market: A Perspective on Trends and Forecasts for U.S. Resort Travel 1982-83* (New York, Ziff-Davis Publishing Co., October 1982), p. 33.

The junior family. Families with parents aged 20–34, having preschool and/or grade-school children only.

Mid-range families. Families with parents aged 35–44, with grade-school and/or high-school children only.

Mature families. Families with parents aged 45 or over, with children who are of high school age and older.

What motivates family pleasure-travel trips? For all three family groups the first priority is to use travel as an educational experience for their children. The second priority is to do something different, and this factor is especially highly rated by mid-range families. The third priority is to use travel to bring the family closer together. Another important motivator is to visit friends and relatives, and this is particularly prevalent with the junior families. The major deterrents to family pleasure-travel are the costs of travel, particularly the cost of transportation, accommodation, and food, the ability of the parents to have privacy from their children, and the problems of organizing and coordinating family pleasure-travel plans. Marketers in destinations appealing to families would therefore be well-advised to promote the experiences that families are seeking and to take steps to lessen the impact or perceptions of the deterrents.

The Elderly

An examination of population trends in North America clearly indicated that the population is aging. There are many more people today of fifty years of age and over, including greater numbers of retirement-age persons in the sixty-five–plus category. These population shifts have made the "elderly" persons pleasure-travel market and its component segments an increasingly lucrative target for tourism destination areas. The strong growth that has occurred in the bus tour and recreational-vehicle market is indicative of the increasing relative importance of the "fifty-plus" market. One startling statistic released in 1976 suggested that approximately 8 million retirement-age Americans were living in recreational vehicles and had adopted the nomadic way of life.

Fig. 5.3 and 5.4 visually demonstrate the aging population trend in the United States and Canada. They also depict the phenomenon of the "baby boom" market, a significant segment of today's North American population that has members who were born approximately within twenty years of the conclusion of World War II. This group, which in 1981 consisted primarily of people in the fifteen to thirty-four age categories, represents the major concentration of the United States and Canadian populations. As the "baby boomers" age further, the "bulge" in the U.S. and Canadian population age distributions will also move towards the older age categories. For example, by 1991 the major concentrations will be in the twenty-five to forty-four age groups.

One of the important elements of the over 50's market are the "empty nesters" who were profiled earlier in Chapter 3. Another group which Crissey[6] isolates are the "active affluents" most of whom are at the same

---

[6]Yvonne Crissey, "Over Forty-Nine: The Active Affluent," in *Research and the Changing World of Travel in the 1980's* (The Travel Research Association Eleventh Annual Conference Proceedings, 1980), pp. 127–33.

FIGURE 5.3   U.S. Population Projections by Age Group: Age Group: 1900-2000

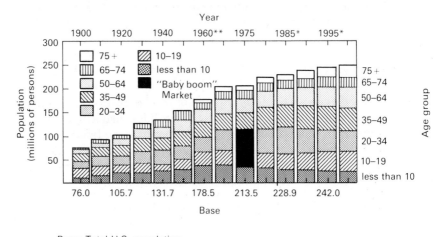

Base: Total U.S. population
*Series III Projections
**65-74 and 75+ age breaks were not
available prior to 1960 date Base

SOURCE: U.S. Bureau of the Census. Adapted from Yvonne Crissey, "Over Forty-Nine: The
Active Affluent," in *Research and the Changing World of Travel in the 1980's* (Travel
Research Association, Eleventh Annual Conference Proceedings, 1980), p. 130.

time "empty nesters." Crissey's conclusions were that 40% of the 53.4
million "50 plus" Americans in 1976 were "active affluents" or people
in this age bracket with the money and the desire to travel extensively.
She stated that the active affluents search for unique experiences, cultural
enrichment, learning and high degrees of participation in their pleasure
travel trips. Other researchers have also found that the older people are
the more emphasis they place on learning experiences, socialization and
activities which lead to self-fulfillment.

Singles and Couples

Another growing segment of the travel market that one resort chain
has targeted to most successfully has members wanting their vacations
to fulfill their "psychological, intellectual, and physical needs" by giving
them the opportunity "to rest, relax, escape the routine of pressures of
daily living, to indulge their fantasies, enjoy the naturalness of life, and
to express total freedom."[7] The chain is Club Mediterranee, and the market
segment consists of singles and couples. The hedonistic appeal of the Club
Med-resort formula, in fact, ties in directly with many of demo-

---

[7]Roz Gibbons, "Singles and Couples," in *Research and the Changing World of Travel in the 1980's*
(The Travel Research Association, Eleventh Annual Conference Proceedings, 1980), pp. 113-16.

FIGURE 5.4 Canadian Population by Age Group: 1976–2001

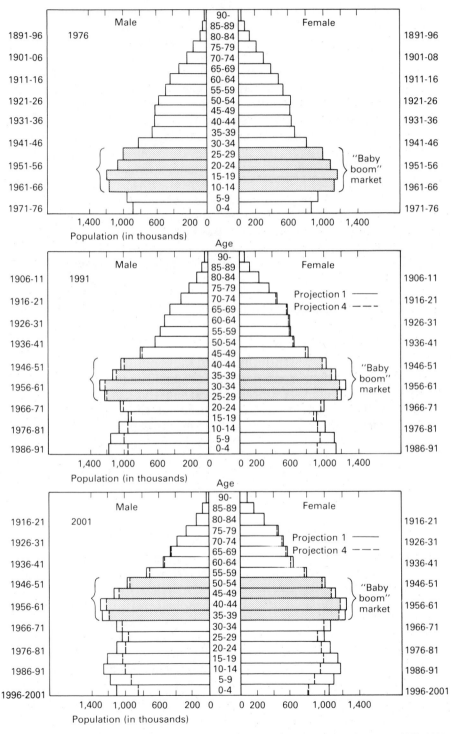

SOURCE: Statistics Canada, *Population Projections for Canada and the Provinces 1976-2001* (Ottawa, Ontario, Statistics Canada, 1979), p. 42.

graphic/socioeconomic and life-style/social changes highlighted earlier. Approximately 60 percent of Club Med vacationers are couples or pairs, and 40 percent are singles vacationing on their own. The average age of Club Med members in 1980 was twenty-nine years, and 50 percent were in the thirty to sixty years age bracket. This is certainly not the family travel market, and indeed many Club Med properties do not allow children to accompany adults. Growth in the numbers of persons visiting Club Med resorts has been spectacular. Also of note is that North Americans account for a growing proportion of Club Med's visitors each year, representing 20.5 percent of the total in 1978–79, compared to 14.2 percent in 1974–75. Club Med is not the only organization to have tapped into the singles and couples pleasure-travel segment. Other resorts and destinations, particularly in the Carribbean region, have initiated the successful Club Med formula or at least learned about this market segment. Club Med's success can be attributed to the fact that there are many more singles and childless married and unmarried couples in the North American market today who have the means and the desire to travel for these "hedonistic" experiences.

Black Pleasure-Travel

The black pleasure-travel market is also growing quickly in North America. The 1979 U.S. Census indicated that approximately 12 percent of the adult population, or approximately 19.6 million people, were blacks. Almost 30 percent of black Americans had household incomes of $15,000 or more in 1978, and 41 percent of the people in this high-income group had graduated from or attended a college or university. The black travel market is expected to continue to grow as the black middle class expands and as education levels continue to rise. Some of the same projections can be made for the large Hispanic population within the United States.

Handicapped Travelers

Handicapped travelers make up another segment of the travel market that is growing and is deservedly receiving greater consideration in the physical design of tourism facilities. Many destination areas have published booklets and guides for handicapped travelers, including the British Tourist Authority that has produced a pamphlet entitled "Britain for the Disabled." The positions of tour operators and wholesalers specializing in arrangements for handicapped people have been created, and organizations such as the March of Dimes are also actively assisting these persons in their travel. The International Year of the Disabled did a great deal to build more public awareness of the needs of those in this particular market segment, and many government agencies have introduced more stringent standards for making buildings more accessible to the handicapped.

Casino Gambling

Traveling for the purpose of casino gambling has increased much in the United States and overseas. The major casino concentrations in the United States are in Las Vegas, Reno, North and South Lake Tahoe, and Atlantic City. Casino gambling is prohibited by law throughout Canada. Nevada has more than two hundred casinos within the state. As of this writing, Atlantic City has ten casinos. The gross win, defined as the total wagering less payouts, in the United States in 1982 was estimated at $4.05 billion, up 11.5 percent from the 1981 figure of $3.63 billion. The chart below clearly shows the spectacular growth trend that has taken place in casino gambling in the continental United States since 1970.

Casino Gaming Revenues—Gross Win (in millions of dollars)

Year	Clark County (Las Vegas)	Total Nevada	Atlantic City	Total U.S.
E1982	1,750	2,675	1,375	4,050
1981	1,676	2,533	1,100	3,633
1980	1,617	2,382	643	3,025
1979	1,424	2,120	325	2,445
1978	1,236	1,846	134	1,980
1977	1,015	1,519	—	1,519
1976	846	1,262	—	1,262
1975	770	1,126	—	1,126
1974	685	1,004	—	1,004
1973	588	858	—	858
1972	476	731	—	731
1971	399	633	—	633
1970	369	575	—	575

E—Estimated by S&P.

SOURCE: State of Nevada Gaming Control Board; Las Vegas Convention/Visitors Authority; New Hersey Casino Control Commission.
Standard & Poor's *Leisure-Time: Basic Analysis* (New York, Standard & Poor's Corporation, September, 1982), p. L15.

Approximately 11.8 million people visited Las Vegas in 1982, which is considered by most to be the casino capital of the United States. Off-shore, the islands of Puerto Rico, Aruba, Dominican Republic, Martinque, and the Bahamas have casinos. Monte Carlo, Madeira, Bophuthatswana, London, Macao, and Mauritius are other international casino locations. One interesting trend that has developed in Atlantic City is the use of short-duration bus tours as a mode of bringing people to the casinos.

Other Growth Markets

In the 1970s and 1980s travel for other new reasons showed spectacular growth rates. Travel was to theme parks, health spa resorts, whitewater rafting operations, tennis resorts, timesharing/resort hotel condominimum projects, wineries, and several other types of places. One source estimates that the total attendance of the twenty-nine major theme parks in the United States was in the range of 78.1 to 85.1 million during the period of 1979 to 1981. One only has to consider the impact of Disneyland, Disney World, and EPCOT to realize that the theme park has created a significant and somewhat novel travel purpose.

The United States and Mexico have between them approximately fourteen major resort spas. These resorts specialize in beauty treatments, weight reduction, physical fitness programs, and restoration/revitalization. There are of course many traditional resort spas in Europe that are based upon the qualities of their mineral waters.

There are over three-hundred white-water rafting companies in operation in the United States; Canada has about thirty-five. This adventure-oriented and relatively high-risk activity has enjoyed almost geometric growth rates in the United States and Canada from the 1960s onward.

There has been significant growth in other specialized resorts, including tennis resorts, and in timesharing and other condominium-resort developments in the United States, Canada, and elsewhere.

REFERENCES

BEHAVIOR SCIENCE CORPORATION, *Developing the Family Travel Market*, undated, p. 2.

BRYANT, BARBARA E., AND ANDREW J. MORRISON, "Travel Market Segmentation and the Implementation of Market Strategies," *Journal of Travel Research*, vol. 19, no. 3, Winter 1980, pp. 2–8.

CANADIAN GOVERNMENT OFFICE OF TOURISM, *Canadian Travel Survey* (Ottawa, Ontario, CTS Research Bulletin No. 10, Canadian Government Office of Tourism, June 1981).

Divorce: Law and the Family in Canada (Ottawa, Ontario,) Statistics Canada, 1983.

ECONOMIC CONSULTING SERVICES, "Developing Successful Theme Recreation Centers," *Real Estate Review*, Winter 1983, pp. 1–4.

FORTIN, PAUL A., J. R. BRENT RITCHIE, AND JULES ARSENAULT, *A Study of the Decision Process of North American Associations Concerning the Choice of a Convention Site, Volume 1, Final Report* (Quebec, Quebec Planning and Development Council, May 1979), p. 9.

GIBBONS, ROZ, "Singles and Couples," in *Research and the Changing World of Travel in the 1980's* (The Travel Research Association, Eleventh Annual Conference Proceedings, 1980), p. 114.

GYUNN, ROBERT, "Elderly Recreational Vehicle Tourists: Motivations for Leisure," *Journal of Travel Research*, Summer 1980, p. 9.

HALSTENRUD, ROBERT J., *Trends in Participation Sports During the Decade of the 70s*, USDA Forest Service (Proceedings of 1980 National Outdoor Recreation Trends Sysmposium, 1980), pp. 195-201.

HENDERSON, FREDDYE, "The Black Travel Market," in *Research and the Changing World of Travel in the 1980's* (The Travel Research Association, Eleventh Annual Conference Proceedings, 1980), pp. 135-142.

HOTEL & TRAVEL INDEX *The U.S. Resort Travel Market: A Perspective on Trends and Forecasts for U.S. Resort Travel 1982-83* (New York, Ziff-Davis Publishing Company, 1982), p. 18.

"Incentive Travel from A to Z," *Meetings and Conventions*, undated, p. 10.

JAMES, GEORGE W., ed., *Airline Economics* (Lexington, MA, Lexington Books, D. C. Health & Co., 1982), p. 28.

JENKINS, ROGER L., "Family Vacation Decision-Making," *Journal of Travel Research*, vol. 17, no. 4, Spring, 1978, pp. 2-7.

KARTUN, DEREK, "Club Meditteranee's Growth and Policies," *International Journal of Tourism Management*, vol. 2, no. 2, June, 1981, pp. 113-20.

KAYNAK, ERDENER, AND UGUR YAVAS, "Segmenting the Tourism Market by Purpose of Trip: A Profile Analysis of Visitors Halifax, Canada," *International Journal of Tourism Management*, vol. 2, no. 2, June 1981, p. 107.

M.P.I., MARKETING RESEARCH INC., *The Meetings Market* (New York, Ziff-Davis Publishing Company, 1980), pp. 8, 70.

PATTERSON, WILLIAM D., "The Big Picture," *ASTA Travel News (annual)*, p. 52.

POWER, JIM, *"Profile of the Profitable Guest,"* *H.S.M.A. World*, 1979, no. 5, p. 13.

SELLERS, PETER, "Dicey Destinations," *Globe & Mail*, May 1982, pp. 16-19.

SHIPKA, BEVERLY D., Practical Applications of Travel Research in Marketing," in *Using Travel Research for Planning and Profits* (The Travel Research Association, Ninth Annual Conference Proceedings, 1978), pp. 95-113.

STANDARD & POOR'S *Leisure-Time: Basic Analysis* (New York, Standard & Poor's Corporation, September, 1982), pp. L15-L17.

"The Business Women: A New Market for the Travel and Hospitality Industry," *H.S.M.A. World*, 1979, no. 6, p. 13.

"The Theory & Practice of Incentive Travel," *Successful Meetings*, June, 1977, pp. 2, 3.

Travel Marketing—1978 (Stamford, CT, Marketing Handbooks, 1978), p. 71.

Travel, Tourism and Outdoor Recreation: A Statistics Digest, 1978 and 1979 (Ottawa, Ontario, Statistics Canada, May 1981), p. 69.

"United Surveys Female Passenger Gains," *Travel Weekly*, September 1978, p. 26.

VAN DOREN, CARLTON S., "Outdoor Recreation Trends in the 1980's: Implications for Society," *Journal of Travel Research*, vol. 20, no. 3, Winter 1981, p. 3.

6

GEOGRAPHY OF TRAVEL:
The Characteristics
of Traveler Flows

Tourist flows, both domestic and international, are not random. The movement of travelers, when measured and explained, can be used as a basis for forecasting future tourist movements. The characteristics of traveler flows is the subject of this chapter.

International tourist movements are described and recent trends noted. One of the most significant trends for North America has been an increase in the number of overseas travelers to Canada, the United States, and Mexico. The origins of these visitors and reasons behind this trend are explored.

The unsteady growth pattern of outbound overseas travel from North America is examined and reasons for this discussed.

Regional flows of tourists (between Canada, the United States, and Mexico) far outweigh flows of overseas visitors to North America. The size and characteristics of travel flow between the three countries in North America are covered in detail.

Domestic travel within North American countries is the next topic of this chapter. The major characteristics of domestic travel are examined; we draw heavily from the findings of the U.S. National Travel Survey and the Canadian Travel Survey.

THEORETICAL MODELS OF TRAVELER FLOWS

The study of traveler flows has been called by many the geography of travel/tourism or simply "tourist geography." As Matley notes, there is quite obviously an "uneven spatial distribution of international tourist activities."[1] He attributed this to the following factors:

> The uneven distribution of tourism resources between destinations
> The wide variety of activities in which travelers participate
> Changes in season
> Weather
> International and domestic political situations
> Economic changes in countries of origin and destination
> Fluctuations in monetary exchange rates
> Increases or decreases in the prices of tourist services
> The staging of special, short duration attractions and events

A number of authors and researchers have attempted to explain past travel-flow patterns and their unevenness by developing and using theoretical models.

The hypothesis put forward by Williams and Zelinsky is that travel flows are not random but have distinctive patterns that can be explained by several identifiable factors.[2] They suggest that these factors include:

1. *Spatial distance*
   The travel time and costs involved when going between origin and destination points.
2. *Presence or absence of past or present international connectivity*
   The existence of economic, military, cultural, and other ties or linkages between countries. The flow of travelers between Canada and the United States and between Canada and the United Kingdom are good examples of strong international connectivity.
3. *Reciprocity of travel flows*
   The belief that a flow in one direction creates a counterflow in the opposite direction. Williams and Zelinsky have found that this is a poor predictor of travel flows between two countries.
4. *Attractiveness of one country for another*
   The attractive features of one country that can induce travel; these include such items as a favorable climate; cultural, historical, and sporting attractions; and so on. The attractiveness of Florida, Hawaii, and the Caribbean

---

[1]Ian M. Mately, *The Geography of International Tourism* (Washington, DC, Association of American Geographers, Resource Paper no. 76-1, 1976), p. 11.

[2]Anthony V. Williams and Wilbur Zelinsky, "On Some Patterns in International Tourist Flows," *Economic Geography*, vol. 46, no. 4, 1970, pp. 549–67.

to North Americans is a good example of this, as is the climatic attractiveness of Spain and other Mediterranean countries to Europeans.

5. *Known or presumed cost of a visit within the destination country*

6. *Influence of intervening opportunities*
The influence of attractions and facilities between the origin and destination points that cause travelers to make intermediate stops and even to forego the journey to their original destination.

7. *Impact of specific, nonrecurring events*
The influence of major international events such as the Olympic Games, the Worlds Fair and the World Cup of Soccer that can cause temporary increases in travel between a destination and various points of origin.

8. *The national character of the citizens of originating countries*

9. *The mental image of the destination country in the minds of the citizens of originating countries*

Williams and Zelinsky developed and tested their hypothesis by examining the flows of travelers between fourteen destinations, including the United States, Japan, the United Kingdom, France, the Netherlands, Benelux, West Germany, Scandinavia, Austria, Switzerland, Italy, Iberia, Greece, and South Africa. These authors illustrated the relationships of the flows between these fourteen destinations through the use of cartograms. They developed a model with which they calculated the actual and expected travel flows between individual pairs of origins and destinations. They then computed a "relative acceptance index" (an "RA") by dividing the difference between the actual and expected flows by the expected flows. Williams and Zelinzky found strong interactions between several origin and destination pairs, including the United States and Japan, the United Kingdom and South Africa, and France and Iberia. It is probable, however, that the authors had created an artificial situation by limiting their analysis to only fourteen countries.

The simplest model of a travel flow consists of an origin point, a destination, and a transportation link. This basic system has been adapted by introducing the two factors of the *resistance of the link* (a function of distance and cost) and the propensity to participate at the origin. The basic equation[3] is that the flow for a link is equal to P (propensity to participate) $\times$ 1/resistance of the link.

Miossec's model of tourist space is shown in Figure 6.1. Both he and Yokeno hypothesize that the pace and intensity of flows decrease as they spread outwards from a generating point of origin. Miossec introduces such variables as negative and positive "deformations," other generat-

---

[3]Michael Chubb, "RECSYS-SYMAP-Michigan's Computerized Simulation Approach to Demand Distribution Prediction," in *Predicting Recreation Demand* (Technical Report No. 7, Michigan State University, 1969), pp. 23–33.

FIGURE 6.1 A Theoretical Model of Tourist Space

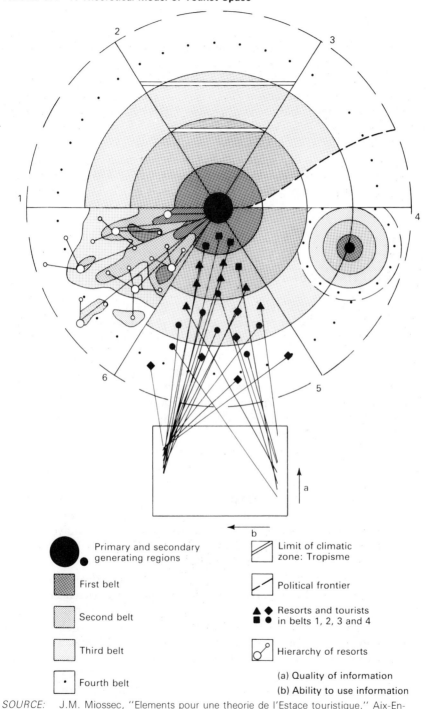

SOURCE: J.M. Miossec, "Elements pour une theorie de l'Estace touristique," Aix-En-Provence: Centre des Hautes Etudes Touristiques, *Les Cahiers Du Tourisme,* C-36, 1976.

ing points, and the quality of travel information to explain abnormalities in his basic model. The pleasant climate of Florida and the Caribbean, for example, is a factor that modifies the basic model of flows of Canadian and U.S. resident travelers in a southerly direction. Climate, therefore, causes a "positive deformation" in these flows; that is, people travel further than the model would predict because of the favorable climate in these destinations.

Yokeno's model of travel flows was somewhat similar to that of Miossec and is shown in Figure 6.2. Yokeno's hypothesis is that destination characteristics such as capital cities, major transportation links, other cities and prices change the pattern suggested in the basic model.

TRAVEL FLOWS

Global Travel Flows

Tourism has been characterized by many people as a strong growth industry with a worldwide character. In 1981 global travel volume reached 2.6 billion people, just over 10 percent of which was due to international arrivals. Over the past ten years there have been, in any given year, five to ten times as many domestic arrivals as international ones.

This varies from region to region. In 1981 there were thirteen times as many domestic tourist arrivals as international ones in North America, and seven times as many in Europe; the proportions were almost equal in Africa and the Middle East.

International tourism receipts in 1981 were $139.3 billion, approximately 15 percent of the total global tourism receipts.

Although international travel has slowed down after having shown unprecedented expansion in the post–World War II era, domestic travel continues its strong growth. This suggests that people increasingly view vacations as requirements rather than luxuries. They may, in poor economic times, travel shorter distances, shorten the length of stay, and economize on transportation and lodging choices.

Regionally Europe continues to account for two-thirds of international arrivals and expenditures. By comparison, North America accounts for one-eighth of international arrivals. This is due to the propensity of Europeans to travel and the fact that countries in Europe are smaller than in other regions of the world. A trip of 100 miles in the United States, for example, might get an individual into another state. This would be recorded as a domestic arrival. In Europe if that 100-mile trip meant traveling to another country it would be classified as an international arrival.

FIGURE 6.2 Locational Patterns of International Travel

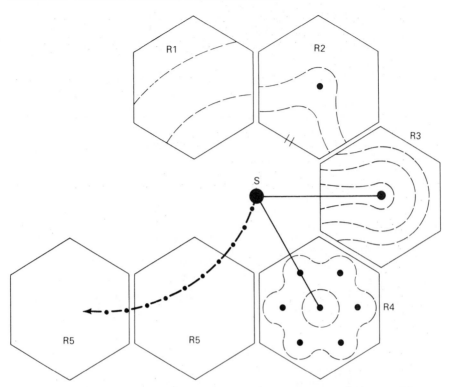

SOURCE: Douglas G. Pearce, "Towards a Geography of Tourism", *Annals of Tourism Research,* .vol. 6, no. 3, July-September 1979, p. 263, adapted from N. Yokeno, "The General Equilibrium System of "Space-Economics" for Tourism", *Reports for the Japan Academic Society of Tourism,* 1974, 8:38-44.

An Organizational Framework

Before moving to the discussion of North American travel flows, definitions of the different types of travel flows must be given. First, all countries have a domestic travel flow created by their own residents traveling within their boundaries. Second, all countries have an international travel flow when foreign residents travel within their boundaries. In North America, it has been a common practice for each of its three nations to divide this international travel flow into two and sometimes three groups, that is into overseas visitors and the residents of the other two North American countries. Finally, each country has an outflow of its own residents to foreign destinations. Again in North America, a differentiation has been made between overseas travelers (those leaving North America) and those visiting the other two North American nations.

We can, therefore, characterize the travel flows to and from the North American nations in the following travel flow market grid:

TABLE 6.1 Travel Flow Market Grid

Flows & Inflows	U.S.A	CANADA	MEXICO
Domestic Travel	—Domestic travel by United States residents `1`	—Domestic travel by Canadian residents `8`	—Domestic travel by Mexican residents `15`
Intra–North American Travel	—Travel by Canadians within the United States `2`	—Travel by United States residents within Canada `9`	—Travel by United States residents within Mexico `16`
International Travel	—Travel by Mexican residents within the United States `3`	—Travel by Mexican residents within Canada `10`	—Travel by Canadian residents within Mexico `17`
Overseas Travel	—Travel by overseas residents within the United States `4`	—Travel by overseas residents within Canada `11`	—Travel by overseas residents within Mexico `18`
Outflows			
Intra–North American Travel	—Travel by United States residents in Canada `5`	—Travel by Canadian residents in the United States `12`	—Travel by Mexican residents in the United States `19`
International Travel	—Travel by United States residents in Mexico `6`	—Travel by Canadian residents in Mexico `13`	—Travel by Mexican residents in Canada `20`
Overseas Travel	—Travel by United States residents in overseas countries `7`	—Travel by Canadian residents in overseas countries `14`	—Travel by Mexican residents in overseas countries `21`

In North America, therefore, there are the following three main categories of travel flows:

Overseas travel (inbound and outbound)
Intra-North American travel (inbound and outbound)
Domestic travel

As seen in Chapters five and seven, these three principal flows are often further subdivided as to the purpose of the trip (business, VFR, pleasure/personal and other) and as to the travel mode to be used. (air, rail, sea, automobile, bus, and other).

During the 1970s there were major shifts in the proportions of international travelers from different countries. Approximately 22 million U.S. residents (flow grids 5, 6, and 7) traveled to foreign countries in 1970, 5.2 million of whom went to overseas nations (flow grid 7). In 1979 these statistics had grown to 23 million U.S. residents traveling internationally, with 7.8 million U.S. travelers going overseas. In the same period, international travelers from West Germany increased from 12 million to almost 23 million. Japan's outbound international travelers showed more than a six-fold increase, from 600,000 in 1973 to 4 million in 1979. The trend towards European predominance in international travel has been even more pronounced when travel expenditures are considered. Expenditures by U.S. international travelers grew by 119 percent, from $4.3 billion in 1971 to $9.4 billion in 1979. West German residents, on the other hand, spent $18 billion in 1979, up 414 percent from their 1971 expenditures of $3.5 billion. Canadians spent $4 billion on international travel in 1979, only 22 percent of the total money spent by the West Germans.

Travel To and From North America

A significant trend of the 1970s that has worked to the benefit of tourism in the United States, Canada, and Mexico has been in the significant increases in overseas travelers to North America. Overseas travelers (flow grid 11) spent $1 billion in Canada in 1979. This was 6.5 times greater than the 1971 foreign spending figure of $154 million. Approximately 2 million overseas visitors (including 41,000 Mexicans) came to Canada in 1979, up by approximately 122 percent since 1972 when just over 902,000 people made the trip. The growth record in the United States was even more spectacular. In 1979, approximately 7.2 million overseas travelers (flow grid 4) visited the United States. In 1971, less than 2.5 million overseas travelers came to the United States, as Figure 6.3 illustrates.

In the 1970s the U.S. "travel gap" became a well-discussed phenomenon in the tourism literature. As the following graph clearly il-

FIGURE 6.3   U.S. Foreign Travelers — Inflow and Outflow

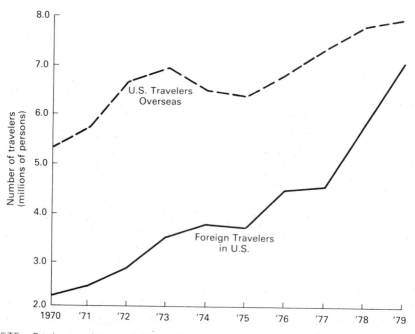

NOTE: Foreign travelers are residents of countries other than the United States, Canada, and Mexico.

SOURCE: The Conference Board, *International Travel* (New York, The Conference Board, January, 1981), p. 2.

lustrates, the period from 1974 onward was one of a narrowing of this "travel gap" between U.S. residents traveling overseas (flow grid 7) and overseas residents traveling to the United States (flow grid 4). A similar graph to that shown above was prepared for Canada, and it is contained in Figure 6.4. Although this shows a less consistent pattern than that for the United States, in 1979, for the first time in the 1970s, overseas visitors to Canada (flow grid 11) outnumbered the numbers of Canadian residents departing for overseas countries (flow grid 14).

Another perspective of the narrowing of the North American travel gap can be gained from a review of overseas travel receipts and expenditures. As Figure 6.5 shows, the "overseas travel dollar gap" appeared to improve in the late 1970s in both the United States and Canada.

Mexico has also made impressive gains in its overseas arrivals since 1970 (flow grid 18). The Bank of Mexico has indicated that its overseas arrivals rose from 91,000 in 1970 to 521,000 in 1979, an increase of 473 percent. When the total overseas travelers were added up for the United States, Canada, and Mexico, a figure of around 9.8 million travelers (flow grids 4, 11, and 18) was arrived at for 1979, compared with a figure of

FIGURE 6.4   Overseas Travelers To and From Canada

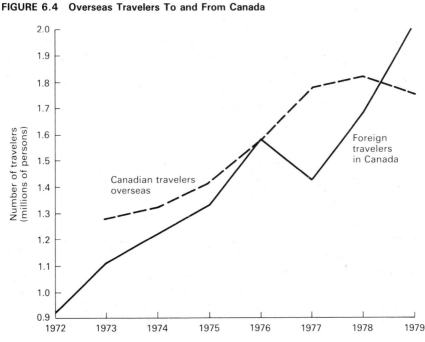

NOTE: Foreign travelers are residents of countries other than Canada, the United States, and Mexico.

SOURCE: Statistics Canada, *Travel, Tourism and Outdoor Recreation: A Statistical Digest: 1978 and 1979* (Ottawa, Statistics Canada, May 1981), pp. 82-83.

less than 3.5 million in 1971. The compound growth rate of overseas travelers to the United States, Mexico, and Canada in the 1973–79 period was therefore somewhat in the range of 14 to 14.5 percent, compared to the 5.9 percent quoted earlier for all international tourism arrivals. Where do the overseas residents who visit North America originate? There are some distinct differences in this respect between the three nations. For example, Mexico is more dependent on the Latin American countries, while Canada draws more heavily from Europe, particularly the United Kingdom. The United States generates the highest proportion of Japanese visitors of the three.

There were some important differences in the growth rates of travelers from the various overseas countries to the North American nations during the 1970s. For example, the number of West Germans visiting Canada increased by 94 percent between 1973 and 1979, while Japanese visitors grew at the even faster rate of 124 percent. Canada also had major gains during this period in visitors from Israel (283 percent), India (164 percent), Switzerland (138 percent), Australia (116 percent), and Sweden (127 percent). The number of Mexico's visitors from Europe showed the highest growth rate among its overseas arrivals in the 1973–74 period, increasing by 117 percent. Japanese visitors to the United States grew very rapidly during the 1970s. Other important growth markets for the United States during that period were Germans, Venezuelans, Africans, and New Zealanders. An approximate ranking of the importance of *all* foreign travelers for the three North American countries at the current time would result in the following top five placements:

U.S.A.	Canada	Mexico
1. Canadians	1. U.S.	1. U.S.
2. Mexicans	2. British	2. Canadians
3. Japanese	3. Germans	3. Latin Americans
4. British	4. Japanese	4. Europeans
5. Germans	5. Australians	5. Others

FIGURE 6.5   Overseas Travel Dollar Gap

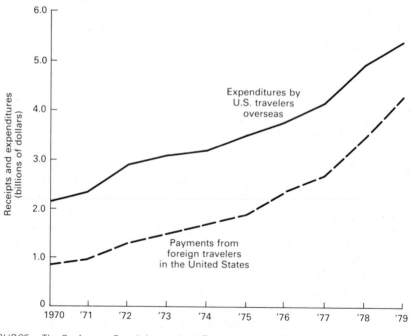

SOURCE: The Conference Board, *International Travel* (New York, The Conference Board) January 1981, p. 2.

	(1) Expenditures by Canadian Residents Traveling Overseas	(2) Expenditures by Overseas Residents Traveling to Canada	Differences (1)-(2)
	($ Millions)	($ Millions)	($ Millions)
1971	N/A	154	N/A
1972	N/A	207	N/A
1973	669	286	383
1974	782	386	396
1975	955	478	477
1976	1,165	584	581
1977	1,386	500	886
1978	1,531	728	803
1979	1,498	1,006	492

SOURCE: Statistics Canada, *Travel Tourism and Outdoor Recreation: A Statistical Digest: 1978 and 1979* (Ottawa, Ontario, Statistics Canada), May 1981, p. 85.

The increasing affluence of other nations, particularly West Germany and Japan, relative to the North American nations, together with fluctuations in currency levels have been suggested by most experts as the reasons for the increased levels of overseas travelers to the United States, Canada, and Mexico. On the other hand high rates of inflation in other countries, together with the declining value of the Canadian dollar, have discouraged greater numbers of Canadian residents from venturing overseas. In the case of the United States, there has been an increased number of inbound vacation-package opportunities available for overseas residents.

By far the major reason for visits by overseas residents to the United States and Mexico is a pleasure/personal one. (Comparable figures are not available for Canada.) It is also believed that there is a higher proportion of leisure vacations relative to VFR traffic than of domestic travel flows in the two countries.

The timing of visits by overseas visitors to the North American countries is a final factor that is useful to evaluate, because it gives an indication of the seasonality in demand from these sources. Figure 6.6 illustrates the pattern of overseas arrivals in Canada in 1978 and 1979. The severe peaking in demand in the summer months is clearly evident. Mexico, which enjoys a much warmer climate than Canada, has a much more even foreign demand pattern throughout the year. Table 6.2 demonstrates this point for 1980 arrivals in Mexico. The reader should realize that this distribution includes U.S. and Canadian residents:

FIGURE 6.6   Overseas Visitors* Entering Canada, 1978 and 1979

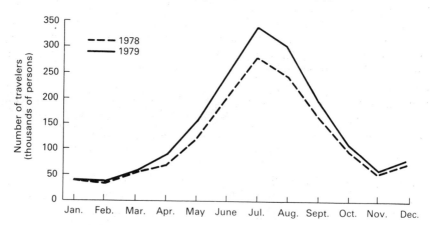

*Excludes same day travelers by land, via the United States. Includes travelers from Mexico.

SOURCE: Statistics Canada, *Travel, Tourism and Outdoor Recreation: A Statistical Digest, 1978 and 1979* (Ottawa, Ontario: Statistics Canada), May 1981, p. 84.

TABLE 6.2   Tourist Arrivals by Month—Mexico

	Percent
January	8.8
February	9.0
March	9.8
April	8.0
May	7.9
June	8.1
July	8.5
August	8.8
September	5.5
October	6.7
November	7.9
December	11.0
	100.0

As we noted earlier, a large percentage of overseas visitors to the United States arrive by air. The distribution of these air arrivals in 1981 showed a peaking in the third quarter of the year (July, August, and September), but this does not seem to be as extreme as in Canada:

1st Quarter:	22 percent
2nd Quarter:	24 percent
3rd Quarter:	31 percent
4th Quarter:	23 percent

Travel Flows from North America

Flow grid items 7, 14, and 21 shown in Table 6.1 represent the other side of the overseas travel picture in North America—the travel by North Americans outside of North America. If we deal first with the overseas destinations of North Americans, the following patterns are evident. The most popular overseas destinations for both U.S. and Canadian residents are Western Europe, the Caribbean, and Central America. The single most popular country of destination overseas is the United Kingdom. When intra–North American travel is considered also, the five most popular foreign destinations for U.S. and Canadian residents appears to be approximately as follows:

U.S. residents	Canadian residents
1. Canada	1. U.S.
2. Mexico	2. U.K.
3. U.K.	3. Italy
4. France	4. Hawaii
5. Germany	5. France

The four Caribbean nations of the Bahamas, Bermuda, Barbados, and Trinidad/Tobago would probably rank as the sixth favorite destination of Canadians. The large Italian segment of the population within Canada undoubtedly contributes to the third-place ranking of Italy, as the strong family ties between Canada and the United Kingdom contribute to second-place ranking of the United Kingdom. Travel by Canadians to Mexico is discussed later, but it appears that, as a single destination country, it would rank sixth in popularity among Canadians.

MAJOR TRENDS: What have been the major trends in outbound overseas travel by the residents of the United States and Canada? There was not a steady growth pattern in the overall volumes of overseas travel by these residents during the 1970s. In fact, corresponding with the start of OPEC-induced "energy crisis" in 1973, the total number of U.S. residents traveling overseas fell in the two consecutive years of 1974 and 1975. By 1977, the U.S. demand had returned to just above pre–energy crisis levels, but it has grown much more slowly since then. The numbers of Canadians traveling overseas grew rapidly between 1974 and 1977, but then slowed and, in fact, fell in the two successive years of 1979 and 1980. Statistics Canada laid the blame for these reversals on the weak state of the Canadian dollar relative to major foreign currencies. The decreases in U.S. volume in 1974 and 1975 have been attached to the impacts of energy supply/demand problems on airline fares and to the pervasive uncertainties that this "crisis" period generated. It should also be realized that both the United States and Canada recorded their poorest economic performance results in 1981 and 1982, and that interest and unemployment rates were running at record-high levels during that time period.

With respect to trends in the overseas destinations of U. S. residents, it appears that there has been a lessening of travel to the United Kingdom. Trips fell by 17.9 percent between 1977 and 1981. Additionally, there was a considerable drop in the number of traveler days spent by U.S. residents overseas during the 1973–77 period. Figure 6.7 traces the average length of stay of U.S. residents at selected overseas destinations. It indi-

FIGURE 6.7   Average Length of Stay of U.S. Travelers in Selected Areas

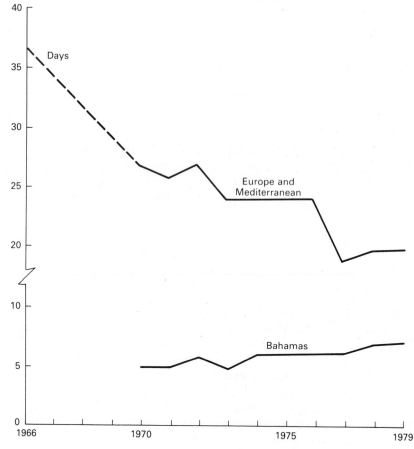

SOURCE: The Conference Board, *International Travel* (New York, The Conference Board, January 1981), pp. 1-4.

cates that average stays in Europe have had a definite downward trend from the mid-1960s through the 1970s.

The time series of Canadian resident departures to overseas nations from 1973–79 clearly indicates that the United Kingdom and the rest of Europe has lost ground to the Caribbean–Central American region and to other non-European destinations, including Hawaii. The pattern of Canadian visitors to the United Kingdom was quite erratic according to Statistics Canada figures, dropping from 483,000 in 1973 to 413,000 in 1974 then back to 528,000 by 1977, only to go down to 477,000 in 1979. There is a strong tendency in the cold winter months for Canadians to journey to warm-weather destinations such as the Caribbean/Bermuda, Hawaii, Mexico, and of course, Florida. Figure 6.8 indicates the twin peaks of overseas travel demand by Canadians, one in the winter and one in the summer. It appears that these "sun-seeking" vacations in the winter months by Canadians have been gained at the expense of the traditional overseas vacations that have been taken primarily during the peak summer months.

Although no comprehensive statistics have yet been made available on the overseas trip purposes of U.S., Canadian, and Mexican residents, it is believed that pleasure/personal reasons, including VFR, predominate as was the case for bound overseas arrivals.

The airplane again is by far the most popular travel mode used by North Americans returning from overseas destinations. About 98.5 percent of Canada's residents returning from overseas have done so by air.

FIGURE 6.8   Canadian Resident Travelers Re-entering from Overseas Countries, 1978 and 1979*

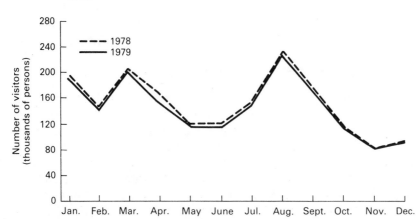

*Includes trips to Mexico.

SOURCE: Statistics Canada, *Travel, Tourism and Outdoor Recreation: A Statistical Digest: 1978 and 1979* (Ottawa, Ontario, Statistics Canada, May 1981) p. 84.

Statistics for the United States and Mexico are not available, but the absolute dominance of the airplane as a mode of travel is felt to hold true there as well.

The annual twin peaks of Canadian overseas travel demand have already been highlighted. No such statistics are available on U.S. outbound overseas travelers, but observation suggests that the pattern may be similar, but less extreme, than that for Canada. The monthly distributions in 1980 for outgoing Mexican nationals are shown in Table 6.3.

TABLE 6.3   Monthly Distributions—Outgoing Mexican Nationals, 1980

	All Departures[1]	Air Departures	Overland Departures[1]
January	5.6		
February	7.2	18.9	22.5
March	8.6		
April	9.7		
May	8.1	20.8	28.2
June	8.2		
July	11.7		
August	9.8	34.8	25.5
September	6.8		
October	6.0		
November	7.4	25.5	23.8
December	10.9		
	100.0	100.0	100.0

NOTE: [1]To all foreign destinations including the United States and Canada.
SOURCE: Banco Nacional de México, S.A.

Although there does not appear to be a very marked seasonality of overseas demand by Mexicans, it seems that the majority of departures take place in the peak summer months and in the early winter.

Intra–North American Travel Flows

Although much of the available tourism literature has concentrated on overseas travel by North Americans, the volumes of intra–North American travel flows are in fact of much greater magnitude and significance. Canadians and Mexicans are the number one and number two international travel markets for the United States. The United States is Canada's major international travel market. Moreover, U.S. and Canadian residents are Mexico's top two international travel generators. Only in the case of Mexicans visiting Canada is there any distinct weakness in intra–North American travel flows.

The North American share of global travel flows is quite significant. The intra–North American travel flows are outlined in Table 6.4.

TABLE 6.4   Intra-North American Travel Flows

Intra-North American Market Elements	1979 Millions of Person Trips	Percent
U.S. residents to Canada: All modes; returning the same day	20,283	28.2
U.S. residents to Canada: All modes; staying one night or more	10,909	15.2
Canadian residents to the United States: All modes; returning the same day	23,866	33.2
Canadian residents to the United States: All modes; staying one night or more	10,516	14.6
U.S. residents to Mexico: All modes[1]	3,430	4.8
Mexican residents to the United States: All modes	2,560	3.6
Canadian residents to Mexico: All modes[2]	188	0.3
Mexican residents to Canada: All modes	103	0.1
	71,855	100.0

NOTES: [1]Visitors to interior only.

[2]Banco Nacionál de México figure was 183,000; Statistics Canada's was 192,000. The difference was halved.

SOURCES: Statistics Canada, pp. 66-67, 69-70.
Banco Nacionál de México, p. 14.

Readers will note the large proportion (61.4 percent) of total person trips taken on a same day basis between Canada and the United States. Although no detailed statistics are available on it, it is believed that a high percentage of the same day travel between the United States and Canada involves trips of less than 100 miles.

U.S. AND CANADA: We begin our discussions on the intra-North American travel flows with the interchange of U.S. and Canadian travelers. This represents the major share of these flows, which were identified in Table 6.1 as flow grid items 2 and 9. When reviewing the statistics and trends that follow, the reader should realize that the two neighbors share an enormously long border and that the U.S. population is about ten times the size of Canada's.

Figure 6.9 depicts the flows of travel between the two countries from 1972 onward. It is quite obvious from this graph that Canadians have a much higher propensity to travel to the United States than U.S. residents have of traveling to Canada. Indeed, in terms of total volumes of visitors, the numbers of United States-bound Canadians outnumbered Canada-bound U.S. residents on overnight stays in 1977 and 1978, and on a same-day travel basis did so from 1975 onward. It is also noticeable that a downward trend in U.S. travel flows (same-day and overnight) began in the energy crisis years of 1973-74 and continued to 1979. Coincident with this trend was a strong growth trend in Canadian travelers

FIGURE 6.9   Travel Flow between the United States and Canada

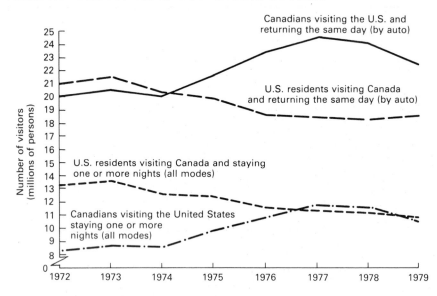

(same-day and overnight) to the United States from 1973–74 to 1977. There are not pat answers for these trends, which have certainly favored the United States, but Canadian and U.S. authorities attribute them to a combination of energy crisis effects, currency fluctuations, and the relative movements of the price levels of accommodation, food, transportation, and other travel services in the two countries. The Canadian Government Office of Tourism, now renamed Tourism Canada, in its tourism sector strategy of 1981 has noted that:[4]

> A central factor in the declining volume of U.S. residents traveling to this country was the more rapid increase in travel prices in Canada versus the U.S. It is only in 1979 that this trend seems to have changed.

It is also notable that there was more than a five-fold increase in the number of Canadians on charter flights to the United States during the 1973–79 period. In 1979, of the 540,625 outbound Canadian air charter passengers to the United States, 46.7 percent went to Florida, 27.6 percent to Hawaii, 15.9 percent to Nevada, 5.5 percent to Puerto Rico, and the remainder to other U.S. destinations.

The most popular destinations of residents in the other countries are as follows:

---

[4]Canadian Government Office of Tourism, *Tourism Sector Strategy* (Ottawa, Ontario, April 1981), p. 26.

Canadian Residents Traveling to the United States 1979	U.S. Residents Traveling to Canada 1978
1. Middle Atlantic (21.9%)	1. Ontario (49.2%)
2. Pacific (18.9%)	2. Quebec (16.7%)
3. New England (14.7%)	3. British Columbia (15.2%)
4. East North Central (11.5%)	4. Atlantic Provinces (7.0%)
5. South Atlantic (10.5%)	5. Alberta (5.1%)

Hawaii and the Pacific region made the greatest gains in Canadian market share during the 1973–79 period, while New England and the South Atlantic regions lost ground. The west coast of Canada, including British Columbia, the Yukon, and the Northwest Territories, made the greatest gains in U.S. market share, and Ontario and Quebec lost some ground. As generators of U.S. travel, the provinces of Ontario and British Columbia have gained in significance, and Quebec and the Atlantic Provinces have decreased in relative terms. As generators of Canadian travel, the New England, Middle Atlantic, and East North Central regions have lost ground, and the Pacific, South Atlantic, West North Central and East South Central have increased in relative terms.

It is clear that the automobile predominates as a mode of transport across the U.S.–Canadian borders, but it steadily lost ground to the other modes during the 1970s. Airborne traffic between the two countries made the greatest gains in market share during the 1970s. U.S. bus traffic into Canada also appeared to be more significant at the close of the 1970s.

Concerning the timing of visits, in both cases it appears that the peak summer months have declined in relative significance and the winter months have increased in significance. It is also notable that a higher proportion of Canadians travel in the first and fourth quarters of the year, whereas the U.S. travelers go to Canada primarily during the spring and summer months. As was the case with the overseas departures by Canadians, there is a twin peak in demand for United States-bound travel as Canada's warm-weather seekers head south in the winter months.

There is a lack of statistical information available to give accurate indications on the trip purposes of U.S. and Canadian residents traveling to their neighboring countries. It is believed, however, that pleasure/personal travel reasons predominate by quite a high margin.

U.S. AND MEXICO: Travel between the United States and Mexico grew rapidly during the 1970s, although there were temporary interruptions during the 1974–76 period. Figure 6.10 shows that, as in the case of Canada, Mexican visitors closed the gap on U.S. visitors from about 1974 onward. This tendency, however, has been reversed due to devaluations of the peso in 1982. The net effect has been to make Mexico a much cheaper

FIGURE 6.10   Travel Flows—United States and Mexico

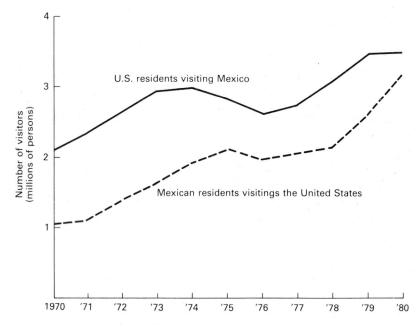

SOURCE: Banco Nacionál de México, S.A, *Basic Tourism Statistics, 1970-1980* (Mexico City, Mexico: Banco Nationál de México, S.A., 1981), pp. 13-14, 56.

place in which to vacation while making it much more expensive for Mexicans to vacation abroad. As a result the gap has been widened, with an increase in the number of U.S. travelers to Mexico and a drastic decline in the other direction. There is very little origin/destination information available on visitors to and from both countries. Mexico, however, has maintained records on the origins of U.S. visitors by state. The top five generating states for Mexico are as follows:

U.S. Residents Traveling to Mexico
1.   Texas
2.   California
3.   Arizona
4.   Florida
5.   Illinois

The proportion of Mexico's U.S. visitors from California, Florida, and Arizona increased over the 1970–80 period, while the greatest relative decline was in New York residents. No origin/destination information on Mexican nationals visiting the United States is available. Additionally, there is no information available on the travel purposes of U.S. residents arriving in Mexico, but it is believed that pleasure/personal reasons predominate by a large margin. The same is true of Mexican visitors to the United States. No comprehensive information is available on the timing of visits through the year by U.S. and Mexican residents to their neighboring countries.

Although there is an almost even split between U.S. residents arriving by land and those arriving by air in Mexico, Mexican overland arrivals in the United States outnumbered air arrivals by about three to one.

MEXICO AND CANADA: Very little information is available on the interchange of visitors between Mexico and Canada. Table 6.5 shows the total number of visitors between the two countries for the 1973–79 period. Although there has been a growth in travel between the two countries during the 1970s, the "energy and recession dips" of 1977 and 1979 have slowed it down. Due to devaluation of the peso, mentioned earlier, fewer Mexicans have been traveling to Canada. The flow south is three times stronger than the flow north.

Domestic Travel Within North American Countries

The final element of travel flows within North America is that of domestic tourism. In terms of the total volumes of trips involved in domestic tourism within the United States and Canada, domestic trips far outstrip the international travel trips of their residents. For example,

TABLE 6.5   Flow of Travelers Between Canada and Mexico

	Canadian Visitors to Mexico	Mexican Visitors to Canada
1972	112,000	N/A
1973	116,000	23,000
1974	131,000	27,000
1975	110,000	35,000
1976	119,000	36,000
1977	155,000	26,000
1978	210,000	35,000
1979	183,000	41,000
1980	170,000	N/A

N/A—Not available.

SOURCE: Banco Nacional de México, S.A., *Basic Tourism Statistics, 1970-1980* (Mexico City, Mexico: Banco National de México, S.A., 1981), pp. 13-14.
Statistics Canada, *Travel, Tourism and Outdoor Recreation: A Statistical Digest: 1978 and 1979* (Ottawa, Ontario: Statistics Canada, May 1981), p. 90.

in 1979 Canadian travel trips (fifty miles or more one-way, away from home) outnumbered all international trips by a ratio of 3.5 to 1. For the United States, the ratio is higher. In 1977 U.S. residents' domestic travel trips exceeded their foreign trips by a ratio of 14.8 to 1.

Two major sources of information are available on the domestic travel patterns of United States and Canadian residents. These are the U.S. National Travel Survey and the Canadian Travel Survey. At the time of preparation of this text, the latest information available for the United States is from the 1981 U.S. National Travel Survey. The survey covers domestic and international trips, of U.S. residents of 100 miles or more (one way) from home. The Canadian Travel Survey began with the third quarter of 1978. It covers trips taken by Canadians of fifty miles or more (one-way) from home. Unlike the U.S. travel survey, it deals only with domestic tourism. From 1982 onward, the Canadian Travel Survey is to have been conducted for each quarter in each even-numbered year. In the United States, the U.S. Travel Data Center conducts a monthly national travel survey. This survey process began in March 1979. Quarterly and annual summaries of the results have been published.

The major characteristics of domestic travel in the United States and Canada from 1979 onward are presented in Figures 6.11 and 6.12. The following broad-scale comments can be made based upon an analysis of these statistics:

> The automobile is the principal transportation mode for domestic travel both in the United States and Canada.

FIGURE 6.11 Profile of U.S. Domestic Travel Flows

	1980	1981
Total Flows		
Millions of person trips	1,045.5[1]	1,165.6[1]
Percent	100	100
Transportation Modes (Percent of Total Person Trips)		
Auto/truck/RV	81	83
Air	15	13
Bus	2	2
Rail	1	1
Other	1	1
Purpose of Trip (Percent)		
Business and convention	14	14
VFR	35	37
Pleasure and personal	38	36
Other	12	13

FIGURE 6.11 *(cont.)*

	1980	1981
Origins (Percent)		
New England	4	5
Eastern Gateway	9	10
George Washington country	9	9
The South	19	19
Great Lakes country	21	20
Mountain West	5	4
Frontier West	18	17
Far West	14	15
Destinations (Percent)		
New England	4	4
Eastern Gateway	5	5
George Washington country	8	8
The South	24	24
Great Lakes country	16	16
Mountain West	6	5
Frontier West	16	16
Far West	14	14
Outside of the United States	7	7
Age Distributions (Percent)		
Under 18 years	21	19
18–24	13	12
25–34	22	20
35–44	15	16
45–54	12	14
55–64	9	12
65 and over	6	7
Family Incomes (Percent)		
Under $10,000	9	9
$10,000 to $19,999	26	22
$20,000 to $29,999	26	22
$30,000 and over	30	35
Not reported	9	12
Sizes of Travel Parties (Percent)		
1 Person	19	20
2 Persons	34	36
3 Persons	17	16
4 Persons	15	17
5 Persons or more	15	11

NOTE: [1]Approximately 7 percent of the total person-trips by U.S. residents of 100 miles or more in both 1980 and 1981 were to destinations outside of the United States.

SOURCE: U.S. Travel Data Center, *1980 & 1981 National Travel Surveys: Full Year Reports* (Washington, DC, U.S. Travel Data Center, 1981 and 1982).

FIGURE 6.12 Profile of Canadian Domestic Travel Flows

	1979	*1980*
Total Flows		
Millions of person trips	114.0	111.0
Percent	100.0	100.0
Transportation Modes (Percent of Total Person Trips)		
Automobile	88.6	88.2
Air	4.6	5.5
Bus	3.9	4.0
Rail	1.3	1.2
Boat and other	1.0	0.6
Not stated	0.6	0.5
	100.0	100.0
Season of Travel (Percent)		
First quarter (January–March)	20.3	19.6
Second quarter (April–June)	24.3	23.3
Third quarter (July–September)	34.8	36.0
Fourth quarter (October–December)	20.6	21.1
	100.0	100.0
Purpose of Trip (Percent)		
Business	16.6	17.3
VFR	33.2	32.4
Pleasure and personal	49.2	49.5
Not stated	1.0	0.8
	100.0	100.0
Origins (Percent)		
Newfoundland	1.8	1.7
Prince Edward Island	0.3	0.2
Nova Scotia	4.0	3.6
New Brunswick	2.5	2.7
Quebec	23.7	24.3
Ontario	35.6	34.1
Manitoba	5.2	5.5
Saskatchewan	6.0	7.0
Alberta	12.4	11.9
British Columbia	8.5	9.0
Yukon and Northwest Territories	—	—
	100.0	100.0
Destinations (Percent)		
Newfoundland	1.7	1.7
Prince Edward Island	0.5	0.5
Nova Scotia	4.0	3.6
New Brunswick	2.4	2.6
Quebec	22.8	23.9
Ontario	33.1	33.9

FIGURE 6.12 (*cont.*)

	1979	1980
Destinations (Percent) Continued		
Manitoba	4.9	4.9
Saskatchewan	5.7	6.5
Alberta	11.2	11.8
British Columbia	9.2	9.7
Yukon and Northwest Territories	—	—
Not stated	4.5	0.9
	100.0	100.0
Type of Expenditure (Percent)		
Total expenditures ($'000)	$9,395,218	$9,510,422
Prepaid package	10.1	8.2
Transportation	29.3	32.0
Local transit	2.3	2.2
Accommodation	11.8	12.0
Food and beverage	25.1	24.8
Recreation and entertainment	9.7	8.8
Other	11.7	12.0
	100.0	100.0
Age Distributions (Percent)		
Under 15 years	21.6	20.3
15–19	7.9	7.7
20–24	11.9	12.1
25–34	21.3	21.8
35–44	13.7	14.9
45–54	10.8	11.0
55–64	8.5	8.0
65 and over	4.3	4.2
	100.0	100.0
Male-Female Ratio (Percent)		
Males 15 and over	42.6	43.3
Females 15 and over	35.8	36.4
Males and females under 15 years	21.6	20.3
	100.0	100.0
Size of Travel Parties (Percent)[1]		
1 Person	54.6	55.1
2 Persons	24.6	25.2
3 Persons	10.3	9.1
4 Persons	7.3	7.5
5 Persons or more	3.2	3.1
	100.0	100.0

NOTE: [1]This table is a percentage based upon total households and not on person trips.

SOURCE: Canadian Government Office of Tourism, Canadian Travel Survey. Authors' calculations.

Approximately half of the trips in the United States are made by persons between the ages of eighteen and forty-four. In Canada, the fifteen to forty-four age group accounts for more than half of the trips.

Ontario and Quebec are the major generators and recipients of domestic travelers in Canada.

The Great Lakes and south regions of the United States are the major generators and recipients of domestic travelers.

Business and convention travel accounts for less than 20 percent of all domestic travel trips in both Canada and the United States.

The VFR segment is the largest trip purpose group in both countries.

In the United States the higher-income families and better-educated persons appear to have a higher propensity to travel than do others.

REFERENCES

ARCHER, BRIAN H., "Forecasting Demand: Quantitative and Intuitive Techniques," *International Journal of Tourism Management* (Guildford, England, March 1980), pp. 5–12.

BANCO NACIONAL DE MÉXICO, S.A., *Basic Tourism Statistics 1970–1980* (Mexico City, Mexico, Banco Nacional de México, S.A., 1981), pp. 13–14, 36, 88.

BEEKHUIS, JEANNE, *The Seventh Annual World Tourism Review* (New York, American Express Publishing Company, 1982), pp. 12–18.

CANADIAN GOVERNMENT OFFICE OF TOURISM, *Tourism Sector Strategy* (Ottawa, Ontario, April 1981), p. 26.

ECONOMIST INTELLIGENCE UNIT, "United States of America: National Report No. 58" (London, England, *International Tourism Quarterly*, 1980), pp. 17–37.

HOTEL & TRAVEL INDEX, *The U.S. Resort Travel Market: A Perspective on Trends and Forecasts for U.S. Resort Travel: 1982–83* (New York, Ziff-Davis Publishing Company, October 1982), pp. 63–71.

MATELY, IAN M., *The Geography of International Tourism* (Washington, DC, Association of American Geographers, Resource Paper No. 76-1, 1976), pp. 1–40.

MIOSSEC, J. M., "Elements Pour Une Theorie de I'Esatce Touristique," Aix-en-Provence: Centre des Hautes Études Touristique, *Les Cahiers Du Tourisme*, C-36, 1976.

PEARCE, DOUGLAS G., "Towards a Geography of Tourism," *Annals of Tourism Research*, vol. 6, no. 3, July/September 1979, pp. 245–272.

ROBINSON, H. *A Geography of Tourism* (London, England, MacDonald and Evans, 1976).

THE CONFERENCE BOARD, *International Travel* (New York, The Conference Board, January 1981), pp. 1–4.

STATISTICS CANADA, *Travel, Tourism and Outdoor Recreation: A Statistical Digest: 1978 and 1979* (Ottawa, Ontario, Statistics Canada, May 1981), pp. 77–95.

"U.S. Travel Expenditure, Abroad," *Tourism International Quarterly,* no. 4, 1978, pp. 15, 16.

WILKINSON, PAUL F., "The Use of Models in Predicting the Consumption of Outdoor Recreation," *Journal of Leisure Research,* vol. 4, no. 3, Summer 1973, pp. 34–48.

WYNEGAR, DON, *1981 International Travel Outlook* (Washington, DC, U.S. Travel Data Center/The Travel Research Association, 1980), pp. 157–74.

YOKENO, N., "The General Equilibrium System of "Space-Economics" for Tourism," *Reports for the Japan Academic Society of Tourism,* 1974, 8:38–44.

7

MODES OF TRAVEL:
People-Mover Alternatives

The means travelers use to reach their destinations is the subject of this chapter. The evolution of transportation is reviewed from the preindustrial and early industrial travel system; through the mature railway, express travel, and automobile-based travel systems, to the modern and post-mobility adjustment era of today.

A model is presented to explain the reasons people select one transportation mode over another. Marketing implications for the various modes are suggested.

An in-depth treatment is provided of each of the travel modes. The rise and fall of travel by rail is chronicled and its competitive edge today defined. The major change through which ocean liners have gone is the shift from scheduled to cruise trips. The reasons and ramifications are explained. Automobile travel is the single most predominant mode in North America. The extent and advantages of automobile travel to the tourist are covered in a section that includes material on recreational vehicles and rental cars. The airplane has had a revolutionary impact on tourism. The history, scope, and significance of travel by air is an important part of this chapter. The importance of bus travel is indicated by the fact that the industry annually carries more passengers and provides service to more destinations than any other common carrier mode.

This subject would not be complete without a consideration of the effects of energy problems on travel modes. A summary of responses to energy problems is given.

A final segment suggests that travel may face competition from a rather unusual source—the telecommunications industry. As people are able to "travel electronically," will the same technological advances that aided travel's growth contribute to its demise?

There can be no doubt that the development of new transportation modes, routes, and alternatives has opened up the world to tourism. People travel either in their own private mode of transportation or alternatively use a group travel mode offered by a common carrier. The following diagram defines today's major people-mover alternatives:

FIGURE 7.1   People-Mover Alternatives

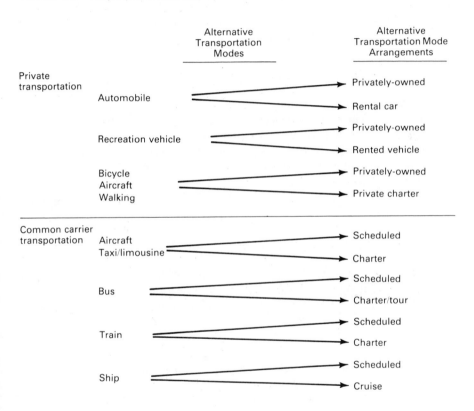

THE TRANSPORTATION AND TRAVEL EVOLUTION

Transportation and travel have been revolutionized since the 1850s to the point at which, as Robinson points out:

> Human conceptions of territorial space, of spacial relationships and of physical distance have undergone a continuing evolution. Today man's concept of territoriality (and especially in the tourist sense) is closely identified with the life and activities of specific places, while his concept of distance is measured rather in the time it takes him to reach his destination than in miles or kilometers.[1]

---

[1]H. Robinson, *A Geography of Tourism* (London, England, MacDonald and Evans, 1976), p. 94.

There has been a partial reversal of this in North America with respect to automobile travel as a result of energy supply/demand problems. This point is further elaborated upon later in this chapter.

It is useful to briefly review the history of transportation and travel as this shows that their evolvement has taken place in several identifiable eras. Lundgren[2] separated these "eras" into six groups, namely the pre-industrial travel system, the early industrial era travel system, the mature railway system, the express travel system, the automobile-based travel system (individual travel diffusion), and the modern tourist travel system. Van Doren[3] added a seventh era to this list in the context of North America, which he termed the "post-mobility adjustment period" of 1974 and thereafter. Van Doren's post-mobility adjustment era was set in motion by the energy-related problems first experienced in 1973–74. In Table 7.1 an attempt has been made to interface Lundgren and Van Doren's hypotheses on the evolution of transportation, travel, and recreation. The reader should note that Van Doren's focus was on the United States, while Lundgren's hypothesis was international in its scope. Van Doren's conclusions nevertheless appear to be quite applicable to Canada as well as to the United States.

A brief review of these seven major transportation evolution eras is provided below.

Pre-industrial Travel System Era

This was the period before widescale industrialization in North America and Europe. It was also before the development of railways within the two continents. There were few, if any, common carriers. There were almost no regularly scheduled transportation services and there was little travel and tourism. Travelers made their own arrangements with many suppliers. Travel was ardous and often dangerous. It was the era of the stagecoach and the wayside inn. Only a small proportion of the population had the money or the reason to travel.

Early Industrial Society Travel System Era

Rapid industrialization and advances in transportation technology brought about road improvements (turnpikes), railways, canals, and steamship services during this era. Common carriers emerged and began to offer more regularly scheduled transportation services. There were more

---

[2]Jan O. J. Lundgren, "The Development of the Tourist Travel Systems," *The Tourist Review*, no. 1, January/March; 1973, pp. 2–14.

[3]Carlton S. Van Doren, "Outdoor Recreation Trends in the 1980's: Implications for Society," *Journal of Travel Research*, vol. 19, no. 3, Winter 1981, pp. 3–10.

persons with the money and the reason for traveling, and thus travel increased.

Mature Railway System Era

This era was one in which the railways began to expand the scope of their operations into running hotels and providing other travel-related services. The railways began to market their services more aggressively. Travel agencies and tour operating companies were formed. Thomas Cook was one of the innovators in this field during this era, beginning his company's activities in the 1840s in the United Kingdom. Again, more people were traveling in this era than in the one before.

Express Travel System Era

During this era express services became increasingly available, meaning that the trains or other forms of transportation did not stop at every station or terminal but only at the major ones. This enhanced the speed of travel and encouraged more travel and tourism than before.

Automobile-based Travel System Era

From about the 1920s onward the influence of the privately owned automobile accelerated in North America and Europe. Although only 109,000 Britons had cars in 1919, over 14 million of them had their own vehicles by 1973. Car ownership also boomed in North America. Motorways, interstate highways, and other trunk highways were developed in the latter half of this era, which spanned the 1920–74 period that was characterized by Van Doren as the mass recreation era or the mass mobility-transience era. In reality, Lundgren's automobile-based travel system era overlapped with the modern tourism-travel system era. However, from the period of 1920 to 1945, the automobile was particularly predominant over other travel modes. Commercial travel by air also had its beginnings during the 1920–45 period.

Modern Tourism Travel System Era

The modern tourism travel system era spanned the period of 1945 to 1974. It is still prevalent today, but some fundamental changes have taken place since the energy crisis years began in 1973 and 1974. Car ownership continued to grow at a rapid rate, mainly at the expense of long-distance rail travel. Mass air travel was another post–World War II phenomenon, and the introduction of wide-bodied jets in 1970 further increased air travel and tourism. The "mass tourism" philosophy and marketing approaches were certainly prevalent during the 1950s and

TABLE 7.1 Recreation/Leisure/Travel Eras

Variable	High Society 1860–1920	Mass Recreation 1920–1958	Mass Mobility–Transience 1958–1974	Post-Mobility Adjustment 1974–
Population Characteristics Trends (U.S.)	Rural Northeast-Midwest 50 million people	Rural-urban Suburbia west coast 130 million people	Urban-nucleated city 70–75 percent of population Sun Belt growth 200 million people	Central city, small town growth, rural, 242 million (1990)
Person/Societal Philosophy	Nuclear large family Puritanical work ethic Self-denial	Smaller family Leisure recreation emergent A privilege to enjoy leisure	Single-parent family Self-gratification, "me" generation Minority actions Changing role of women, ERA	Leisure recreation, a right Individual awareness Self-actualization Self-improvement
Time	Sixty-hour workweek Sunday free	Fifty-hour workweek Saturday free Paid vacation	Forty-hour workweek Three-day weekends	Thirty-eight-hour workweek Moonlighting Do-it-yourself home repairs
Income, Money	Hourly wages	Salaries	High disposable income Era of credit Two-income families	Inflation Zero growth Cost consciousness Electronic money
Activities and Equipment	Church-centered Bicycle, golf, tennis	Family-centered Improved equipment Boats, camping equipment, etc.	Social group Specialized activity/ equipment ORVs Back-to-nature movement	Electronic games Human energy Physical fitness High-risk sports
Political Action	Conservation/ preservation Leadership/ management of natural resources	Environment management public use	Reactionary leadership Environmental awareness, ecological ethics, congestion in parks	Public involvement leadership Localized congestion

Public/Private Organization	Professional sports Public recreation movement City/national parks Amusement parks	Amateur sports State parks TVA-C of E Regional parks	Disneyland-theme parks Mission 66 Individualized travel	Airline deregulation Tourism caucus Package tours
Technology and Communication	Photography Movies, wireless Mass production Literature	Radio, television Plastics, super alloys Air conditioning Computers, electronics	Instant photography Satellite communciation Computer management	Videophone Cottage electronics
Mobility	Coal and steam Railroad, ship, mass transportation	Automobile Airplane, small group transportation	Interstate highways RV, sub-sonic aircraft	Supersonic travel? Mass transit?
Facilities/Services	Luxury hotel resorts Second homes, wealthy Overseas travel	Motels Second homes, middle class	Private campgrounds, lodging Franchises, fast foods Full-service campgrounds	Family camping, time-sharing, cruise ships, one-stop vacations, reservations to enter parks

Lundgren's Transportation Eras

1. Pre-industrial Travel System
2. Early Industrial Travel System
3. Mature Railway System

4. Express Travel System
5. Automobile-based Travel System

5. Automobile-based Travel System
6. Modern Tourist Travel System

7. Post-mobility Adjustment

SOURCES: Carlton S. Van Doren, "Outdoor Recreation Trends in the 1980's: Implications for Society," *Journal of Travel Research*, vol. 19, no. 3, Winter 1981, p. 4.

Jan. O. J. Lundgren, "The Development of the Tourist Travel Systems, *The Tourist Review*, no. 1, January/March 1973, pp. 2-14.

1960s. The period of 1945 to 1965 is generally considered to be the baby-boom era, when a large segment of today's population was born and these people passed through their childhoods.

Post-Mobility Adjustment Era

Van Doren's post-mobility adjustment era was initiated in 1973–74 as a result of the OPEC-generated oil embargo and the fastly increasing fuel prices that ensued. This author's point was that the events of the energy crisis fundamentally modified travel patterns in North America and elsewhere. The material presented later in this chapter certainly supports his hypothesis. But as the information presented in Table 7.1 indicates, there have been other fundamental influences or trends in the economy, population, society, values, and life-styles that have jointly contributed to the post-1973 fashioning of travel trends. The present era is one in which travelers have and will continue to look in increasing numbers to alternative, group-oriented modes of transportation.

Transportation and travel have then evolved over the years in six or perhaps seven distinct eras. The first six eras were marked by continuing growth in travel, both for business and pleasure/personal reasons, and by constant advances in transportation and communications technology. In the modern era, although technological advances are still with us, the growth curves of travel and tourism have experienced some reverses or at least shown some moderation in the rates of growth.

TRANSPORTATION MODE SELECTION DECISIONS

Model

Why do people select one transportation mode over another for their business and pleasure/personal trips? Many theories have been put forward on mode selection decision processes. Most theorists, however, consistently identify availability, frequency, cost/price, speed/time, and comfort/luxury as the mode decision variables. Other factors that have been suggested are safety, convenience, ground services, terminal facilities and locations, status and prestige, and departure and arrival times. People in different segments of the travel market place varying degrees of value or utility on these criteria. For example, a business traveler is unlikely to have the same value perceptions as a pleasure traveler. Speed/time and departure/arrival times may be all-important to the business traveler, while cost/price may be the pleasure traveler's first criterion. One useful classification of selection variables and values has been put forward by

Sheth.[4] He suggests that travelers choose a travel mode based upon their psychological weighting of five factors, namely the functional, aesthetic/emotional, social/organizational, situational, and curiosity utilities of the alternative modes. The functional utility of a mode is simply its likely performance for a specific purpose. Departure and arrival times, safety records, the directness of routes, and the absence of stops or transfers are examples of functional considerations. Aesthetic/emotional reasons relate to such things as fear, social concern, style, luxury, comfort, and other personal feelings that the alternative travel modes evoke. Travel modes can attract stereotypes or be perceived to attract stereotypes on such lines as sex, racial origin, income, price/cost, education, and occupation. For example, bus tours and cruises have been stereotyped as being a mode of transportation and vacation type for persons of retirement age. This may dissuade younger people from taking bus tours and cruises. Situational utility reasons primarily relate to the locational convenience of the mode and its terminal facilities to the traveler. Curiosity utility concerns the traveler's perceived need to do something new and different. For example, flying transatlantic on the Concorde may have a high curiosity value for many business travelers.

Sheth's explanation of the transportation mode selection decision-making process is illustrated in Figure 7.2. It shows that certain supply-oriented determinants and trip-purpose/traveler-profile factors influence the traveler's utility assessments.

Travel by Train

It seems fitting to begin our review of individual transportation modes by talking about trains. They opened up the North American continent from its Atlantic to Pacific coasts, and they were the major stimulant in the nineteenth and early twentieth centuries to vacations within the United States, Canada, and Europe. The first transcontinental route in the United States was completed in 1869. Britain had its first organized tour on the train in 1841 when Thomas Cook put together an excursion between Leicester and Loughborough. In 1851, 3 million English took the train to the Great Exhibition that was being staged in London. The train was also instrumental in Britain for spurring the development of many of its seaside resorts.

In the United States in 1929, the first year for which comprehensive statistics are available, approximately 780.5 million paying passengers

---

[4]Jagdish N. Sheth, "A Psychological Model of Travel Mode Selection," in *Advances in Consumer Research, vol. 3* (Proceedings of the Association for Consumer Research, Sixth Annual Conference, 1975), p. 426.

FIGURE 7.2   Travel Mode Selection Model

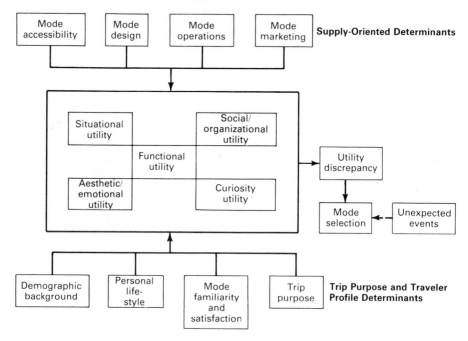

*Needed to account for occasional deviations from regular mode usage.

ADAPTED FROM: Jagdish N. Sheth, "A Psychological Model of Travel Mode Selection," in *Advances in Consumer Research, vol. 3* (Proceedings of the Association for Consumer Research, Sixth Annual Conference, 1975), p. 426.

took the train. This number had fallen to about 268.9 million by 1975. In fact the heydays of the train in most of the major developed countries lasted approximately one-hundred years from the 1830s to the 1930s. This period corresponds to Lundgren's early industrial society travel system, mature railway system, and express travel system eras. In the 1920s and 1930s the automobile began to gain more popularity as a passenger transportation mode, mainly drawing away traffic from the train. Rail passenger traffic in the United States began to decline in the 1920s during what some persons have called the "age of abundant energy." It was not until the mid-1970s to the early 1980s, which could be referred to as the "age of uncertain energy," that the slide in the popularity of the train as a passenger transportation mode seemed to be halted. Although the U.S. railroads had accounted for approximately 77 percent of the nation's common carrier passenger miles in 1929, this market share had slid to about 7 percent by 1970.

The demise of the railway as a passenger travel mode was so alarming that in 1958 the U.S. Interstate Commerce Commission (ICC) ordered a detailed study of the situation. The results of this study became known as the Hosmer Report, and it predicted the eventual disappearance of the train in the United States as a passenger travel mode. The recommendations of the Hosmer Report were never officially accepted, and it was not until 1970 that the federal government took some concrete action to improve the failing rail-passenger travel business. In October 1970, the Rail Passenger Service Act became law. The act created the National Railroad Passenger Corporation, now commonly known as Amtrak. Amtrak began its operations in May 1971, and it was intended to be a profit-making corporation. Canada's equivalent of Amtrak, Via Rail Canada, was created in 1977 in the form of a crown corporation.

Both Amtrak and Via Rail have the sole national responsibility for marketing and providing intercity passenger rail transportation. Since their inception both organizations have been successful in increasing passenger volumes that had been falling continuously beforehand. They have done so primarily by improving the equipment and services they offer, and by promoting the benefits of traveling by train more effectively.

Several attempts have been made to determine why travelers select the train as a transportation mode. Four factors seem to emerge consistently; these are cost/price, comfort, safety, and the ability to see the area through which the train is passing. Via Rail's on-board surveys of business travelers have identified user cost, convenience, travel time, and comfort as being of prime importance. A survey of Amtrak users has indicated that travelers favored the train for the following reasons:

Safety
Ability to look out of train and see interesting things enroute
Ability to get up and walk around
Arriving at the destination rested and relaxed
Personal comfort

Negative factors often associated or perceived with rail travel are slowness in reaching the destination, relatively inflexible departure times, and a lack of quality in food service. Trains are certainly perceived as being a very safe mode of transportation and are thought to attract a significant "fear of flying" market. Recent promotions by Via Rail and Amtrak have emphasized the rest and relaxation benefits of taking the train. They have also begun to point out that the downtown-to-downtown routing of trains actually saves passengers time.

In West Germany, France, and Japan, high-speed trains have been developed and are in operation. These trains travel faster than the automobile, and they actually cut down on the time that passengers would take to drive between major cities. For example, the Train Grande Vitesse in France travels at over two-hundred kilometers per hour between Paris and Lyons, reducing this trip to about two hours. (A comparable trip by car takes a minimum of five hours.) Via Rail was planning on introducing some of these LRC (light, rapid, comfortable) trains to Canada in 1984.

In the early 1980s, intercity train travel was beginning to show significant increases. Via Rail's passenger loads for example, grew at about 25 percent per year. In the period of 1980–81, business travelers using its first-class service grew even more quickly. The upward effect of energy cost increases on airline ticket prices was considered to be a major contributor to this trend, along with the improved rail service being offered and the more effective selling of the train's benefits.

Before leaving the subject of rail travel, the role of railways as tourist attractions should be highlighted. Short-duration train excursions through scenic surroundings have proven to be major attractions to pleasure travelers in recent years. For example, two major excursions of this type in Canada, the Algoma Central Railway in Ontario and the Royal Hudson Steam Train in British Columbia, carried 163,000 passengers between them during the summer of 1981. The Strasburg Railroad in Pennsylvania is a U.S. example of a popular train excursion of this type. The experience of riding aboard the Orient Express, made famous by Agatha Christie, was reintroduced in 1983 after a complete restoration of the train had been completed.

Travel by Water

Travel by ship did in fact precede travel by train, but it was not until the mid-nineteenth century that travel by ocean liner began to show its greatest prominence. Although ocean liners used to provide an important link for passengers between continents, water transport today plays two main roles in travel and tourism—ferrying and cruising.

The steamship era had its beginnings in the 1840s. Sir Samuel Cunard pioneered the first transatlantic scheduled liner trips at that time. Just as the automobile led to the demise of the train, the introduction of intercontinental commercial airline service precipitated the rapid decline in the use of ships as a scheduled passenger transportation mode. In 1957, transatlantic ship traffic reached a new post–World War II high as some 1,036,000 passengers were transported on ocean liners. Although travel by ship remained strong for several years thereafter, the aircraft had by 1958 eclipsed it in terms of volumes of transatlantic passengers.

Transatlantic scheduled passenger ship traffic declined rapidly. Passenger departures from New York fell from approximately 500,000 in 1960 to 50,000 in 1975. So great has been the decline in scheduled liner passenger transport volumes that it has almost completely disappeared in this modern-day era.

Cruising has taken the place of scheduled liner services. In 1982 the worldwide cruise market was approaching the 2 million passenger mark. Forty-five cruise line companies had 125 passenger ships with a total of 72,000 berths.

It is predicted that another 15,000 cruise ship berths will have been added by the mid-1980s to the 72,000 in existence. The largest ocean cruise liner is the *Norway*, which is operated by Norweigan Caribbean Lines and has 2,000 berths.

Cruises share a kinship with other unique transportation offerings such as traveling on the Orient Express train in that they are more of a vacation experience than a transportation mode. The romance of cruising has been heavily promoted, and this has been helped along by a popular television program known as *Love Boat*. Today cruise ships are like portable resort hotels that ply the waters of the Caribbean, Mediterranean, and other regions.

Cruises can be divided into three main categories depending on the duration of the trips. Short cruises are of one week or less. Intermediate-length departures last approximately one to four weeks, and long cruises are the round-the-world variety covering a one- to three-month period. Short-duration cruises appear to be gaining in popularity as they require less vacation time and are less expensive. There are many examples of these taken in North America, including three-night cruises from Los Angeles to Mexico and cruises on the St. Lawrence River on vessels such as the *Canadian Empress*.

Another reason for the growing popularity of short- and intermediate-length cruises appears to be the effectiveness of innovative programming and theming that many of the cruise lines have been doing. In many ways this recent marketing thrust parallels that which many destination resorts have been practicing for several years. Special interest or hobby-type cruises have grown, packaging such things as the theater, gourmet dining, bridge, flower arranging, aquasports, jazz, country and western music, and many other themes and activities. This ties in closely with the trend toward more vacation travel for the purpose of learning or improving upon a leisure time or recreation activity. Another growth area has been in incentive-travel cruises. Cruise travel by groups has increased, as have shipboard conventions and meetings.

These trends in cruise offerings demonstrate the higher level of market segmentation that the cruise lines are practicing today and underscore the observation that the pleasure and business travel market is becoming increasingly capable of segmentation. "Cruises to nowhere" are another cruise innovation appealing to those seeking adventure in their vacation travel. Here the passengers do not know their itineraries prior to the departure of the ship. Fly cruise packages have grown in popularity as well, combining the speed and efficiency of jet travel, with the relaxing, romantic attributes of cruise ships.

Although cruising made impressive gains in popularity during the 1970s and early 1980s, its penetration of the total North American travel market has been quite small. One survey of the U.S. population has indicated that less than 10 percent have ever taken a cruise. However, about 85 percent of those who have been on cruises are likely to repeat the experience. Like destination resorts, cruise lines have successfully developed their own loyal repeat clienteles that average in the 30 to 40 percent range of total passenger volumes. As mentioned earlier, the global total of cruise passengers was in the two million range in 1982.

The ship remains an important passenger transportation mode in its role as a ferry service. The "floating bridge" is an essential complement to the automobile, recreational vehicle, and bus in many parts of the world, including the English Channel, the Irish Sea, the Hebridean Islands of Scotland, the North Sea, the Maritime provinces and British Columbian coast in Canada, and on the Great Lakes.

As with its "partner" in history, the train, the ship also has considerable importance in tourism as an attraction. Examples of short-duration sightseeing cruise-ship attractions are abundant in North America and elsewhere. Characteristically, these cruises are for a day or for an even shorter period of length. Viewing scenic surroundings is the major focus of many of these operations, including those featuring the Thousand Islands (New York-Ontario), the Mississippi River, Muskoka Lakes (Ontario), Niagara Falls (New York-Ontario) and many others. Other cruises combine nostalgia with scenic viewing. Steamer and riverboat cruises are examples of these. One study of a restored steamer sightseeing cruise operation indicated that its appeals were in learning about the history of steamships and the history of the surrounding area, seeing the scenic beauty of the area, watching the visible operations of steam engines, and using its dining/bar service.

In summary, the modern era of travel by water is characterized by boats, ships, hovercraft, and jet foils performing cruising and ferrying roles. This period seems to overlap with Lundgren's modern tourist travel system and Van Doren's post-mobility adjustment periods. In the period of 1840 to the late 1950s the heyday of scheduled liner passenger services paralleled that of the train.

Travel by Automobile

The introduction of the automobile precipitated the demise of the train in most developed countries. As mentioned earlier, the automobile as a passenger travel mode gained its momentum as far back as the 1920s. Lundgren refers to the period after this as the automobile-based travel-system era characterized by "individual travel diffusion." He explained this point as follows:

The private motor car siphoned off a larger portion of the potential travel market from the established mechanisms and routes toward a new tour destination concept with quite different distance dimensions. Thus, the (international) tourist dollar became diffused over wider territories.[5]

The advent of the automobile, therefore, spread the benefits of tourism more widely and provided more and more people with the means to travel individually or in private, smaller groups. Nonprivate group travel had been a characteristic of the railway and steamship era that preceded the automobile. Due to the nature of the railroad's infrastructure and the limited routing possibilities by water, travel patterns were very predictable. People could only get to the destinations to which the trains and steamships would take them. Many famous resort areas, resort hotels, and city center hotels flourished at important destination and staging points for the trains and steamships. With the increased popularity of the automobile, the attractiveness of these areas and facilities began to decline and many of them suffered significantly.

The automobile brought about a more random pattern of travel movements, opened up new destinations, and spurred the development of elaborate networks of new automobile-oriented facilities and services along highways and roads. The tourist court, motel, and the motor hotel were three of the new facility types that developed in the United States and Canada after World War II. In fact, the whole development pattern in North America was fashioned directly and indirectly to accommodate the private automobile.

Traveling by automobile is now the single most predominant travel mode in North America. Most travel surveys have shown that automobile trips account for 90 percent or more of the pleasure/personal and business trips taken by Canadians and U.S. residents. The nuclear family unit traveling by private automobile has been the major source of pleasure/personal travel demand and marketing target for a majority of tourist-oriented businesses in the United States and Canada. It is not difficult to see why, considering the statistics that have been discussed earlier.

Just as they have done with the train, many experts have tried to explain why the automobile is selected over other modes of transportation. One such report[6] found the major attractive attributes of the automobile to be as follows:

Control of the route and the stops enroute
Control of departure times

---

[5]Jan O. J. Lundgren, "The Development of the Tourist Travel Systems," *The Tourist Review*, January 1973, p. 10.

[6]Marcia Stockton and Harriet Thiele, *Group Transportation to Public Recreation Areas: Literature Review* (Madison, WI, University of Wisconsin Extension, May 1980).

Ability to carry baggage and equipment easily
Low out-of-pocket expense of traveling with three or more persons
Freedom to use the automobile once the destination is reached

Other surveys have shown that many persons perceive the automobile to be a relatively safe mode of transportation, and others indicate that people like driving as a recreational experience.

Two other important aspects of automobile travel that remain to be discussed are recreation vehicles and car rentals, or as they are called in Britain "car hires." These two areas have developed so extensively in North America and elsewhere that they are now both significant elements of tourism.

The recreation vehicle, or RV for short, was a further extension of North Americans' love affair with the automobile. The Survey Research Center at the University of Michigan stated that 7.3 percent of all households in the United States in 1980 owned one or more recreation vehicles. This ratio is even higher in Canada as 12.4 percent of its households had some form of recreation vehicle in 1978. Approximately 906,000 Canadian and 6 million U.S. households owned one or more recreation vehicles in 1978.

The trends in production and ownership of RVs in the 1970s were closely tied to the "energy crisis" pattern, as the graphs shown in Figure 7.3 indicates. This figure indicates that the major drops in RV production in the United States occurred in 1974 and 1979 following the main "crisis" periods in 1973 and early 1979. Ownership has now increased since 1979.

The Recreation Vehicle Industry Association identifies eleven types of recreation-vehicle models available (conventional travel trailer, park trailer, fifth-wheel travel trailer, folding camping trailer, truck camper, multiuse van conversion, conventional motor home, van camper, mini chopped van, low profile chopped van, and the compact chopped van). These are commonly separated into distinct groups, such as travel trailers, motor homes, tent/fold-down camping trailers, truck/slide-in campers, and vans/multiuse vehicles. The Survey Research Center study mentioned earlier estimated that 35 percent of RV owners owned travel trailers, 14 percent had motor-homes, 14 percent had tent/fold-down camping trailers, 20 percent had truck/slide-in campers, and 17 percent had vans/multiuse vehicles. The Canadian figures for 1978 showed that the travel trailers had a 36.4 percent market share, tent/fold-down camping trailers had 33.9 percent share, truck/slide-in campers had a 22.4 percent share, and motor homes and vans/multiuse vehicles had a combined share of 7.3 percent.

Since World War II, camping has rapidly grown in popularity in North America and elsewhere. The United States has more than 14,000 public/private parks and commercial campgrounds containing about a mil-

FIGURE 7.3   Trends in Shipments of Recreational Vehicles in the United States, 1969–1979

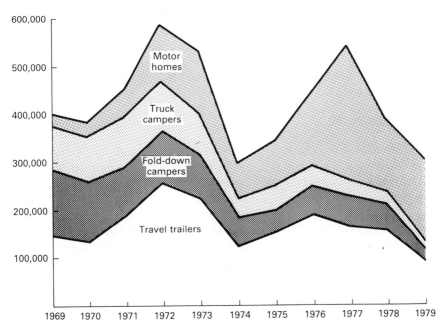

NOTE: 1976-79 shipments of motor homes includes B-2 chassis estimates.

SOURCES: Automotive News 1979 Data Book Issue (from Recreation Vehicle Industry Association).
Canadian Government Office of Tourism, *Planning for the 80's: A Perspective of
Canada's Private Campground Industry* (Ottawa, Ontario, Canadian Government Office of Tourism, 1980).

lion campsites. Canada has been said to have 250,000 campsites and Mexico 10,000 campsites. The increasing popularity of the RV led directly to
a number of new camping phenomena during the 1970s, including the fran-
chised, condominium, and time-sharing condominium campgrounds.

Yet another phenomenon to which the RV has led is that of many
European visitors to Canada and the United States renting these vehicles
for cross-continent trips. Many companies have been formed to provide
this service to overseas pleasure travelers.

The rental of automobiles was another sector of the tourism industry
that demonstrated rapid growth in the 1960s and 1970s. The revenues
earned by U.S. car rental firms increased by ten times during the period
of 1960–1978. The highest utilization of rental cars takes place on Mondays to Fridays and by business travelers (about 75 percent of the total
business). Weekend demand comes primarily from pleasure/personal
travelers. A high proportion of car rentals takes place at airport terminals

in North America and, therefore, it is understandable that the fortunes of this business are closely tied to that of the airline industry.

Recent changes in the rental car business have included significant shifts in car fleets towards smaller and more fuel-efficient models. Fly-drive packages offering rental cars together with flights have made significant gains in popularity as more travelers have begun to substitute air travel for travel by the private automobile.

Travel by Air

Continuing our chronology of transportation modes, the airplane had a revolutionary impact on tourism from World War II onward. This point was already highlighted in Chapter Six where the plane's refashioning of the global travel market was mentioned.

The history of air transportation can be divided into at least three parts, pre–World War II, World War II, and post–World War II. The first period, from 1918 to 1938, was a period of infancy for the scheduled airlines of North America, while the modern era can be termed the mass air-travel era. The present era has been marked by steadily improving aircraft technology and the advent of air charters and of the packaged vacation, or as it has sometimes been called, the "inclusive" or "all-inclusive vacation."

A few dates in history allow us to put the facts discussed later in perspective:

> The first scheduled domestic air service in the United States was in 1918 on the New York-Philadelphia-Washington route.
>
> In 1939 Pan American operated the first transatlantic passenger flight using a "clipper" flying boat.
>
> BOAC (now British Airways) offered its first transatlantic passenger service in 1946.
>
> BEA (now also a part of British Airways) offered its first passenger service to Europe in 1946.
>
> The first of the wide-bodied jets was introduced into service in 1970.

As was pointed out above, the modern era of air travel really began at the end of World War II. Between 1945 and 1960 we have seen that travelers increasingly switched from trains and ships to automobiles and airplanes. In the 1960s this trend continued, and airfare reductions further stimulated air travel. The 1970s was the decade of the wide-bodied jets, and it was then that the "mass tourism" phrase was coined.

By the early 1980s the airplane was the predominant common carrier passenger transportation mode in the United States and Canada, and in international travel to and from the continents. Air travel grew rapidly on an international level during the 1960s and 1970s. The transatlantic route is very significant to the growth of international air travel. In 1948, only 183,000 U.S. citizens flew by transatlantic airplanes to Europe. This figure had mushroomed to 3.8 million people in 1973. The total air passenger traffic on the North Atlantic had risen to over 19 million in 1981, with 90.6 percent of these passengers being on scheduled services and the remaining 9.4 percent, or 1.79 million, on charters.

The other major aspect to air travel in North America is the domestic air-travel market. As Figure 7.4 indicates, scheduled air travel is of much greater significance in the United States and Canada than in other major countries. Domestic air travel exceeded international air travel in the United States, Canada, and Japan in 1978. The reverse was true of the major European countries. Obviously, the sheer size of the United States and Canada relative to their far smaller European neighbors is a major contributor to these differences.

In Canada, the Canadian airlines had a total of 44.9 billion passenger kilometers in 1979. Approximately 77 percent of these were on scheduled services, and the remaining 23 percent were on charters. The average annual rate of growth in scheduled passenger kilometers was 10.9 percent during the 1966–79 period in Canada. The average annual growth rate for charter traffic was much higher at 24.3 percent.

The Canadian scheduled air services market is dominated by the national airline, Air Canada. In 1979 it accounted for 62 percent of the total operating revenues of all the Canadian airlines, a figure three times greater than its biggest competition, CP Air.

As a result of regulatory changes introduced in 1978, Canada's airlines have been allowed to introduce certain types of discounted air fares. These include fares referred to as Seat Sales, Skybus, Night Hawk, and Advance Booking Charters. A Canadian Transportation Commission research study found that these new fares have had a positive effect on domestic air travel within Canada stating that:

> The overall observation suggested by this research is that the domestic low fare experiment has stimulated considerable experimentation by the scheduled carriers. Using low fare concepts, scheduled carriers have been successful in spreading peak loads, improving overall load factors and expanding the market. Consumers have benefited from the availability of considerably lower prices and, at least in major markets, increased variety of choice.[7]

The low-price air fares available in Canada can be divided into two groups, scheduled services (surplus seats and dedicated services) and charter services (advance booking charters and inclusive tour charters).

The experience has been quite similar with domestic air travel in the United States. The deregulation of the U.S. airline industry in 1978, dis-

---

[7]Canadian Transport Commission, *Transport Review: Trends and Selected Issues* (Ottawa, Ontario, Canadian Transport Commission, November 1981), pp. 35–41.

FIGURE 7.4   Air Passenger-kilometers for Scheduled Services: 1968 and 1978

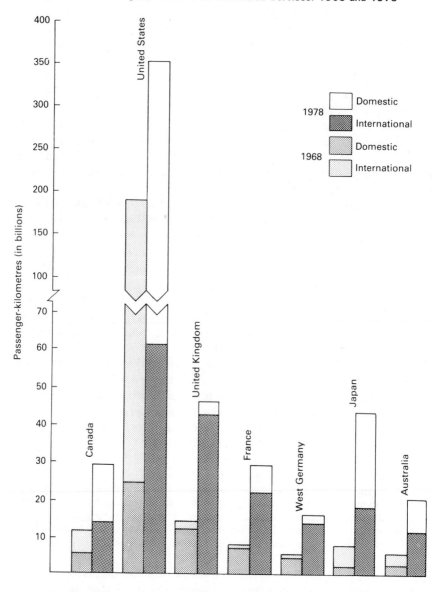

SOURCES: United Nations Statistical Yearbook.
Canadian Transport Commission, *Transport Review: Trends and Selected Issues,
1981* (Ottawa, Ontario, Canadian Transport Commission, November 1981), p. 74.

cussed in detail in Chapter Twelve, had a major effect on the types of air fares available, as well as on airline routes and the numbers of airline companies. U.S. domestic scheduled air-service volumes were 6.5 times higher in 1979 than they were in 1960, representing an average annual growth rate of around 27 percent during this period.

It was estimated in 1979 that the commercial airline companies of all nations, excluding the U.S.S.R., had an inventory of around 6,000 airplanes. It is projected that 50 percent of the current fleet will be retired by 1990 and another 5,000 new planes will be added, bringing the estimated total of planes in 1990 to 8,000. It is expected that by 1990, half of the world commercial airplane fleet will be of the wide-body variety (DC-10, L-1011, and 747) and the other half will be of the smaller, single-aisle variety.

The commercial airline industry in North America has several different types of operators (defined by the CAB) and these are as follows:

United States	Canada
1. Major carriers (annual revenues over $1 billion)	1. Trunk carriers (Level I)
2. National carriers (annual revenues of $75 million to $1 billion)	2. Regional carriers (Level II)
3. Large regional carriers (annual revenues of $10 million to $75 million)	3. Commuter carriers (Level III)
4. Commuter airline carriers	4. Charter airline carriers
5. Charter airline carriers	

In the United States in 1980 there were seventeen airline companies in the first three scheduled air-service categories (Eastern, Delta, United, American, TWA, Braniff, Western, Northwest, Continental, Pan American, USAir, Republic, Frontier, Piedmont, Hughes Air West, Texas International, and Ozark Air). Canada has only six Level I and Level II carriers.

As a result of the deregulation of the airline industry in the United States, there has been significant growth in the numbers of regional and commuter carriers, such as Air New England, Air Florida, and New York Air.

The charter airline carriers in the United States include World, Capitol, Transamerica, Evergreen, Zantop, and Rich. Since deregulation, several of these charter companies have also begun to operate scheduled services as well. Canada has one major charter airline, Wardair, and one smaller one, Worldways Canada. There are also several airline companies offering services in Alaska and Hawaii. The U.S. airlines together have had 2,542, or 42 percent of the world's (excluding U.S.S.R.) airplanes in 1979, and they have accounted for approximately 38 percent of world passenger traffic.

During the 1970s the charter air-travel market became increasingly important to the world's commercial airlines. The following facts further illustrate this point:

For non-United States carriers, charter services have represented 13.2 percent of revenue passenger miles in 1979.

Within Europe, 40 percent of the passengers and more than 50 percent of passenger miles have been accounted for by charters.

In 1976, 16 percent of arriving passengers in the United States were on charters. About 25 percent of those arriving from Europe were on charters.

In 1976, 13 percent of departing passengers from the United States were on charters. Some 23 percent of those departing for Europe were on charters.

In 1979, about 18 percent of the Canadians flying to the United States were on charters.

32.6 percent of the air revenue passengers carried between Canada and overseas countries in 1979 were on charters. Some 27.6 percent of passengers on Canada-Europe routes were on charters.

The major charter routes in the world include the transatlantic crossing and the air corridors between the United Kingdom and the rest of Europe to Spain and other Mediterranean countries.

Deregulation and competitive pricing by North American airlines have subsequently reduced the advantages to the consumer of flying by charter.

Who chooses to fly on airplanes? One of the answers would, of course, be anyone who wishes to go overseas from Canada and the United States, since scheduled transatlantic ship services have almost disappeared. The U.S. Air Transport Association (ATA) has been conducting a survey for several years now on the frequency of flying among the U.S. adult population. Over two-thirds of adult Americans have flown on a commercial airline. Groups with the highest propensities to fly are those in professional and business occupations, residents of the western United States, those in the twenty-five to forty-nine age group, and those with family incomes of $40,000 or more. About half of those who fly take only one trip a year, while the frequent fliers, representing 4 percent of those who fly, take 36 percent of the trips. The moderate fliers (two to twelve trips in previous year), accounting for 48 percent of those who have flown during the previous year, generate 50 percent of the trips. The ATA survey also indicated that 55 percent of the air trips taken were for business purposes and 45 percent for pleasure/personal reasons.

In summary, the airplane has in the post–World War II era taken over as the major international and intercontinental transportation mode. It also predominates among the common carriers in domestic transportation in the United States and Canada. It is a particularly important mode for the business travelers who have the time factor as a major consideration. Additionally, charter flights, since their introduction, have become increasingly important as vacation travel modes, particularly in Europe.

Travel by Bus/Motor Coach

The third principal common carrier mode is the bus. Although it does not share the glamour of the jet, the motor coach nevertheless plays a vital role in tourism. As one spokesman of the U.S. bus industry has stated:

> In 1979, the bus industry carried 360 million passengers; the airlines carried 295 million; Amtrak carried 21.5 million. The bus industry provided service to 14,000 communities; the airlines served 700 communities; Amtrak served 550 communities.[8]

In North America and elsewhere the coach performs two key roles. The first is to provide a regular schedule of intercity passenger transportation services. The second is to provide charter and tour services. The 1979 ridership figure on U.S. buses increased to 378 million passengers in 1981. Of this total, 203 million passengers, or 53.7 percent, were on charters and tours, and the remaining 175 million were on regular scheduled intercity bus services. As the chart in Figure 7.5 shows, there was a decline in the passenger volumes carried by U.S. buses on their regularly scheduled routes, although some gains were made during the main energy crisis periods in 1974 and 1979. On the other hand, there has been substantial growth in the bus charter and tour business, particularly with the bus tours. The National Tour Association estimated that in 1981, the bus charters and tours created economic benefits of $8.2 billion in the United States. A major trend in this respect is the increasing popularity of bus tours among elderly persons.

It is estimated that 90 percent of U.S. and 85 percent of Canadian bus ridership is accounted for by persons on pleasure/personal trips. Business travelers, on the other hand, constitute only 10 percent to 15 per-

---

[8]Stuart N. Robinson, *1981 Outlook for Bus Travel* (Washington, DC, U.S. Travel Data Center/The Travel Research Association, December 1980), pp. 107–27.

FIGURE 7.5   Breakdown of U.S. Bus Traffic: 1969–1979

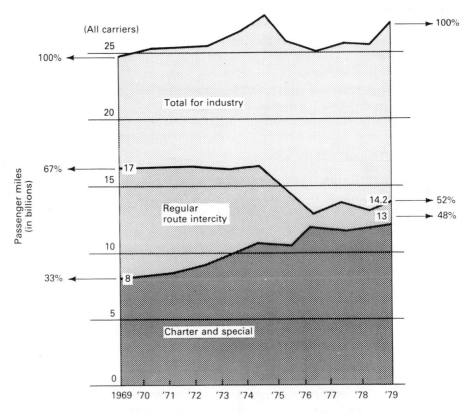

SOURCES: Marketing Support Services, Inc./American Bus Association.
Stuart N. Robinson, *1981 Outlook for Bus Travel* (Washington, DC, U.S. Travel Data Center/The Travel Research Association, 1980), p. 123.

cent of the bus travel market. Surveys have shown that bus passengers in North America are predominantly either young or old. Buses also attract a larger share of the lower-income groups than do the other common carriers. Another interesting fact is that women riders of the bus significantly outnumbered men. Recent advertising indicates that bus companies are targeting their marketing programs towards the family summer vacation market, young couples, older people on summer and fall vacations, and the "empty nesters."

One Ontario-based bus-tour operator has surveyed past bus-tour patrons and others and concluded that the major perceived advantages and disadvantages of bus tours are as follows:

Why People Take Bus Tours	Why People Don't Take Bus Tours
1. Value	1. Don't have time
2. Access	2. Bus tours are perceived as being for
3. Total experience, including social aspects	senior citizens.
4. Continuous sightseeing and learning experience	3. Bus tours are perceived as not going to destinations where people want to go.
5. Convenience	
6. Easy and quick to organize	
7. Group size	

As the information presented on domestic travel within the United States and Canada in Chapter Six clearly indicated, the bus has been increasingly utilized as a pleasure/personal travel mode in recent years.

ENERGY PROBLEMS AND THEIR EFFECTS

The effects of the energy crises of the seventies can be summarized as follows:

> Since the first energy crisis in 1973–74, we have entered the post-mobility adjustment period. In this period, the travel patterns of travelers in North America and elsewhere have undergone fundamental changes. One such change is toward greater use of the common carriers (train, bus, and plane) for long-distance travel.
>
> There has been a distinct move in North America toward the use of smaller, lighter, and more fuel-efficient automobiles.
>
> The family automobile touring type of vacation has been on the decline relative to single-destination trips.
>
> Travel trips in the automobile are being taken closer to home.
>
> There has been a distinct trend towards more intermodality, that is, fly/drive, fly/cruise, and rail/drive packages.
>
> Recreation vehicle sales suffered severe reversals during the energy crisis periods. Smaller, lighter, and more fuel-efficient RVs have increased in popularity as a result.
>
> Rental-car agencies have moved towards smaller, lighter, and more fuel-efficient cars in their fleets.
>
> There have been temporary declines in air travel volumes on certain routes during the energy crisis periods.

Because of the pace of change in other factors external to passenger transportation and travel, great caution has to be exercised in relating travel volume changes directly to the energy crisis. As McCool correctly has stated about one study dealing with the relationship of vacation travel and fuel shortages:

The authors have casually inferred that changes in vacation travel patterns between 1973 and 1975 are due to energy availability and cost. Other influences are also possible. These include economic conditions, family life cycle, and weather. To identify cause-effect relationships, sophisticated research methods are often necessary and frequently must be used to control for extraneous influences.[9]

Other authors have stressed the need to give separate consideration to the prospects of higher fuel prices, rationing, and increased fears over the availability of gasoline. The prospects of rationing and fears about the availability of gasoline certainly appeared to have an immediate market effect on automobile-based pleasure travel when the energy crises were at their peaks in 1973–74 and 1979. There was an almost instantaneous switch towards the common carrier modes at that time.

The train ridership figures discussed earlier indicated that there also appeared to be a switch towards rail travel at the time the energy problems were at their height. Whether these movements were temporary reactions to the problem and not permanent shifts in mode preferences is still the subject of much academic debate.

Another important aspect of the energy question is the price of fuel and the "fuel price elasticity of demand" with respect to individual travel modes and travel purposes. Some authors have suggested that non-convention-meeting, business, and VFR travel trips are relatively inelastic and, therefore, should not be affected greatly by increases in gasoline prices. On the other hand, they indicate that convention-meeting, business travel, and non-VFR pleasure trips in the automobile are quite elastic and will be adversely affected by increases in gasoline prices. Again, these hypotheses remain to be verified conclusively.

The future impacts of energy transportation modes and travel remain very uncertain. Fears still remain about the future availability of gasoline and transportation companies, and private individuals have done a great deal to make their equipment more fuel-efficient.

TRAVEL AT HOME: TELECOMMUNICATIONS AND TRAVEL

It is now conceivable that the telecommunications technology, that did so much to aid the development of tourism, will begin to detract from it. One might begin to believe this after reading the following quote from *Sales & Marketing Management* magazine:

---

[9]Stephen F. McCool, "Vacation Travel and Fuel Shortages: A Critical Comment," *Journal of Travel Research*, vol. 19, no. 2, Fall 1980, pp. 18–19.

SALES MEETINGS ENTER THE ELECTRONIC AGE

Advances in communications technology and falling prices are persuading more companies to use teleconferences for sales and meetings. A survey by Runzheimer and Co., Rochester, WI, reveals that 15% of U.S. companies used video to cut business travel costs. A new study by Quantum Science Corp., New York City, predicts that the number of business teleconferences will explode from 89,400 in 1981 to 1.8 million by 1986, says Christine H. Ehrenbard, associate director of the consulting company's communications and teleconferencing strategy program.

Gary Badoud, president, Video-Net, Woodland Hills, CA, a producer of tele-conferences, says that costs of teleconferences have dropped from 23% to 29% between 1980 and 1982, depending upon the number of cities used. He says costs are being pushed down by the increased availability of satellite receiving equipment, expanding supply of portable equipment, installation of permanent receiving facilities at more major hotels, and adaptation of cable TV for teleconferences.[10]

"Electronic travel" may indeed be one of the hallmarks of the 1980s and 1990s, as corporations and perhaps even individual pleasure travelers move toward it to avoid the steadily escalating costs of conventional travel. Some spokesmen for the teleconference industry believe that it will eventually grab a 5 to 20 percent share of the corporate-meeting travel market as the costs of teleconferencing continue to fall relative to the traditional travel alternatives. It may not be too far-fetched to suggest now that people will watch travelogues in their own homes on oversized TV screens rather than actually traveling to the destination at a higher cost.

REFERENCES

ANTON, G. MYRON, "Technological Resources for the Airframe/Airline Industries: The Changing Characteristics of Airplanes," in *Research and the Changing World of Travel in the 1980's* (The Travel Research Association, Eleventh Annual Conference Proceedings, 1980), pp. 19–27.

BEEKHUIS, JEANNE, *The Seventh Annual World Tourism Review* (New York, American Express Publishing Co., 1982), p. 44.

"Bus Industry Adds it All Up," *The Travel Agent*, April 16, 1982, p. 29.

CANADIAN GOVERNMENT OFFICE OF TOURISM, *Planning for the 80's: A Perspective of Canada's Private Campground Industry* (Ottawa, Ontario, Canadian Government Office of Tourism, 1980).

CANADIAN TRANSPORT COMMISSION, *A Study of Amtrak's Effectiveness* (Ottawa, Ontario, Canadian Transport Commission, Report 119, November 1974), p. 11.

---

[10]"What it Costs to Get into Teleconferencing," *Sales and Marketing Management*, February 1983, pp. 24–25.

CURTIN, RICHARD T., *The RV Consumer: Current Trends and Future Prospects* (Chantilly, VA, Recreation Vehicle Industry Association, June 1980), pp. 1–46.

FARRIS, MARTIN T., AND FORREST E. HARDING, *Passenger Transportation* (Englewood Cliffs, NJ, Prentice-Hall, Inc., 1976), p. 16.

GREEN, F. B., "Recreation Vehicles: A Perspective," *Annals of Tourism Research*, October/December 1978, pp. 429–39.

JAMES, GEORGE W. ed., *Airline Economics* (Lexington, MA, Lexington Books, 1982), pp. 23–34.

KAMP, B. DAN, JOHN L. CROMPTON, AND DAVID M. HENSARLING, "The Reactions of Travelers to Gasoline Rationing and to Increases in Gasoline Prices," *Journal of Travel Research*, Summer 1979, pp. 37–41.

MATHIEU, SUSAN M., *The S. S. Segwun: Marketing of a Successful Attraction* (Ottawa, Ontario, Recreation Canada, December 1981), pp. 34–38.

ROBINSON, H., *A Geography of Tourism* (London, England, MacDonald and Evans, 1976), p. 101.

ROBINSON, STUART N., "What Happens When the Intercity Bus Industry is Deregulated," in *A Decade of Achievement* (The Travel Research Association, Tenth Annual Conference Proceedings, 1979), pp. 193–212.

SCHANZ, WILLIAM, "The Cruise Market," in *Research for Changing Travel Patterns: Interpretation and Utilization* (The Travel Research Association, Fourth Annual Conference Proceedings, August 1973), pp. 173–76.

STANSFIELD, JR., CHARLES A., "Evolving Patterns of International Sea Passenger Ports in Eastern United States," *The Tourist Review*, no. 3, July/September 1975, pp. 105–11.

TANEJA, NAWAL K., *Airlines in Transition* (Lexington, MA, Lexington Books, 1981), pp. 37–38.

TANEJA, NAWAL K., *The Commercial Airline Industry: Managerial Practices and Regulatory Policies* (Lexington, MA, Lexington Books, 1976), pp. 1–20.

"The Cruise Business Part 2: Special Report No. 43," *International Tourism Quarterly*, no. 3, 1982, pp. 68–87.

"Tour Brokers Out to Raise Client Consciousness," *The Travel Agent*, April 16, 1982, p. 29.

Travel Marketing—1978 (Stamford, CT, Marketing Handbooks, 1978), pp. 35, 47–49, 65.

Travel, Tourism and Outdoor Recreation: A Statistical Digest: 1978 and 1979 (Ottawa, Ontario, Statistics Canada, May 1981), pp. 16, 92, 101.

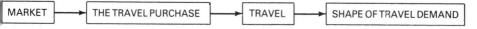

The second part of *The Tourism System* ends with the arrival of tourists at the destination. This third part of the system looks in detail at a destination.

The aspects that define a destination are identified, and standards for the attractions and services necessary for tourism are given. (Chapter Eight). Chapter Nine explores the reasons that people at destinations seek tourism and considers the economic and social effects of tourism on those at a destination. Guidelines are given to ensure the "best" type of development from the destination's viewpoint.

In order to get the most benefits from tourism while minimizing the negatives, people at a destination must establish a policy (Chapter Ten) within the confines of the regulatory framework (Chapter Eleven). Having done this, those people at the destination are free to plan (Chapter Twelve) and develop (Chapter Thirteen) tourism resources for the long-term benefit of the destination.

Although planning and development must take into account the characteristics of the potential tourists, the major emphasis on tourists occurs when people at the destination seek to move tourists round *The Tourism System* from origin to destination. To sell travel requires the implementation of a marketing plan. That plan can only be formulated and implemented once those at the destination have developed a policy, a plan, and a development strategy for tourism.

READINGS

This reading analyzes tourist flows from the viewpoint of a geographer. It is an all-inclusive study of the characteristics of people and places from a tourism outlook.

This reading is a chapter in a Resource Paper (No. 76-1, 1976) written by Ian M. Matley, Professor of Geography at Michigan State University, and titled *The Geography of International Tourism*. The authors wish to thank the Association of American Geographers for permission to reprint this reading.

Physical and Cultural Factors
Influencing the Location of Tourism

The study and analysis of tourist flows and their patterns on the surface of the earth form the core of the geography of international tourism. We have seen the various forms of transportation which permit the rapid and widespread movement of tourists around the world. We have also looked at the methodology for the study of these flows and at the impact of tourism on the economy of places and regions. However, people do not travel considerable distances and are not willing to expend money and experience discomfort to get to a specific destination unless that place offers certain attractions which their own place of residence does not possess. In other words, flows and patterns of tourism result because of a variety of physical and cultural attractions possessed by different places which appeal to people with different backgrounds, tastes and needs. The uneven distribution of tourism on the surface of the earth is explained to a great extent by the complex interrelationships between attractions of various types and the interests and desires of tourists.

In order to be able to explain these interrelationships and in turn the tourist movements which develop from them, the geographer needs to know the various characteristics of the people and places involved. Therefore, it is necessary to look at the various factors which make a place attractive for tourism and also at the way in which people perceive a place as attractive or not.

SUN, SEA, AND THE RESORT

Of all the factors influencing the location of tourist activities, the most important are the physical. The mass development of tourism in Europe derives from the existence, on one hand, of urbanized regions with a cool, cloudy climate and, on the other, of relatively underpopulated regions with a warm, sunny climate. It has been said that the large migration of Germans to Spain and Italy is not a reflection of an interest in Latin culture, but of the shortness and coldness of Germany's coastline (Simpson: 1968, p. 233). A large number or resorts[1] ring the Mediterranean coast for housing and feeding the worshipers of sun and sea from Northern Europe. Other amusements and entertainments may be provided, but they are sidelines to the major attractions of the sun and the beach. To many tourists the country matters little. Spain may have bullfights and flamenco dancers and Italy may have Latin lovers and the Leaning Tower of Pisa, but what matters to most is the promise of reliable sunshine, warm temperatures, a beach to lie on, warm water to swim in, and clean but cheap hotels and restaurants. In fact the relative popularity of Spain in the last couple of decades over Italy and the south of France has been attributed to its relatively low prices. Yugoslavia, Romania, and Bulgaria have been the latest countries to develop their coasts for tourism and to offer low cost vacations to sun-hungry northerners. The complex of new hotels stretching along the Black Sea coasts of Romania and Bulgaria is a good example of development designed primarily to exploit warm summer temperatures and broad sandy beaches which slope gently into a sea free from dangerous currents and jellyfish. Foreigners are housed in hotels according to nationality and language and, although trips can be made to various inland natural and cultural attractions, contact between the guest and the local people is limited.

PROBLEMS OF COASTAL RESORTS

This isolation of resort visitors from the surrounding native people is also a phenomenon of modern tourist development in areas other than Eastern Europe. In many countries new resorts and hotels are being built from scratch on empty coastlines, with tourists, waiters, cooks and maids all coming from outside the area. This can produce an "ocean liner" atmosphere, insulated from the outside world (Simpson: 1968, pp. 233–34). It is probably true that many people like it this way, as it limits the need to communicate with foreigners and reduces contacts with possibly unpleasant or perhaps puzzling aspects of local life.

This tendency towards isolating tourists from local life runs counter to the view of tourism often propagated by writers in the communist countries. A Romanian view is that "tourism in general, including tourist geography, serves a high humanistic ideal of education, of progress and peace between peoples" (Iancu: 1976, p. 374). To a Soviet writer tourism is "a form of cultural contact between peoples of different countries" and "tourism between socialist countries plays an important role in develop-

---

[1]Place visited by people for the purpose of recreation, health, etc.

ing social connections between them and helps to develop the world system of socialism" (Anan'yev: 1968, pp. 11-12). This somewhat idealistic view of tourism, difficult to associate with present trends in mass tourism, is tempered by the warning that "the Soviet people constantly remember that tourist exchange between socialist and capitalist countries takes place at the same time in the arena of a political and ideological struggle with its own specific features" (Anan'yev: 1968, p. 13). This last remark would suggest the advisability of isolating tourists from capitalist lands as much as possible from contacts with the local population. In fact, the attraction of the tourist mark or dollar for the governments of many of the communist countries is offset by the dangers of excessive contact between their peoples and Western tourists.

Although the Mediterranean beaches of Southern Europe and North Africa, along with those of the Black, North, and Baltic Seas, have virtually monopolized the seaside tourist trade of the Old World (Figure 7[2]), other continents are beginning to develop their resources. The United States has seen the development of the Florida beaches along with those of the Carolinas, and California. Mexico has its Acapulco, and the Caribbean Islands have developed their resorts at a rapid rate during the last two decades. Uruguay attracts other Latin Americans with its excellent beaches and casinos. In West Africa, the Ivory Coast is developing a major coastal resort for foreign tourists.

This development of seaside resorts in sunnier climates has had considerable repercussions on resorts in northern Europe. With an increase in the number of persons able to afford vacations which occurred during the Victorian period in Great Britain, a number of major seaside resorts had developed. They were located mainly near large urban concentrations, the most notable being Brighton, serving the London area, and Blackpool, serving the industrial North. Their growth was speeded by the development of rapid railroad transportation (Robinson: 1972, p. 384). On the continent similar types of resorts arose, such as Scheveningen serving the Hague, Ostend serving Brussels, Deauville serving Paris, and Le Touquet serving Paris and Brussels, whereas in the United States, Atlantic City served the New York-Philadelphia region. Apart from offering the visitor a beach and the sea, and, with luck, some sunshine, these resorts developed various other attractions, such as promenades, piers, amusement galleries, dance-halls, casinos, and theaters, and accommodations ranged from cheap bed-and-breakfast establishments to giant luxury hotels. The development of resorts in the Mediterranean and other sunnier and warmer regions, along with the ability of more people to afford longer vacation journeys, has led to the demise of many of the seaside

---

[2]Readers may find Figure 1 useful in locating the various place names of European and Mediterranean resort areas.

resorts of northern Europe. Luxury hotels have been closed or converted to other uses and many resorts rely now for their income on the day tripper, whose range of activity has been increased greatly by the automobile, or on a more stable population of retired persons. Because of the great increase in day tourism by car and the resultant traffic congestion in resort towns, many tourists are seeking small, unspoiled villages and towns, which, in their turn, will become overcrowded.

It should be noted that the transition from northern to southern European resorts involves factors other than purely climatic ones. The earliest resort development in the Mediterranean region took place on the French Côte d'Azur. The period from 1865 until World War I saw the rise of Nice and Cannes as winter resorts for the moneyed classes from northern Europe and England in particular. These luxury resorts have undergone considerable changes since World War II, as a new class of tourist has arisen with different tastes and more limited finances than the prewar group. The new group consists mainly of working people, who have their vacations in the summer months, a fact which has changed Nice into a predominantly summer resort (Latouche: 1963, pp. 369-70). The rich have in turn joined the "jet set," who now seek the more exotic and distant shores of Acapulco or Tahiti. Nice and Cannes have lost their old glory and must now compete in the field of the new mass tourism not only with newer resorts on the French Mediterranean coast, especially in the Languedoc-Roussillon region, but with a host of others in neighboring countries. Between the war and 1955 the French Riviera had some competition from the Spanish Costa Brava and the Biarritz-San Sebastian area on the Bay of Biscay. During the period 1955-1965, however, new resorts began to appear in Corsica, on the Costa del Sol and the Costa Blanca in Spain, along the Italian Riviera di Ponente and di Levante, on the Adriatic coast north of Rimini, in the Naples-Capri area and in Sardinia, and on the Dalmatian coast of Yugoslavia. Since 1965 new developments have taken place on the Costa Dorada of Spain and on the Balearic Islands, especially Majorca, in Portugal on the Algarve coast and in the north, in Calabria and Sicily in Italy and on the Greek islands, including Corfu and Rhodes. A large number of new hotels have been built on the Yugoslav coast, while Morocco, Tunisia and Turkey have been investing in the development of several major new resorts. The rapid growth of the Black Sea resorts of Bulgaria and Romania also began during this period. During the last few years the European tourist agencies have added Madeira and the Canary Islands to their lists, especially for the wealthier winter tourists.

This move away from the traditional vacation of the past is a reflection not only of a search for exotic sunny shores, but also of the development of cheap air transportation, mainly organized on a charter basis. The lower costs of accommodations and food in many of the economical-

EXHIBIT A   Major Tourist Resorts of Europe and the Mediterranean.

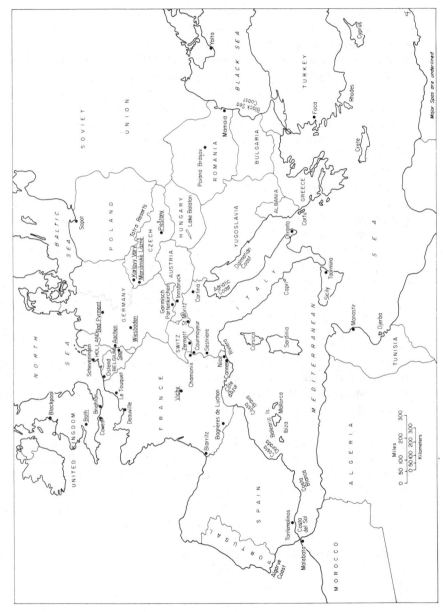

ly less developed regions on the fringes of the Mediterranean also make
it possible for tourist agencies to offer attractive package vacations within the financial ability of many working-class families in northern Europe.
Tourist organizations and agencies in many north European countries
have organized hotels and other facilities in southern resorts for the exclusive use of their own nationals. For example, the Dutch have developed
hotels in the Spanish resorts of Torremolinos and Benalmadena on the
Costa del Sol and Dutch tourists arrive in large numbers by charter plane
during the summer. Some have bought houses, apartments, or land in the
area for vacation use or for retirement, and a small but growing Dutch
colony is developing. These people are bringing a steady stream of foreign
currency in exchange for services into a region which offers few alternatives for employment.

Most resorts owe their development to government activity and investment and the tourist industry is to a great extent nationalized. For
example, the French government is involved in the development of six
resorts in Languedoc to house two million tourists (Lavery: 1974, p. 193).
Only a few individuals, such as Baron Edmond de Rothschild, who is aid-
ing the development of a resort at Caesarea in Israel, and the Aga Khan,
who is backing a resort in Sardinia, can afford the necessary investments
(Simpson: 1968, p. 240, footnote 18). In the developing countries, in particular, investment in the tourist industry by the government is essential if any development is to take place at all and in some countries the
development of tourist facilities stands very high on the list of investment priorities. As Christaller pointed out, it is precisely in the peripheral
regions of Europe and in the underdeveloped countries that tourism has
most to offer in terms of economic development (1964, pp. 95–103). It is
in these regions that the greatest expansion of the "sun and fun" variety
of mass tourism should be expected in the future.

A recent development of significance for the future of tourism in the
Mediterranean and beyond is the development of organizations such as
the "Club Méditerranée." The concept of this club is based somewhat on
the holiday camp as devised by Butlin in Great Britain. The Butlin holiday camps, first started at Skegness in 1936, consist of villages of chalets,
with communal restaurants and amusements, located near the sea. The
keynote of the holiday camp, however, is organized entertainment and
activities, whereas the Club Méditerranée, although using the village format, does not attempt to organize the vacations of its members to the
same degree. The aim of its founder, the Belgian Gerard Blitz, is to create
an atmosphere directly opposed to that of life in a large urban center. Life
in the villages is informal and democracy is stressed, and sports form the
major occupation of the guests.

The first village was started in 1949 on Majorca and at the moment
there are over 75, stretching from Tahiti to Senegal, including villages

in such diverse places as Egypt, Israel, Cuba, Spain, Morocco, Turkey, Hawaii, and Mexico. There are several winter sports resorts. The Club is trying to attract American tourists by developing bilingual villages where English is spoken along with French. About nine percent of the Club's one million members are North Americans. The Club Méditerranée is now a public company, with Baron Edmond de Rothschild and a company owned by Giovanni Agnelli of the Fiat corporation as major stockholders.

The village resorts of the Club Méditerranée are open to the same criticism as most other modern resorts which have appeared along the coasts of the developing countries; they are self-contained, isolated islands of middle-class European or American urbanites who have little contact with the local people. The Club does not encourage members to leave the premises of the resort except on conducted tours (Francke: 1976, p. 47).

Although long hours of sunshine and warmth are the basic ingredients for a successful seaside resort, another aspect of the physical environment, although independent of the climate, cannot be neglected. This is the quality of the beach. Such resorts as Copacabana, Palm Beach, Mamaia in Romania, Muizenberg in South Africa, and Montego Bay in Jamaica offer the combination of sunshine and fine sandy beaches. The sandy, dune-backed beaches of the Dutch and the Belgian coasts are good enough to offset the disadvantages of climate for the thousands of Germans from the Ruhr industrial region who invade them during the summer. In the British Isles the quality of the beaches varies from one resort to another and can be an important factor in attracting families with children, who are looking for a sandy beach where the children can dig and build sand castles and which has a gentle slope into a sea without dangerous currents.

The character and slope of the beach creates the necessary conditions for surfing, which has increased greatly in popularity in recent years. Although suitable conditions for the sport exist at locations in California, Hawaii, South Africa and other regions, the major area of development is in Australia. For example, a twenty-five mile stretch of coast south of Brisbane has been developed as a surfing and water sports area, known as the Goldcoast. This region, with Surfers Paradise as its center, now contains over 2,600 hotels and has begun to attract foreign tourists, including Japanese.

The nature of the coastline may be important in the development of resorts, apart from the presence or absence of good beaches. Boating and sailing have played a major role in the development of some coastal resorts and the existence of a sheltered bay or channel, the lack of reefs or rocks, and the presence of a good harbor, natural or otherwise, are favorable for the sport of sailing. The resort of Cowes on the Isle of Wight in southern England has the above features and has become a major center for international yachting. Marinas, which provide mooring, provisions, repairs, and in some cases overnight accommodations and other services for yachtsmen, are beginning to appear in increasing numbers along the coasts of many countries. Although sunshine and warmth make sailing more pleasant, warm temperatures are not as important for sailing as for swimming and many of the northern countries offer good conditions for the sport.

Pollution

A major problem which may have a limiting effect on the development of seaside resorts in the future is that of pollution, both of beaches and of the adjacent waters. Beach users are major polluters. Their litter is not only unsightly but creates hazards such as broken glass and tin cans which can cause injury to the feet of bathers. More serious, because less easy to control and to remove, is the pollution caused by oil spills from passing ships, either in the form of deliberate release of oil or because of an accident. Several serious oil spills along the coasts of the United States and the British Isles have received considerable publicity in recent years. Although the damage to sea birds and other fauna has been stressed, the threat to a resort beach from even a small spill can be serious.

The dumping of industrial waste, sewage, and garbage into the sea close to resort beaches can make swimming not only unpleasant but also dangerous to health by increasing the possibility of infectious diseases. It also limits the possibility of safe recreational fishing in many coastal areas because of the danger of eating the polluted fish.

Some tourist countries are already seriously affected by pollution. Almost two-thirds of the beaches of Italy have been polluted to some degree by sewage and garbage. Some Eastern Mediterranean countries, such as Israel and Lebanon, also report that pollution is becoming a major problem facing the future development of their tourist industry. So far Greek, Yugoslav, and Turkish resorts have not yet encountered serious pollution, but they will have to exercise extreme caution to prevent the present situation from deteriorating. Pollution is also affecting inland waters. For example, in Switzerland no swimming is permitted on Lake Lugano, and some beaches have been closed on the shores of Lake Geneva.

Apart from environmental pollution, the seaside resort may suffer from what is often referred to as "visual pollution." Many of the nineteenth century resorts were built with taste and style and some modern resorts, such as the villages of the Club Méditerranée, make an attempt to blend with the local architectural styles and physical environment. However, many resorts are characterized by poorly designed and shoddily built hotels, restaurants, other recreational buildings, garish advertisements and signs, and a general lack of control of architectural style. Some Mediterranean coastal resorts consist of rows of apartments constructed en masse with cheap and rapid construction techniques. In some cases overcrowding has resulted in a second row of apartment blocks from which it is impossible to obtain a view of the sea. There is a sameness to many of these resorts which makes it difficult at times to know in which country one might be.

WINTER RESORTS

Although warm summer temperatures may be the major component of climate affecting the location of tourist development, cold winter temperatures are also important. Although the majority of people employed in a modern industrial society take their vacations during the summer there are more and more who find it possible to take some time off from their work in the winter. Some summer resorts keep hotels and facilities open for a clientele seeking relief from northern winters and who benefit from cheaper off-season rates both in accommodations and transportation. This is especially true of the more southerly resorts in North Africa, Madeira, and the Canary Islands. It was, in fact, the warm winters of the French Riviera which led to its early development as a tourist region. However, cold winter temperatures are more significant than warm ones in the development and location of modern winter tourism and the growth in popularity of winter sports is one of the most noteworthy developments of the tourist industry of the last few decades.

Of all the modern winter sports activities, skiing is by far the most popular. Skiing as a form of winter transportation has an ancient history, but as a sport it is of relatively recent vintage. Skating is an older sport, being popular in northern Europe, especially in Holland, in the seventeenth century. The lack of long periods of freezing temperatures results in a rather limited skating season in England or Holland, but no major skating resorts were ever developed in countries with a more suitable climate. This was partly because of the relative unpopularity of skating as a modern sport and partly because of the development of the artificial indoor ice rink, which made skating a sport independent of climate. Skiing requires quite different physical conditions from skating. First of all, it is an outdoor sport and second, it requires a good snow cover and a mountainous or, at least, hilly terrain. The last item is not so necessary for cross-country skiing as practiced in the Nordic countries, a type of skiing which is becoming rapidly more popular in the Alpine countries and North America. However, few skiing resorts have been developed in areas which do not have a hill in the vicinity. Modern skiing as a mass sport developed in the Alps and Alpine-type downhill skiing still forms the model for the sport in most parts of the world.

The use of mountain regions as areas for recreation and tourism is of relatively recent origin. It was only in the eighteenth century that Europeans began to perceive mountains as anything but regions of danger and horror. Mountain climbing in the Alps began in the late eighteenth century and skiing was introduced from Norway by the English to the Swiss Alps in the 1890's. The development of the ski lift in the 1930's led not only to the rapid development of skiing for sport, but opened up the Alps to all forms of tourism. By giving access to higher slopes and glaciers it has enabled resorts such as Chamonix and Zermatt to develop a summer skiing season.

Because of differences in climate and terrain between the different mountain regions of Europe, conditions for developing winter sports vary considerably from region to region. The lack of sufficient snow for long periods makes much of the southern Alps unsuitable for skiing, although a few resorts have recently been developed in this region. Even in the northern Alps weather and snow conditions can be quite variable depending on the time of the year and the altitude. For this reason some resorts can offer guaranteed good conditions for skiing from Christmas until Easter, whereas others have a more restricted season. In the Norwegian mountains, on the other hand, snow conditions are more uniform from place to place throughout the winter, but the short daylight hours of the winter months along with the cold temperatures reduce the popularity of Norwegian resorts with the foreign tourist until the spring (Heller: 1969, pp. 60–61). Scotland has seen more commercial development of its winter sports facilities in recent years, but suffers from the variable weather associated with a west-coast marine climate, with a resultant uncertainty about snow and weather conditions at any given time in the winter (Perry: 1971, pp. 197–201). In fact, commercially organized skiing in Scotland is only really practical in the snow-filled corries and gullies of the major mountain ranges, such as the Grampians. Scottish skiing, however, attracts few tourists from outside Britain. Other mountain regions of Europe have varied conditions for winter sport development. The Pyrenees have some centers, such as Bagnères de Luchon and Barèges on the French side, but in general the Pyrenees are not easily accessible from the main urbanized regions of Europe; and in the western Pyrenees the snow cover is uncertain (Ritter: 1966, pp. 227–28). In Eastern Europe the best conditions for skiing are found in the Carpathians, in particular in the Tatra mountains between Poland and Czechoslovakia. Some resorts in Romania and Yugoslavia attract some foreign visitors, but very few from the West.

North American skiing has so far attracted few foreigners, although the Laurentian region of Quebec and some other Canadian resorts attract U.S. tourists from the East and Midwest. The other continents have seen some development of their winter sports potential in recent years, but this is mainly of regional or national rather than international importance. In South America the ski resorts of the Andean region of Chile and Argentina have some potential to attract tourists from other Latin American countries.

Development of Winter Sports Resorts and Centers

It should be noted that suitable conditions of climate, snow, and terrain are not enough to guarantee the success of a particular location as a winter sports resort. Much capital must be invested in the form of hotels with central heating, ski lifts, snow plows to keep access roads clear, and special care for the ski slopes (Blanchard: 1958, p. 202). At some resorts snow-making machines are used to reinforce inadequate snow cover on the slopes or snow may even be brought in from areas where it is abundant. Besides, the prospect of good skiing is not enough to attract many people to a winter sports resort, and night clubs, restaurants, and bars are important features of most of the larger resorts. There are, however, two main types of winter sports bases: the village, with a self-contained life and transportation system, which can best be thought of as a "resort" and the much larger area, with ski lift stations far apart and linked by public transportation, which has more of the nature of a "center." A variant of the latter is the "created center," built from scratch on an empty mountain side (Heller: 1969, p. 49). The "created center" is found in its most extreme form in France and Italy, where small urban-type settlements with skyscrapers have been developed virtually in the wilderness. One of the most spectacular of these is La Plagne in the Tarantaise Valley of Savoie, with skyscraper apartment buildings, a shopping center with covered arcades, including boutiques with the latest fashions, and a central plaza where all the ski runs end. In Italy, Sestriere has been developed along the same lines. These "created centers" are more compact than some of the other large centers such as Davos and St. Moritz, but they are typical Latin developments in the sense that they are an attempt to reproduce an urban way of life in the wilds. In Austria and Switzerland the architecture of resorts and centers is more traditional and in keeping with the rest of the human landscape. Austria in particular encourages the natural growth of existing villages rather than the construction of new centers. In general the large center appeals to the tourist who wishes a sophisticated after-ski night life, and the smaller resort may appeal to the person who desires only good skiing.

Some winter sports resorts have been moving from the development of hotels as the main form of lodging for tourists to the construction of apartments and condominiums. In the United States complexes of condominiums have been built near major ski resorts in mountain states such as Colorado, but have not proved as popular as hoped. In some European ski resorts the richer clientele from the big cities often own their own apartments which they use themselves or rent to others.

Safety is one of the problems inherent in the development of new centers. Apart from the question of preventing accidents on the slopes, there is the much more serious problem of avalanches. Recent major tragedies, in the French Alps in particular, where avalanches overwhelmed ski resorts causing destruction of buildings and loss of life, have drawn attention to the lack of safety planning in locating new ski resorts and centers.

Earlier we mentioned cross-country skiing, which has recently become very popular in North America. Although ski touring and cross-country ski racing has been extremely popular for many years in Scandinavia, it was virtually unknown in North America and Alpine Europe until the early 1970's. Its main attractions are that equipment is considerably cheaper than for downhill skiing; it is good exercise in the fresh air in pleasant surroundings; it is not dangerous; and as long as there is some snow, it can be carried out on almost any type of terrain, including flat country. It is this last feature that makes cross-country skiing independent of resorts. It does not require ski lifts and prepared runs and as long as some accessible country can be found, the skier may not have to travel far from home. Cross-country skiing, thus, is much more important as a local form of recreation than as an attractor of foreign tourists. Downhill skiing still remains much more significant as a generator of international tourist traffic.

Some mention should be made of snowmobiling, a winter sport which has shown such rapid growth in North America recently. So far this sport has been confined mainly to the flat or slightly hilly regions of the northern United States and Canada. Apart from North America the only region where snowmobiling has seen some growth, principally as a means of transportation, is northern Scandinavia. It is not a sport which can be carried on effectively in mountainous areas, and being mechanized, requires considerable service facilities. It has become necessary to control the use of these potentially dangerous machines and special terrain and trails are being developed for their use. Damage to the environment and excessive noise are also problems which are difficult to control. Snowmobiling has not yet developed into a sport attracting foreign tourists in any number and it is doubtful if it will ever challenge skiing as a major international sport. It offers little as a form of exercise and requires little skill in return for a large financial expenditure on equipment.

Mountain regions do not always rely exclusively on their winter climate to attract visitors. Local people in regions adjacent to mountainous areas use the mountains to escape the summer heat. Darjeeling and Simla in the Himalayas were developed as summer resorts for the British seeking relief from the summers of the plains, and the Blue Mountains of Australia and the Adirondacks and Catskill Mountains of New York State contain resorts serving the populations of the Sydney and New York metropolitan areas, respectively. Although these resorts were developed mainly to serve a regional population, in some cases they attract foreign tourists as well.

The importance of climatic factors in the location of tourism has much to do with the seasonal nature of tourism. The summer still remains the peak period of tourist activity and in industrial Europe and North America June, July, and August are the main vacation period. This is, of course, not only because the summer is the warmest period of the year, but because most persons are given their vacations from work at that time. In some countries, such as France, the Scandianvian countries and New Zealand, almost the entire nation takes it vacation during a one-month period in the summer, with a resultant strain on tourist and transportation facilities. As noted above, the tourist facilities which cater to summer tourism are often not the ones which serve the winter tourist. Thus, many tourist resorts have a short but intensive season. Winter tourism appeals mainly to the young and to the sportsman and even with the great rise of interest in winter sports it may never have the popularity of the more varied activities that can be carried on in summer. The winter season does not compete in intensity of tourist activity with the summer.

That the southern hemisphere experiences its seasons at the opposite time to those of the northern hemisphere might suggest the possibility of refugees from the northern winter seeking the sun south of the equator, but this difference in seasons has little influence on the pattern of world tourism at the moment (Zachinyayev and Fal'kovich: 1972, pp. 44–45).

THE ATTRACTIONS OF THE LANDSCAPE

Apart from climate and terrain, there are other aspects of the physical environment which are important in the development of tourism. In particular, the landscape or scenery of a region has much to do with its attraction for the tourist. The word "landscape" is used here in the sense of a tract of country considered as scenery. A seaside resort or a winter sports center adds to its attractions if the countryside around it creates a pleasant impression. The beauty of the Alps not only adds to the popularity of its winter sports resorts, but attracts many visitors to these same resorts during the summer months, when the excitement of skiing is replaced by the quieter pleasures of walking amid spectacular scenery. The growth of the popularity of the Dalmatian coast of Yugoslavia is due not only to the sun and the beaches but also to the rugged beauty of the coastal mountains. Many regions, which offer little in the way of good climate or exciting sports, have built up a tourist industry virtually on scenery alone. Such regions are the Scottish Highlands, the English Lake District, the Norwegian fjords, Iceland, and, to a lesser extent, the Rocky Mountains. Resorts have arisen in some of these regions which offer little else than scenery, such as Pitlochry in Scotland, Interlaken in Switzerland and Keswick in the Lake District.

Water plays an important role in forming an attractive landscape. The sea, lakes, and rivers not only add to the visual beauty of a region but also offer the possibilities of swimming, sailing, canoeing, and fishing. Hence, the popularity not only of the sea coast and other large bodies of water, such as the Great Lakes, the Lake of Geneva or Lake Balaton, but also of such regions as the Finnish lakes, the Scottish lochs, the Italian lakes, and the Andean lake district of Bariloche. Forest areas also have considerable attractions for relaxation and sport. In North America the development of state parks and wilderness areas has taken place largely in response to demand for forest scenery. In the case of wilderness areas there is the added attraction, at least for some people, of isolation and solitude combined with an element of "roughing it." For more information on the use and misuse of wilderness areas, see *Wilderness as Sacred Space*, by Linda H. Graber (1976).

Apart from the pleasures of viewing the scenery of a region in general, there are certain specific natural phenomena which may draw tourists, such as volcanoes, waterfalls, caves, and canyons. Examples are the Grand Canyon in the U.S., Vesuvius in Italy, Niagara Falls in the U.S. and Canada, Mammoth Caves in Kentucky, the geysers of Iceland and New Zealand, the Great Barrier Reef of Australia, or the Plitvice Lakes of northern Yugoslavia. Some of these phenomena, such as Niagara Falls or the Grand Canyon, are impressive enough to be a major attraction on their own, but in most cases they are visited in the course of a general tour. This is especially true if they are located in a region which also offers other features of interest to the tourist.

The particular fauna or flora of a region sometimes draw tourists. In Kenya and other countries of southern Africa wildlife safaris are rapidly increasing in popularity, the camera being substituted in most cases for the gun. Game reserves often provide accommodations and services for tourists. The Arctic and Antarctic regions attract a small but significant number of tourists to view the icy wastes, the polar bears, or the penguins. The Amazon, with its exotic rainforest vegetation and its wildlife, is also seeing an increase in its tourist trade. On a less exotic level, the tulip fields of Holland or cherry blossom time in Japan or Washington, D.C. are added attractions to the other sights.

HUNTING AND FISHING

Apart from the pleasure of viewing animals in their natural habitat, there is the added attraction for some people of hunting them. Although hunting remains basically a local sport, there are persons who are willing to pay for the privilege of shooting big game in Africa, bear, boar and chamois in the Caucasus, or grouse in Scotland. In particular the Soviet Union and other East European countries, such as Poland and Hungary, offer hunting vacations to Western tourists who are willing to pay the high prices. The attraction is the possibility of shooting species of animals which have vanished or are in short supply in Western countries. For example, the Polish government permits a limited hunting of the European bison which at one time was almost extinct and is now increasing in numbers in a forest preserve in eastern Poland.

Fishing attracts tourists to both the sea and to inland waters. Again, fishing is primarily a local pastime, but several countries have developed it as a significant branch of tourism. In Europe countries such as Ireland, Scotland, and Norway attract foreigners to fish their salmon and trout rivers and streams, and many Americans travel to Canada for the pleasure of fishing in unspoiled waters and wild natural surroundings. River and lake fishing is limited primarily to the northern countries where physical conditions are conducive to the breeding of sport fish such as trout and salmon.

Sea fishing as a sport of international significance is located mainly in the tropics or sub-tropics. The deep-sea game fish, such as swordfish or tuna, are found in southern waters. Attempts to popularize shark fishing in northern waters have not proved very successful. Spearfishing by divers equipped with snorkels or breathing apparatus is also a predominantly southern sport, but is confined to onshore waters and does not involve game fish.

Although hunting and fishing may constitute very important branches of a country's internal tourism, they have less significance as attractors of foreign tourists.

The physical attractions of a particular region may appeal to some persons and not to others. Attitudes may vary from individual to individual within a particular culture, depending on perception of an attractive place or environment in which to spend a vacation. Although the sea, and lakes or rivers are usually perceived as desirable features for vacation resorts, there are people who are not interested in the presence of water and who may even find it distasteful. The author has heard the view expressed that a seaside resort is only "half a place" because its hinterland is only half that of an inland resort. Some persons find a mountain landscape too confining and may even experience a type of claustrophobia in mountain valleys.

The perception of the attractiveness of places from the point of view of tourism has been little studied as a phenomenon. The work of Gould and White (1974) on the subject of mental maps suggests the possibility of constructing mental maps of a country, region or continent which would indicate the most desirable places for a vacation as perceived by the population of selected places or regions. In many cases these mental maps would not differ greatly from those which indicate preferences for areas for living and working. However, mental maps have generally been constructed on the basis of a single country, whereas mental maps for the purposes of international tourism would involve the perception of foreign areas and places. Gould and White touch on the theme of perception of residential desirability in Europe from the point of view of Swedes, West Germans and Italians (1974, pp. 181–86).

Although attitudes may vary from individual to individual within a particular culture, there are still clearly identifiable attitudes towards the natural environment which differ from culture to culture (Lowenthal: 1962–63, pp. 19–23). The seaside has a particular attraction for the British, partly because of their long association with the sea and partly because of its relative accessibility. The forests are particularly popular with the Swedes and Finns, who value the isolation of a forest cottage during the summer months. The love of northern nature among the Scandinavians is, however, balanced by a love of the southern sun, which sends them in large numbers to the south of Europe, if possible during the long, dark northern winter. The Italians and some other peoples of Latin culture have neither a particular admiration for untamed nature nor a desire for isolation, and prefer more sophisticated pleasures. Hence the urbanized nature of most Italian winter sports centers and the necessity of good restaurants and cafes in resorts catering to Italian tourists. Tourists from Moslem countries also have a perception of recreational attractions which are characteristically different from those of the inhabitants of other culture regions (Ritter, 1974). In spite of these differences in national attitudes, the modern tourist industry has by advertising created a mass demand for sun or snow which embraces the nationals of most countries of the industrialized West.

SPAS AND HEALTH RESORTS

One component of the physical environment which was once a major attractor of tourists, but which has a more limited significance, is mineralized water, found in springs or tapped by wells. By the seventeenth century people developed a widespread conviction of the medicinal value of various varieties of mineral waters, either for drinking or for bathing and began to visit such spas, the general name given to places where these waters occurred. As the name suggests, Spa in Belgium was one of the earliest of these medicinal watering-places, but the spa saw much early development in England. Bath and Tunbridge Wells became the most fashionable. The clientele of the spas can be numbered among the earliest tourists in Europe (Robinson: 1972, p. 383). On the continent certain spas became world-famous and attracted a rich and fashionable clientele from abroad, especially during the latter half of the nineteenth century. In general, spas also offered their clientele parks and gardens, concerts, theatrical performances, and other recreation, the quality of which helped to determine a spa's popularity. English and American spas in particular were more social than therapeutic (Lowenthal: 1962, p. 127).

With the development of modern methods of medical treatment and a lack of faith in the curative powers of mineral waters, the spas have ceased to attract the clientele of the past. This is particularly true in Great Britain and the United States, whereas in Central and Eastern Europe some spas still retain considerable popularity. For example, the Czech spa of Karlovy Vary (Karlsbad) still attracts a large number of tourists, not only from the Soviet bloc countries, but also from West Germany. The Germans in particular retain a strong belief in the curative powers of mineral springs and Karlovy Vary offers a cheaper vacation than does a German spa. Pieštany in Slovakia treats rheumatic complaints with mudbaths and, strangely enough, has a large clientele from the Arab countries. The necessity of visiting spas to drink the water is offset to a great extent by the practice of bottling the waters and selling them cheaply to a wide public.

Along with the spa can be classed the sanatorium, which, although scarcely a tourist attraction, nevertheless uses a "healthy" climate to attract persons suffering from certain diseases, especially those of the lungs. The Alpine region, and Switzerland in particular, contains a large number of sanatoria specializing in the treatment of tuberculosis. These sanatoria achieved their greatest popularity among foreigners during the inter-war period, before the development of antibiotics. In recent years the necessity of sanatorium treatment has greatly diminished, although some sanatoria are used as convalescent homes or as health resorts for children. The sanatorium has ceased to be a major attractor of foreign visitors.

URBAN CULTURAL AND HISTORICAL ATTRACTIONS

It is impossible to estimate with any accuracy the number of tourists who move from one country to another in response to the attractions of the physical environment alone. There are few countries which do not have some man-made attractions to offer the visitor, and in any decision to visit another country cultural factors have a certain influence. This influence may be the major one, as in the case of a person who visits a city to attend the theater or visit the art galleries, or marginal, as in the case of the visitor to a Spanish beach resort who attends a bullfight. In the case of a large number of tourists who simply want a couple of weeks on the beach in the sun, the choice of country is probably dictated by the cheapest package deal which they can get from a tourist agency. As already noted, the isolation of many resorts from the surrounding region and its population makes it immaterial to many tourists which country they are visiting. However, even the most isolated and self-contained resort usually arranges some cultural attractions for the tourist. For example, the resort of Mamaia on the Black Sea coast of Romania provides special plane and bus trips for its visitors to such places as Bucharest, the Danube Delta, and the monasteries of northern Moldavia.

Urban Tourism

Apart from the large numbers of tourists who travel abroad to find a natural environment which they do not have at home, there are many who visit other countries primarily because of their cultural attractions. Many of these tourists find what they are seeking in urban centers rather than in the countryside. These people form the basis of the important urban tourist industry.

It is difficult to itemize all the factors which attract people to certain cities. Apart from the buildings, churches, art galleries, museums, theaters, restaurants, and shops which individually or collectively interest and attract tourists, many cities have an individual character and atmosphere which transcend the mere sum of their buildings and other physical attractions. An obvious example is Paris. It is doubtful if the average tourist visits the city with the specific intention of seeing the Eiffel Tower or visiting the Louvre or the Folies Bergère. He does so because he wishes to experience the atmosphere and spirit of the legendary city, about which he has heard so much in song and story. The same is true to a certain degree of other world cities, such as London, Rome, Venice, New York, or Amsterdam. This atmosphere is difficult to define, being a combination of visual impressions based on pleasant or characteristic architecture, attractively laid-out streets or pcituresque canals, along with restaurants and cafés serving good food and drink and also the life-style of the inhabitants. The organizations and agencies responsible for propagating urban tourism know the characteristics of these places well and their advertising stresses the atmosphere and the character of the city they wish to sell to the tourist.

From the viewpoint of tourism, cities can be divided into two major groups: old and modern. Old cities, such as Rome, Athens, Venice, or Jerusalem attract the tourist mainly with their ancient ruins, castles, classical architecture, palaces, museums, and art galleries, whereas modern cities, such as New York, Chicago, West Berlin, or Düsseldorf, offer modern architecture, theaters, department stores, boutiques, luxury hotels, restaurants, and night clubs. Of course, many old cities combine the attractions of old and new, such as Paris, Rome, London, or Amsterdam. These cities are the main centers of mass urban tourism. Many tourists not only visit these cities while on tour, but may regard a stay in one of them as their main tourist goal. Many visitors to France or Great Britain see little of these countries outside Paris or London, although the increased mobility of the modern tourist has resulted in shorter stays in more places in a given country.

Apart from the world cities of major interest to tourists, there are many smaller cities of historical or cultural interest, which are generally visited as part of a wider tour of a country or region. Such are York, Stratford-on-Avon, and Oxford in England, Edinburgh in Scotland, Bruges and Ghent in Belgium, Florence and Pisa in Italy, Granada in Spain, and Heidelberg in Germany, to name only a few. In some cases these towns are known for a particular feature of attraction, such as the Leaning Tower of Pisa, the Alhambra in Granada, or the Castle and Holyrood Palace in Edinburgh.

Youth Tourism

An aspect of western urban tourism of recent origin is the so-called "youth" tourism. Although numbers of young people with packs, bundles, or suitcases can be found hitchhiking along most of the main highways of Europe, their goal is generally the city. Cities such as Paris, London, Copenhagen, and, above all, Amsterdam became the rallying-points for young people from many countries, including the United States, during the 1960's. They formed the clientele for cheap hotels and hostels and in the summer slept in the parks and streets, local police permitting. In Amsterdam the Vondelpark was virtually turned into a dormitory for the young tourists in the summer months. Some countries attempted to restrict this "youth" tourism as it brought in little money and created problems, such as drug use and theft. In the case of Amsterdam, however, many conventional tourists came considerable distances to be shocked by the "hippies," who in themselves had become a tourist attraction.

This type of youth tourism has changed considerably in the 1970's. The hippies have been replaced largely by a more conventional type of young traveller who is less willing to sleep under a tree in a park, but who nevertheless is looking for cheap lodgings and restaurants and is willing to hitchhike. The travel agencies and transportation companies are aware of this market and have offered cheap air fares, special prices for passes on the European railroads, and other attractions. Special guidebooks on several countries have been written for young tourists with information on inexpensive eating-places, night-life, how to meet the opposite sex, and other useful hints.

A sub-category of cities with tourist attractions are the cities of the non-Western world, with their exotic architecture, food and customs. These are the Moslem cities of the Middle East and Africa, such as Tangier, Marrakesh, Tunis, or Istanbul, cities of the Far East, such as Tokyo, Hong Kong, or Bangkok, and cities of Latin America, such as Rio de Janeiro, Bogota, or Mexico City. These cities may combine aspects of ancient and modern, but it is the exotic elements of these places that attract most Western tourists.

Some urban areas offer what are best described as "economic" attractions. These include such features as ports and harbors, airports and trade fairs, as well as interesting industries, such as automobile factories, salt mines, and breweries (Christaller: 1955, p. 3). In many port cities groups can take organized tours of the harbor by boat, and visits to large airports to watch the planes take off and land are a popular form of family recreation with many city people. These "economic" attractions are of little significance in international tourism, except for the trade fairs, such as the Leipziger Messe, which provides about the only reason for foreigners to visit that city. A few foreign tourists visit such places as Wieliczka salt mines near Cracow in Poland or the Chartreuse distilleries in France, but most of these visits are only incidents on a tour with other major objectives.

Religious Pilgrimages

Some urban centers have an ancient history as sites of objects of religious veneration and thus have become the object of pilgrimages. Classic examples for the Christian world are the tombs of the Apostles at Rome, the relics of the Three Kings at Cologne, Germany, the tomb of St. James at Santiago de Compostela in Spain, the tomb of St. Thomas in Canterbury, England, the house of the Virgin at Loreto in Italy, and the highest goal of all medieval Christians, the Holy Sepulchre in Jerusalem. Of these, only Rome and the Holy Land still attract pilgrims from abroad in any numbers. Of much greater significance in terms of modern religious tourism are the shrines of more recent origin, such as Fatima in Portugal and Lourdes in France. The latter shrine is the supreme example of an object of religious veneration forming the basis of a major tourist industry. Special trians bring the sick and the faithful from all over Europe and their needs are catered to by many hotels, boarding houses, hospitals and nursing homes, restaurants, and shops selling religious souvenirs. Numerous Americans visit Lourdes and Fatima on organized trips.

The Moslem world has several places of religious pilgrimage, such as the mosque in Kairouan in Tunisia and the Dome of the Rock in Jerusalem, but these are overshadowed by the great pilgrimage of *hajj* to Mecca. Large numbers of pilgrims still visit Mecca annually, coming not only from the Middle East and North Africa but from Pakistan, Bangladesh, Malaysia, and Indonesia. The pilgrims travel in ships, often highly overcrowded, to the Red Sea port of Jidda, which is connected by rail with Mecca, or by charter plane directly to Mecca. For the average pilgrim, accommodations in Mecca are primitive, consisting usually of a tent in a large camp, although in recent years the Saudi Arabian government has improved accommodations and services in the city. The places of pilgrimage of other religions, such as Banaras for the Hindus, or Buddha's footprint in Ceylon for the Buddhists, have little significance as centers for international tourism.

RURAL HISTORICAL AND CULTURAL ATTRACTIONS

Apart from buildings of historical interest in urban areas, either because of their architecture or their connection with historical characters or events, there are many places in the country with historical associations. Chief among these are castles, palaces, abbeys, monasteries, and country houses, either of architectural interest or associated with a particular person, family or period. Examples are the French chateaux of the Loire Valley, Malmaison near Paris, with its relics of Napoleon, the castle of Chillon in Switzerland, immortalized by Byron, and the many palaces and country houses open to the public in the British Isles. In order to add to the attractions of country houses with no particular historical significance and to pay for the expenses of their upkeep, many of their owners have devised added entertainments for the visitors. The Marquis of Beaulieu has opened a zoo and a museum of old cars on his estate in Hampshire, U. K., while other country houses offer medieval style dinners or tea with the duke.

Apart from buildings and estates there are other places of historical importance in the countryside. Battlefields, such as Waterloo (Belgium), Verdun and the Somme (France), and Gettysburg (U.S.), and the military cemeteries associated with them are of interest to many tourists, especially those with family connections in the case of more recent battles. The sites of concentration camps from World War II still receive many visitors. Oswięcim (Auschwitz) near Cracow is still of major interest to tourists visiting Poland.

In the developing countries the major historical tourist attractions are mainly the ruins of ancient civilizations, such as the Pyramids and Sphinx of Egypt, Angkor Wat in Cambodia, Borobodur in Java, Machu Picchu in Peru, or Palmyra in Syria. A lack of knowledge of the more recent histories of the countries of Asia and Africa limits the interest of the American or European tourist in more modern monuments and relics.

Just as a beautiful natural landscape may please the tourist, so may a cultural one. Part of the attraction of the Alps lies in the contrast between wild nature and the cozy, comfortable villages of the inhabitants. The highly artificial, well-organized landscapes of the polderlands of the Netherlands or the rice-lands of the Far East have a charm of their own, while many picturesque villages in the British Isles, such as those of the Cotswolds or Devon, are in themselves objects of tourism.

"Ethnic" Tourism

Some rural areas offer what might be described as "ethnic" attractions, such as a colorful folk-life, native costumes, house-types, customs, regional foods and drink, fiestas, and wine festivals. In Europe many folk costumes and customs are maintained specially for the tourist, and folkloric events, such as dance or song festivals, are purposely organized to attract visitors, although in some cases the local people are genuinely interested in their own folklore. Much of this rural culture has been transferred to the city and many East European countries in particular maintain dance groups, choirs, and folk orchestras in the major cities to entertain the foreign tourists. In Asia, Africa, and Latin America, where an active folk-life still exists in the rural areas of many countries, this artificial stimulus is not so necessary. In North America about the only areas with genuine ethnic attractions are the Southwest, with its Indian and Mexican population, and French Canada. Other ethnic attractions, such as offered by German, Dutch, or Swiss communities in the Northeast and Midwest may be artificial and some are not even authentic.

Another type of "ethnic" tourism consists of the return of people to the country of their origin. Much of the flow of American tourists to Ireland is made up of immigrants and other persons of Irish origin paying a nostalgic visit to the old country. Immigrant societies organize charter flights for their members to a number of countries, including the countries of Eastern Europe. In recent years even the Soviet Union has organized tours of the Ukraine and the Baltic States designed to attract persons originally from these regions or with family connections there.

SPORTING EVENTS

Major sporting events such as the Olympic Games or, to a lesser degree, the Wimbledon tennis championships or international soccer matches, attract visitors who may also spend some extra time in the country for sightseeing. However, the proximity of the site of the event to major regions of tourist origin will influence the number of visitors. For example, the

Winter Olympics at Sapporo in northern Japan were too distant to attract a large number of European tourists.

ARTIFICIALLY CREATED ATTRACTIONS

Some mention should be made of the artificially created attractions of such institutions as Disneyland in California and Disney World in Florida. These amusement centers, which have proved to be prime attractions for foreign visitors to the United States, including heads of state, are an elaboration on the traditional urban amusement park, such as the old Vauxhall Gardens in London or Tivoli in Copenhagen, with a suggestion of the open-air museum, such as Skansen in Stockholm or Greenfield Village in Detroit. They Disney creations are, however, highly artificial in that all their indoor and outdoor exhibits and amusements rely little on the physical and cultural features of the areas where they have been developed, except that the sites have been located in areas with a good climate all the year round. Disneyland and its counterparts, including some of the "Western" towns inhabited by "cowboys" which one finds scattered throughout the Midwest and West of the United States, are a new development in the tourist field, in that they can create a major tourist attraction in an area which has virtually no physical or cultural features of note.

A less desirable, but nevertheless important aspect of tourism must not be overlooked. This is the number of establishments often found in frontier areas devoted to gambling, drinking, prostitution or the sale of goods or services unobtainable or more expensive in the neighboring country. In North America this situation not only exists between the United States on one hand and Canada and Mexico on the other, but between the states themselves. Examples are the gambling casinos of Reno and Las Vegas, Nevada, the bars along the state lines which attract minors from one state who are of legal drinking age in the next state, and the supermarkets of northern Illinois which sell margarine to Wisconsin housewives who cannot buy it legally in their own state.

On the international level the red-light districts of such towns as Tijuana, Ciudad Juarez, Nuevo Laredo, and others just over the Mexican border are said to bring in an annual revenue of $900 million, or 60 percent of Mexico's tourist revenue, and attract some 90 million Americans (Young: 1973, p. 122). These figures are probably exaggerated as it must be difficult to distinguish this type of tourist from the many other Americans who cross the border for more innocent pleasures. Besides, statistics for visitors to Mexico by car are not accurate. The phenomenon of "frontier prostitution" exists also along the Belgian side of the Belgian-Dutch border, where a number of red-light cafés cater to the Dutch from the towns of the southern Netherlands. A strange twist to this situation is the existence of the large number of sex-shops and pornographic book-stores which have been opened in towns on the Dutch side of the border to cater to Belgian tourists. This type of tourist traffic is generally the result of differences in national or local laws or sometimes in national attitudes and customs.

Crossing a national frontier to get cheaper drink or food or to be free of legal restrictions on drinking hours is an important factor in a limited number of cases. One example in North America is the small detached fragment of the state of Washington known as Point Roberts, which is located at the end of a small peninsula south of Vancouver in British Columbia. This two-mile long, three-mile wide strip of U.S. territory has some 200 inhabitants, but over one and a half million Canadians a year visit it. The reason is that dancing is not permitted in bars in British Columbia and they are closed on Sundays. A couple of the largest bars in the United States are located in Point Roberts, offering dancing every night to well-known bands. On a larger scale, this type of tourism exists between England and some of the French and Belgian channel ports, such as Calais, Boulogne, and Ostend, where tourists from Dover and other southern English towns on cheap day or other short-period trips can drink inexpensive drinks all day and night, generally starting on the boat, where drinks are free of the high British taxes on liquor, wine, and beer. This type of "alcoholic tourism" has very questionable value. It generally attracts the worst type of tourist and often results in drunkenness, disturbance of the peace, and even violence or vandalism, and alienates the local inhabitants, whose opinion of a particular nation may be formed from the tourists which they encounter.

A more innocuous form of border tourist is the shopper who wishes to take advantage of cheaper prices in a foreign country. An example is Calexico, California, which attracts shoppers from Mexicali in Mexico. In 1974 the stores of the town, which has a population of 13,000, had total receipts of $54 million. Every day some 50,000 Mexicans cross the border to buy eggs, meat, and groceries because of their better quality and lower price. Mexican peddlers from the rural areas come by train and bus to Mexicali, cross the border to shop for goods which they later sell back in their local villages. On a broader front, the same phenomenon can be seen in border areas in Europe. For example, Trieste in Italy attracts shoppers from Yugoslavia. New tariff agreements between West European countries have limited this type of tourism in recent years.

OTHER FACTORS OF ATTRACTION OR REPULSION

Apart from the major physical and cultural factors which attract tourists to a particular country or region there are a few minor, but nevertheless important, ones which should be mentioned. One of these is the economic level of development of the country to be visited. Low prices compared with those of the country of origin or with those of competing tourist countries may be a strong attraction for tourists. For example, the very low level of the Argentinian peso compared with the U.S. dollar during 1975 and 1976 has attracted a large number of tourists from surrounding Latin American countries who enjoy a cheap vacation and return laden with goods bought in Argentina. In Europe, many people choose Austria for a winter vacation because of the relatively low level of prices compared with West Germany and Switzerland. The lower prices of the East European countries also partially account for their increasing popularity with West European and American tourists. The drop in the value of the British pound has made Britain an attractive country for foreign visitors.

However, a low level of prices may reflect a low standard of living, and this in turn may be associated in many people's minds with poor food, unsafe drinking water, a lack of hygiene in restaurants, or dirty bed linen. It must be admitted that in some cases this association is true, and many a person's vacation has been ruined by intestinal disorders or even serious illness. The fact that many of the developing countries which are trying to attract tourists are located in the tropics means that disease can be a serious hazard and many tourists are not keen to visit a country for which innoculations against various diseases are necessary. This problem has been partially overcome in some areas by the developing self-contained resorts, where the developer can exercise some control over hygiene, food preparation, and laundry.

The general standard of tourist services is also important. If hotels are badly built, faucets do not work, hot water is not available, roads are bad, and gasoline stations few, the news spreads by word of mouth or through travel articles in newspapers. Potential visitors may decide that the physical attractions of the place may not be sufficient to outweigh these other factors. In other words, factors of repulsion may be as important in some cases as factors of attraction in explaining tourist flows.

REFERENCES

ANAN'YEV, M. A., 1968, *Mezhdunarodnyy Turizm* (International Tourism), Moscow: Izdatel'stovo "Mezhdunarodnyye otnosheniya."

BLANCHARD RAOUL, 1958, *Les Alpes et Leur Destin* (The Alps and their Destiny), Paris: Librairie Arthème Fayrad.

CHRISTALLER, WALTER, 1955, "Beitrage zu einer Geographie des Fremdenverkehrs" (Contributions to a Geography of Tourism), *Erdkunde*, vol. 9, no. 1, pp. 1-19.

FRANCKE, LINDA, 1976, "Sun Spots," *Newsweek*, January 5, pp. 44-50.

GOULD, PETER, AND RODNEY WHITE, 1974, *Mental Maps*, Harmondsworth: Penguin Books.

GRABER, LINDA H., 1976, *Wilderness as Sacred Space*, Monograph No. 8. Washington, DC: Association of American Geographers.

HELLER, MARK, 1969, *Ski*, London: Faber and Faber.

IANCU, MIHAI AND SILVIA, 1967, "Citeva consideratii asupra geografiei turismului" (Several considerations about the geography of tourism), *Studia Universitatis Babes-Bolayi*, series geologia-geographia, no. 2, pp. 371-75.

LATOUCHE, ROBERT, 1963, "Un colloque scientifique sur le tourisme à Nice" (A scientific colloquy on tourism in Nice), *Revue de Geographie Alpine*, vol. 51, no. 2, pp. 369-70.

LAVERY, PATRICK, 1974, "Resorts and Recreation," in P. Lavery (ed.), *Recreational Geography*, New York: John Wiley and Sons, pp. 167-96.

LOWENTHAL, DAVID, 1962, "Tourists and Thermalists," *Geographical Review*, vol. LII, no. 1, pp. 124-27.

PERRY, ALLEN H., 1971, "Climatic Influences on the Scottish Ski-ing Industry," *Scottish Geographical Magazine*, vol. 87, no. 3, pp. 197-201.

RITTER, WIGAND, 1966, *Fremdenverkehr in Europa* (Tourism in Europe), Leiden: A. W. Sijthoff.

ROBINSON, H., 1972, *Geography for Business Studies*, London: Macdonald and Evans.

SIMPSON, ANTHONY, 1968, *The New Europeans*, London: Hodder and Stoughton.

YOUNG, GEORGE, 1973, *Tourism: Blessing or Blight?* Harmondsworth: Penguin Books.

ZACHINYAYEV, P. N., AND N. S. FAL'KOVICH, 1972, *Geografiya Mezhdunarodnogo Turizma* (Geography of International Tourism), Moscow: Izdatel'stvo "Mysl'."

8

THE DESTINATION MIX:
Attractions and Services
for the Traveler

At a destination there is a mix of interdependent elements. The elements are interdependent because in order to produce a satisfying vacation experience, all elements must be present.

The destination is composed of:

Attractions

Facilities

Infrastructure

Transportation

Hospitality

Attractions draw visitors to an area. Facilities serve the needs of the visitors while away from home. Infrastructure and transportation are necessary to help ensure accessibility of the destination to the visitor. Hospitality is concerned with the way in which tourist services are delivered to the visitor.

THE TOURISM SYSTEM

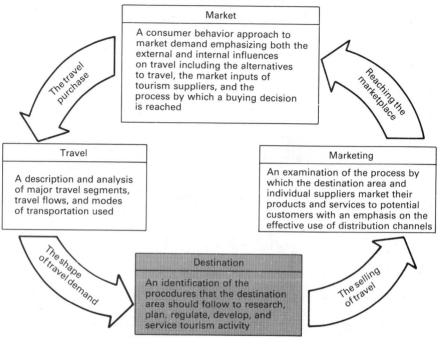

ATTRACTIONS

The central aspects of tourism are attractions. Attractions, by definition, have the ability to draw people to them. Although attractions for the tourist concern the satisfactions perceived from various experiences, the task for the developer and designer is to create an environment made up in part of "attractions" that will provide an opportunity for the tourist to enjoy a visit. The addition at a site of factors (services, transportation, hospitality) other than attractions will help ensure that enjoyment.

Attractions have many characteristics. As mentioned above, they tend to draw visitors to them—they aim to serve the recreational needs of visitors. They can to a large extent be developed anywhere and act as a growth inducer, tending to be developed first in a tourist region.

Scope

The way in which attractions are characterized has implications for development and marketing. Attractions can be characterized in terms of their scope, ownership, permanency, and drawing power. A typology is suggested in Figure 8.1. Destinations may be primary or secondary

FIGURE 8.1 Typology of Attractions

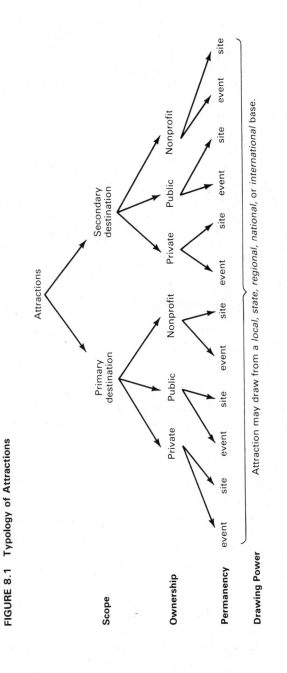

Scope

Ownership

Permanency

Drawing Power

Attraction may draw from a *local, state, regional, national,* or *international* base.

(sometimes called stopover or touring destinations). A primary destination is one that is attractive enough to be the primary motivation for tourism visits, and one that is aimed at satisfying tourists for several days or longer. A secondary or stopover destination is either an interesting or a necessary place to visit on the way to a primary destination, and it aims at satisfying tourists for one to two days. It may be interesting enough to attract tourists on their way somewhere else, or it may, in fact, be a required stop on the way to a final destination. Certain areas can be primary destinations for one segment of the market or stopover destinations for other segments.

Attractions at a primary destination have to have sufficient breadth of appeals to appeal to tourists for many days. There have to be sufficient things to do and see to keep all members of the party occupied. At a stopover destination, the length of stay will be shorter and the need for a diversity of attractions is less. From a marketing viewpoint, the primary destination or attraction seeks fewer tourists staying longer periods of time, compared to the secondary destination that relies on attracting larger numbers for shorter periods of time. In terms of location, primary destinations tend to be oriented towards the location of the market (Disney World) or to the site of the resource (Aspen). Secondary destinations, although located between tourists and resources, are more reliant on their accessibility to transportation networks.

Ownership

The form of ownership of the attraction has great implications for tourism. Approximately 85 percent of all outdoor recreation lands in the U.S. are owned by the federal government. The agencies that manage this land often do not have tourism as a primary use of the land. Their outlook will determine the degree to which tourism and recreation are encouraged.

The nonprofit sector is usually oriented to some aspect of the social good. Yet when nonprofit organizations get involved in work for the social good such as historical preservation, their efforts can have great implications for tourism. Limited tourism may be a vehicle for getting sufficient revenue to continue the historical work. Care must be taken to ensure that the means does not become the end. The nonprofit organization involved may back out of the project and the resource may become overcommercialized and lose its original appeal.

The private sector's motivation is that of profit-making. The wise manager will realize that short-run profit maximization may be detrimental to the long-run success of the attraction and the destination.

Permanency

Site attractions concern attractions of a physical nature. They are largely permanent, with their locations being fixed. Event attractions are rather short in duration, and their location can be changed. Site attractions are more dependent upon the resource base. Event attractions can be developed at places more convenient to the market. Because site attractions cost more to develop in terms of both time and money than do event attractions, new tourist regions can conceivably develop event attractions as a way of publicizing the area and bringing in cash to help finance more permanent site attractions.

Drawing Power

Attractions may also be defined in terms of the distance from which they are able to draw people. Attractions may be locally, state-wide, regionally, nationally, or internationally significant. The rating is inclusive in that a national attraction will draw from the state and local level also. If proposed and existing attractions can be objectively viewed in terms of their drawing power, appropriate strategies for the marketing of existing attractions and the development mix of future attractions can be developed. Attractions do not become attractions for the purpose of tourism until a certain amount of development has occurred to make the natural resource accessible to and attractive for tourists.

Although tourists are motivated to visit a destination to satisfy various needs and wants, they are also motivated to visit a destination because of certain characteristics. The characteristics that attract tourists are:

Natural resources

Climate

Culture

History

Ethnicity

Accessibility

NATURAL RESOURCES. The natural resources of a destination provide an excellent asset to sell to tourists. When studying the landscape or scenery of an area it is important to note not only the natural resources but also the human imprints on the area, for this is also part of the scenery. In this respect it is important to point out that any change in one aspect of the scenery changes the whole landscape.

For many markets, an outstanding natural resource has been, and still is, sandy beaches. In urban areas, where children do not have the opportunity to run free in safety or the chance to see the sea, an exodus occurs on weekends and holidays to spots offering such attractions. So it is that Jones Beach becomes a weekend mecca for Manhattan residents while Manitoba advertises 100,000 lakes, together with soft warm sands and sparkling blue waters.

Two important points should be stressed when considering scenery. First, from the visitor's viewpoint, there is no cost for it. A beautiful sunset, Niagara Falls, the Grand Canyon—these cost the tourist nothing. The second point is concerned with the variety of scenery. Variety in an area can be an important selling point. In this way, Britain with a variety of views and types of countryside every few hundred yards can compete—successfully so—with such dwarfing structures as the Canadian Rockies and the Swiss Alps.

CLIMATE. Climate is perhaps the most common marketing theme used as the basis for selling a tourism area, once it has suitable tourist attractions. Although a region in some cases can be sold largely on the basis of climate, for maximum effect the area must be readily accessible to large concentrations of population. One reason for the popularity of California's coastline resorts is their proximity via automobile to millions of people. Florida, meanwhile, to attract vacationers from the northeastern and the north central states must advertise that its sun is only an hour or so away by plane.

In addition to ready accessibility, the destination area should promise something that tourists cannot get at home. In a populous center, where most people live with enough disposable income to travel, one market segment may be attracted by warm sunshine at a time when it is cold and gloomy at home while another segment may seek accentuated winter conditions of a ski resort. Conversely, when the population centers are sweltering with summer heat, one market segment may head for the seashore—Maine, Oregon, Florida, or even the Caribbean—for cooling breezes while another segment wants a mountain area, whether it's New Hampshire, the Canadian Rockies, Scotland, or Switzerland.

When considering summer weather, the most comfortable living is in the populous temperate zones of the Mediterranean, which have warm, sunny, and dry climates. Tropical conditions are too hot and too wet to sell solely on this asset, so that selling of tropical climates must be amplified with a number of other attractions, which is the case of the Caribbean.

An interesting corollary of climate advertising is that those who have left home want to be kept informed about the bad conditions they have fled. In Florida and Puerto Rico, hotels post weather conditions in northern cities during the winter. In summer, it may also be cooler in Florida and Puerto Rico than it is back home because of ocean breezes.

Recreational activities are undertaken considering the combination of natural resources and climate on hand. Over the past several years we have seen a remarkable growth in recreational pursuits in general and participative recreational pursuits in particular. This has resulted in a decline in the business of many sedentary holiday areas and the upsurge of resorts offering sporting facilities. The type of recreation facilities offered is usually determined by the nature of the surrounding countryside—skiing requires mountains, water sports need water, and so on. However, we are seeing the introduction of artificial ski slopes, "dry" ski slopes, artificial lakes for boating and fishing, and artificially stocked waters and bird and hunting grounds.

The important point to remember in selling an area on its recreational facilities is to sell a variety of pursuits, not just one. This way one does not rely solely on one sport, one market, or one season for one's business.

CULTURE. Each country has its own unique culture—a state of manners, taste, and intellectual development. Some countries are found to be more interesting culturally and better developed than others. Culture is, for practical tourism purposes, interwoven with history. Today's way of life is tomorrow's culture.

Thus, although one can "sell" the way of life of the people of a foreign land, that way of life must be radically different from the visitor's own to induce excitement and the desire to view it.

America and the Americans have always exhibited, perhaps because of their relatively young existence, an almost insatiable appetite for historical culture. With a fusing in this country of so many races from so many different lands, these groups have jealously clung to preserving their own ethnic culture. Today, however, these cultures are not guarded quite so tightly, but are sold to the rest of the country. Williamsburg, the Pennsylvania Dutch, and western ranch country demonstrate this feature remarkably well.

HISTORICAL RESOURCES. Historical resources may be defined by function into the following subdivisions: 1.) war, 2.) religion, 3.) habitation, and 4.) government. Past wars hold a fascination for many people. Depending on the chronological distance from the event, the emotions aroused range from morbid curiosity and excitement to sorrow and remembrance. Thus, people throng to the Tower of London and Edinburgh Castle to see the chamber of horrors and the bottleneck dungeons, excited by the thought of such distant gory deeds. The most popular World War II sites in Europe are Margraten in the Netherlands, Omaha Beach Ceremony in France on the site of the D-day landings in Normandy in 1944, and the Luxembourg City Ceremony, where General George S. Patton, Jr. lies buried. In America, the popularity of Arlington Cemetery in Washington, D.C., attests to the national feeling of remembrance for those who died for their country.

Since the times of the earliest pilgrimages and the travelers in Chaucer's *Canterbury Tales* pilgrims have made journeys to shrines, monuments, and cathedrals in the name of their Lord. Although religion can be a tremendous selling force, it can act negatively for the country. The obvious present example is in Northern Ireland where past demonstrations against parades commemorating William of Oranges's defeat of the militant Catholics have erupted into long, and sometimes bloody, battles that have served to disrupt trade, industry, and tourism from progressing into the area. (An interesting side-note is that after the 1967 Israeli six-day war, the number of travelers to Israel actually increased.)

Religion forms the basis for the Outdoor Biblical Museum at Nymegen, Holland, which is a beautiful and moving attempt to bring all faiths to a point where they can worship together. Visitors walk along narrow paths cut through a forest to arrive at a scene from the Bible. A minimum of figures and a natural landscape leave the visitor awestruck by the simplicity of it all.

From the simple house tour to the elaborate view of Buckingham Palace, man's natural curiosity to see the trappings of others' homes is a marketable item. Thousands will flock to the homes of Anne Hathaway and William Shakespeare, or to the houses of George Washington and Abe Lincoln, in an attempt to achieve some sense of rapport with the memory of these famous people. However, one need not be numbered amongst the dead to enjoy this admiration and visitation. The White House and Buckingham Palace are favorite tourist stops while, in Britain, many stately homes are being opened to the public and the promise of dining with a duke and thereafter spending the night in one of the state rooms is an appealing attraction to many. After the success of the movie *Mary, Queen of Scots*, the Scottish Tourist Board ran a promotion centered around "Mary, Queen of Scots country."

Visitors can also be encouraged to visit places where ficticious people lived. World Travel Tours also advertise special *Song of Norway* tours and *Sound of Music* trips to Norway and Austria, respectively. Pan Am has run tours to Dracula's Transylvania (now a part of Romania).

A nation's capital will always hold a fascination for those who desire to see where the decisions are made. The Houses of Parliament are as well known as the House of Representatives and the Kremlin. The chance to see the country's leaders in session is an experience few visitors would miss. Even on the state and local levels, council sessions can become the focal point of an educational tour, while the City Hall "you can't fight" may also be visited.

ETHNICITY. The United States is a cosmopolitan mixture of first-, second-, and third-generation Scots, Irish, Dutch, German, Russian, and so on. As such, it is easy to appeal to people's basic sentimentality to coax them "back to the homeland." The ethnic groups may be classified as first and later generations. For the first generation, no development is needed at all, for these people wish to see the area they left just as they left it.

However, first-generation travelers will generally stay with friends, and one finds that it is the later generations that will spend more money in a particular spot. This latter group of travelers, experiencing a different environment, will require some of the creature comforts afforded them at home. It should not be thought, however, that the only viable market for this kind of promotion consists of present-day U.S. citizens, though many examples of such marketing exist. One of the definite movement channels that can be readily traced is that from Ireland to New York and Boston.

In North America itself, Michigan's Tulip Festival, the Highland Games at Alma, the Beer Festival at Frankenmuth, and the weekly summer ethnic concerts in downtown Detroit show the success of a campaign on this asset.

It is possible also to spotlight movements within a country. In the United States, it is estimated that one out of every five Americans moves each year. Nor are these movements random. States like Florida, Nevada, Arizona, and California have attracted decennial population increases in the order of 50 to 80 percent, and states like Arkansas and West Virginia have suffered population decreases in the order of 6 to 10 percent. There may well be a significant market to be reached through the sentimental pull of old friends and places.

ACCESSIBILITY. The last item to consider in this section is accessibility. Though germane to every asset listed above, certain areas owe their popularity—and some their very being—to the fact that they are readily accessible to large urban areas. The development of Brighton, England, as a weekend and holiday resort despite its completely stony beach is due to its proximity to London with a potential market of 8 million people.

The accessibility of an area to a particular market should be measured in terms of time, cost, frequency, and comfort. Although attention should be paid to each factor, an area can sell on its comparative advantage in providing exceptional service in one or a combination of several of the above factors at the expense of another.

Traveling to Europe by plane, for instance, may cost more and be less comfortable than land or sea travel, but Europe is more accessible in terms of time and frequency of service. An advertisement for a sea ferry declares, "All that divides Scotland and Ireland is two-and-a-half hours." The motorist immediately knows how long it will take him to get to Ireland, and a seemingly large and time-consuming obstacle—the Irish Sea—becomes a mere two-and-a-half hour expressway.

Part of Mexico's appeal to the American market is its accessibility in terms of cost—not necessarily in terms of cost to reach the country, but in terms of what can be bought there. A two-week vacation in Mexico may be more accessible in terms of cost than fourteen days in the United States.

Other areas have become attractions because of the difficulty in reaching them. In those few cases in which lack of accessibility increases the attractiveness, the end result (the destination) should be somewhat spectacular—a magnificent view, great food, or a wonderful culture.

Development and Design

Gunn has suggested several design principles to guide the development of attractions.[1] It is important to remember that the dependencies of the attraction vary. Certain types of attractions, such as ski areas and battlefields are extremely dependent upon the resource base, but others, such as theme parks, are much less so. All attractions are, to some extent, dependent upon their relationship to the tourist's origin, upon their accessibility, and upon the number of facilities and services available. In terms of the tourist origin, the time relationship may be more important than the distance relationship. Zones of tourist origin will differ, depending upon the mode of transportation considered. A two-hour zone, for example, may include tourists 100 miles away by car and 500 miles away by plane.

As noted earlier, accessibility, although important, is more crucial to the touring destination because the time available is a major constraint.

Services and facilities tend to grow up to support the developed attraction. However, if a service center is already developed, its location may effect the development of a new attraction.

Attractions tend to be clustered for several reasons. First, there is an increased desire on the part of tourists to do more in one place. Second, clustering allows a destination a better opportunity to satisfy more people. To fully explore a major theme, a variety of different attractions may be required. A group of museums each exploring part of an overall

---

[1]Gunn, *Tourism Planning*, and Clare A. Gunn, *Vacationscape: Designing Tourist Regions* (Austin, Texas, The University of Texas, 1972).

theme is more effective than one. A cluster of different but related historic buildings may be necessary to fully explore and explain a particular time in history. Different rides, clustered into a theme park, are necessary to appeal to all of the senses.

The extent of clustering depends upon the type of destination involved. For the primary destination, clustering is obviously more important. This is particularly true if accessibility is dependent upon modes of transportation oriented towards mass tourism. Destinations that rely on tourists arriving by plane, boat, or train will be apt to develop more clusters of attractions than those appealing to the motorist.

Events

Events can be developed for several reasons. Events may be staged to make money, to celebrate particular holidays, seasons, or historical events, to provide cultural or educational experiences, or to unite and give a feeling of pride to a particular community. An event may seek to combine these reasons. It is important that objectives be developed, agreed upon, and ranked in order that subsequent conflicts over strategy can be solved by referring to the action that will help to achieve the most important objective.

An examination of special events in Illinois revealed that most events included from eight to sixteen different activities. The most common activities were parades, queen and beauty contests, carnivals with featured entertainers, lunches and dinners, musical entertainments, dancing, and children's activities.

In approximately one-third of the cases, a nonprofit corporation takes major planning responsibility. The planning of the event can take anywhere from a month to over a year. Most groups used from five to eleven committees to organize the event that involved a total of 12 to 350 people, almost all of them volunteers.

FACILITIES

While attractions draw visitors from their homes, facilities are necessary to serve these visitors away from home. Facilities tend to be oriented to attractions in their location because of the need to locate close to where the market will be. They tend to support rather than induce growth and, hence, they tend to be developed at the same time as or after the attractions are developed.

It is possible for an attraction to be a facility. A case in point would be a well-known resort hotel that not only serves to draw people to an area but satisfies their needs as well.

Lodging

While away from home, the tourist needs to eat and sleep. Sleeping accommodations can range from hotels of an international standard and condominiums, to campgrounds and the homes of friends and relatives. Lodging accounts for between one-fifth and one-fourth of total tourist expenditures, despite the fact that almost half of U.S. tourists stay in the homes of friends and relatives when taking a trip. It is vital to the success of a tourist region that a sufficient quantity of accommodations of the right quality be provided for tourist needs.

The type of accommodation provided will be determined primarily by the characteristics of the market segment being sought. Some prefer the full-amenity type of property. In destination areas these properties will tend to have greater demands placed on them in terms of room size and services offered because guests will be staying a long time. Tourists whose prime motivation is to visit friends and relatives will likely stay with them.

The type of accommodation provided is also partly determined by what the competitors are providing. A key concept to remember in marketing is that the facilities provided should at least equal those provided by the competition for the same market. The type of lodging is also determined by the transportation used by visitors to the destination. In Roman times, resting places were determined when the horse, not the rider, was tired. In the United States in the early seventeenth century, taverns were located about fifteen miles, or one day's carriage ride apart. The development of rail travel led to accommodation clusters near the stations. An increase in auto travel encouraged the roadside motel, but the growth of air travel has led to clusters of hotels and motels around airports.

Food and Beverage

More of the tourist dollar is spent on food and beverage than on any other service. It is probably of no coincidence that those states highest in per capita eating place sales are also top tourist states.

The type of food service provided will be related to tourist needs. Many areas have successfully developed menus indigenous to the area to promote local economy foods, while they also use the local items as a unique selling point.

Support Industries

Support industries refer to the facilities provided for tourists in addition to lodging, food, and beverage. These may include souvenir or duty-free shops (for goods), laundries and guides (for services), and festival areas and recreational facilities (for activities).

Support industries can be either subsistence-related by providing staple needs or requirements or pleasure-related by providing impulse or entertainment purchase opportunities.

For tourism, support industries tend to be small businesses. This fact can be both positive and negative for the destination area. It can be positive in that the encouragement of small businesses will allow for the wide distribution and sharing of the financial benefits of tourism with those in the community. On the other hand, small businesses may lack the capital and expertise required to provide a quality part of the vacation experience. Several considerations can assist in maximizing the potential of support industries. It is important that the support industries be located in places accessible to tourists. It will be necessary to observe or predict tourist movement patterns to optimally locate facilities to serve them. The number and types of facilities offered will also have to be determined relative to tourist needs. Facilities should be provided that match the quality and price level of lodging, food, and beverage operations that should themselves be provided in light of visitor expenditure levels.

If a sufficient number and mix of services is provided, the supply may actually stimulate demand or increase the length of stay of visitors by offering such a number of attractive alternatives that they will have enough things to buy and do to encourage them to stay longer. At the same time, too many facilities at one place may mean that there is insufficient sales volume to assure a reasonable rate of return for the businesses involved.

The two primary techniques for helping assure the effective development of support industries are:

Zoning and operating regulations enforced by law

Ownership or control exercised through leasing of facilities to individual entrepreneurs

The methods can in fact be combined with good results. People at destination areas may designate certain areas as being appropriate for tourist-support industries, and within those areas they may lay down restrictions as to theme, design, building height, and density; and they may place restrictions on signs in order to ensure the development of a destination that has attractions and facilities that meet expectations of the tourist market sought. The problem can also be effectively managed if a developer or public agency can own a large tract and establish control through requirements in the lease agreement.

INFRASTRUCTURE: TRANSPORTATION

Attractions and facilities are not accessible to tourists' use until basic infrastructural needs of the destination have been met. Infrastructure consists of all the underground and surface developmental construction of a region and comprises:

Water systems
Communication networks
Health care facilities
Transportation terminals
Power sources
Sewage/drainage areas
Streets/highways
Security systems

There has been some criticism of tourism's overreliance on a fully developed infrastructure. In certain parts of the world newly discovered tourist destinations may be able to satisfy tourist needs without developing a full infrastructural system. The lack of modern highways may, in fact, be an added attraction for some kinds of tourists. As a destination attracts more tourists, the increase in numbers may actually stimulate the development of the infrastructure. In most cases, the reverse is true. Infrastructural development is necessary to stimulate the development of tourism.

The infrastructure of an area is shared by both tourists and residents. An upgrading of the elements of the infrastructure primarily for the purpose of attracting tourists will benefit the host population.

The development of infrastructure is almost always a public-sector responsibility. It is one way that the public sector has created a climate suitable for tourism development.

The development of a proper infrastructure requires engineering input, but it is wise to consider the reports of engineers in light of the effects on tourism. The best placement from an engineering perspective of a coast road may not be the best route for tourist viewing.

It is necessary also that visitors receive enough communication so that their questions about travel within the state are answered. Because of federal pressure in the United States to restrict billboards on the highway, various alternatives have been explored. Vermont has developed a successful travel information system comprised of the following parts:

1. Local chambers of commerce are located in many Vermont communities, with manned offices or booths.
2. Vermont visitors handbooks, containing details on the facilities offered by over 600 Vermont traveler-oriented businesses, can be obtained from local chambers of commerce.

3. Official state maps, containing historic sites, museums, golf courses, campgrounds, and ski areas are offered. These maps, highway route numbers, and town destination signs will guide the visitor between towns. Once the desired town is reached . . .

4. Official business directional signs replace billboards for services available in that town and may indicate the number of miles to a hostelry or other service. These signs are located just before road junctions that require the visitor to change direction from one numbered highway to another, except at congested intersections and other important locations, and on interstate highways at rest areas, where these signs are replaced by listings on . . .

5. Travel information plazas, from which are dispensed the area . . .

6. Travelers services guides, pertaining to the section of Vermont in which the dispensing plaza is located. These guides provide directions to businesses that are listed on each plaza where the guide's dispenser is located.

The important parts of a tourist infrastructure are the following:

Water—Sufficient quantities of pure water are essential. A typical resort requires 350 to 400 gallons of water per room per day. An eighteen-hole golf course will require 600,000 to 1 million gallons of water per day, depending on the region in which it is located.

Power—The important considerations are that adequate supplies of power be available to meet peak-load requirements, that continuity of service be assured, and that, if possible, the type of power supplied be compatible with that used by the target markets of the destination.

Communication—Despite the fact that many tourists may wish to get away from it all, it is necessary for most that telephone and/or telegraph service be available. The lack of telephones in hotel rooms will often deter visitors from staying at a particular property because of the security aspect.

Sewage/drainage—Sewer demand is often placed at 90 percent of domestic water demand. Although water-storage resevoirs and sewage treatment plants can be designed on the basis of maximum average demand, transmission lines must be designed on a basis of maximum peak demand.

Health care—The type of health-care facilities provided will depend on the number of visitors expected, their ages, the type of activities in which they will engage, and local geographic factors. Ski areas will tend to specialize in broken bones, for example.

Streets/highways—The availability of first-class roads adds greatly to the accessibility of a region. Some areas have in fact refused to upgrade their road systems in order to slow down tourism development. The effect of a highway system was noted by the U.S. Department of Transportation when it estimated that the development of the U.S. interstate system meant that the distance that could be safely driven in one day increased from 350 to 500 miles. There are certain ways to make use of the highway more interesting for tourists:

1. Provide close-range view of local scenes.
2. Change the elevation.
3. Develop viewpoints and overlooks.
4. Independently align dual-lane highways to fit into the land contour.

5. Selectively thin trees to reveal views. It is crucial to consider to what extent resident (or local) traffic is to be integrated with tourist (or regional) traffic. It may be desirable to design a dual system of higher-speed lanes flanked by roads for low-speed local traffic. Roads should be engineered for safety, taking appropriate measures designed to safeguard the highway user.

Transportation terminals—A report by the U.S. Department of Transportation identified the following problems in terminal facilities and ground transportation.[2]

General—There is an almost complete lack of coordination between the three modes of air, rail, and bus. In addition, there is a noticeable lack of consistency in standards and procedures within each mode.

—Directional and informational signs are often difficult to see; signs are not uniform throughout the system; public-address announcements are often unintelligible.

Air—Long walks are required in many terminals.

Rail—Parking is inconvenient and inadequate near larger terminals; use of facilities by local transients and inadequate cleaning procedures lead to crowded, unsanitary waiting rooms and restrooms; security to prevent thefts is lacking; information and directional maps are not provided in most rail terminals; special transportation to and from rail terminals is not provided, and the urban transit and taxi service is often inadequate.

Bus—Terminals are dirty and crowded due to use by unauthorized people and to inadequate cleaning procedures; boarding gates lack a system of orderly procedures resulting in crowding when passengers are boarding; inadequate protection is afforded to passengers against traffic.

The following suggestions regarding terminals and ground facilities have been made and serve as a guide to the provision of adequate services:

1. Full information about facilities, terminal location, and local transportation at destination should be made available to all originating passengers.

2. A security system should be provided to prevent theft and misclaiming of checked baggage at terminals.

3. The information system should provide data on connecting or alternative rail and bus service, including information on fares and schedules.

4. A system of standard signs and symbols should be developed and installed in all air terminals.

5. Rapid updated arrival and departure information should be available on posted information boards, through public address announcements, and to telephone callers.

6. Personnel should always be available to assist passengers, particularly the aged, the handicapped, and non–English speaking.

7. Complete information should be provided on the location, fares, schedules, and routes of local transportation services.

---

[2]*Evaluation of Traveler Service Problems*, Department of Transportation Office of Facilitation and Office for Consumer Affairs, May 1972.

8. City maps should be made available to passengers.

Security—While on vacation tourists are in an unfamiliar environment. Because of this, the need for assurances regarding their safety is important. Especially when traveling long distances and to foreign countries, the image gained of the destination may be distorted. Europeans, for example, are fed television programs that sensationalize the American crime scene. This creates an image of the United States as a place filled with violence. In addition, the costs of medical care are so expensive that concerns about health in foreign countries may generate additional fears. Insecurities about food, water, or police protection may dissuade visitors from visiting. It is necessary that the basic needs for security and safety be considered and assured to make the potential tourist feel secure prior to and during the vacation.

HOSPITALITY RESOURCES

Hospitality resources refers to the general feeling of welcome that visitors receive while visiting a destination area. It is the way that tourist services are delivered by service providers, as well as the general feeling of warmth from the general resident population. It is a combination of a certain amount of knowledge and a positive attitude that results in specific hospitable behaviors. The way in which services are delivered is particularly important because tourism is consumed "on the spot." Sales and service occur at the same time. Although excellent service cannot totally make up for a hard bed, tough steak, bumpy bus ride, or rainy weather, poor service can certainly spoil an otherwise excellent vacation experience. In the broader sense, tourists will have a much more rewarding vacation if they feel welcomed by the host population and will certainly feel awkward and unhappy if they feel resented.

Hospitality resources can be improved by, in effect, training tourism personnel to be hospitable and encouraging positive feelings towards tourism and tourists on the part of the general public. These two aspects will be dealt with separately.

Hospitality Training

A program of hospitality training is generally aimed at motivating service providers to be hospitable in their dealings with tourists. The assumption is that providing more hospitable service will result in a more satisfied tourist who will be inclined to return and/or spread positive reactions through word-of-mouth advertising to other potential tourists. To achieve hospitable service on the part of service providers it may be necessary to change their present behavior. Many believe that a change in behavior is brought about by a change in attitude and an increase in the level of knowledge. The three aspects of attitude are toward self, toward others, and toward the subject matter.

ATTITUDE TOWARD SELF. If an individual's self-esteem, or attitude toward self, is low, that individual will tend to behave in such a way that the feedback from others will confirm this low opinion of himself or herself. Traditionally the tourism industries have lacked prestige. Those who work in the tourism industries have, by association, lacked prestige. Behavior is thus precipitated that will reinforce this feeling. The key then is to change the individual's perception of self in order to improve behaviors. If service providers can be made to believe that their work and they themselves are important, the hope is that their work and specifically their actions toward tourists will reflect this new feeling. This aspect can be put into practice by highlighting the vital part that service providers play in ensuring a positive vacation experience. If service providers can be viewed as hosts and hostesses rather than as "just" employees, their self-image may be raised. Stress should be placed on the fact that dealing with and serving people is, indeed, a most difficult task. Visitors often bring demands with them that are difficult to satisfy. Although it is relatively easy to deal with a satisfied guest, it is very challenging to deal with visitors who are dissatisfied or extra demanding. The ability to create a satisfied guest is a very demanding task. Those people who can do this have skills that should be highly regarded by themselves as well as by others.

ATTITUDE TOWARD OTHERS. The second aspect of attitude relates to attitude toward others. An individual's feelings toward people that she or he comes into contact with will affect, positively or negatively, behavior toward them. The task is to assist the service provider in developing positive feelings toward fellow employees and tourists that will result in positive behavior toward the tourists. This can be achieved by training the individual in the importance of teamwork and interdependence in getting the job done. Oftentimes employees are not aware of all the people and actions that are necessary to ensure a satisfied guest. It is important that employees see where they fit into the big picture of a satisfied tourist, not only to see how important their role is, but also to be aware of the interfacing roles of others.

It is obviously important to consider the employee's attitude toward visitors. The key to the development of positive attitudes toward visitors is being able to develop the ability to put oneself in the visitor's place. Role-playing can be successfully used for this purpose. If a service provider can empathize with the tourist, accept tourists as they are, understand that for them this vacation is something that they have saved for all year, and appreciate how tired they may be after a long trip, then the attitude is likely to be more positive.

ATTITUDE TOWARD SUBJECT MATTER. The third aspect of attitude concerns attitude toward subject matter. The individual who does not believe in the work being done will display a negative attitude that will be reflected in poor service toward the guest. A positive attitude on the part of service providers toward tourists can come about only when employees are made aware of how important tourism is to their state, country, city, and property. By being aware of the amount of revenue, jobs, and taxes generated and the dispersion of the tourist dollar throughout the community, employees may become convinced of the economic and social significance of the industry of which they are a part.

The hope is that more hospitable behavior will come, in part, from a better self-image, more empathy with others, and a positive attitude about tourism's role in the community.

To precipitate a change in attitude, it is necessary to raise the knowledge level of the individual. This may be done in group sessions or through a variety of audiovisual means.

Teaching Specific Behaviors

A second theory of behavior change is that a change in behavior affects attitudes. If people can be trained in specific desired behaviors and act them out, the positive feedback they receive will result in a positive attitude. The task is to develop specific behaviors that will be termed "hospitable" and instruct employees in these behaviors. If the employees act out these hospitable behaviors, the positive reactions (tips, recognition, advancement, and so on) will result in positive attitudes toward hospitality. To this end, employees can familiarize themselves with the surrounding attractions and services (to be able to give advice or direction). Some attractions will have an open house for those involved in tourism to acquaint them by means of a mini-familiarization tour. Sessions can cover both verbal and nonverbal behavior. Employees are often unaware of the negative messages their facial expressions or posture give.

By means of this joint approach—attempting to change attitudes about the self, others, and tourism through increasing the level of knowledge and teaching specific hospitable behaviors—an attempt is made to raise the hospitality behavior level of service providers.

Community Awareness Programs

Although the tourist is most directly affected by the degree of hospitality shown by service providers, the overall feeling of welcome within a community will also enhance or detract from the vacation experience. Residents of a destination area cannot be trained to act in a hospitable way toward tourists, but a community awareness program can help develop a more positive attitude toward the tourist on their part. The objectives of such a program are twofold—to build acceptance of tourism and to build an understanding of the tourist.

An acceptance of tourism cannot be built unless the benefits of tourism are made relevant to members of the community. The benefits of tourism are many, yet many people do not realize that they are positively affected by it. To some it may mean a summer job, while to others tourism may ensure that a playhouse can survive year-round for the cultural benefit of the community. It is necessary to communicate to each part of the community messages that are important and relevant to them.

An understanding of who the tourist is can assist in a greater acceptance of the visitor. Knowing why people visit the area might result in a renewed civic pride.

There are different ways to communicate with the local community. Public meetings can be held to discuss particular problems. Some areas have successfully organized a speaker's bureau consisting of tourism community leaders who talk to community groups. Information sheets and newsletters, though infrequently used, can be distributed to the general public. Some communities have shown the effect of tourism by giving two-dollar bills in change to tourists to distribute throughout the area. In the off-season in Niagara Falls, Ontario community groups can tour many of the tourist attractions free of charge. Whatever methods are used, the objective remains to create a feeling of welcome for the tourist within the community.

REFERENCES

Destination U.S.A., Vol. III, Implementation: Visitor Services (The University of Missouri, 1978), pp. 14–20, 89.

GUNN, CLARE A., *Tourism Planning* (New York, Crane Russak & Company, Inc., 1979), pp. 54–61, 76, 83–86.

"It's All Up to You," Facilitator's Training Manual, Gulf Coast Community College, Florida, undated.

KAISER JR., CHARLES, AND LARRY E. HELBER, *Tourism Planning and Development*, (Boston, CBI Publishing Company, Inc., 1978), pp. 28–29, 61, 169, 191, 193–94.

KASTARLAK, BULENT, "Planning Tourism Growth," *Cornell Hotel and Restaurant Administration Quarterly*, February 1971, pp. 27–29.

MCINTOSH, ROBERT W., *Tourism: Principles, Practices, Philosophies*, 2nd ed. (Columbus, OH, Grid Inc., 1977), p. 127.

Planning Community-Wide Special Events (University of Illinois at Urbana-Champaign, Cooperative Extension Service, undated).

9

impacts

Social
economic

TOURISM
AND ECONOMIC/SOCIAL
PLANNING:
The Contributions
of the Travel Industry

Tourism can have a significant impact upon a destination country. This chapter explores the potential economic and social effects of tourism upon a destination and suggests appropriate strategies to maximize tourism's economic effects.

It is recognized that tourism may be one of several development options open to a location. The characteristics of tourism compared to other development possibilities are therefore examined. The full effect of tourism on the economy in terms of foreign exchange, income, and employment is detailed.

Although tourism can bring economic advantages to a destination country, it can also bring social changes. The possibilities are outlined.

The effect of tourism on the U.S. economy is detailed, and suggestions are given to help those at a destination develop policies to maximize tourism's economic effect.

TOURISM'S ROLE IN ECONOMIC DEVELOPMENT

Tourism development has been advanced as a policy alternative, particularly for developing countries, to aid economic growth. There are several arguments for this. First, the demand for international travel continues to grow in developed countries. Second, as incomes in the developed countries increase, the income elasticity of demand for international travel will mean that it will increase at a faster rate. Third, developing nations need foreign exchange earnings to aid their own economic development to satisfy the rising expectations of their growing populations.

Developing countries have tended to rely upon agriculture and other primary industries for economic growth. Indeed, the World Bank, indicating that between fifty percent and seventy percent of the population of middle- and low-income developing countries is directly dependent on agriculture, supports the necessity for full agricultural growth as a key to industrialization and further economic and employment growth. Noting that almost all developing countries have followed import-substitution (the substitution of locally produced products for those presently imported), they stress the need to reward exports with incentives. A basic problem, however, with a reliance on agriculture development is that the developing country can easily be overly dependent on a few primary products. The price of primary products is unpredictable and dependent on such things as weather, disease, and outside manipulation by large buyers from the developed countries.

The development of the manufacturing sector is not always a viable option. Problems include the fact that:

The processing of raw materials—in increase local value-added—is related directly to the base amount available in the area, and possible projects are likely to be few for all but the most richly endowed nations

For industries aimed at import substitution, the relatively small size of many domestic markets restricts growth

Developing countries are characterized by a chronic shortage of skilled labor

For export-oriented industries, their products will have to face full international competition, in terms of price and quality, as well as in terms of marketing techniques used

This is not to say that the development of tourism does not face similar problems for a developing country. Yet each country has the "raw material" for tourism within its borders. In most cases, there are fewer restrictions on international travel than on international trade. The distance of the destination from the market is becoming less of a problem and may in itself be an attraction. Also, prices charged are more under the control of the seller than of the buyer in tourist-related industries compared with primary industries. The Organization for Economic Cooperation and Development has concluded, in fact, that tourism provides a major opportunity for growth for countries that find themselves at the intermediate stage of economic development and that are experiencing rather fast economic growth and increasingly require more foreign-exchange earnings. They also caution that "there are few if any developing countries which could or perhaps even should rely principally on tourism for their economic salvation."[1]

Tourism is an invisible export that differs from international trade in several ways:

1. The "consumer" collects the product from the exporting country, thereby eliminating any freight costs for the exporter, except in cases in which the airlines used are those of the tourist receiving country.

2. The demand for the pleasure segment of tourism is highly dependent on non-economic factors, such as local disturbances, political troubles, and changes in the fashionability of resorts/countries created mostly by media coverage. At the same time international tourism is usually both price elastic and income elastic. Changes in either of these two variables normally result in a more-than-proportional change in pleasure travel.

3. By using specific fiscal measures, the exporting (tourist receiving) country can manipulate exchange rates so that those for tourists are higher or lower (normally the latter in order to attract a greater number of tourists) than those at other foreign trade markets. Also, tourists are permitted to buy in domestic markets at the prices prevailing for the local residents (the exceptions being the duty-free tourist shops operated in many Caribbean islands and elsewhere).

4. Tourism is a multifaceted industry that directly affects several sectors in the economy (such as hotels and other forms of accommodations, shops, restaurants, local transport firms, entertainment establishments, and handicraft producers) and indirectly affects many others (such as equipment manufacturers and utilities).

5. Tourism brings many more nonpecuniary benefits and costs (that is, social and cultural) than other export industries.

ECONOMIC IMPACT

Foreign Exchange

Because of the findings stated above, many countries have embraced tourism as a way to increase foreign exchange earnings to produce the investment necessary to finance economic growth. This certainly can and does occur. Some countries even require tourists to bring in a certain amount of foreign currency for each day of their stay and do not allow them to take it out of the country at the end of their vacation.

However, the foreign exchange earnings generated by tourism can be overstated unless the import factor is known. The value of goods and

---

[1]Robert Erbes, *International Tourism and the Economy of Developing Countries*, OECD, June 1973, p. 4.

services that must be imported to service the needs of tourism is referred to as leakage. The money spent leaks from the host economy and must be subtracted from foreign exchange earnings to determine the true impact.

Leakage occurs from a variety of sources. The extent to which a destination can minimize these effects will determine the size of the foreign exchange earnings. Leakage occurs first from the cost of goods and services that must be purchased to satisfy the needs of tourists. If a tourist wishes a steak and if that steak is imported, the cost of the steak is an import cost set against earnings. Local industries may also import part of their raw materials to produce goods for tourists. This also is a cost. A second cost may occur when importing goods and materials for infrastructure and buildings required for tourism development. The use of materials indigenous to the area will not only reduce import cost but will also add a distinctive look to the facilities. Payments to foreign factors of production represent another import cost. Commissions might have to be paid to overseas tour operators. If foreign capital is invested in the country's tourism, plant interest payments, rent, or profit may have to be paid to those outside the country. The amount of local ownership and control is crucial in this regard. Foreign-owned chain hotels will often be staffed, stocked, and furnished by people, food, furnishings, fixtures, and equipment from a central foreign source. A fourth area of cost is in direct expenditure for promotion, publicity, and similar services abroad. The cost, for example, of setting up a national tourist office is a large expense to be set against earnings. There are several ways that transfer pricing can reduce foreign exchange earnings. If tourists make purchases in the country of origin for services to be delivered at the destination, the transfer payments need not be made for the services provided. If a tourism company is multinational, payments may be recorded in the country of tourist origin rather than in the destination country, thereby reducing profits and taxes in the destination country. In a similar situation, purchases by a foreign-owned hotel at the destination country may be made from a foreign-owned subsidiary at inflated rates to again reduce the taxable income in the destination country. The use of credit cards and traveler's checks can mean that local banks will not be able to participate in the exchange. Last, foreign exchange earnings can be reduced when host governments exempt duties or taxes on foreign-owned companies or offer financial inducements to them to attract investment.

A critical issue for destination areas is to determine the *net* foreign exchange earnings from different types of tourists. High-income tourists may be few in number and may spend large amounts of money, but they may require a substantial infrastructure and facilities resulting in a high import cost. Is this better for the destination country than the mass market that comes in greater numbers and spends less per person, but that requires fewer import goods and services? The answer comes from a rather complex economic analysis. It breaks down tourism earnings into component economic sectors and then determines to what extent each of the sectors depends on imports. Countries can be characterized as follows on the basis of the proportion of net foreign exchange earnings (subtracting the import content) from tourism:

> Less than 10 percent: Totally Import reliant (such as Mauritius)
>
> 10–50 percent: Heavily import reliant (such as the less-developed Caribbean and South Pacific islands)
>
> 50–70 percent: Import luxuries and a few necessities (such as the better developed Caribbean islands)
>
> 70–90 percent: Import principally luxuries; have advanced manufacturing sectors with good resources (such as Kenya, Tunisia, Greece, and Yugoslavia)[2]

There are relatively few studies in this area, and the works that exist do not use the same methodology. However, a certain pattern seems to be true regarding foreign exchange earnings. The foreign exchange cost will be high initially as a country begins to develop its tourism potential. Materials will probably have to be imported and incentives given to attract investment. After this heavy initial cost period, the foreign exchange cost will gradually diminish for a period and then will tend to increase again. This is due in great part to what is known as the demonstration effect. The demonstration effect describes the process by which local residents, exposed to goods imported for tourist use, begin to demand those goods for themselves. This automatically increases the demand for imports. This is illustrated in Figure 9.1. To what extent this cost should be "charged" to tourism is debatable. As incomes rise and as communications relay messages to residents, they increasingly have the means for and are exposed to many new products. Tourism may be said to hasten the process by exposing at first-hand such goods and services to the local residents.

Income

MULTIPLIER.   The tourism industry obviously generates income within a destination country. The amount of income generated, however, is difficult to determine. The difficulty arises from the fact that the tourism industry is comprised of many different sectors of the economy. Additionally, many small businesses are involved, which leads to great difficulty in getting precise data.

---

[2]Robert Cleverdon, *The Economic and Social Impact of International Tourism on Developing Countries* (E.I.U. Special Report No. 60, The Economist Intelligence Unit Ltd., May 1979), p. 32.

FIGURE 9.1 Foreign Exchange Cost over Time

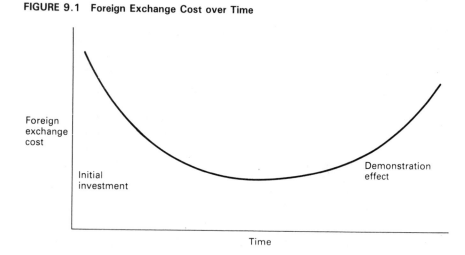

Probably the most common method for estimating the income generated from tourism is by determining the multiplier for a destination. The multiplier effect is illustrated in Figure 9.2. A tourist makes an initial expenditure into the community. This expenditure is received as income by local tour operators, handicrafts store owners, hoteliers, and taxicab drivers. In the first round of transactions, a hotelier may use some money received to buy some supplies, pay some wages, and retain some profits. The income in the second round may be spent or saved, while the employee who has received payment for services rendered may spend some of that on rent and some on food, and may put some into savings. The money spent on supplies in the third round of spending, goes for things such as seed, fertilizer, and imported raw materials. Any income spent on imports has leaked out of the local economy. This process continues until the additional income generated by a new round of spending essentially becomes zero. The multiplier is given by:

$$K = \frac{Y}{E}$$

where

K = the multiplier
Y = the change in income generated by E
E = the change in expenditure (the initial sum spent by the tourist)

(Because of the difficulties in generating the data for an additional unit of expenditure, the analysis is generally conducted relative to an average unit of spending.)

FIGURE 9.2   Multiplier Effect

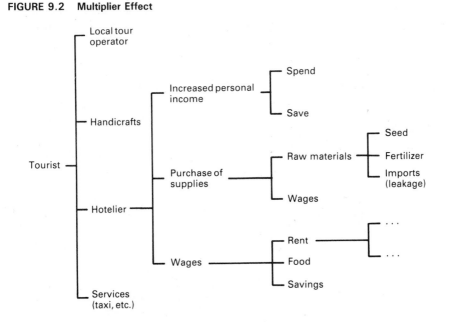

The size of the multiplier depends upon the extent to which the various sectors of the economy are linked to one another. This is largely a function of the diversity of activities within the destination. When the tourism sectors buy heavily from other local economic sectors for goods and services, there will be a correspondingly smaller propensity to import, and the multiplier will be greater than if the reverse were true.

A simplified formula for the multiplier is:

$$K = \frac{1 - L}{1 - (c - c_j - t_i c)(1 - t_d - b) + m}$$

where

K = the multiplier
L = the direct first-round leakages
c = the propensity to consume
c_j = the proportion of that propensity spent abroad
$t_i c$ = the indirect tax
t_d = the value of direct deductions (income tax, national insurance, and so on)
b = the level of government benefits
m = the value of imports[3]

---

[3]Robert Cleverdon, pp. 134–35.

Most island economies have an income multiplier range between 0.6 and 1.2, while developed economies have a range between 1.7 and 2.0.[4]

The simple multiplier has come under criticism for several reasons. It is suitable for use in only small countries with relatively small economies for two reasons. First, the model does not take into account the fact that the destination country may increase export sales to other countries from which it presently imports. Although it may be necessary to import certain items to cater to visitors, once these former tourists return to their home country they may desire foods or other items from the country visited. Second, the model fails to take into account the fact that the additional income generated may produce investment in the destination country.

A more serious criticism of the simplified multiplier formula, however, has to do with the assumption that each type of income injected into the economy has the same general effect. To remedy this it is necessary to break the increase in expenditure into its component elements in order to analyze the effect of each element separately. This is done through input-output analysis. An input-output table shows how transactions flow through an economy in a given time period. A matrix is developed, the rows of which show the total value of all the sales made by each sector of the economy to all the other sectors, the columns of which show the purchases made by each sector from each of the other sectors. Input-output analysis is a method of looking at these interactions and determining the effects of any possible changes. Here again, problems exist. It is extremely difficult to get sufficient data for a detailed model, largely because tourist spending affects so many sectors of the economy. Analysis is suitable for only the short- and medium-term. Last, it is argued, input-output analysis makes too many unrealistic assumptions. It assumes that supply is elastic. Any increases in demand will require more output that can be met by purchases from the economic sectors that supplied the previous supply. It is unlikely that this will happen in the short-run because of production hindrances. It also assumes that production functions are linear in form and that trade patterns are stable. It assumes that when production increases, purchases of imports will be made in the same proportions and from the same sources as before, negating any thought of economies of scale. Additionally, it is assumed that increases in income will be spent on the same items and in the same proportions as previously. In reality, none of these assumptions are likely.

Certainly input-output analysis can show the economic impacts of different kinds of visitors, which will assist in target market selection. It can also show short-term economic effects compared with the effects

---

[4]Brian Archer, "Input-Output Analysis: Its Strengths, Limitations and Weaknesses," in *The 80's: Its Impact on Travel and Tourism Marketing* (The Travel Research Association, Eighth Annual Conference Proceedings, June 1977), p. 98, and Cleverdon, p. 33.

of other sectors of the economy. Other tools, however, are needed to demonstrate the best long-term policy option for investment in the various available economic sectors.

COST/BENEFIT ANALYSIS. Cost/benefit analysis is a technique used to determine which economic sector will produce the most benefit in terms of foreign exchange, employment, taxes, or income generated relative to the costs of development. The factors of production are valued at their opportunity cost—the marginal value of their next best use. It is then possible to compare several investment options. The social cost/benefit analysis of a project determines the average annual rate at which benefits accrue to society. Such an analysis also draws critics who argue that the results are too dependent upon how appropriate are the assumptions made. It is not possible to check actual performance against prediction. Certainly, it does appear possible to make value judgments that will produce the appropriate results.

STRUCTURAL ANALYSIS. As growth takes place, long-term changes in the economy can be determined through structural analysis. It is necessary to determine and study three different processes:

1. Accumulation processes
   (investment, government revenue, education)
2. Resource allocation processes
   (structure of domestic demand, production and trade)
3. Demographic and distributional processes
   (labor allocation, urbanization, demographic transition, income distribution)

In recent years, countries have tended to become primary or industrial specialists, have balanced production and trade, or have moved through the process of import substitution. Insufficient work has been done to determine the development pattern of a country's economy as it builds its tourism sector. Early work suggests that there is a danger of developing the tourism sector at the expense of other exports such as agriculture. For maximum economic impact, care must be taken to achieve as much integration of tourism with the internal economy as possible.

Employment

A principal argument made for encouraging the development of tourism is that it produces many jobs. Tourism creates primary or direct employment in such areas as lodging, restaurants, and sightseeing operations. Indirect employment can also be created in construction, agriculture, and manufacturing industries. The amount of indirect or secondary employment generated depends upon the extent to which the tourism sector is integrated with the rest of the local economy. The more integration and diversification that occurs, the more indirect employment that is generated.

It is argued that tourism is more labor intensive than other industries, and for this reason it deserves developmental support. The degree of labor intensity can be measured in terms of the cost per job created or the employment/output ratio. The employment/output ratio is the number of workers employed divided by the contribution of tourism to the national income. Although research conclusions are not unanimous, for the most part they agree that the cost per job created in tourism is no less than in other sectors of the economy. A major reason for this is the fact that tourism is also capital intensive. The heavy costs of providing necessary infrastructure drastically increase the cost of creating jobs.

In the early stages of tourism development, the cost per job created is likely to be rather high due to the costs described previously. Similarly, the capital/output ratio will also be high because of the low volume of tourists in the initial stages of tourism development. As the destination country develops and as more tourists are attracted, the capital/output ratio declines. The cost per job created will also be reduced due to the experience and organization of those at the destination. In addition, as tourism increases, physical development takes place in facilities that is less costly than the construction of hotels. Jobs can thus be created at a lower average cost. In the third stage of tourism development, the average cost per job created may increase due to higher land prices and increased engineering costs because of the necessity of using sites that are more difficult to develop. Also, as tourism increases in importance a greater infrastructure may be necessary, because the tourism plant will be geographically spread out. Also, greater infrastructural demands may be made by larger numbers of tourists.

The cost per job created obviously depends upon the type of facility constructed. The cost will be greater for a luxury hotel than for a smaller, more modest property. Also, the luxury hotel will offer more job opportunities per room and higher employment/output ratios than will the smaller properties. The larger properties are more inclined to use imported labor, at least for managerial positions. The key to maximizing the economic and job returns for the destination is to use materials and personnel indigenous to the region while maintaining a quality standard acceptable to the target market.

Can tourism development be an aid to regional development by producing income and jobs in areas previously lacking in economic development opportunities? Many people feel that this is a key role for the tourism industry. The fact, however, that the tourism industry requires a heavy infrastructure means that the cost of developing tourism in a rural, outlying area may be as great as for developing its agricultural or industrial market potential.

Several additional criticisms of the tourism industry as an employer have been made. In many areas, tourism is a seasonal business. To ensure a balance between market demand and staff requirements, a business tends to adopt one of two strategies. Either employees are laid off during the low season, or additional employees are imported from other regions during the high season. In the former situation, tourism cannot provide a meaningful job to a resident. In the latter situation, there is an increased need for housing for employees who will spend most of their wages outside of the destination region. Thus, jobs and income are lost to the local area.

Because the tourism industry relies so heavily upon people for delivering a service, productivity gains are difficult to come by. The national output may be difficult to improve if tourism becomes a dominant part of the economy, particularly if the destination lacks a strong industrial sector, where productivity gains are easier to obtain.

SOCIOECONOMIC IMPACT.   Tourism development does indeed change the economic structure of the host country. Although such changes can easily be integrated into the developed economy, the effects in a lesser-developed country are more profound. Stresses can occur when the old and the new exist side by side. Traditional methods of farming and primitive industries contrast with modern hotels and polished tourist entertainment. This, in fact, causes a movement away from traditional forms of employment. The fisherman turned tour-boat entrepreneur and farm girl turned waitress undergo not only a change in income but a change in status. The fisherman's catch is lost to the local people, but his own income may improve. The waitress may view her task of serving as a throwback to earlier colonial times or may look at the new found job as a cleaner and less arduous way to earn a living. The satisfaction for locals may well depend upon the range and type of jobs available together with the opportunity for advancement. The problem of seasonality is a major concern.

As with any other development industry, tourism encourages workforce migration, with the corresponding possibility of breaking down the traditional family unit. It does appear, however, that, even though migration occurs, family ties and responsibilities are maintained.

Because of the tourism industry, profound changes can occur within society in terms of economic power. To the extent that tourism businesses attract women and young people, they gain an economic independence previously unheard of. Particularly in traditional societies, great tension can occur because of this shift in the economic resources within a destination region. There is inconclusive evidence to show that such changes may or may not result in negative effects upon the family.

Finally, tourism does change both the value and the ownership pattern of land. As tourism is developed, the value of potential sites increases. Land sold to outsiders results in a short-term profit to the local landowner. However, the land may be lost to agricultural production or local recreational use, and control of the land goes out of the community. Some destination regions take steps to prevent unhealthy (from the viewpoint of the destination) land speculation.

Tourism obviously has certain impacts upon the host region. Many of these impacts are direct—such as the raising of land values—while others are indirect—such as the increase in imports brought about by local exposure to goods imported for tourist consumption. Many of these changes would occur no matter what type of economic development took place. Whether these changes are good or bad is often a value judgment. The important point is to realize that these impacts are likely to occur, decide whether or not they are desirable for the destination in question, and plan accordingly.

SOCIAL EFFECT OF TOURISM

Tourism is concerned with the movement of, and contact between, people in different geographical locations. In sociological terms this involves:[5]

1. Social relations between people who would not normally meet
2. The confrontation of different cultures, ethnic groups, life-styles, (possibly) languages, levels of prosperity, and so on
3. The behavior of people released from many of the social and economic constraints of everyday life
4. The behavior of the host population, which has to reconcile economic gain and benefits with the costs of living with strangers

The degree to which conflict will occur between host and guest depends upon the similarity in their standards of living, the number of tourists at any one time, and the extent to which the tourists adapt to local norms.

Sociocultural Impact

The sociocultural impact of tourism can be both positive and negative. If host regions recognize that indigenous culture will attract tourists and serve as a unique factor in distinguishing one destination from another, attempts may be made to keep the culture alive. In some cases, traditional ways and goods may be restored because willing buyers

---

[5]"Tourism Supply in the Caribbean: A Study for the World Bank by the Shankland Cox Partnership," November 1974, p. 84.

(tourists) can be found. The Aaraya women of Cuna, Panama, had to be taught to sew the traditional dress of their culture. The skill had been lost. In London, England, many theaters can survive only because of the influx of tourists. In other areas, festivals are produced for tourists by the community which is thus encouraged to keep its culture alive. Thus, entertaining the tourist may be the impetus for the performing of cultural activities or the production of goods, but the effect on the local community is that of preserving part of the old culture.

There are two negative sides to this. First, a process of cultural involution can take place. The modernization of an area and a people can be halted because of tourist demand for the old ways. Tourism in essence can encourage the host people to remain artisans at the expense of their industrial modernization. Second, the authenticity of culture packaged for the tourist may be questionable. Many people feel that when a cultural event is prepared for tourist consumption its original, often spiritual, meaning is lost. In the United States, the moving of certain historic celebrations (Columbus Day, Washington's Birthday, and so on) to Mondays to give more three-day weekends throughout the year delighted many people in the tourism industry. The purpose of the celebrations, however, was lost. In a smaller destination such changes in festivals, foods, and traditional ways of life have a greater impact.

Tourism's effect on architecture has largely been to the detriment of local styles. Part of this pressure comes from tourist demands, part from the transnational companies that seek economies of scale in construction, and part from the host countries themselves who see the building of Western-type hotels as a step toward modernity. A decision to build in the local style using materials indigenous to the area gives the region a different selling point while reducing economic leakage.

Tourism appears to act as a medium for social change (because of the contact between host and guest) rather than as the cause itself. The host/guest interaction offers the opportunity for each to learn more of the other, and as such, it can contribute to a greater understanding between peoples. Each destination region must weigh the cultural gains to be had—revived arts, theater, exposure to new ideas—against the losses to be had—overcrowding, a cheapening of the culture, possible social change.

TOURISM IN THE U.S. ECONOMY

Economic Impact

Any attempt to develop economic impact data for the United States has been hampered by the cost involved. Because tourism cuts across so many industries, the expense of obtaining accurate and detailed figures is considerable.

The U.S. Travel Data Center has developed the travel economic impact model designed to estimate the economic effects of tourism at the national, regional, and local levels. Their work indicates that approximately 30 percent of the U.S. resident and foreign visitor spending is initially for food, and about 20 percent is spent on private and public transportation. Expenditures on lodging are about 15 percent of the total. Incidentals, entertainment, and recreation cost account for less than 10 percent each of visitor expenditures. Domestic expenditures are approximately seventeen times that of foreign visitor totals. Approximately 40 percent of the states account for over 70 percent of the expenditures. The major states in income and jobs generated are, in order, California, Florida, New York, and Texas.

The food-service industry is by far the major recipient of jobs created by tourism. Approximately 50 percent of all travel-related employment in the United States is in the food-service industry. Lodging accounts for less than 20 percent of all of the jobs. Public transportation, entertainment, and recreation each account for about 10 percent of the jobs.

The impact of tourism jobs is felt greatest in states such as Nevada and Vermont and least in the larger, more industrialized states that have more diversified economies. In about three-quarters of the states, tourism is among the top three private-industry employers and is the first private-industry employer in over 25 percent of the states.

Input/Output Analysis

Input/output analysis has been conducted for the United States.[6] Each dollar spent by a domestic traveler requires a direct output of $1.45 from various industries. Although many industries (185) have been impacted during the first-round transactions, most have felt very little impact. Almost half of the output has been produced in five industries: retail trade (30 cents), airlines (13 cents), hotels and lodging places (9 cents), motion pictures and amusements (9 cents), and petroleum refining (8 cents).

Benefits are also felt by the government in terms of increased taxes. Each traveler dollar spent has generated 30 cents in taxes. Approximately 86 percent of this goes to the federal government in the form of personal income tax, corporate profit tax, and contributions for social security. The remaining 14 percent goes to state and local governments in the form of personal income tax, corporate profit tax, and indirect business tax.

In sum, the impact of domestic travel expenditures touches many industries, although the service industries feel they are the major bene-

---

[6]Bill Anthony, "Industry Effect of Domestic Travel Expenditures: An Input-Outpu   '
(Workshop presentation for The Travel Research Association, Eighth Annual Conference, June 1977).

ficiaries. Each dollar spent requires $1.45 worth of output in the first round. Indirect effects account for another 49 cents. Travel spending generates income for people in the industry who spend this income on other goods and services. The total effect is $2.13 of output. The gross national product multiplier related to travel expenditure is estimated to be 1.62.

Cost/Benefit Analysis

Almost half the states have generated cost/benefit ratios for travel/tourism. These vary from 13 to 1 for Georgia to 2000 to 1 for Rhode Island. Two prominent tourism states, Florida and Texas, have indicated cost/benefit ratios of 869 to 1 and 300 to 1, respectively. Although the methodology has not been reported and undoubtedly differs from state to state, it is promising that this technique is being tested and used by so many states.

MAXIMIZING TOURISM'S ECONOMIC EFFECT

Growth Philosophy

Traditional economic growth theories have suggested one of two strategies to maximize economic inpact within a region. Supporters of *balanced growth* suggest that tourism be viewed as an essential part of a broad-based economy. This philosophy stresses that tourism supply (the goods and services delivered as tourism) needs the support of other interrelated industries. To obtain the maximum economic benefit, these inputs should be locally produced. This necessitates a significant economic effort. The objective is thus to integrate tourism with the other economic activities.

Proponents of *unbalanced growth*, on the other hand, see tourism as the spark to economic growth. Although balanced growth supporters emphasize the development of supply, unbalanced growth proponents stress the need to expand demand. As demand is established through the vigorous development of tourism, other industries will see the need for their products and services and will move to provide them locally, thus expanding the economic base of the region. The dangers of relying upon tourism have been mentioned earlier. Certainly, it is preferable to develop tourism along with industrial activity.

A compromise strategy is that of *coordinate growth*. Economic efforts are concentrated into areas that "either provide a promising or existing base (i.e., the balanced growth concept) or . . . exhibit valid, yet incomplete, recreational opportunities and/or substantial market flow (utilizing tourism as the linchpin industry in an unbalanced situation, but limiting implementation to those cases where the proposed project can have considerable spillover effects upon the other, existing tourism elements in the area"[7] (for example, the developmet of a convention center to alleviate problems of seasonality).

Strategies

It would seem that the key to maximizing the economic effect of tourism is to maximize the amount of revenue and jobs developed within a region. This entails developing and marketing to bring tourist money in and organizing the tourism sector to minimize leakage of both money and jobs. Developing and marketing will be dealt with in remaining chapters of this text. Strategies for minimizing leakage will form the basis for the remainder of this chapter.

IMPORT SUBSTITUTION. A major economic problem, especially for lesser-developed countries, is the lack of linkages from the tourism industry to other industries within the economy. Foreign exchange earnings can be increased if ties can be developed between the tourism industry and primary, industrial, and other service industries. The economic feasibility of local development can be investigated in industries ranging from handicrafts to furniture. The industries showing most promise can be supported through specific subsidies, grants, or loans. Also, quotas or tariffs can be placed on the importation of goods that can be developed locally. This latter strategy may invite retaliation from other countries or regions, however. Last, it may be possible to encourage the use of local architecture, design, and materials by means of incentives.

INCENTIVES. The wise use of incentives can encourage the influx of capital, both local and foreign, necessary to develop tourism supply. The common forms of incentives are:[8]

1. Tax exemptions/reduction on imported equipment, machinery, materials, and so on
2. Reduction in company taxation by means of favorable depreciation allowances on investment, or special treatment in relation to excise taxes, sales taxes, income taxes, turnover taxes, profits taxes, or property taxes
3. Tax holidays (limited period)
4. Guarantee of stabilization of tax conditions (for up to twenty years)
5. Grants (for up to 30 percent of total capital costs)
6. Subsidies (guaranteeing minimum level of profit, occupancy, and so on)
7. Loans at low rates of interest
8. Provision of land freehold at nominal or little cost or at low rents

---

[7]*Tennessee Tourism Investment Study*, Leisure Systems Inc., February 1975, p. 12.

[8]Robert Cleverdon, *Economic Impact*, p. 47.

9. Free and unrestricted repatriation of all or part of invested capital, profits, dividends, and interest, subject to tax provisions
10. Guarantees against nationalization or appropriation

Incentives are often offered on the basis of what the competition is offering rather than on what is best for the destination region. As a result, capital intensive activities may be encouraged when, for many destinations, the problem is a surplus of labor. Several other difficulties can arise. The easy importation of materials may make it more difficult for local industries to develop. Destination regions have also found that it is difficult to phase out tax concessions. Managers may lose interest in the project or let the quality standards run down as the tax holiday comes to a close. Care must be taken to ensure that the burden of risk is borne not only by the local government, but by local or outside investors as well. Overall, the specific affect of incentives in encouraging development has not been demonstrated.

Before implementing an incentive strategy a destination should:

1. Examine the performance of other countries' schemes in the light of their resources and development objectives
2. Research the actual needs of investors
3. Design codes of investment concessions related to specific development objectives, with precise requirements of the investors (such as in terms of job creation)
4. Establish targets of achievement and periodically monitor and assess the level of realization of such targets

TRANSNATIONAL CONTROL.   As tourism has developed among nations, the opportunity has arisen for international expansion of businesses in three areas—hotels, airlines, and tour operations. Much criticism has been leveled at the transnational businesses (transnationals) that, it has been charged, operate to benefit their own operations at the expense of the destination region.

Overwhelmingly, transnationals have their home offices in developed countries. Approximately 80 percent of the hotels abroad are accounted for by companies headquartered in the United States, France, and the United Kingdom. Most problems for the destination countries have resulted when the transnational corporations have had no financial investment in the hotels. Most overseas properties are operated without any foreign equity involvement, which is a trend that is increasing. Control is exercised through management contracts, or to a far lesser extent, through franchise agreements.

Although it is true that a foreign-owned hotel may engage in policies that run counter to the national tourist plan, it is impossible to identify this activity as a trend. The chances of this happening are lessened by a direct financial involvement of the overseas company. Likewise, criticisms stating that a type of international property is out of context with the host country must be viewed in the larger scope of the target market. If a country has correctly identified the type of tourists it is seeking, it may seek a larger "international-type" of facility. In general, however, transnational corporation hotels usually generate lower foreign exchange receipts than do local hotels, especially the smaller locally owned and managed properties. The charge that foreign-owned properties import too much seems to be ill-founded. The import content of constructing, equipping, and operating a hotel in a lesser-developed country has been analyzed as follows:[9]

	Cost Component Analysis (percent)	Import Content (percent)
Construction and capital equipment	87.5 to 92.5	50 to 80
Furniture and furnishings	4 to 6	10 to 50
Hotel operating equipment	4 to 6	20 to 70
Overall	100	45 to 80 (average 60)

There has been no clear evidence, however, that the import content would have been less if the hotel had been developed by a local developer. Hotels seem to be willing to purchase food locally if prices are competitive and supplies are assured.

Another concern among host countries has been that a foreign-owned hotel allows limited opportunity for local employees to reach positions of responsibility. International hotel chains usually have a core expatriate management team of three in a 100-room hotel, five in a 250-room hotel, and eight in a 350-room hotel. The wage bill however is proportionally higher than the number of employees. Some management contracts will stipulate that within, say, three to five years the management team must be made up of locals.

It appears that foreign ownership of hotels is of greatest benefit to the host country in the early stages of tourism development. At this point, the destination can really benefit from the foreign know-how. Maximization of benefits comes from direct financial involvement of the transnational business in the development of local managerial and supervisory talent.

Most countries have a national airline, although the airline may be owned and operated by a foreign company. Tourists will generally prefer

[9]Robert Cleverdon, p. 59.

to travel by the airline of their country of origin rather than by the airline of the destination country. This is particularly true, because of the perception of quality and safety, in the event of travel to a lesser-developed country. To protect their investment, destination countries have attempted to develop pooling agreements whereby technical services may be reciprocated or revenue earned and costs incurred on a route shared by the airlines serving that route. Lately, attempts have been made by the United States to dismantle this procedure on the grounds of antitrust violations. Virtually every charter airline is owned and operated by companies in developed countries. If an airline is a charter operation of another country, the host country receives less than 10 percent of the airline's revenue in the form of landing fees, fuel costs, and passenger handling. This figure may be as low as 2 to 3 percent if fuel is excluded. Although some countries have successfully banned charter aircraft from their airports, the development of mass tourism usually, though not always, requires the development of charter traffic.

Tour operators can wield a great deal of influence over destinations. Operators have the ability to direct large numbers of tourists to particular destinations. If a country has made a decision to develop tourism to the masses, and if it has consequently built the infrastructure and facilities to service these tourists, it must attract sufficient numbers of visitors to utilize and pay for the facilities. This type of country can become dependent on large tour operators who have the ability to sharply influence where the masses will vacation. In both Europe and the United States a large percentage of the charter tour market is increasingly controlled by a small number of companies. The larger foreign operator dealing with the mass market is much more likely to bypass local tour operators and deal directly with the local hotels. If hotel owners are in a situation in which supply is greater than demand, they can be forced to promise rooms at uneconomic rates or else face a total loss of business. If destinations are dependent on foreign-based tour operators, they have lost control of their own development. Also, the foreign exchange revenues may suffer. Destination regions benefit more from short-haul tourism than from long-haul. In addition, by dealing with smaller operators who specialize in a smaller but more discriminating market, there is more chance that local operators will be used.

FOREIGN EXCHANGE.   To maximize foreign exchange earnings, many countries have placed restrictions on spending. Countries have limited the amount of their own currency that tourists can both bring in and take out of the destination in order to ensure that foreign currency is used to pay bills in the host region. Tourists may be required to pay hotel bills in foreign currency. Before being allowed into the country, visitors may have to show that they have enough money for their stay, or they may even be required to enter with a specified amount of foreign currency for each day of their visit. Foreign tour operators will often barter with operators of local facilities to avoid an exchange of cash. Destination countries may require that tour operators pay in foreign currencies for services in the host country. In other cases, tour operators may issue vouchers in the country of origin for services to be provided at the destination. Some destination countries will require that these vouchers be cashed by the service provider inside the host country. Although there has been some talk of a number of destination countries issuing, on a regional basis, their own credit card or traveler's check program, the idea has not yet been implemented.

REFERENCES

ARCHER, BRIAN, "Input-Output Analysis," pp. 93–95.

CLEVERDON, ROBERT, *Economic Impact,* pp. 10–11, 13, 32, 38–39, 59, 64, 66, 70, 74, 115.

"Development in Perspective: World Bank Assessment," *Tourism International Air-Letter,* August 1979, p. 2.

GRAY, H. PETER, *International Tourism: International Trade* (Lexington, MA, D. C. Heath & Co., 1971), p. 131.

OECD, *Tourism Development and Economic Growth,* May 1966.

SMITH, VALENE L., ed., *Hosts and Guests: The Anthropology of Tourism* (Philadelphia, The University of Pennsylvania Press, Inc., 1976), pp. 8–12.

The Impact of Travel on State Economies, 1977–78 (U.S. Travel Data Center, Washington, DC, 1978).

"The Role of Tourism in Economic Development," Special Article No. 8, *International Tourism Quarterly,* no. 2, 1973, p. 57.

"Transnationals in Developing Country Tourism," Special Report No. 39, *International Tourism Quarterly,* no. 1, 1981, p. 43.

UNITED STATES TRAVEL SERVICE, *Tourism: State Structure, Organization and Support—A Technical Study,* 1978, p. 25.

10

THE TOURISM POLICY
FORMULATION:
The Political Framework
for Travel Industry Development

To guide the development of tourism at a destination area it is necessary to establish a tourism policy. Because of the potential importance of tourism to the destination area, public-sector involvement is often desirable for setting and carrying out that policy.

This chapter examines the political framework within which tourism policy is established and implemented. The various roles played by members of the public sector in tourism are reviewed and a model for establishing tourism policy is given.

Tourism policy is implemented through the efforts of tourism organizations. The functions of international, regional, and national organizations are examined in regard to their role in carrying out tourism policy.

The efforts of the U.S. public sector to establish tourism policy are traced from 1940 to the present, and problems with and primary functions of organizations at the national, state, and local levels are outlined.

REASONS FOR PUBLIC SECTOR INVOLVEMENT

There are several reasons why the public sector should be involved in tourism. First, there are political reasons. Tourism by its nature involves travel across national boundaries. Government must get involved in terms of policies relating to the procedures regarding the entry and exit of travelers and nationals. The encouragement of tourism can be used for political purposes—as a means of furthering international relations between two countries, or as a means of enhancing the national and international image of a particular destination.

Second, there are environmental reasons for public-sector involvement. Tourism "sells" such things as the scenery, history, and cultural heritage of a region. One of the dangers of tourism is that in attempting to make the national environment more acceptable to a foreign market, the true nature of that environment, physical or cultural, may be lost.

Last, there are economic reasons for public-sector involvement in tourism. It is an export industry. In order to maximize tourism's economic advantages to the host country, the government, to some extent, must get involved.

The type and amount of government involvement will vary from country to country. The greater the importance that the government attaches to tourism, the greater will be the involvement. The conditions existing in the country will also affect the type and amount of government involvement. The political/economic/constitutional system is an important factor. We would expect the level of involvement of a socialist government to be greater than in a country that has a predominantly free-enterprise philosophy. The level of socioeconomic development is another important factor determining the level of a government's involvement. The greater the economic development of a region, the less the need for government involvement. In connection with this, the maturity and financial capabilities of the private sector will have to be considered. The greater the capabilities of the private sector, the less the need for public-sector involvement.

PUBLIC-SECTOR ROLES

Coordination

The public sector often plays a coordinating function. Coordination is necessary among the many governmental bodies concerned with different aspects of tourism. Immigration may, for example, wish to relax the frontier formalities in order to expedite the entry of tourists into a country. This obviously will aid tourism. The appropriate agency for drug enforcement may be against this proposal of relaxation, though, for fear that it will increase the flow of drugs as well as tourists into the host country. Some kind of coordination is obviously necessary. Coordination is also necessary among government at the federal, state, and local levels. To be truly effective, tourism within a country must be coordinated so that all regions are moving toward the same goals. For the same reason, coordination is necessary between the public sector and the private sector as well as between the public sector and nonprofit organizations. Many educational and cultural organizations, although they do not have tourism as their major focus, do much to provide resources that attract tourists. The private sector is obviously very involved in tourism. To avoid duplication of effort, it is vital that goals and strategies be coordinated.

Planning

In countries such as Algeria and Israel, government gets into the planning of tourism development. National tourism development plans are drawn up in which the government decides which sectors of the various tourism-related industries will be developed, what the appropriate rate of growth will be, and who will provide the needed capital for expansion. The key is to balance the development of supply (attractions, facilities, and infrastructure) and the promotion of demand (the number of tourists).

Legislation and Regulation

An important role of government is that of legislator and regulator. Government legislation can affect the number of paid vacation days during the year and hence the amount of discretionary paid time available for vacations. Policies on passports and visas have to be determined. A visa is required for tourists from Europe entering the United States; the reverse is not true. The appropriate policy is determined by the government. Government influence may also be felt in the regulations necessary to run a tourism business. In some countries, guides must be licensed. Businesses may have safety and health regulations to abide by; they may also have to meet zoning, building, and licensing requirements. The need to protect the resources that attract tourists may result in restrictions regarding entry to and use of fragile natural resources. Tourists are no longer allowed to enter certain European monuments, and in the United States the national parks have certain areas set aside as wilderness, the use of which is severely limited.

Entrepreneur

The public sector will generally provide the infrastructure for tourism development in a region. In addition, however, government gets involved in owning and running attractions and services. Many countries operate state-owned airlines, and in Greece, Spain, and Portugal the government owns and operates hotels.

Stimulator

A government can stimulate tourism within a country, state, or locality in one of three ways. First, financial incentives, such as low-interest loans or nonpayment of taxes for a specified period of time, may be offered to induce private-sector investment. Second, the public sector may sponsor research that will benefit an industry in general rather than one company in particular. For instance, research may be conducted on the characteristics of a particular foreign market. The results then can be made available to those in the private sector who can develop their own plans to attract this market to use each particular facility. Last, government can stimulate tourism by spending money on promotion. The effort should be aimed at promoting the entire county or state, and it usually consists of travel promotion aimed at generating tourist demand. In some cases, it may also involve investment promotion aimed at inducing capital investment for tourism attractions and facilities.

ESTABLISHING A TOURISM POLICY

It should be clear that whether those in the public sector like it or not, they are involved in tourism. To guide its actions and the actions of those in the private and nonprofit sectors, it is advisable to establish a tourism policy.

The policy acts as a set of guidelines to determine which specific objectives and actions should be pursued to meet the needs of those in the particular destination areas under consideration.

A MODEL FOR TOURISM POLICY

The model presented in Figure 10.1 illustrates the process by which tourism policy is formulated. The many needs of a region are identified by using appropriate research techniques. Tourism goals reflect these needs, but they are constrained by the existing market and resource factors. A series of programs or strategies will flow from the overall policy that is aimed at achieving goals and satisfying previously identified needs. Also, the constraints of market and resource will be changed as a result of feedback resulting from the generated policy. The model will now be explored in greater depth.

Goals

Goals for tourism have to be set before policy can be developed. However, it is crucial that goals for the tourism sector not be set in isolation. For example, there is a very close link between tourism and recreation.

FIGURE 10.1   Tourism Policy Model

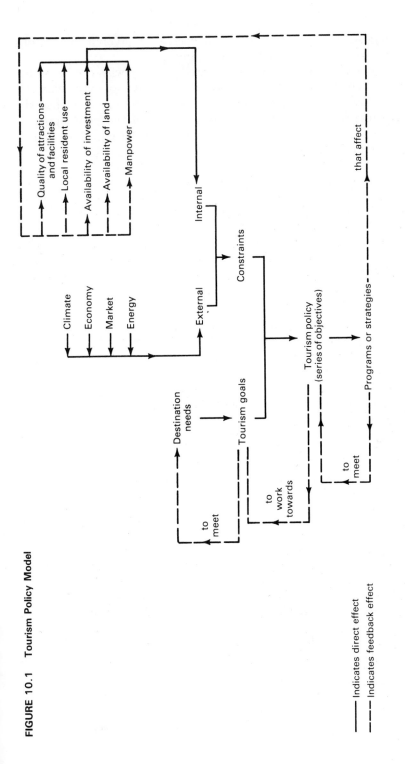

ADAPTED FROM: Harry G. Matthews, *International Tourism: A Political and Social Analysis* (Cambridge, MA, Schenkman Publishing Company, 1978). Scottish Tourist Board, *Planning for Tourism in Scotland: Preliminary National Strategy,* 1975. U.S. Senate, "National Tourism Policy Study: Ascertainment Phase," *Committee on Commerce, Science and Transportation,* 1978.

It can be argued that tourism is a form of recreation involving overnight travel or a certain distance away from home.

Tourism goals must also be formulated to agree with the broad national interest and to complement the specific objectives of national, state, and local bodies in related fields. A recent U.S. study has identified the following principles of national public policy by which the federal government achieves a consensus for guiding federal legislation.[1] They can be used as an expression of the U.S. national interest:

> Energy conservation
> Full employment
> Economic growth with minimum inflation
> Improved operation of the federal government
> Environmental protection
> Judicious use of natural resources
> Urban revitalization
> Preservation of national heritage resources
> Consumer protection
> Equal opportunities for people in disadvantaged segments of the population
> Improved physical and mental health
> Reduced international trade deficits
> Equitable taxation
> Economic viability of small businesses
> Minimum regulation of private industry
> Improved international goodwill
> Balanced national transportation system

Against this backdrop of national interests, tourism goals can be developed along four lines—economic, consumer, national resource/environmental, and government operations.

Constraints

Before specific objectives can be developed in the four above-mentioned areas, it is necessary to consider some constraining factors. Constraints may be external or internal to the host destination. External constraints are those outside the control of the host destination.

EXTERNAL. Because the volume of demand for vacations is closely related to levels of disposable income, policy is constrained by general economic conditions in the tourist-generating countries. A stagnant economic situation suggests that one plan for, at best, limited growth and

---

[1]U.S. Senate, "National Tourism Policy Study: Ascertainment Phase," *Committee on Commerce, Science and Transportation*, 1977, p. 30.

a policy of improved quality rather than quantity of resources.

Policy is also constrained by the world energy situation. The price and supply of gasoline particularly affects destination regions that rely upon auto tourists. The overall effect of an increase in the price of gas or uncertainty over gasoline supplies may be a reduction in the number of auto-based tourists, a redistribution of tourists to more accessible areas, and a more center-based vacation than a touring one. Such a situation will have important policy implications for the development of facilities and the encouragement of public transportation.

The travel potential of various segments of the market will also influence policy. For example, the best potential, for increased package holidays to Scotland is from Southern England because of rapid access by public transportation, particularly by air. This suggests that one make policies regarding the development of public transportation.

Climatic factors constrain the types of tourism that can be developed. For example, the climate of Scotland is regarded unfavorably by many people in Britain. To a certain extent the image is not totally justified and may be remedied by promoting the seasons when the climate is conducive to vacations. If poor weather limits vacation activities, the obvious implication for policy makers is to develop more wet-weather facilities.

INTERNAL. Internal constraints, although influencing tourism policy, can be modified as the result of the policy created.

The quality of attractions and available facilities limits, for example, the type of vacationers that can reasonably be attracted. The U.S. market is very accustomed to private bathrooms in hotels. If these are lacking, a policy implication may be to allow financial incentives to modernize existing facilities by building more rooms with private bathrooms. Facilities that have been built without private bathrooms will not be eligible for such aid.

It has been noted earlier that tourism policy cannot be separated from recreation and leisure policy. The use of attractions and facilities by the local population has to be considered as a possible constraint to tourism policy. In and around urban areas it may be that only a small portion of the recreational capacity will be available for tourists, particularly on weekends. On the other hand, certain cultural and recreational facilities may be viable and available to the local community only because of the support from tourist demand. The extensive theater facilities in London are a prime example. Many of these theaters rely upon tourist traffic to make them commercially viable. If this demand were not present, many theaters would be forced to close and this resource would be lost to the local population.

The availability of both land and investment is also of concern to destination areas. Particularly in small areas, difficult decisions must be made regarding appropriate land use. In the United States considerable controversy has arisen over the use of public land for wilderness or recreational use. The scarcity of investment money raises particular problems for a destination country. The lack of money for investment will prevent tourism development, but the encouragement of capital from outside the area will result in a loss of local control. This problem is felt not only by countries but also by local areas within a country that seek financing from domestic sources of capital. Decisions to expand, contract, build, or close facilities—decisions that vitally affect the local community—are decided by people outside the community.

The availability of manpower also acts as a constraint to tourism policy. Tourism is a people industry. The characteristics of the tourism industry create particular employment problems. Tourism jobs are often seasonal and low-paying. In order to deal with the public from another social class and culture, it may be necessary to learn different behaviors or different ways of serving food than those used in the home. In some cases, U.S. hotel companies, prior to the opening of an overseas property, have had to support the development of a school for training local employees in methods of serving the American market.

Tourism Goals

The tourism goals set will be tempered by the constraints already discussed. Typical tourism goals are:[2]

Economic—To optimize the contribution of tourism and recreation to economic prosperity, full employment, regional economic development, and improved international balance of payments.

Consumer—To make the opportunity for and the benefits of travel and recreation universally accessible to residents and visitors.

—To contribute to the personal growth and education of the population and encourage their appreciation of the geography, history, and ethnic diversity of the nation.

—To encourage the free and welcome entry of foreigners, while balancing this goal with the need to monitor persons and goods entering the country with laws protecting public health.

Environmental and natural resource—To protect and preserve the historical and cultural foundations of the nation as a living part of community life and development, and to insure future generations an opportunity to enjoy the rich heritage of the nation.

—To insure the compatability of tourism, recreational, and activity policies with other national interests in energy development and conservation, environmental protection, and judicious use of natural resources.

Government operations—To harmonize to the maximum extent possible all federal activities supporting tourism and recreation; to support the needs of the general public and the public and private sectors of industries involved with tourism and recreation; to take a leadership role with all those concerned with tourism, recreation, and national heritage conservation.

---

[2]"National Tourism Policy Study," p. 31.

Tourism Objectives

Once the above-stated broad goals are made, conflicts arise when specific objectives are set. Conflicts may arise between goals or within goals. For example, should casino gambling be encouraged? To do so may be consistent with an economic goal, but it may conflict with a consumer goal. Trinidad and Tobago have decided that permission will not be granted for the operation of gambling casinos. Although they recognize the earning potential of casinos, it is felt that the social cost will be too great. Similar fears for their citizens have stopped several U.S. states from allowing casino gambling. Similar conflicts can arise within goals. For example, encouraging foreigners to visit existing tourist ports of entry, the international balance of payments may be improved, thus helping achieve part of an economic goal, but it will not be compatible with a desire to maximize regional economic development.

Only when local interests weigh what is best for their community, what meets the community needs, will such conflicts be solved in the best interests of the community.

Tourism Policy

The agreed-upon objectives, formulated to meet set goals, constitute the tourism policy of a destination area. The many alternative ways to meet tourism's goals have been resolved by Trinidad and Tobago in such a way to arrive at a basic policy statement:[3]

Because the country's resources and facilities must be directed primarily to serving the needs, comforts, and enjoyment of its own citizens, the general public is guaranteed access to all beaches in the country and no discrimination is allowed against any person on the grounds of race, color, class, or religion.

Although the likely earning potential of casinos is great, because the social cost is too high a price to pay, permission will not be granted for the operation of gambling casinos.

Although the major attraction for tourism arises out of the culture of the islands, any program for tourism development must include positive measures to protect the country's art forms and the artists who perform them from wanton destruction.

Because tourism employs either directly or indirectly a large number of persons, it is important that clear evidence exist that a person of any race, class, color, or religion be expected on merit to aspire to the highest positions of employment in the industry.

A fair share of the investment in tourism must be reserved for the small entrepreneur, either by way of participation in larger projects or by way of small hotels and guest houses.

[3]Max Cuffie, "Tourism," in *Patterns of Progress: Trinidad & Tobago 10 Years of Independence* (Key Caribbean Publications, undated).

Firms engaged in tourism development will be required to show that effective decision making is vested in citizens of the country.

The entire industry must take steps to reverse the trend of relying heavily on imports, and it must more vigorously seek to maximize the use of local goods and services, particularly in the fields of food, drink, entertainment, and professional and consulting services.

Tourism Programs

Working with the set policy, developers will set up programs to meet the stated objectives. Examples include programs establishing specific investment incentives, programs setting immigration rules, programs organizing the tax structure, and promotional campaigns aiming at a specific target market. The successful completion of these programs will result in the objectives being met. This in turn will affect the internal constraint as it moves toward meeting the agreed-upon tourism goals. As stated earlier, these goals are set in line with the needs of the community.

TOURISM ORGANIZATIONS

World Tourism Organization

Many types of organizations have formed at the international, national, and local levels to develop and implement tourism policy. The only organization that represents governmental tourist interests is the World Tourism Organization, which is based in Madrid. Formed in 1975 from the International Union of Official Travel Organizations, WTO is the official tourism voice to the United Nations. The organization generally aims to promote and develop tourism and specifically pays attention to the interests of developing countries. To this end, the WTO collects information and issues publications on such subjects as world tourism trends, marketing approaches, and the protection of natural and cultural resources. Training programs are conducted and work is undertaken to make foreign travel easier in such ways as reducing the number of passport and visa requirements and standardizing the travel signs.

International Civil Aviation Organization

Established in 1944, the International Civil Aviation Organization (ICAO) is made up of representatives from the governments of eighty countries. The principal task of the ICAO is to promote worldwide civil aviation. To achieve this, international standards and practices regarding air navigation have been adopted. Proposals have been developed for the construction of facilities and the reduction of frontier formalities to help ensure the growth of international civil aviation in a safe and orderly way.

Regional Organizations

Many organizations have come into being to assist in the development of tourism in different regions of the world. Some, such as the Organization for Economic Cooperation and Development (OECD) were established for reasons of general economic growth and stability. Within OECD a tourism committee was established to deal specifically with tourism, including the assessment of the effect of member country policies on tourism.

In other cases, organizations have been created to implement policies to develop, promote, and facilitate travel to specific regions of the world. PATA, the Pacific Area Travel Association, was organized in 1951 to promote travel in the Pacific area.Similarly, the Caribbean Tourism Organization and the European Travel Commission have been organized to assist the Caribbean islands and Europe, respectively.

National Organizations

The tourism policies of a country are developed by and implemented through a national tourism organization (NTO). An NTO is the official body responsible for the development and marketing of tourism. The functions of the official tourism organization will vary according to the governmental status it is given. First, it may be governmental—part of a civil service system as either an independent ministry, such as the State Secretariat for Tourism in Mexico, or as a part of another related ministry. In France the State Secretariat for Tourism is part of the Ministry of Cultural Affairs and the Environment, but in Spain the Ministry of Commerce and Tourism contains the national tourism organization. Approximately 30 percent of World Tourism Organization members have an independent ministry for tourism.

Second, the official tourism organization may be a government agency or bureau responsible for tourism and set within a larger department. Tourism Canada, formerly the Canadian Government Office of Tourism, is located within the Department of Regional Industrial Expansion, but the Japanese Department of Tourism finds itself as part of the Department of Transportation. The government agency has, in general, less influence and status than the ministry form described above. Mexico, for example, has an independent government agency called the National Tourism Council that is responsible for international promotion but that reports to and receives policy guidance from the above-mentioned State Tourism Secretariat. Tourism bodies that have governmental status have the broadest range of functions of NTOs.

Third, the official tourism organization may be a quasi-public government-funded corporation, board, or authority, such as the Hong Kong Tourist Association, the Irish Tourist Board, or the British Tourist Authority. A key advantage of the government-funded board is that it has greater management flexibility in dealing with the commercial aspects of tourism development and promotion. A closer liaison with the private sector and the consuming public is possible. In fact, members of the private sector are often asked to serve as board directors.

Last, the official tourism organization may be a private industry association indirectly supported by government funding, such as the Japan Tourist Association. Less than ten percent of WTO members have a national tourism organization that has nongovernmental status. A primary advantage of having a government agency as a national tourist organization is that the NTO has the authority within government to represent tourism and develop and interpret tourism policy.

FUNCTIONS—SUPPLY. As the text has noted, the functions of the NTO will vary depending upon the governmental status given to it. To some extent, the NTO will be involved with the supply of and demand for tourism facilities and attractions. This involves conducting an inventory of resources prior to the formulation of a general plan for tourism development. In fewer cases, the NTO will get involved with maintaining the quality of the tourism product. This may include protecting the environment that tourists come to view or setting standards in hotels or for tour guides. NTOs in free-enterprise countries tend to have less input into any of the aspects of quality control. The input of the NTO in free-enterprise economies will probably be limited to the giving of advice on the effects of industry practices on tourism. When another agency sets policy that affects tourism, the NTO may have some advisory input into that policy.

Although the state's role in economic activities in free-market economies is generally confined to legislation and regulation, the role of the state in socialist countries is quite different. In such countries the government may actually get involved in owning and managing tourist facilities. Developing countries that lack private industry capital and expertise have often found it necessary for the state to develop, own, and manage facilities and attractions. To further ensure the proper development of supply, it may be necessary for the government to get involved in the areas of financial incentives to ensure facility development and manpower development to produce sufficient numbers of qualified personnel. Table 10.1 contains the results of a comparative study by Arthur D. Little of the tourism functions of supply of eight countries.

TABLE 10.1 Comparison of Tourism Technical Assistance, Planning, Development, and Regulatory Programs of the Eight Foreign Governments Surveyed

Country	Existence of Industry Technical Assistance Programs	Existence of Comprehensive Tourism Planning Program	Existence of Government Financial Support for Tourism Development	Tourism Industry Sectors Regulated by the NTO
Canada	Yes	Pilot program for national tourism planning incomplete	Yes	None
Mexico	Yes	Currently developing a national tourism plan	Yes; grants, loans, and loan guarantees	Price regulation of hotels, restaurants, tourist guides, tourism equipment rental firms, travel agencies
United Kingdom	Yes	Identification of national development areas; first attempts at comprehensive regional tourism planning underway	Yes; grants, loans, and implicit loan guarantees	None (Tour operators regulated by Civil Aviation Authority)
Ireland	Yes	Comprehensive national and regional tourism land-use plan completed	Yes; grants and loans	Registration and quality rating of hotels
France	Yes	Regional tourism development planning within the context of five-year economic development plans	Yes; grants and loans	Licensing of travel agents; regulation of price and quality of hotels
Spain	Yes	Identification of national tourism development areas; completed national inventory of tourism resources	Yes; grants and loans	Licensing of travel agents and hotels; quality grading of hotels
Hong Kong	Yes	None	None explicitly for tourism development	None
Japan	Yes	Site-specific planning for tourism facilities and recreational areas	Yes; grants and loans	Licensing of travel agents; examination of guide-interpreters

SOURCE: Arthur D. Little, Inc., *National Tourism Policy Study Final Report* (U.S. Senate Committee on Commerce, Science and Transportation, Phase III Report, April 1978), p. 209.

FUNCTIONS–DEMAND. On the demand side, NTOs tend to get involved in matters of facilitation, promotion, market research, and representation at the international level. The role of the NTO in facilitation tends to be an advisory one, commenting on the effect of government policies regarding visas, passports, and custom formalities on tourist demand. National tourism organizations are primarily known for their role in marketing.

The specific functions of both supply and demand will be examined in greater detail in Chapters Twelve, Fourteen, and Sixteen.

UNITED STATES GOVERNMENT INVOLVEMENT IN TOURISM

Historical Review[4]

Prior to World War II the federal government of the United States had done little to involve itself with either domestic or international tourism. In 1940, however, the Domestic Travel Act was passed. This act authorized the National Park Service, a part of the Department of the Interior, to promote and administer tourism functions of the department. World War II halted any plans the NPS might have had. After the war the National Park Service was faced with restrictions of budget and a need to expand park facilities to meet the increasing numbers of park visitors. Thus, travel activities were given no attention.

At the same time, two developments led to a tourism balance of payments deficit for the United States. First, Americans were encouraged to visit Europe to help the devasted European economies. This was partly justified by the argument that the inflow of U.S. dollars would better enable Europe to purchase American goods. Second, many foreign countries, because of their need to acquire American dollars, restricted foreign travel by their own citizens in the immediate postwar years.

In 1960, President Eisenhower proclaimed a "Visit U.S.A. Year," but felt that, although government involvement in tourism could be justified on economic grounds, it was not a proper function of government to advertise and promote travel. Pushed initially by the Senate Commerce Committee, the International Travel Act, passed by Congress in 1961, established the United States Travel Service within the Department of Commerce. The USTS represented the first real attempt to promote the United States to foreigners. The office was authorized to set up overseas offices and to promote and advertise U.S. travel destinations in foreign countries. The goals of the USTS were to:

Contribute to the maximum extent possible to the balance of payments position of the United States

---

[4]This section is abstracted from *Destination U.S.A.*, final report of the National Tourism Resources Review Commission, Vol. 4, "Federal Role," June 1973.

Contribute to the maximum extent possible to the health and well-being of the American people

Contribute to the maximum extent possible to international goodwill and understanding

Emphasis was placed on the economic goal of achieving as favorable a balance of payments position as possible.

By the mid-1960s the travel deficit had increased to $1.6 billion. In an attempt to reduce this, President Johnson proposed in 1968 the imposition of a tax on international tickets and a reduction in the duty-free allowance upon return to the United States. The proposal was not enacted because of the widespread opposition generated. Recognizing that a travel deficit could be reduced not only by discouraging American travel abroad but also by encouraging foreign travel to the United States, Congress in 1970 amended the 1961 International Travel Act to authorize matching funds to states or nonprofit organizations for projects aimed at promoting foreign travel to the United States. At the same time the position of director of the USTS was elevated to that of assistant secretary of commerce for tourism.

In 1975, the authority for domestic tourism that the secretary of the interior had agreed to transfer to the secretary of commerce was given to the United States Travel Service, which was later renamed the U.S. Travel and Tourism Administration. Passage of the National Tourism Policy Act in 1981 ended an eight-year industry lobbying effort. The act, which survived strong objections from the executive branch including a presidential veto, has resulted in the U.S. Travel and Tourism Administration being headed by an undersecretary of tourism, which is an elevation in status from an assistant secretary. Funding, however, has been kept at a level so low, having declined from $30 million in 1977 to a proposed $0 in 1984 (this will probably result in a compromise of about $6.5 million), that meaningful activities at the federal level have been effectively stymied.

Present Role

PROBLEMS. The tourism system is comprised of natural resources, attractions, facilities, services, transportation, facilitation, and marketing. The blend of these factors determines the effectiveness of the system. A major difficulty in the United States is that the role of the federal government in tourism is so fragmented that integration of the various tourism elements is exceedingly difficult.

There appear to be over one-hundred different programs in approximately fifty different departments or agencies that directly affect tourism, travel, or recreation. The difficulties caused by this fragmentation are obviously felt in problems of communication. A study by Arthur D. Little found a "widespread lack of understanding among Federal officials of the degree of their agencies' current involvement in and/or impacts on tourism and travel."[5] The study team also found that the federal interagency coordination on travel and tourism was poor to nonexistent. Little or no coordination existed between those agencies viewed as influencing tourism and the USTTA. There was general agreement that there were too many federal programs involved in an aspect of tourism and no effective means of coordinating existing efforts, resulting in an ineffective federal involvement.

MARKETING. The marketing aspect of tourism lies in the hands of the U.S. Travel and Tourism Administration, which is a part of the Department of Commerce. The agency is primarily concerned with overseas promotion, although a certain amount of market research has culminated in a variety of publications being made available to the public at a nominal charge. Programs range from promotional campaigns aimed at attracting conventions and sponsorship of international trade shows, to the development of gateway reception areas to provide language assistance to the international visitor.

NATURAL RESOURCES. The natural resources of the United States are the responsibility of the Department of the Interior, the Department of Agriculture, and the Department of Defense, and additional independent government offices. The primary research, development, and planning function is undertaken by the former Bureau of Outdoor Recreation, now the Heritage Conservation and Recreation Service (HCRS). HCRS has the primary responsibility of maintaining a comprehensive nationwide outdoor recreation plan. The agency can only make recommendations on recreation policy, planning, and research, and it has no authority to manage land, water, and recreation areas.

The link between tourism and recreation is again shown by the fact that of the 760 million acres of land owned by the federal government, 447 million acres have been set aside for recreation use by tourists. Federal lands represent approximately 85 percent of the recreation space in the United States. The principal agencies that manage federal lands for recreation and tourism are the Corps of Engineers, the U.S. Forest Service, and the National Park Service.

The Corps of Engineers is responsible for navigation, beach erosion control, hurricane flood protection, major drainage, flood control, and water resources on both federal land waterways and improved inland and intercoastal waterways. The corps takes recreation into account in their

---

[5]U.S. Senate, "National Tourism Policy Study: Ascertainment Phase," *Committee on Commerce, Science and Transportation*, 1977, p. 15.

cost/benefit analysis to determine whether or not a project should be undertaken. Although recreation sites at project sites are operated by the corps, the agency prefers to turn over operation to nonfederal units.

The U.S. Forest Service controls both national forest areas and national grasslands areas. Recreation is a major activity on forest land, as is timber harvesting, mining, livestock grazing, and protecting wildlife. Approximately half of the nation's ski areas operate under permit from the U.S. Forest Service.

The original purpose of the National Park Service (NPS) was to preserve the unique natural wonders of the country for the use and pleasure of all people. Later legislation added historic preservation, intensive outdoor recreation, and cultural activities to that mandate. NPS areas serve as attractions for hundreds of thousands of visitors every year.

A major problem as far as tourism is concerned is the question of preservation versus development. The agencies mentioned above are very concerned about the resources they manage. Critics argue that a certain level of development is necessary to service the visitors that travel to the natural resource attractions. This is answered by those who are concerned that too much development will ruin the attraction of the natural resources. Although tourism is heavily dependent on the proper management of the natural resources of land and water, it also relies upon physical improvement of the base. The controversy arises over this balance.

FACILITATION. The Departments of State, Transportation, Treasury, and Justice are concerned with the movement of tourists. The U.S. Travel and Tourism Administration is authorized to encourage the simplification, reduction, or elimination of travel barriers. In reality, apart from transportation, the influence of arguments for encouraging tourism is very low.

In summary, the problem tourism faces at the federal level is that the programs of many government departments and agencies affect it, but these same departments attach little importance to tourism. Additionally, an insufficient coordinating mechanism exists to ensure a concerted federal action on behalf of tourism.

ROLE OF STATE GOVERNMENTS

Structure

Within the many states, tourism's role within each state and the corresponding role of each state in tourism is recognized to varying degrees. Essentially three types of organization structures are present:

1. A public or quasi-public travel commission or bureau
2. An independent or semi-independent travel development department
3. Travel development within another department

Hawaii and Michigan are examples of the first type of structure. In Hawaii, leadership is given by the private Hawaii Visitors Bureau. The organizational chart for the bureau is shown in Figure 10.2. A senior vice-president and a vice-president for finance and administration report to the president who in turn is responsible to a board of directors. The vice-president for finance and administration is responsible for accounting and administrative support. He or she is also responsible for attracting conventions. This officer in addition to three directors—for special events and promotions, for information services, and for sales and service—report directly to the senior vice-president as does an outside advertising agency. The directors of visitor satisfaction and of research and marketing report directly to the president. In the case of Michigan, as shown in Figure 10.3, leadership comes from the public sector. The Michigan Travel Commission acts as the board of directors and is made up of representatives of convention bureaus, representatives of the state travel bureau, and consumer representatives appointed by the governor. Located within the Department of Commerce, the Travel Bureau is organized into three divisions. The Marketing and Promotion Division is responsible for publicity, advertising, publications, sales offices outside the state, special projects, and information services. The Product Development Division liaises with local, state, and federal governments while it prospects for new business developments. In addition it handles traveler services, consmer protection, and product satisfaction. The Programs and Administration Division is responsible for research and program development, market analysis, administrative services, and the administration of grants.

The state of Tennessee has a Department of Tourism Development with an independent cabinet-level status as is shown in Figure 10.4. This allows for a simplification of the decision-making process because of the access that the commissioner of tourism development has to the governor due to his position as a member of the governor's cabinet. Another important plus is the advantage the commission has, especially at the time of the budget, in dealing with the state legislature as a full department. Reporting to the deputy commissioner are four distinct divisions. The Fiscal Services Division regulates all fiscal and personnel management of the commission. The Travel Promotion Division is responsible for promoting tourism in Tennessee. This includes working with various intermediaries to help produce packages and selecting and placing all advertising materials, including brochures, publications, and maps. Within the Information and Media Services Division feature articles and news items are developed and placed in magazines, newspapers, and trade publications to promote the state. This division supervises the State Photographic Laboratory and liaises with Memphis State University in

FIGURE 10.2 Organizational Structure, Hawaii Visitors Bureau

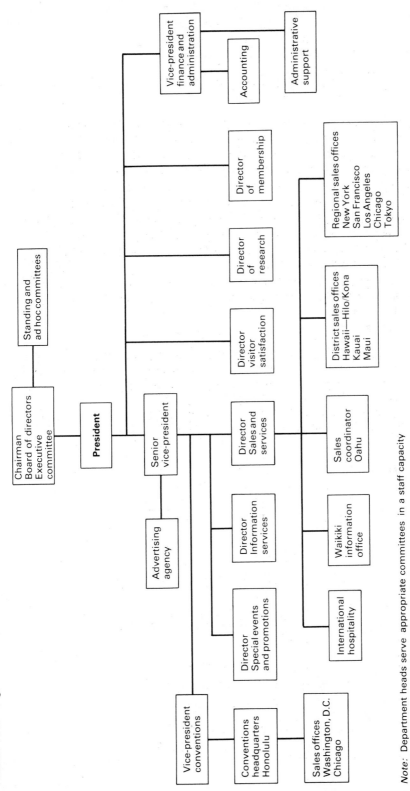

Note: Department heads serve appropriate committees in a staff capacity

SOURCE: USTS Tourism: State Structure, Organization and Support, A Technical Study, 1978, p. 50.

FIGURE 10.3   Organizational Structure, Michigan Travel Bureau

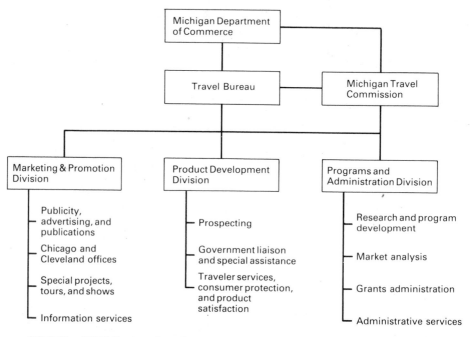

SOURCE: USTS Tourism: State Structure, Organization and Support, A Technical Study, 1978,
p. 51.

the development of a research program concerning relevant statistical data. The Support Services Division is responsible for upgrading hotel and restaurant facilities and educating managers about the value of tourism to the state. The division is also responsible for staffing and operating the state's welcome centers.

The State of Montana represents the third type of structure, as shown in Figure 10.5. The parent of the travel promotion unit is the Department of Highways. Three divisions exist within the unit—those of film location, tour, and photo and publicity. A major concern in this type of structure is that tourism is regarded as secondary to the main purpose of the department and may have to struggle for attention.

Those states that have the most active travel and tourism programs have certain characteristics:

1. They have the personal interest and active support of either the governor or lieutenant governor and the legislature.
2. A committee of the legislature deals specifically with travel and tourism.
3. A program of research and evaluation is carried out to indicate the effectiveness of the marketing effort and the impact of tourism on the state.

FIGURE 10.4 Organizational Structure, Tennessee Department of Tourism Development

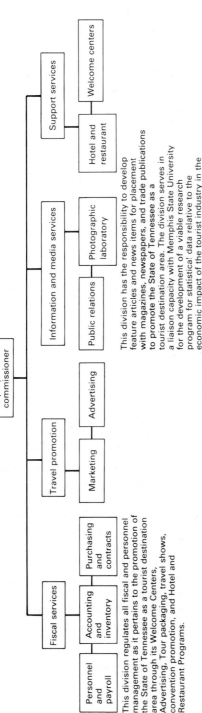

Department of Tourist Development

This division regulates all fiscal and personnel management as it pertains to the promotion of the State of Tennessee as a tourist destination area through its Welcome Centers, Advertising, Tour packaging, travel shows, convention promotion, and Hotel and Restaurant Programs.

This division has the responsibility to promote the scenic, historic, natural and man-made tourist attractions in Tennessee. The division conducts special promotion programs in key markets for tourists to Tennessee to develop individual family auto vacations and group movement of tourists via a common carrier. Also, the division works closely with industry-related organizations, travel agents, tour brokers, and tour operations to package Tennessee vacations for sale both domestically and internally. Additionally the travel promotion division is responsible for the selection and placement of all advertising materials. This includes brochures, publications, booklets, maps, and promotional literature.

This division has the responsibility to develop feature articles and news items for placement with magazines, newspapers, and trade publications to promote the State of Tennessee as a tourist destination area. The division serves in a liaison capacity with Memphis State University for the development of a viable research program for statistical data relative to the economic impact of the tourist industry in the State of Tennessee. Additionally, the division has the managerial and supervisory responsibility for the State of Tennessee Photographic Laboratory.

This division has the responsibility for coordinating the efforts of upgrading Hotel and Restaurant facilities in Tennessee. Also the division educated the management of these facilities on the value of the tourist industry. Additionally this division is responsible for the staffing and operation of the eight Welcome Center facilities across the state, which operate seven days a week, twenty-four hours a day.

SOURCE: *USTS Tourism: State State Structure, Organization and Support, A Technical Study*, 1978, p. 52.

FIGURE 10.5   Organization Chart of Travel Promotion Unit—Montana

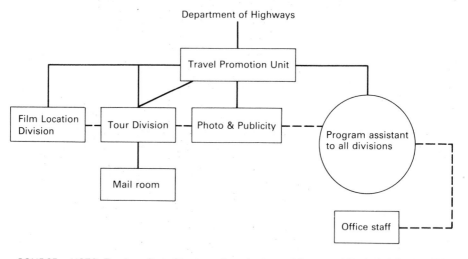

SOURCE: USTS, *Tourism: State Structure, Organization and Support, A Technical Study,* 1978, p. 54.

4. The economic development aspects of tourism are emphasized.
5. Active advisory councils or commissions are present, and the liason between the private and the public sectors is strong.
6. State travel/tourism plans are part of the planning/budgeting process.
7. Spending of promotional dollars has shifted from promoting the natural resources to promoting urban, convention, and man-made attractions.

Functions[6]

All of the fifty states have some kind of official government agency responsible for tourism development. In recent years, at various times, California and Maine have not had a state travel office. Approximately 90 percent of the states retain advertising agencies to handle their promotional program. In order to stretch state tourist dollars, approximately thirty states have a matching formula, usually on a fifty-fifty basis, with private businesses, regional travel organizations, and city convention and visitor bureaus. Magazines and newspapers are the preferred media to use for state travel advertising. Radio is used by approximately 10 percent of the states, and television is used even less. Most states participate in travel shows, and approximately one-quarter operate out-of-state information centers. Although all states have a special travel pro-

---

[6]This section is abstracted from *Survey of State Travel Offices,* an annual report published by the United States Travel Data Center.

motion or theme, less than one in six states have different themes directed to separate market segments.

Although almost 90 percent of state travel offices have programs devoted to package-tour development, only one-third of them publish and distribute state package-tour catalogs. About two-thirds of all states operate familiarization tours for tour operators and retail travel agents.

About two-thirds of the states publish travel-oriented newsletters. They are generally distributed monthly. In slightly over half the cases the newsletter is distributed to the public.

Almost all states employ a public relations or press information officer, while about three-quarters of the states conduct press or travel writer tours.

In just over half the states there is a staff member assigned to travel research, although for more than half of the members this is a part-time responsibility. In approximately 40 percent of the states, research is conducted by university faculty members, and in about one-quarter of the states this function is undertaken by employees in other agencies of state government. In about one-third of the states, private research organizations are hired to conduct research. In nine out of ten states, travel data is gathered on a continuous basis, usually through welcome centers and/or vehicle counts.

ORGANIZING FOR TOURISM AT THE DESTINATION

Within a state it is desirable for local communities, under the umbrella of the state effort, to initiate their own policies and strategies for the effective development of tourism. This may involve regional organizations, as in Michigan, where four tourist associations are responsible for encouraging visitors to their part of the state. Funded in part by a state grant and in part by contributions from private businesses, these regional organizations supplement the effort at the state level while encouraging a joint public/private sector involvement.

At the local community level a tourism organization typically evolves in the following way:

1. A small, informal group of people (most likely a special-interest group) interested in increasing tourism in the community gets together to seek additional support and help by visiting governmental or community agencies such as the city council.
2. Once the agencies are made aware of the many things involved in the community affecting and affected by tourism, there develops the realization that a proper community involvement is necessary; a subcommittee on tourism is formed as part of the chamber of commerce or city council.
3. When it is realized that certain jobs can best be accomplished by people who share the same priorities, an association forms either as a part of the chamber

of commerce, as a part of the local government under the city council, or as an independent entity; as the quantity of work increases, a regular office and secretary may be established to complement the volunteer leadership.

4. At the final stage a full-time executive director is hired to direct the organization's work.

The way an organization forms depends in great part upon the tradition within the community, the resources that are available, the organizational structure in the community, the strength of the local chamber of commerce, and the amount of confidence in the local elected officials. At the state level, cooperation may be given to local communities in one of two ways:

1. States may assist local efforts by passing legislation enabling communities to collect taxes to support local promotional activities; this is usually in the form of a bed tax, but some cities derive support from a tax on mixed drinks, entertainment, or tickets, or from an earmarked sales tax.

2. The states may provide matching funds, either for general purposes or for activities specified by the state government; these activities are usually such things as promotion and public relations, familiarization tours for travel brokers and writers, preparation of information materials, and technical assistance and research.

Structure and Function

An organizational structure for a destination-area tourism council is suggested in Figure 10.6. The tourism council establishes the philosophy for the community and sets the overall goal for the master plan. Assisted by input from related organizations, the council develops policies that are carried out by a full-time staff. Eight primary planning committees are represented in addition to the two basic functionaries of research and data collection and promotion and public relations. The Committee on Community Involvement and Leadership is responsible for maximizing the involvement of community leaders in the work of the council. The Committee on Development of Tourist Attractions seeks to identify new attraction opportunities and develop them. Similar tasks are undertaken by the Committee on Support Facilities in regard to the need for both private and public facilities to support the goals of tourism development.

The role of the Budget and Finance Committee is to identify and evaluate the various ways of financing the operations of the council. This may be accomplished through various means. As mentioned above, a bed or transient guest tax is a common method of obtaining funding. This usually requires passage of a city ordinance after state enabling legislation has authorized such a tax. This tax is usually resisted by local lodging groups as an unfair tax on only one segment of the industry, although residents are inclined to support it since it is a tax paid by the visitor.

To a lesser, though rather considerable extent, communities receive allocation from the general funds of the city, county, or state. A major limitation is that cities are often reluctant to allocate general revenue funds to agencies over which they have no control—in some cases it may not even be legal. A number of states will provide matching funds for the purpose of attracting tourists from outside the state. Provisions may be placed on the use of such funds to ensure that they are used for advertising rather than for staff salaries and that they are used for specific objectives, for example, attracting out-of-state businesses that the state supports.

The most common method of financing local efforts is through membership dues. The dues may be on a sliding scale, depending upon the volume of business or the number of employees. A major responsibility of the director or president of such an organization is to convince local businesses that it is worth their time and money to belong to such an organization. Some communities will organize special events—such as races and auctions—to raise funds. These activities usually require a great deal of organization by the local staff as well as the support of many local people and businesses. It does, however, provide a focal point for galvanizing community support. It is often possible, although not often undertaken, to have property owners vote a mill levy on their real estate property to be specifically used for tourism development. Monies so collected do not reflect the pressures of inflation unless new properties are constructed.

The Research and Data Collection Committee determines the amount of research needed and what data should be collected. An important, though often overlooked function, is that of ensuring that the level of service given visitors at the destination is of sufficiently high quality. The Education and Training Committee is concerned with determining the best ways that employees in the various tourism businesses can be trained. This is usually done by the individual operation, but in some cases it may be more efficient to have a group training session on, for instance, fire safety or the importance of customer service.

The Public Relations Committee seeks to develop the best ways of communicating with the different publics of the community. This involves getting press releases and articles in newspapers and magazines, handling tourist complaints, and determining how best to promote the destination. The last committee, the Evaluations Committee, is responsible for determining how to evaluate each part of the tourism program.

Because of the economic and social importance of tourism, the public sector has, to some extent, taken a role in organizing tourism. The amount of involvement will depend upon factors such as the political philosophy of the government and the degree of maturity of the destination area. The case has been made for establishing a clear tourism policy to guide the

FIGURE 10.6   Destination Area Tourism Council Organizational Structure

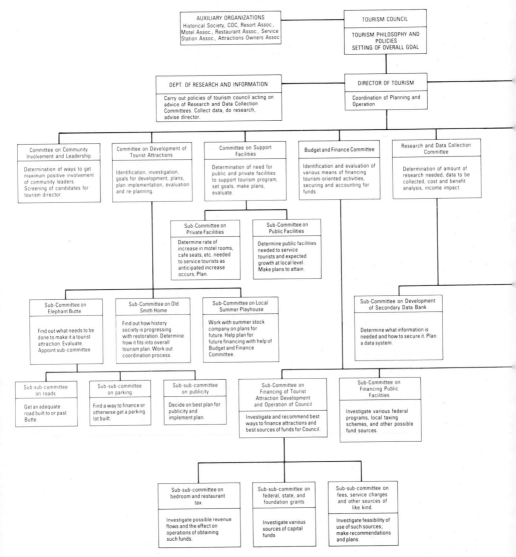

266

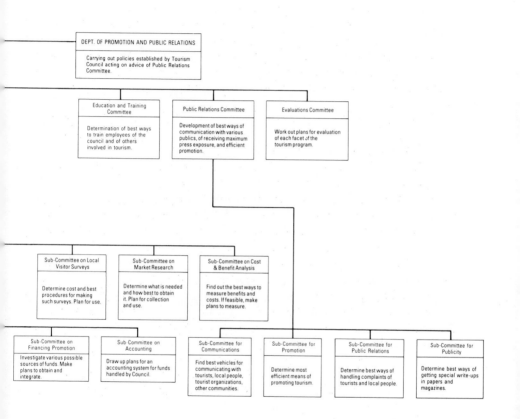

DEPT. OF PROMOTION AND PUBLIC RELATIONS

Carrying out policies established by Tourism Council acting on advice of Public Relations Committee.

Education and Training Committee

Determination of best ways to train employees of the council and of others involved in tourism.

Public Relations Committee

Development of best ways of communication with various publics, of receiving maximum press exposure, and efficient promotion.

Evaluations Committee

Work out plans for evaluation of each facet of the tourism program.

Sub-Committee on Local Visitor Surveys

Determine cost and best procedures for making such surveys. Plan for use.

Sub-Committee on Market Research

Determine what is needed and how best to obtain it. Plan for collection and use.

Sub-Committee on Cost & Benefit Analysis

Find out the best ways to measure benefits and costs. If feasible, make plans to measure.

Sub-Committee on Financing Promotion

Investigate various possible sources of funds. Make plans to obtain and integrate.

Sub-Committee on Accounting

Draw up plans for an accounting system for funds handled by Council.

Sub-Committee for Communications

Find best vehicles for communicating with tourists, local people, tourist organizations, other communities.

Sub-Committee for Promotion

Determine most efficient means of promoting tourism.

Sub-Committee for Public Relations

Determine best ways of handling complaints of tourists and local people.

Sub-Committee for Publicity

Determine best ways of getting special write-ups in papers and magazines.

tourism destiny of the region, and a model for establishing the policy has been suggested.

To implement tourism policy it is necessary to have an organization. A tourism organization may be the World Tourism Organization, which has a province that is worldwide, or a regional or national organization, or a mechanism at the local level. At each level, the possible functions and roles of the tourism organizations are delineated.

Without a policy and a mechanism for implementing it, tourism will increase or decline at the destination in a haphazard manner.

REFERENCES

"America's Best Kept Secret: The Tourism Industry" (Address before the National Conference of Lieutenant Governors), *Vital Speeches*, 42(24), pp. 756–57.

Destination U.S.A., vol. 4, "Federal Role," June 1973, p. 9.

MCINTOSH, ROBERT W., *Tourism: Principles, Practices and Philosophies* (Columbus, OH, Grid Inc., 1977), p. 128.

U.S. SENATE, "National Tourism Policy Study: Ascertainment Phase," Committee on Commerce, Science and Transportation, 1977, p. 28.

UNITED STATES TRAVEL SERVICE, *Planning for Tourism*, vol. 2, "Development," 1978, pp. 2–3.

UNITED STATES TRAVEL SERVICE, *Tourism: State Structure, Organization and Support, A Technical Study*, 1978, pp. 56, 89–90.

WAHAB, SALAH ABDEL, "Aspects of Organization for Tourism at the Destination End," *Tourist Review*, no. 2, April/June 1975, pp. 49–57.

11

TOURISM REGULATION: Controlling the Tourism Industries

The role of the public sector in regulating tourism is regarded by many as essential and by most as controversial. This chapter explores the many ways in which tourism is regulated by the public sector. Tourism legislation and regulation in the United States is examined in depth. The role of regulatory agencies is discussed, and arguments for and against regulation from the viewpoints of consumers, government, and industry are given. Legislation and regulation in Canada is described in full, and the situation is compared with that in the United States.

Beyond the national level, there are a number of international regulations that affect tourism. The most significant of these involve air travel between countries. The specifics of how such agreements are reached are discussed.

The chapter concludes that governments act primarily to protect the resources of the destination area as well as the visiting tourist. Thus, their role in tourism is a positive one. However, the lack of cooperation and coordination between the government agencies that directly or indirectly affect tourism means that the public sector is too often unable to react with the speed desired by the private sector.

CONTROLLING THE TRAVEL INDUSTRY

Introduction

In Chapter Ten it was pointed out that one of the public sector's roles in tourism was that of setting and enforcing various forms of legislation and regulations. This role is at the same time essential and controversial in most free-enterprise-system destination areas. It is thought to be essential because governments cannot totally rely upon the private sector to effectively control and regulate its activities; it is often controversial because the private sector feels that the public sector goes too far in enforcing its regulations. For example, in Canada a major private-sector task force has reached the following conclusions on government regulations:

> The tourism industry . . . could optimize its contribution to the Canadian economy if there were less intervention from all levels of government. Regulations have largely impeded the growth of tourism, rather than hastened its growth. There is a requirement to modernize these regulatory processes and have them respond to needs of the industry and the market rather than as a policing function.[1]

In the United States as well as in Canada a multitude of government agencies have programs and regulations that directly or indirectly affect tourism. Other countries, especially those with socialist or communist governments, regulate tourism even more comprehensively. The complexity of the tourism regulatory framework in most destination areas is a direct reflection of tourism itself; tourists cross international borders, are exposed to all of the cultural, historic, man-made, and natural resources of the destination area, and must be catered to in a safe, secure, and hygienic fashion. It follows, therefore, that a variety of government agencies have tourism-related programs and regulations and not just one.

As Chapter Ten has pointed out, those in the public sector generally get involved in tourism for political, environmental, and economic reasons. The specific functions of governments normally encompass coordination, planning, legislation/regulation, entrepreneurial ventures, and tourism-industry stimulation. The degree of emphasis given to each of these five principal roles varies from destination to destination, but it is usually directly related to the importance attached to tourism as an economic activity. It is important to realize that the actions of those in the public sector have to be supported by various bodies of law (legislation) and specific regulations to have legitimacy in democratic societies. It is with the actual enforcement of the laws and with the structuring of regulations

---

[1]Tourism Sector Consultative Task Force, *A Report By the Sector Task Force On the Canadian Tourism Industry* (Ottawa, Ontario, Department of Industry, Trade and Commerce, 1978), p. 126.

that the most controversy and conflict occurs between the private and public sectors of the tourism system.

A Taxonomy of Tourism Legislation and Regulations

Before the specific types of legislation and regulations that have been introduced in the United States, Canada, and elsewhere are described, it will be useful to classify them as they are commonly found in most destination areas. One method of classification is to group the tourism legislation and regulations into functional areas, such as those related to the protection of the environment, those related to economic development, those related to frontier controls, and so on. The material on the United States is organized in this way. Another means of classification is to group on an industry sector basis by identifying the legislation and regulations that relate to airlines, hotels, travel agents, and so on. In this respect, "horizontal" legislation or regulations are those items that affect every industrial sector, whether it be a tourism or nontourism one, such as income tax and labor legislation. "Specific" legislation or regulations are those items that relate directly to an industrial sector. An example of this is a grading system for hotels. The following chart illustrates commonly found legislation and regulations classified on a sector-by-sector basis in tourism:

ACCOMMODATION ESTABLISHMENTS

Classification and grading/rating of hotels and other establishment types
Fire safety regulations and codes
Health safety regulations and codes
Building and zoning codes
Issuance of operating and liquor licenses and other regulations of the terms
    and conditions of operation
Liability laws with respect to guests and their belongings
Labor and taxation legislation

TRAVEL AGENTS, TOUR WHOLESALERS, AND OPERATORS

Regulations and licensing of travel agents, tour wholesalers, and operators
Definition of responsibilities and limitations
Regulations of promotions
Labor and taxation legislation

AIRLINES, RAILWAYS, BUSES, SHIPS, AND OTHER CARRIERS

Control of fares and tariffs
Licensing of carriers
Regulation of safety procedures
Control of route entry and exit

Limitation of weights and capacities
Negotiations of services
Subsidization of routes
Labor and taxation legislation

Other sectors of the tourism industry, including retailers, car rental agencies, commercial attractions operators, and other businesses, have their own specific legislation and regulations in addition to the horizonal laws and regulations that apply to all.

The Legislation and Regulation of Tourism in the United States

The role taken by the U.S. federal government in preparing legislation and regulations relative to tourism reflects the country's national interests in tourism and tourism's interrelationship with other aspects of U.S. society and business. The U.S. Senate Committee on Commerce has identified these national interests related to tourism as follows:[2]

1. Health and other aspects of the quality of life:
    a. The national interest in public health
    b. Other aspects of the quality of life
    c. Protection of the quality of the tourism experience
    d. Ensuring opportunities for participation in tourism
2. Tourism as an economic activity
    a. The efficient satisfaction of consumer demand
    b. Increasing employment, income, and regional development
3. Meeting business travel demand
4. Facilitation of international tourism
5. Tourism's impact on publicly-owned lands

In addition to recognizing tourism's direct impact and interrelationship with these five factors, the committee has also recognized that tourism interacts with the national economy, the functioning of the transportation system, the system of social and economic statistics, the forms of environmental protection, the clearance of international visitors, the public revenues, and the forms of consumer protection.

It is obvious from these expressed national interests and interactions that tourism is perceived as having a broad-scale and pervasive impact on U.S. society, as in most destination areas that have embraced it as an important economic activity. The broad scope of these impacts is mir-

---

[2]U.S. Senate, *A Conceptual Basis for the National Tourism Policy: Appendix B* (Washington, DC, U.S. Government Printing Office, 1976), pp. 23–27.

rored by a diverse range of legislation and regulations that directly and indirectly affect tourism within the United States.

The most comprehensive analysis of federal legislation in the United States was completed in 1976 as part of the National Tourism Policy Study.[3] One of the major conclusions emerging from this analysis was that "Federal legislation has seldom been addressed explicitly to national interests in travel or tourism. . . ." The Senate Commerce Committee separated the existing tourism legislation in the United States into two main categories, namely federal tourism legislation and federal tourism-related legislation. The committee also identified the following nine subcategories of federal legislation:

FEDERAL TOURISM LEGISLATION

1. Tourism promotion and development legislation
2. Tourism resources legislation

FEDERAL TOURISM-RELATED LEGISLATION

3. Interstate transport investment and regulation
4. Nonimmigrant visa and customs legislation
5. Economic development legislation
6. Environmental quality control legislation
7. Energy legislation
8. Land-use legislation
9. Tax legislation

Within these subcategories, there are forty-five existing or proposed acts that have had some impact on tourism within the United States.

It is quite obvious, and the U.S. Senate Commerce Committee has confirmed it, that the major direct pieces of tourism legislation in the United States, that is, the domestic and international travel acts, have been structured without sufficient regard to other legislation and the programs of affected federal agencies. The reverse is also true, since the programs and legislated mandates of other agencies have not given sufficient attention to tourism. This situation is not uncommon among those at destination areas, as few of them have systematically developed legislation on an effectively coordinated fashion. As is discussed later in this chapter, Canada for example, has moved to ease its regulatory and legislative overlaps and conflicts by forming an Interdepartmental Committee on Tourism.

We turn our attention now to regulation as opposed to legislation. Governments have two common methods of enforcing regulations, namely by establishing regulatory agencies and by utilizing regulatory tech-

---

[3]*A Conceptual Basis for the National Tourism Policy Study,* pp. 5–70.

niques. In the United States, the regulatory agencies currently include the Civil Aeronautics Board (CAB), the Federal Aviation Administration (FAA), the Interstate Commerce Commission (ICC), the Federal Highway Administration (FHWA), the National Highway Traffic Safety Administration (NHTSA), the Federal Maritime Commission (FMC), the United States Coast Guard (USCG), and the Federal Trade Commission (FTC). The CAB is scheduled to be completely phased out by the end of 1984 and represents the federal government's first attempt to drastically deregulate a once closely regulated business sector. The regulatory techniques used by governments include, among others, establishing land-use controls, setting admission policies, and withholding government funds.

Many of the regulatory agencies in existence in the United States have been created as a result of the passage of federal tourism-related legislation. For example, the CAB was established in 1938 through the Civil Aeronautics Act. Its mandate was to protect the safety of the public and to maintain the viability of the U.S. airline industry. The CAB was given the authority to determine which airlines could operate in the United States, which routes they could operate on, and what fares they could charge. It was given powers over airline schedules, airline profit margins, and the types of working relationships permissible. Since its inception, the CAB has probably been the most influential regulatory agency in the United States with respect to its impact on tourism within the nation. The successful passage of the Airline Deregulation Act in October 1978 was, therefore, a most significant event in terms of U.S. tourism. This act was historically unique since it was the first time ever that the federal government virtually abolished its role in the economic regulation of an industry. The decision to wind up the powerful CAB came after much public criticism of the agency and of its perceived overregulation of the airline industry. The general concern was that the CAB had gone too far in trying to maintain the viability of the airline industry and was beginning to engage in activities that were not beneficial to the traveling public. The following statement succinctly expressed the paradox that the CAB represented:

> The CAB in recent months has been accused of sheltering the airline industry, stifling competition, fueling inflation, discriminating against the charter of the marketplace.
>
> It has also been praised for presiding over the development of one of the finest and most efficient air transportation networks anywhere in the world.[4]

Another major problem with the CAB was its tardiness in responding to proposals presented by individual airline companies. During the long lag time, airlines often changed their minds about their proposals

---

⁴Bill Poling, *Behind the Scenes at the CAB* (New York, *Travel Weekly*, Ziff-Davis Publishing Co., Inc., 1975), p. 15.

or they lost the benefit of the marketing opportunity they were seeking. Because of the apparent inability of government regulatory agencies to react with the speed which the private sector requires, a great deal of friction has existed within the tourism system. Thus, as has been the case with the CAB, it is often not a question of regulations being good *or* bad for the industry, but of their being good *and* bad. In other words, the private sector sometimes may agree wholeheartedly with the underlying principles behind the regulations, but often they will be opposed to the manner and to the degree with which the regulations are enforced.

The Airline Deregulation Act of 1978 envisaged that the CAB would be completely phased out by January 1985. The CAB "sunset" timetable included the loss of its authority over route entry in 1982 and its jurisdiction over tariffs and pricing in 1983.

The air travel experiment in the United States, which was motivated by the desire to let the marketplace operate more freely to the ultimate benefit of travelers, has had its advantages and disadvantages. George James of the Air Transport Association has identified these advantages and disadvantages in the context of the three parties affected, namely consumers, government, and airline companies:[5]

ADVANTAGES	DISADVANTAGES
Consumers	
More discounts	Diminished jet service to small and
New entrants	midsize communities
Increased service in dense markets	Sharp base-fare increases (in past
Increased commuter service	year)
	Reservations, terminals, and
	planes more crowded
	Peak period capacity saturated
Government	
A major free-enterprise move	Small- and medium-size
Commuter industry growth	community concern
	Rising cost of essential service
	Major airport saturation/slots for
	aircraft
Airlines	
Increased management options on	Airlines find themselves with a
scheduling, pricing, markets,	mismatch of equipment on
personnel, and aircraft	routes
Freedom of exit	Labor protective provisions of
Increased market aggressiveness	Deregulation Act limits flexibility
Increased flexibility in cost control,	Growing interlining problems
long-range growth	Remaining economic regulation—
Increased new entry, new entrants	airlines don't have complete
	freedom yet

[5]Karen Rubin, "How's Business?" *The Travel Agent*, November 1980, p. 82.

As a result of the deregulation of the airline industry, several new airline companies have emerged and have been certified by the CAB. More discounted fares have become available and the existing airline companies have been better able to rationalize their route systems. Overcrowded planes and airports, and the overbooking of flights were the most frequent criticisms of the results of deregulation.

The roles of other U.S. regulatory agencies are as follows:

FEDERAL AVIATION ADMINISTRATION (FAA)

Regulates the manufacturing, operation, and maintenance of aircraft
Determines and certifies the technical proficiency and physical fitness of flight crews
Certifies airports
Inspects air navigation facilities

INTERSTATE COMMERCE COMMISSION (ICC)

Regulates railroads, bus lines, water carriers, and express agencies in interstate and foreign commerce

FEDERAL HIGHWAY ADMINISTRATION (FHWA)

Develops highway safety standards
Identifies and monitors locations where serious accidents have occurred
Involves itself in highway design, construction, and maintenance
Investigates common carrier accidents
Reviews commercial driver qualifications
Inspects common carrier terminals and vehicles for safety
Runs safety education programs

NATIONAL HIGHWAY TRAFFIC SAFETY ADMINISTRATION (NHTSA)

Regulates vehicle safety standards

FEDERAL MARITIME COMMISSION (FMC)

Regulates common carriers in domestic offshore commerce and U.S. flag-ships in foreign commerce

UNITED STATES COAST GUARD (USCG)

Polices coastal and inland waters and navigable rivers of the United States for water pollution by ships and boats
Sets uniform standards for safety and inspects recreational boats for compliance with these
Educates small boat operators in safe operation
Controls traffic

FEDERAL TRADE COMMISSION (FTC)

Has authority to prevent deceptive advertising

The other method that the public sector uses to enforce its regulations is regulatory technique. Normally these techniques are concerned with the use of land. They include setting access or user quotas based upon a resource's carrying capacity, establishing reservation systems, making restrictive convenants on property ownership transfers, and in the United States using "eminent domain" that enables the federal government to take over endangered lands and historic sites. In the United States these techniques are exercised mainly in lands owned by the federal government.

State, regional/county, and municipal governments in the United States also have legislation and regulations that affect tourism either directly or indirectly. Although the U.S. Constitution provides the federal government with specific powers, state governments automatically have the responsibility for all areas left unspecified. These responsibilities include the authority to regulate land uses and to acquire land within the state. Historically, these powers have been passed on to local governments at the city, town, and county levels. Cities, towns, and counties within the United States exercise these powers through zoning and the structuring of municipal plans.

Like the federal government, state governments have legislation and regulations specifically dealing with state-owned lands, including state parks. Certain states have also enacted legislation that deals specifically with sectors of the tourism industry. A common characteristic of this sectoral legislation is that it has been motivated by a desire to protect the interests of consumers. Rhode Island, for example, passed a Travel Agency Act in 1977 giving the state the power to license retail travel agencies. The law was passed as a result of serious complaints from consumers about their experiences with certain agencies. Rhode Island was the first state in the United States to introduce such legislation, while Puerto Rico had done so earlier in 1974. Several Canadian provinces did likewise during the 1970s. Another part of the tourism industries that has received considerable attention has been the condominium real estate developments within resort areas, particularly timesharing projects. Nebraska was the first state to introduce a timesharing act to protect its citizens against any misleading claims of timesharing resort developers in Nebraska and elsewhere.

The Legislation and Regulation of Tourism in Canada

Like its larger neighbor to the south, Canada has a myriad of legislation and regulations at both the federal, provincial, and municipal levels that directly or indirectly impinge upon tourism. As mentioned at the beginning of this chapter, the Sector Task Force on the Canadian Tourism Industry concluded in 1978 that the industry would be more effective economically if some of these laws and regulations were dismantled or updated. In response to this suggestion, the Canadian government established the Interdepartmental Committee on Tourism (IDCT). In addition Canada's national tourism office, Tourism Canada, has accepted as one of its basic goals the improvement in levels of cooperation and coordination between government agencies and the private sector. It has established its own coordination secretariat to liaise and consult with other federal agencies through the IDCT. It should also be noted that the Conference of Canadian Tourism Officials (CCTO) and the Federal/Provincial Conference of Tourism Ministers have been formed to improve federal/provincial government coordination and cooperation relative to tourism.

Tourism Canada has recognized that due to the diversity of the tourism system within Canada many federal agencies have established regulations, policies, and programs that affect tourism. In their tourism sector strategy of 1981, Tourism Canada stated that the activities of these agencies

> In some cases, . . . address the particular needs of the tourism industry. In others, the pursuit of goals different from those of the tourism industry exacerbate current industry problems or constrain the industry's ability to respond to opportunities. Tourism industry concerns have focussed on several government horizontal policy measures . . . namely labor legislation, manpower policy, taxation policy, transportation regulations, environmental control, and the myriad of regulations at the federal, provincial, and municipal levels affecting facilities development.[6]

As in the United States, Canada's tourism legislation and regulations have their roots in the late nineteenth century. The Rocky Mountain Parks Act of 1887 established the first national park surrounding Banff, Alberta. This was the parallel in history to the Yellowstone National Park Act of 1872 in the United States. The National Parks Act followed in Canada in 1930, and in 1953 the Historic Sites and Monuments Act was passed. The 1930 act stated that only such uses would be permitted within national parks that would "leave them unimpaired for the enjoyment of future generations."[7] This clause has been quite controversial since certain of Canada's national parks, such as Banff and Jasper, are clearly among the nation's major tourist attractions and most favored destinations, particularly with respect to the desires of foreign visitors. The private sector of the Canadian tourism industry via the Sector Task Force

---

[6]Canadian Government Office of Tourism, *Tourism Sector Strategy* (Ottawa, Canadian Government Office of Tourism, April 1981), pp. 59–68.

[7]Parks Canada, *Parks Canada Policy* (Ottawa, Parks Canada, 1979), p. 7.

on the Canadian Tourism Industry stated that these visitor needs and potentials were not being satisfied due to unnecessarily stringent development controls on the part of Parks Canada. This is a classic case of conservation versus development in tourism and of the unavoidable, inherent conflicts between the private sector and certain parts of the public sector of the tourism system.

In addition to Parks Canada, located within the Department of the Environment, at least sixteen other federal departments have tourism-related legislation and regulations. These include Regional Industrial Expansion (that includes Tourism Canada), Energy, Mines and Resources, External Affairs, Finance, Indian and Northern Affairs, Employment and Immigration, Health and Welfare, the Secretary of State, Transport, Agriculture, Consumer and Corporate Affairs, National Defence, Labour, Public Works, and Fisheries and Oceans.

There are several regulatory agencies within Canada whose mandates impact upon tourism. Principal among these is the Canadian Transport Commission (CTC), which is Canada's parallel organization to the CAB. The Air Transport Committee (ATC) is the specific group within CTC that makes airline regulatory decisions. The history of airline regulations within Canada has been quite different from that of the United States, primarily due to the existence of a nationally owned airline, Air Canada. The Canadian government established Air Canada through an act of Parliament which gave the authority for its operation to a crown corporation. Although regulations were eased over the years to allow private airline companies to provide scheduled services within Canada, Air Canada (originally established as Trans Canada Airlines) has always been preeminent, and the scheduled air service market could therefore be described as being one of "regulated competition." This is in sharp contrast to the open market situation that has developed in the United States as a result of airline deregulation. The CTC is also responsible for the regulation of railways and merchant shipping in Canada. The Canadian Coast Guard, located within Transport Canada, regulates nonmerchant boats and ships traveling in Canadian waters, including recreational crafts and cruise/sightseeing vessels.

As in the United States, the ten Canadian provinces and two territories have legislation and regulations that affect tourism directly and indirectly. Several of the provinces have specific tourism acts that give them the authority to license and, in some cases, to inspect tourism businesses. The province of Quebec, for example, has the power through its tourism act to inspect and grade commercial accommodation facilities. Additionally, certain provinces, including Ontario and Quebec, have legislation that permits them to license and regulate retail travel agencies. All of the provinces and territories have considerable legislation governing the use of their parks and other natural resource areas.

Multinational Regulations Affecting the Travel Industry

In addition to the layers of national, state/provincial, regional/county, and city/town legislation and regulations affecting tourism, there are certain agreements that have been reached between foreign countries which have a direct impact upon travel.

Perhaps the most significant of these agreements are those which relate to air travel between countries. The embryonic period for these air travel agreements was during World War II. The "five freedoms" of international air travel were first discussed at an international civil aviation conference in Chicago in 1944. These five freedoms were:

1. Right of transit—The freedom to fly over another country without stopping
2. Right of technical stop—The right to stop at another country's airport for fuel and servicing
3. Right to discharge passengers at another country's airport
4. Right to pick up passengers from another country's airport and return them to their homes
5. Right to discharge passengers at another country's airport and to then load passengers for countries farther on

Although these freedoms had considerable support, especially from the United States, they were never agreed to universally. This meant that there was a need to establish bilateral agreements between countries. The Bermuda Agreement of 1946 was the first of these, and it dealt with air travel between the United States and Britain. The formation of the International Civil Aviation Organization (ICAO) in 1944 and the International Air Transport Association (IATA) in 1945 paved the way for these types of agreements. ICAO is an organization of national governments; IATA represents the airlines. Approximately eighty countries including the United States, Canada, and the United Kingdom belong to ICAO. Its objectives are

1. To adopt international standards and recommended practices for regulating air navigation
2. To recommend installation of navigation facilities by member countries
3. To set forth proposals for the reduction of customs and immigration formalities
4. To plan for the safe and orderly growth of international civil aviation throughout the world
5. To encourage the improvement of the art of aircraft design and operation for peaceful purposes
6. To seek the development of airways, airports, and air navigation facilities for international civil aviation
7. To provide for safe, regular, efficient, and economical air transportation
8. To discourage unreasonable competition

9. To insure that the rights of contracting countries are fully respected and that every member country has a fair opportunity to operate international airlines
10. To discourage discrimination between contracting countries
11. To promote the development of all aspects of international civil aeronautics

More than 110 scheduled airline companies belong to IATA, some of which are nationally owned airlines such as Air Canada and British Airways. Any company offering a scheduled international air service may belong to IATA. The association's purpose is basically to resolve problems that the airline companies would not be able to resolve if they acted individually. Its objectives are to encourage safe, regular, and economical international air services, to encourage international air commerce, and to research problems and issues affecting the industry.

One of IATA's key roles is that of setting rates on international routes to which all member airlines agree. It also acts as a clearing house for air-ticket coupons that allow passengers to fly internationally on several airlines while requiring only one flight coupon. It acts in an advisory capacity on mutual problems, such as fuel shortages, hijacking, navigation, and safety. Also, IATA is an important source of statistics on international air travel. Unlike the national regulatory agencies such as the Civil Aeronautics Board (CAB) in the United States and the Canadian Transport Commission (CTC), IATA does not certify airlines, award routes, or act on market exit decisions. These powers remain with the national governments and their regulatory authorities, such as the CAB and the CTC. Bilateral air agreements are struck between governments addressing these matters; the United Kingdom-United States Bermuda agreement of 1946 is the forerunner of these.

These bilateral agreements are frequently somewhat loose and often mask ongoing disputes between two countries over transborder air services. The 1973 bilateral agreement between the United States and Canada is a good example of this latter point. It is indicative of the inherent problems of a tourism system in which the market or political philosophies of nations are quite different. Since 1977 the United States has deregulated its airline industry and has been a strong proponent of an "open skies" airline policy internationally. In contrast, Canada has maintained a highly protectionist stance with respect to its airline companies. Canada's refusal to completely open up the international air border between itself and the United States led in 1983 to a serious dispute over a proposed package of heavily discounted fares to be offered by Air Canada to several cities in the southern United States. The CAB's obstinacy in not allowing these fare schedules caused many Canadians prebooked on these flights to cancel their trips. Quite obviously the destination areas within the southern United States suffered because of the loss of potential income from the Canadian travelers.

Before leaving the subject of international air travel regulations and agreements, mention must be made of the many pacts that have been made between countries with respect to airlines' liabilities for passenger injuries and damage or loss of baggage. Historically, there have been three such major agreements—the Warsaw Convention, the Hague Protocol, and the Montreal Agreement. The Warsaw Convention dates back to 1929 and constitutes the main body of international rules in this respect. The United States accepted the Warsaw Convention regulations in 1934; Canada and the United Kingdom are other adherents to it. Several Central American and South American countries are not members of the treaty. The Hague Protocol and the Montreal Agreement represent international agreements that have raised the dollar limit on an airline's liability to an individual passenger.

Hotel classification on an international level also represents a tacit attempt by several nations to regulate standards within another important component of the tourism system. The World Tourism Organization (WTO) has taken the lead role in this regard. It was given this authority in 1963 when the United Nations Conference on International Travel and Tourism asked it to draft these standards. The main rationale for setting these was as follows:

> Traveling problems can be eased to a considerable extent if hotels of a particular category in all countries were to present more or less the same characteristics of comfort and service.[8]

Although many countries appear to agree in principle with the classification method and criteria that the WTO has developed, many have chosen to create their own classification and grading/rating systems since they have found the WTO guidelines to be too broad for their purposes.

In addition to these specific agreements, there are a plethora of treaties and agreements governing trade and travel/customs procedures between nations and groups of nations. Although they are too numerous to mention, they also play a key role in the tourism regulatory framework of destination areas.

The Need for Government Regulation of Tourism in Destination Areas

A close analysis of the legislation and regulations described above would clearly show that governments are acting in the general interests of their citizens. They do so primarily to protect and conserve their destination area's natural, historical, and cultural resources, to ensure the health

---

[8]World Tourism Organization, *International Hotel Classification* (Madrid, Spain, World Tourism Organization, 1969), p. 2.

and safety of visitors, and to protect the visitors from unscrupulous business practices. In these respects, the value of a government's role cannot be questioned.

From time to time, however, governments are accused of being overly bureaucratic, of developing unnecessary "red tape," and of going too far in their policing efforts. This is especially true when the political pendulum and public sentiment swing more toward the free-enterprise approach, as they have in the U.S. airline industry. It is also true of Canada where those in the tourism industry have sharply criticized governments for hindering the development of tourism destination areas because of their lengthy and complex project approval processes. Certainly, government agencies seldom appear to act or react with the speed with which the private sector requires.

The lack of coordination and cooperation between government agencies in their policies and programs is often quite prevalent in tourism. This is a reflection of the diversity of the tourism system itself and of the inherent and unavoidable conflicts between the goals of some agencies, such as natural resource conservation versus tourism promotion and development agencies. Any destination area with a vital interest in tourism should undertake steps to bring about the highest amount of coordination and cooperation among its government agencies. It seems logical that the national and state/provincial offices should take the lead role in this respect.

REFERENCES

Destination U.S.A., Report of the National Tourism Resources Review Commission, vol. 4, Federal Role, June 1973, p. 12.

HUDMAN, LLOYD E., *Tourism: A Shrinking World* (Columbus, OH, Grid Inc., 1980), p. 74.

JOHNSTON, EVERETT E., AND J. R. BRENT RITCHIE, "Regulation of Air Travel: A Canadian Perspective," *Journal of Travel Research*, vol. 20, no. 2, Fall 1981, p. 9.

SOLBERG, CARL, *Conquest of the Skies: A History of Commercial Aviation in America* (Boston, Little, Brown & Co., 1979), p. 286.

TOURISM SECTOR CONSULTATIVE TASK FORCE, *A Report By the Sector Task Force On the Canadian Tourism Industry* (Ottawa, Ontario, Department of Industry, Trade and Commerce, 1978), p. 125.

U.S. SENATE, *A Conceptual Basis for the National Tourism Policy Study: Appendix C* (Washington, DC, U.S. Government Printing Office, 1976), pp. 82, 92.

12

TOURISM PLANNING:
Selecting among Alternatives
for the Travel Industry

Because of the wide-ranging effects of tourism on a destination area it is vital that development be undertaken within the context of a plan. This chapter deals with the planning process as a method for selecting among alternatives for the destination.

A comparison is made between planned and the unplanned destination areas and reasons are given why planning should take place. The consequences of unplanned development are noted.

The purposes of planning are laid out and barriers to planning examined in an attempt to understand why the planning stage is often avoided.

A process for planning tourism is detailed, and an examination of each step in the process is undertaken to provide a road map for the destination planner.

THE DESTINATION AREA WITH
AND WITHOUT TOURISM PLANNING

Tourism planning is an essential activity for every destination area, especially in today's fastly changing business environments. Although it is true that some destinations have flourished without any conscious planning, many have eventually suffered serious consequences for not carefully considering future events and their impacts.

Planning refers to the selection between alternative courses of action. All planning involves an analysis of the future. It also involves setting the basic goals and objectives for the destination area, which is the point which other supportive actions follow.

Reasons for Tourism Planning

There are many valid reasons for tourism planning. One of these relates to the destination life-cycle concept as defined by Plog.[1] Plog's hypothesis is that destination areas tend to rise and fall in popularity according to the whims of those in the predominant "psychographic" groups to which they appeal at different stages in their development histories. This concept is somewhat similar to the product life-cycle and product adoption curve ideas discussed in most basic marketing texts (see Figure 12.1), except that it relates certain personality profiles to the destination area's stages of growth. Thus, a new and/or exotic destination tends to appeal first to Plog's "allocentric" group—the innovators in the travel market that seek out uncrowded and unique destinations. As the destination area becomes more widely publicized and better known, it loses its appeal to the allocentrics and they are replaced by the "mid-centrics," who greatly outnumber the allocentrics in the population in general. Plog relates the mid-centric appeal stage in the destination area's history to the maturity phase of the product life-cycle where sales volumes are at their peak. Basically, the destination area can be said to have mass market appeal at this point. Eventually as time progresses, this destination area also loses its appeal to the mid-centrics, and they are replaced by the "psychocentrics" who, like the allocentrics, represent a much smaller proportion of the population. According to Plog, the psychocentric stage is the final point in the destination area's life-cycle; it has lost its appeal to both the market innovators and the mass market. One of the most important messages of the Plog hypothesis is that destination areas can "carry with them the potential seeds of their own destruction" if they allow themselves to become over-commercialized and to forsake the unique appeals which made them popular in the first place.

---

[1]Stanley C. Plog, "Why Destination Areas Rise and Fall in Popularity," *Cornell Hotel and Restaurant Administration Quarterly*, Ithaca, New York, 1973, pp. 13–16.

FIGURE 12.1 (a) Lazer's Product Life Cycle; (b) Plog's Destination Life Cycle; (c) Rogers' Product Adoption Curve

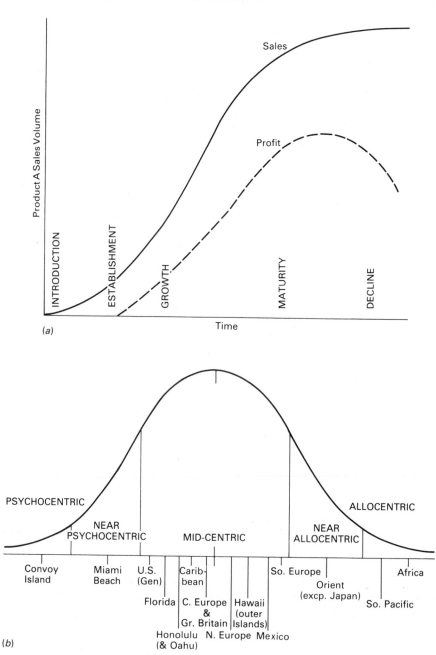

(a)

(b)

286

FIGURE 12.1 *(cont.)*

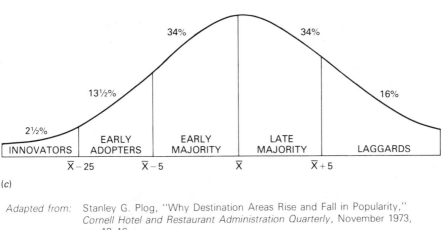

(c)

Adapted from: Stanley G. Plog, "Why Destination Areas Rise and Fall in Popularity,"
Cornell Hotel and Restaurant Administration Quarterly, November 1973,
pp. 13-16.
Everett M. Rogers, *Diffusion of Innovation* (New York, Free Press of Glen-
coe, 1962), p. 162.
William Lazer, *Marketing Management: A Systems Perspective* (New York,
John Wiley & Sons, 1971), p. 272.

Although Plog's concept appears to suggest that all destination areas
eventually face the same fate, the years of experience which have been
gained since it was first publicized have shown that there have been several
exceptions to this rule. This experience indicates that destination life-
cycles can be extended if change is anticipated; and if steps are taken to
adapt to the change. One of the core functions of tourism planning is to
provide the basic framework to allow the destination area to cope with
change.

The point is that both the external and internal variables mentioned
in a previous chapter are constantly changing. The destination has two
choices: (1) react to changes after they occur; or (2) develop a method or
plan to assess the present situation, forecast the future situation, and
select an appropriate course of action to make the most of available
opportunities.

Consequences of Unplanned Development

What can happen if a destination area does not involve itself in
tourism planning? The examples are numerous and often well-documented,
especially as they relate to tourism's impact on the physical environment.
Some of the symptoms of a lack of tourism planning may include the
following:

PHYSICAL IMPACTS

Damage or permanent alteration of the physical environment
Damage or permanent alteration of historical/cultural landmarks and resources
Overcrowding and congestion
Pollution
Traffic problems

HUMAN IMPACTS

Less accessibility to services and tourist attractions for local residents resulting in local resentment
Dislike of tourists on the part of local residents
Loss of cultural identities
Lack of education of tourism employees in skills and hospitality
Lack of awareness of the benefits of tourism to the destination area

MARKETING IMPACTS

Failure to capitalize on new marketing opportunities
Erosion of market shares due to the actions of competitive destination areas
Lack of sufficient awareness in prime markets
Lack of a clear image of destination area in potential markets
Lack of cooperative advertising among individual operators
Inadequate capitalization on packaging opportunities

ORGANIZATIONAL IMPACTS

Fragmented approach to the marketing and development of tourism, often involving "competitive" splinter groups
Lack of cooperation among individual operators
Inadequate representation of the tourism industry's interests
Lack of support from local public authorities
Failure to act upon important issues, problems, and opportunities of common interest to the industry

OTHER IMPACTS

Inadequate signage programs
Lack of sufficient attractions and events
High seasonality and short lengths of stay
Poor or deteriorating quality of facilities and services
Poor or inadequate travel information services

Although the critics of tourism as an economic activity have made much of these negatives, particularly as they relate to environmental conservation and negative cultural/social effects, the blame can more properly be attached to the lack of tourism planning than to the inherent nature of tourism itself.

THE PLANNING CONTEXT

Tourism activity in a destination area is generated through the existence of unique attractions. These can include beaches, natural scenery, parks, historical buildings and landmarks, unique cultural characteristics, unique local events/activities, outdoor sports areas, and so on. It follows that if the destination area wishes to maintain tourism as a long-term economic activity, it must show its concern through planning to preserve and enhance these special factors that make it different from all other destinations. Planning in this context has five basic purposes:

1. Identifying alternative approaches to

Marketing
Development
Industry organization
Tourism awareness
Support services and activities

2. Adapting to the unexpected in

General economic conditions
Energy supply/demand situation
Values and life-styles
Fortunes of individual industries
Other factors in the external environment

3. Maintaining uniqueness in

Natural features and resources
Local cultural and social fabric
Local architecture
Historical monuments and landmarks
Local events and activities
Parks and outdoor sports areas
Other features of the destination area

4. Creating the desirable, such as in

High level of awareness of benefits of tourism
Clear and positive image of area as a tourism destination
Effective industry organization
High level of cooperation among individual operators
Effective marketing, signage, and travel information programs
Other objectives

5. Avoiding the undesirable, such as in

Friction and unnecessary competition among individual tourism
   operators

Hostile and unfriendly attitudes of local residents toward tourists

Damage or undesirable, permanent alteration of natural features
   and historical resources

Loss of cultural identities

Loss of market share

Stoppage of unique local events and activities

Overcrowding, congestion, and traffic problems

Pollution

High seasonality

Other factors

As the reader will quickly realize, the purposes of tourism planning
are basically to avoid the negative physical, human, marketing, organizational, and other impacts that can occur when planning is not practiced.
Although the authors do not advocate that tourism is necessarily the
answer to every destination area's economic and social problems, or indeed
that every community should pursue it, tourism is much more likely to
be a successful activity if planning is pursued.

Roles and Responsibilities for Tourism Planning

In communist-bloc countries all planning is done by the national
government. As such clear centralization of power and responsibility is
not found in noncommunist countries, the roles of the public sector
(government) and the private sector (tourism industry) are much less easily
demarcated. Clearly in a democratic nation, there is a valid role to be
played in tourism planning by both the public and private sectors. Experience has shown that the process of joint participation and close industry
government cooperation produces the best results and that plans are more
likely to be successfully implemented if the private sector is actively involved in the planning process.

Historically, tourism planning appears to have originated in Europe,
quickly being adopted thereafter in several developing nations in Africa
and Asia. France, Eire, and the United Kingdom were among the pioneers
of the technology of tourism planning, with all three nations being involved
in some form of planning for tourism in the early 1960s. Canada has also
been in the forefront of tourism planning, its efforts originating in the
late 1960s and early 1970s. The United States has seen little organized
tourism planning to date and certainly lags badly behind its northern
neighbor in this respect.

Tourism planning should take place at many levels within a country.
The starting point for the tourism planning process in any country should

be development of a national tourism policy. In Chapter Ten a tourism policy model was described (see Figure 10.1), and it was suggested that a national tourism policy represented an amalgam of the principles upon which a nationwide course of action for tourism is based. As such, the tourism policy represents the basic foundation from which more specific goals, strategies, objectives, and plans are developed. It follows that all planning efforts should be complementary to the national tourism policy. A national tourism policy as well as all tourism plans should be given finite time spans and be reviewed and modified at the expiration of these time periods. Because change is inevitable and continuous, it follows that tourism policymaking and planning have to be dynamic processes. Because policies tend to be more broad-scale than tourism plans, they usually are valid for a greater number of years. The life span of a tourism plan is normally not more than five years.

Barriers to Planning

There are often many barriers to tourism planning and problems associated with it. First, many people are against planning in principle, particularly within the free-enterprise system. This is especially true in North America, where the tourism industry has developed and existed for many years without tourism planning. Many business people view tourism planning as an encroachment into their domain of activity, and they are quite skeptical of its ultimate value. Cost is a second barrier to tourism planning. Because effective tourism planning must be based upon detailed resource analysis and market research, it inevitably means that it has to be funded by one or more groups. The public sector generally funds the planning efforts on behalf of itself and the private sector. A third barrier is the complexity and diversity of the industry and the large number of government departments that have activities that impinge upon tourism. Unlike, say, the automobile manufacturing business, the tourism business is not a readily identifiable industry. Although the front-line recipients of tourists' expenditures—such as hotels, motels, resorts, airlines, car rental agencies, campgrounds, commercial attractions, and restaurants—are quite obvious, others—including retail stores, banks, and municipal governments—are not normally seen as being part of the "industry." Another complication is that many tourism businesses receive their income both from visitors and from local residents. In the public sector, the complexity is no less great, as was noted earlier.

The situation in Canada is the same, as the programs of a multiplicity of departments and agencies have some effect on tourism. Tourism planning is often made more difficult because the policies of these departments are not coordinated and indeed are sometimes in direct conflict with one another.

A fourth barrier to planning is the fact that tourism usually is characterized by a few large businesses and a multitude of smaller enterprises. There is also a tendency for individual operators to categorize themselves as being in the campground industry, or the hotel industry, or the restaurant industry rather than accepting their broader role in the tourism industry.

Other problems encountered in planning tourism include the seasonality of business activity and the relatively high ownership turnover in the industry.

Despite these barriers to tourism planning, an increasing number of plans are produced each year around the world. Indications are that tourism planning will be given a higher priority in the future and that more destinations will become involved in this important process. As they become involved, they will have at their disposal the previous planning experience of many other areas and thus a more refined "technology" of tourism planning. The remainder of this chapter is devoted to the steps in the tourism planning process itself.

STEPS IN THE TOURISM PLANNING PROCESS

As was pointed out earlier, tourism planning in a destination country should take place at a variety of levels. The approaches utilized in producing the plans, however, should follow a similar step-by-step pattern. Figure 12.2 provides an illustration of a conceptual model for the tourism planning process incorporating these steps. Actual experience has shown that some of the elements of the conceptual model have been overlooked in some past planning efforts and that varying degrees of emphasis have been attached to the individual phases of the planning process.

There are five essential phases in the tourism planning process and these are as follows:

1. Background analysis phase
2. Detailed research and analysis phase
3. Synthesis phase
4. Goal-setting, strategy selection, and objective-setting phase
5. Plan development phase

Each of the five phases involves a variety of activities, participants, and outcomes, and these are illustrated in Figure 12.2.

Background Analysis Phase

The first phase in the tourism planning process could be classified as being a situational analysis that produces the basic direction for the succeeding phases. Because most destination areas, be they countries, states, provinces, regions, or local communities, have some level of existing tourism activity and regulatory/policy framework for the industry, this is a logical launching point for most tourism plans.

In establishing a national tourism plan, the national tourism policy must be first considered and interpreted. Also, if a state or province has a tourism policy, then it should be carefully reviewed at the outset of the plan. In Chapter Ten, it was stated that tourism policy goals normally fall into four categories—economic, consumer/social, resource/environmental, and government operations. In the province of Ontario, the Ministry of Tourism and Recreation identified the "economic" policy goal as being its prime mandate. It defined this goal as follows:

> To stimulate employment, income and economic development through the systematic improvement, development and marketing of Ontario's tourism industry.[2]

In tourism policymaking and planning there is a hierarchy of goals and objectives. The tourism policy goal or goals, like those of Ontario, are the long-term targets in the destination area that provide the framework and rationale for supporting goals and objectives (See Figure 12.3). At each level in the hierarchy the goals and objectives become more specific and more action oriented. Using the Ontario example again, the Ministry of Tourism and Recreation defined two policy objectives and six subobjectives on the basis of the policy goals as follows:

POLICY OBJECTIVE 1.　To increase the volume and diversity of tourism opportunities throughout Ontario.

SUBOBJECTIVES

1.1　To develop a system of attractions and events of provincial and regional significance
1.2　To provide traveler support services (accomodation, food, transportation, information) in response to existing and projected consumption patterns
1.3　To ensure the existence of an effective and efficient infrastructure to complement provincial tourism resources

POLICY OBJECTIVE 2:　To increase the quality of the tourism experience in Ontario.

SUBOBJECTIVES

2.1　To encourage orderly growth and increased efficiency within the tourism industry

---

[2]Balmer, Crapo & Associates, Inc., *Tourism Development in Ontario: A Framework for Opportunity* (Waterloo, Ontario, Ontario Ministry of Tourism and Recreation, 1977).

FIGURE 12.2 Tourism Planning Model

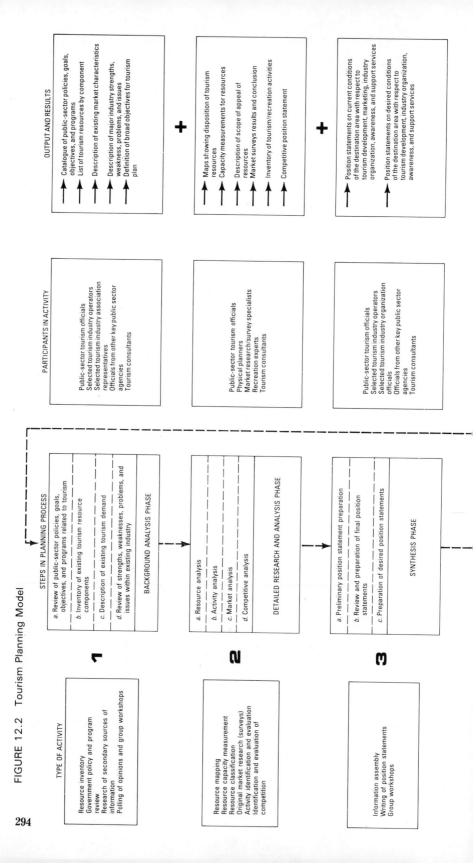

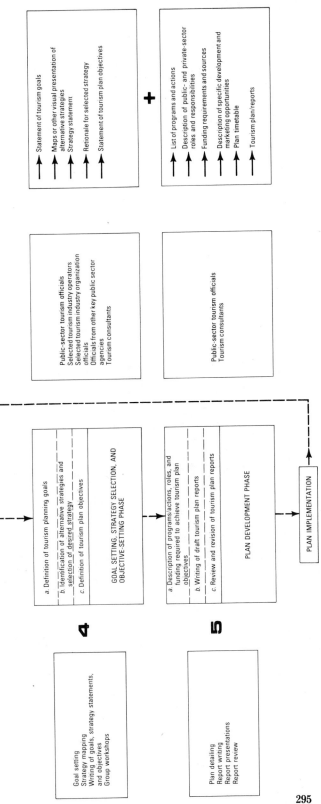

Goal setting
Strategy mapping
Writing of goals, strategy statements, and objectives
Group workshops

4

a. Definition of tourism planning goals

b. Identification of alternative strategies and selection of desired strategy

c. Definition of tourism plan objectives

GOAL SETTING, STRATEGY SELECTION, AND OBJECTIVE-SETTING PHASE

Public-sector tourism officials
Selected tourism industry operators
Selected tourism industry organization officials
Officials from other key public sector agencies
Tourism consultants

→ Statement of tourism goals
→ Maps or other visual presentation of alternative strategies
→ Strategy statement
→ Rationale for selected strategy
→ Statement of tourism plan objectives

+

Plan detailing
Report writing
Report presentations
Report review

5

a. Description of programs/actions, roles, and funding required to achieve tourism plan objectives

b. Writing of draft tourism plan reports

c. Review and revision of tourism plan reports

PLAN DEVELOPMENT PHASE

Public-sector tourism officials
Tourism consultants

→ List of programs and actions
→ Description of public- and private-sector roles and responsibilities
→ Funding requirements and sources
→ Description of specific development and marketing opportunities
→ Plan timetable
→ Tourism plan/reports

PLAN IMPLEMENTATION

FIGURE 12.3   A Hierachy of Tourism Policy and Planning Goals and Objectives

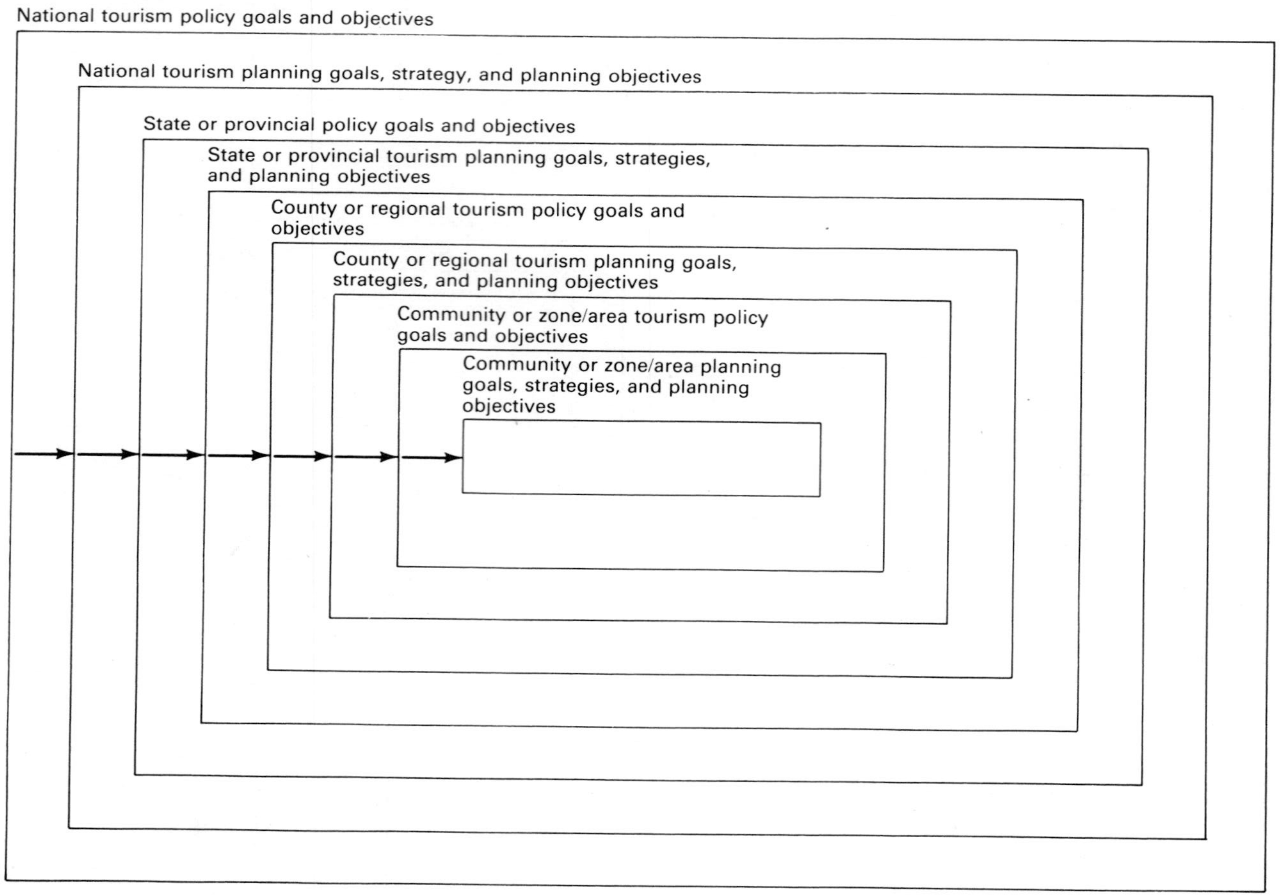

National tourism policy goals and objectives

National tourism planning goals, strategy, and planning objectives

State or provincial policy goals and objectives

State or provincial tourism planning goals, strategies, and planning objectives

County or regional tourism policy goals and objectives

County or regional tourism planning goals, strategies, and planning objectives

Community or zone/area tourism policy goals and objectives

Community or zone/area planning goals, strategies, and planning objectives

2.2 To assist in upgrading the tourism plant

2.3 To encourage integration of supply components to better satisfy tourism requirements

Because other public sector agencies normally have policies, goals, and objectives that impact upon tourism, these must be considered in the background analysis stage. Existing tourism-related programs or activities of public and private sector organizations should also be identified.

The background analysis should produce an inventory or listing of the destination area's tourism resource components. Figure 12.4 provides a basic categorization of these tourism resource components and their subcomponents. These resource components and subcomponents constitute the existing tourism "product" of the destination area.

FIGURE 12.4 Categorization of Tourism Resource Components

Component	Subcomponent
Natural Features	Landscapes Scenery Unique features Flora and fauna
Historical and Cultural Features	Buildings Sites Themes Communities/subcommunities
Tourist Operations and Facilities	Attractions Accommodation Food service Events
Hospitality Services	Information centers Reservation systems Commercial stores and services (banks, retail stores)
Infrastructure	Transportation systems: road rail airport boat Underground services
Human Resources	Population and work force Ethnic community Attitude toward tourism
General Socioeconomic	Employment/unemployment Industries Economic conditions Social problems
Present Land Uses	Land ownership Planning and zoning regulations Future growth and development

SOURCE: The Economic Planning Group of Canada.

The third step in the background analysis normally involves a description of existing tourism demand in the destination area utilizing readily available secondary (published) sources of information. Ideally this information will give a profile of demand along the following lines:

Modes of travel to and within the destination area and past usage volumes (aircraft, bus, train, ship, private automobile, etc.)

Visitation volumes and patterns by month or season

Geographical origins of tourists

Geographical destinations of tourists

Tourist demographics (such as age, sex, income, education, occupations, and travel party composition)

Trip purposes

Activity participation

Market segments (families with children, singles, tour groups, business groups, etc.)

Lengths of stay in area

Tourist expenditures within area

Usage of facilities (such as accommodation, attractions, events, and recreation facilities)

The quantity and quality of this information will be determined by the priority that the destination area has attached to tourism market research in the past. If gaps are found in the available information, these are usually identified in this first phase and an attempt is made to fill them in the detailed research phase.

The final step in the background analysis phase should be a review of the major strengths, weaknesses, problems, and issues within the destination area's existing tourism industry. This is an important scene-setting step for the remainder of the tourism planning process, and it should be both introspective, critical, and objective. It should involve a variety of individuals, including public sector tourism officials, officials from other key public sector agencies, selected tourism industry operators, and selected tourism industry organization representatives. This exercise is likely to be most objective and productive if a broad variety of opinions and interests are sought. In North America, private consulting organizations specializing in tourism are often utilized in the planning process. These organizations inject a degree of objectivity and broad industry experience that may not be readily available in the area itself.

Another step that is taken in some tourism plans at this point is that of staging a series of public meetings with citizen groups in the destination area. These sessions can be useful in determining community attitudes and awareness levels of tourism, and the type of future direction citizens wish for tourism in their locales.

Detailed Research and Analysis Phase

A valid tourism plan cannot be formulated without research. Tourism plans developed without research tend to reflect the subjective opinions of their authors and to perpetuate existing situations. As the Scottish Tourist Board has noted,[3] these types of plans normally "provide what seems to be most in demand at the time" but they do not necessarily lead to the achievement of tourism policy goals and objectives.

Research should be concentrated in four distinct areas—resources, markets, activities, and competition. The very basic level of research carried out during the background analysis phase should have helped to pinpoint where the more detailed research should be focused.

Using the inventory of tourism resource components as a base, the first step in the resource analysis involves the preparation of maps identifying the location of key resources. With the mapping completed, the capacities of the various tourism resources are then measured. Although the capacities of some of the tourism resource components are easily measured (such as in guest rooms, restaurant seats, camp sites, and golf courses) the capacities of others (such as boating lakes/rivers, beaches, and historical landmarks) are not.

The final stage of the resource analysis could be referred to as resource classification. Basically, this represents a ranking or grading of the scope of appeal of the tourism resources of the destination area. Thus, individual resources or zones within the destination are normally defined as being of international, national, regional, or local significance, or as having international, national, regional, or local market appeal. Two examples can be used to illustrate this process. In the Auvergne region of central France, the classification was done on an area-by-area basis. Three classifications were developed—class A areas having tourist attractions of national and international importance, class B areas having regionally important attractions capable of attracting people from the rest of France, and class C areas having attractions of only regional or interregional importance. Another example is illustrated in Figure 12.5, which is taken from a tourism development plan prepared for the Collingwood-Midland-Orillia Zone in Ontario. This plan has classified the various resource components as having local, regional, provincial, Canadian/U.S., or international appeal with respect to both the existing, desired, and potential markets.

The second component of the detailed research phase is the activity analysis. Activities include all of the things that the tourist can do while visiting the destination area, ranging from outdoor recreational pursuits

---

[3]P. A. Taylor and M. R. Carter, "Using Tourism in Regional Development: Planning for Tourism in Scotland," in *Tourism Planning and Development Issues* (George Washington University, 1980), p. 309.

FIGURE 12.5 Recreational Opportunities/Market Associations

Honey Harbour Region

TOURISM RECREATION OPPORTUNITY				RESOURCE OPPORT	EXISTING MARKET					DESIRED MARKET					POTENT MARKET				
					Local	Regional	Provincial	National/U.S.	International	Local	Regional	Provincial	National/U.S.	International	Local	Regional	Provincial	National	International
NATURAL RESOURCES	Water-based Recreation Opportunities	Boating	Sailing	◐	●	○				●	●				●	●			
			Power Boating/Touring	◐	●	○				●	○				●	●			
			Ice Boating	○	○					○					○	○			
			Canoeing	○	○														
			Windsurfing	◐	○										●	○			
		Fishing	Sportfishing	○	○					●					○				
			Icefishing	○	○	○				○	○				○	○			
		Swimming/Bathing		●	●	○				●	○				●	●	○		
		Water Skiing		○	○					○					●	○			
		Scuba Diving/Snorkeling		○	○					○					●	●			
	Land-Based Recreation Opportunities	Skiing	Alpine																
			Cross-Country	●	●	●				●	●				●	○			
		Hunting	Big Game	○	●	○				●	○				●	○			
			Small Game	◐	●	○				●	○				●	○			
			Water Fowl	○	●	●				●	●				●	◐			
		Camping	Auto Touring	○	○					○	○				●	○			
			Wilderness	○	○					○	○				○				
		Hiking/Backpacking	Day	◐	○					○	○				●	●			
			Overnight	○	○					○	○				○	○			
			Snowshoeing	○	○					○	○				●	○			
		Rock Climbing																	
		Cave Exploring																	
		Picnicking		◐	○	○				○	○				○	○			
		Cottaging/Chalet		●	●	○				●	●				●	●	◐	○	
		Snowmobiling		◐	●	○				●	●				●	●			
		Cycling		◐	○	○				○	●				○	●			
		Equestrian Trails		◐	○	○				●	●				●	●			
	Land and Water-Based Recreation Opportunities	Viewing Natural Attractions		◐	○	○				●	●				●	●			
		Gathering/Collecting		○	○	○				○	○				○	○			
		Photography/Painting		◐	○	○				○	○				●	●			
	Air-Based Recreation Opportunities	Hang Gliding																	
		Hot Air Ballooning		◐	○	○				○	○								
		Gliding		◐	○	○				○	○				○				
MAN-DEVELOPED MAN-CONTROLLED RESOURCES	Natural Resource Opportunities	Natural Parks and Sites	National																
			Provincial	●	○	●				●	●				●	●			
			Crown Land	○	○	○				○	○				●	●			
		Game Sanctuaries Reserves		◐	○	●				●	●				●	○			
		Game Farms																	
	Historical Resource Opportunities	Historic Parks and Sites	National																
			Provincial	◐	○	○				●	●				○				
			Local	○	○	○				●	●				○				
		Archaeological Attractions	Existing	●	○	●				○	●				○				
			Potential	◐	○	○				○	○				○				
	Cultural Resource Opportunities	Population Centres	Cities/Towns	○	○	○				●	○								
			Ethnic Settlements	◐	○	○				●	●				○				
		Cultural Attractions	Fairs/Celebrations	○	●	○				●	○				○				
			Crafts/Events	◐	●	○				●	○				●	○			
			Museums/Galleries																
	Recreation/Leisure Developments	Accommodation Recreation Resorts	Hotel/Motel/Cottage	○	○	○				○	●				○	●	○	○	
			Vacation Farm	◐											○				
			Ski Developments																
			Marina Developments	○						○	○				○	○			
			Convention Centres																
		Travel/Touring Corridors	Air	◐	○	○				○	○				○	○			
			Rail																
			Boat	◐	●	○				●	○				●	○			
			Car	◐	●	○				●	○				●	○			
		Recreation/Leisure Developments	Ski Developments - Alpine																
			Ski Developments - Cross Country	●	●	○				●	●				●	○			
			Marina/Boating Developments	○	●	○				●	○				●	○			
			Golf Courses	○	●	○				●	●				●	○			
			Campgrounds/Trailer Parks	○	●	●				○	●				○	◐			
			Beaches	◐	○	○				○	●				○	◐			
	Attractions			◐	●	○				●	●				●	◐			

a. RESOURCE OPPORTUNITIES
- ● Abundant resource opportunities; existing and/or potential.
- ◐ Moderate resource opportunities; existing and/or potential.
- ○ Limited resource opportunities; existing and/or potential.
- ☐ No resource opportunities.

b. EXISTING MARKET
- ● Heavy use/demand
- ○ Limited use/demand
- ☐ No use/demand

c. DESIRED MARKET
- ● Strong desire to attract as a primary market.
- ○ Limited desire to attract as a primary market.
- ☐ No desire to attract as a primary market.

d. POTENTIAL MARKET
- ● Strong market attraction for this activity.
- ○ Weak market attraction for this activity.
- ☐ No market attraction for this activity.

FIGURE 12.5 (cont.)

Midland/Penetanguishene Region

			RESOURCE OPPORT.	EXISTING MARKET					DESIRED MARKET					POTENT MARKET				
TOURISM RECREATION OPPORTUNITY				Local	Regional	Provincial	National/U.S.	International	Local	Regional	Provincial	National/U.S.	International	Local	Regional	Provincial	National	International

NATURAL RESOURCES

Water-based Recreation Opportunities	Boating	Sailing
		Power Boating/Touring
		Ice Boating
		Canoeing
		Windsurfing
Land-Based Recreation Opportunities	Fishing	Sportfishing
		Icefishing
	Swimming/Bathing	
	Water Skiing	
	Scuba Diving/Snorkeling	
	Skiing	Alpine
		Cross-Country
	Hunting	Big Game
		Small Game
		Water Fowl
	Camping	Auto Touring
		Wilderness
	Hiking/Backpacking	Day
		Overnight
		Snowshoeing
	Rock Climbing	
	Cave Exploring	
	Picnicking	
	Cottaging/Chalet	
	Snowmobiling	
	Cycling	
	Equestrian Trails	
Land and Water-Based Recreation Opportunities	Viewing Natural Attractions	
	Gathering/Collecting	
	Photography/Painting	
Air-Based Recreation Opportunities	Hang Gliding	
	Hot Air Ballooning	
	Gliding	

MAN-DEVELOPED MAN-CONTROLLED RESOURCES

Natural Resource Opportunities	Natural Parks and Sites	National
		Provincial
		Crown Land
	Game Sanctuaries Reserves	
	Game Farms	
Historical Resource Opportunities	Historic Parks and Sites	National
		Provincial
		Local
	Archaeological Attractions	Existing
		Potential
Cultural Resource Opportunities	Population Centres	Cities Towns
		Ethnic Settlements
	Cultural Attractions	Fairs/Celebrations
		Crafts Events
		Museums Galleries
Recreation Leisure Developments	Accommodation Recreation Resorts	Hotel Motel Cottage
		Vacation Farm
		Ski Developments
		Marina Developments
		Convention Centres
	Travel Touring Corridors	Air
		Rail
		Boat
		Car
	Recreation Leisure Developments	Ski Developments - Alpine
		Ski Developments - Cross Country
		Marina Boating Developments
		Golf Courses
		Campgrounds Trailer Parks
		Beaches
Attractions		

a. RESOURCE OPPORTUNITIES
- ● Abundant resource opportunities; existing and/or potential.
- ◐ Moderate resource opportunities; existing and/or potential.
- ○ Limited resource opportunities; existing and/or potential.
- ☐ No resource opportunities.

b. EXISTING MARKET
- ● Heavy use/demand
- ○ Limited use/demand
- ☐ No use/demand

c. DESIRED MARKET
- ● Strong desire to attract as a primary market.
- ○ Limited desire to attract as a primary market.
- ☐ No desire to attract as a primary market.

d. POTENTIAL MARKET
- ● Strong market attraction for this activity
- ○ Weak market attraction for this activity.
- ☐ No market attraction for this activity.

FIGURE 12.5 (cont.)

Tiny Shoreline Region

Legend symbols: ● abundant/heavy/strong · ◐ moderate · ○ limited/weak · (blank) none

TOURISM RECREATION OPPORTUNITY				RESOURCE OPPORT	EX Local	EX Regional	EX Provincial	EX National/U.S.	EX International	DES Local	DES Regional	DES Provincial	DES National/U.S.	DES International	POT Local	POT Regional	POT Provincial	POT National	POT International
NATURAL RESOURCES	Water-based Recreation Opportunities	Boating	Sailing	●	●	●	○	○		●	●				●	●	○	○	
			Power Boating/Touring	●	●	●	●	○	○	●	●				●	●	○	○	
			Ice Boating	○		○	○				○				●	●			
			Canoeing	●	●	●	●			●	●				●	●			
			Windsurfing	●	●	●	●			●	●				●	●			
		Fishing	Sportfishing	◐	●	●				●	●				●	●			
			Icefishing	○		●	●				●	○			●	○			
	Land-Based Recreation Opportunities		Swimming/Bathing	◐	●	●				●	●	○			●	●	○		
			Water Skiing	◐	●	●				●	●				●	●			
			Scuba Diving/Snorkeling	◐	●	●	○			●	●	○			●	●	○	○	
		Skiing	Alpine																
			Cross-Country	●	●	●	○			●	●	○			●	○	○		
		Hunting	Big Game	◐	●	●				●	●				●	●			
			Small Game	◐	●	○				●	○				●	○			
			Water Fowl	◐	●	○				●	○				●	○			
		Camping	Auto Touring	○	○	○				○	○				○	●	○	○	
			Wilderness	●	○	○				○	○				○	●	○	○	
		Hiking/Backpacking	Day	○	○	○				○	○				○	●			
			Overnight	●	○	○				○	○				○	●			
			Snowshoeing	◐	○	○				○	○				○	●			
			Rock Climbing													○			
			Cave Exploring																
			Picnicking	●	●	○				●	●				●				
			Cottaging/Chalet	●	○	●		○		○	●				○	●	○	○	
			Snowmobiling	●	●	●				○	●				○	●			
			Cycling	○	○	○				○	○				○	●			
			Equestrian Trails	○	○	○				○	○				○	○			
	Land and Water-Based Recreation Opportunities		Viewing Natural Attractions	●	●	●	●	○	○	●	●	○	○		●	●	○	○	○
			Gathering/Collecting	◐	○	○				○	○				○	○			
			Photography/Painting	●	●	●	○			●	●	○	○		●	●	○	○	
	Air-Based Recreation Opportunities		Hang Gliding																
			Hot Air Ballooning																
			Gliding		○	○	○			○	○				○				
MAN-DEVELOPED MAN-CONTROLLED RESOURCES	Natural Resource Opportunities	Natural Parks and Sites	National	●	○	●	●	○	○	●	●	●	○		●	●	●	○	
			Provincial	◐	●	●				●	●				●	●	○	○	
			Crown Land	●	●	○				●	○				●	○	○		
		Game Sanctuaries/Reserves		●	●	●				●	●				●	●	○		
		Game Farms																	
	Historical Resource Opportunities	Historic Parks and Sites	National	◐	○	●	●	○	○	●	●	○	○					
			Provincial	○	●	●	○			●	●				●				
			Local	○	●	○				●	○				●				
		Archaeological Attractions	Existing																
			Potential		○	○	○			○	○				○	○			
	Cultural Resource Opportunities	Population Centres	Cities/Towns	○	●	●	●	○	○	●	●	●	○		●	●	○	○	
			Ethnic Settlements	○	○	○				○	○				○	○			
		Cultural Attractions	Fairs/Celebrations	○	●	○				●	●				●	○			
			Crafts/Events	○	●	●				●	●				●	○			
			Museums/Galleries																
	Recreation Leisure Developments	Accommodation Recreation Resorts	Hotel Motel Cottage	◐	○	●	○	○	○	●	●	●	○	●	●	●	
			Vacation Farm																
			Ski Developments																
			Marina Developments	◐											●	○	○		
			Convention Centres	○											○	○			
		Travel Touring Corridors	Air		○	○	○			○	○				○	○	○	○	
			Rail		○	○	○			○	○				○				
			Boat	●	●	●	○	○		●	●	○	○		●	●	○	○	
			Car	◐	○	●	○			○	●				●	●	●	○	
		Recreation Leisure Developments	Ski Developments - Alpine																
			Ski Developments - Cross Country	◐	●	○				●	●				●	○			
			Marina Boating Developments	●	●	●	○	○		●	●	○	○		●	●	○	○	
			Golf Courses	○	●	○				●	○				●	●			
			Campgrounds Trailer Parks	●	○	●	○	○		○	●				○	●	○	○	
			Beaches	○						○	○				○	○			
	Attractions			◐	○	○				○	○				○	○			

Legend

a. RESOURCE OPPORTUNITIES
- ● Abundant resource opportunities; existing and/or potential.
- ◐ Moderate resource opportunities; existing and/or potential.
- ○ Limited resource opportunities; existing and/or potential.
- ☐ No resource opportunities.

b. EXISTING MARKET
- ● Heavy use/demand
- ○ Limited use/demand
- ☐ No use/demand

c. DESIRED MARKET
- ● Strong desire to attract as a primary market.
- ○ Limited desire to attract as a primary market.
- ☐ No desire to attract as a primary market.

d. POTENTIAL MARKET
- ● Strong market attraction for this activity.
- ○ Weak market attraction for this activity.
- ☐ No market attraction for this activity.

such as alpine skiing to more passive pursuits such as shopping and viewing scenery. Every destination area has a variety of existing activities and potential activities not yet being capitalized upon. As the activity or activities available at the destination are often a prime motivating factor to travel, this exercise can be most useful in highlighting new demand generation opportunities. Again, it is necessary to classify the activities in terms of their range of appeal (see Figure 12.5). It also is essential to identify the months of the year in which the activities can be pursued (see Figure 12.6). Because many destination areas suffer from a seasonality of demand problem, this part of the analysis helps to pinpoint those activities that will generate demand outside of peak periods.

A good tourism plan will incorporate some original research on the existing and potential markets for the destination area. As will be recalled, the market-related research carried out in the first phase was based upon already available information. The original research is done by carrying out one or more surveys of existing tourists and potential tourists. Surveys of existing tourists are normally carried on while they are traveling within the destination area, and they are useful in producing information of the following types:

> Overall degrees of satisfaction with trips
> Evaluations and ratings of attractions, facilities, services, and other resource components
> Likelihood of return visits
> Awareness levels of area attractions and other resource components
> Motivations for travel to area
> Identification of items that would increase likelihood of return visits
> Sources of information utilized in planning trips
> Major constraints or barriers to return visits
> Images of the destination area

Normally the personal interview technique is utilized in these surveys of existing visitors, either at exit/entry points or at key tourism facilities.

The background analysis phase and the detailed resource/activity analyses should have provided some clues as to the sources of potential new market demand for the destination area. If the tourist market in an area is first divided into its business- and pleasure-travel components, then its market potential will have the following seven major components:

> The attraction of *pleasure travelers* from *other geographical markets* than those which are currently being drawn from
> The attraction of *pleasure travelers* from *other segments of the pleasure-travel market* than those which are currently being drawn from
> The *increased penetration* of those *geographical markets* from which *pleasure travelers* are currently being drawn from

The *increased penetration* of those *segments of the pleasure-travel market* which are currently being drawn from

The *increased penetration* of those *segments of the business travel market* which are currently being drawn from

The attraction of *current business travelers* as *future pleasure travelers*

The attraction of *current pleasure travelers* as *future pleasure travelers* (that is, repeat patronage)

A variety of survey techniques are available and can be utilized to research these potential markets. These include personal interviews, focus group sessions, telephone interviews, and mail-out, mail-back questionnaires. They can be directed towards the individual pleasure travelers in a specific geographic market (household surveys) and/or be aimed at the channels of distribution (tour wholesalers/operators and travel agents) and other travel influencers (convention planners, club/affinity group executives, corporate travel departments, and so on). This research helps to determine attitudes toward future travel to the subject destination area, levels of awareness of the area's tourism resource components, images of the area, the major competitive destinations, and the steps needed to be taken to attract patronage from these potential visitors. It can also provide an opportunity to "market test" new tourism attraction/packaging/activity ideas that those in the destination area have identified earlier in the planning process.

Another important aspect of the detailed market analysis should be an evaluation of the likely impact of future travel trends on the destination area. The information on these trends comes from a variety of available "futures" research studies and ongoing "tracking" research programs on travel trends. It is a fairly common practice at this point in the tourism planning process to forecast tourism demand volumes for the period covering the term of the tourism. A number of techniques can be utilized in such forecasting, and these are described later in Chapter Thirteen. When the forecasts have been completed, a supply (capacities of resource components) demand (forecast demand volumes) matching exercise is normally carried out. This step helps those in the destination area determine where there are likely to be shortfalls in different tourism resources and where there could be problems in preserving tourism resources due to excessive demand levels.

No destination area is without competition, and thus a tourism plan must consider the competitive advantages and future plans of other areas as well as its own. Normally, it is most useful to define competitive markets in terms of their relative distance from prime geographic markets. Those destination areas closer to a prime market are often referred to as being "intervening opportunities"—the tourist must pass them to reach the subject destination area. The detailed market research described earlier can assist in identifying the most competitive destinations, their individual strengths and weaknesses, and the steps that can be taken to make the subject destination area unique among its competitors.

Certain other avenues of research and analysis may also be incorporated in the second phase of tourism planning. These may include an evaluation of the tourism industry organization, tourism awareness levels, and the tourism marketing programs of the destination area. The background analysis phase will indicate the degree of emphasis to be given to these factors. For example, in some areas, organizational problems or conflicts may be so acute that they require detailed research and evaluation

Synthesis Phase

The third phase of the tourism planning process represents the point in which the major conclusions regarding all of the previous work are formulated. Some tourism planning experts consider it to be one of the most important and creative stages in the process. A comprehensive tourism plan will produce conclusions on five distinct subjects:

1. Tourism development
2. Tourism marketing
3. Tourism industry organization
4. Tourism awareness
5. Other tourism support services and activities

The first step in the synthesis phase should be the preparation of position statements on each of these five subjects. The position statement indicates "where we are now" with respect to development, marketing, industry organization, awareness, and other support services. One of the participating groups is given the responsibility for preparing preliminary position statements, usually either the tourism consultants or the public sector tourism officials. These are then reviewed and discussed by all participants, and a consensus is reached on the final wording of the statements. Position statements may be simply expressed in one sentence or be documented in several pages of text. A simple position statement on development could be "our destination area has historically been developed to appeal to a summer/warm weather market; facilities to attract tourism at other times of the year have not been constructed."

The second step is that of determining "where we would like to be" or the desired future situation. Again, it is useful for the destination area

FIGURE 12.6 List of Potential Travel/Recreation Activities By Session

Activity	April	May	June	July	Aug.	Sept.	Oct.	Nov.	Dec.	Jan.	Feb.	Mar.	Present Availability
Boating													
General													*
Sailing													*
Canoeing													*
Ice sailing													Z
Cruise boat trips													Z
House boat rentals													Z
Fishing													
General													*
Ice fishing													*
Hunting													
Grouse and duck													*
Bear													*
Moose													*
Deer													*
Camping													*

Outdoor Recreation		
Swimming		* *
Scuba diving		N *
Water skiing		N *
Windsurfing		* *
Hiking		* *
Snowmobiling		*
Cross-country skiing		*
Downhill skiing		N
Orienteering		*
Wilderness survival		*
Snowshoeing		*
Golf		*
Tennis		*
Horseback riding		*

Key:

——— Prime months for the activity

- - - Activity possible in these months, but not as popular as in prime time

** Activity/facilities available in quantity in the area

* Limited availability of activity/facilities in the area — some room for expansion

N Activity/facilities not available presently in the area

SOURCE: *A Strategy and Action Plan for Tourism in Atikokon Area* (Waterloo, Ontario, Balmer, Crapo & Associates, Inc., 1979), p. 66.

to verbalize these desired states in terms of tourism development, marketing, industry organization, awareness, and support services. In our simple example this could be "it is our desire to have year-round tourism facilities in our destination area."

Tourism strategies and plans provide the "bridge" between the present situation and desired future situations in a destination area. They provide the means to the end.

Before we move on to the fourth phase of the planning process, some classification of tourism planning terminology is necessary. First, it should be realized that the terms "tourism plan" and "tourism strategy" are often used to refer to the same thing. In this text, we refer to the entire task described in this chapter as being tourism planning, irrespective of whether the eventual outcome is called a tourism strategy or a tourism plan. Under our definition all tourism planning exercises produce alternative tourism strategies and a tourism plan. The tourism plan itself is a very specific course of action, and the tourism strategies are the alternative approaches available to achieve the tourism planning goals. The strategies therefore precede the plan in chronological order.

Goal-setting, Strategy Selection, and Objective-Setting

Now that the destination area has decided upon the fundamental future directions for tourism, tourism planning goals, alternative strategies, and plan objectives can be defined. The planning goals, strategies, and plan objectives must be complementary to policy goals and objectives.

In the Ontario example cited earlier, the major policy goal for tourism was "to stimulate employment, income and economic development through the systematic improvement, development and marketing of Ontario's tourism industry." This can be classified as an economy-oriented approach to tourism. Another destination area suffering from overcrowding or an already too rapid pace of development may have chosen a more conservation-oriented approach. Remember that a tourism plan has a relatively short life span, usually five years, and its planning goals should be achievable within that time period. A destination area with an economy-oriented policy approach may wish to obtain the maximum economic impact from tourism within the term of the plan. This area will therefore probably adopt a planning goal that emphasizes the development and marketing of those subareas or specific resource components likely to produce the greatest economic return within the planning period; it will concentrate on its major strengths. Yet another destination may have an economy-oriented approach but be more concerned with spreading the economic benefits of tourism more evenly throughout its subareas. Its planning goals might therefore be to concentrate upon the development and marketing of those subareas with the lowest levels of existing tourism activity.

Once the planning goals have been set, there are usually a variety of approaches or strategies that can be employed to achieve them. Within a specific destination area, it should also be realized that different approaches or strategies may be utilized for the subareas within it—some subareas may have economy-oriented strategies and some may have conservation-oriented strategies.

A commonly found tourism development strategy in North America involves dividing the destination into destination zones, touring corridors, and other areas (see Figure 12.7). This type of strategy was utilized in Ontario and was later adopted by other Canadian provinces and certain states of the United States. It can be applied to many geographic areas, including countries, states/provinces, counties, and regions within counties. As well as being visually displayed in this fashion, a strategy is usually verbalized in a series of strategy statements. A comprehensive strategy will incorporate in these statements the five elements of development, marketing, industry organization, awareness, and support services. Once more it should be mentioned that a strategy is an approach to translating the current conditions in these five fields into the desired situations. For example, a destination area highly dependent on one specific geographic market for its demand, may wish to adopt a strategy of diversifying its geographic markets, thereby reducing its dependence on one market. Those in a destination area with the planning goal of increasing the economic benefits of tourism to a specific subarea may select a strategy to increase visitation to that subarea.

The tourism plan objectives flow logically from the selected strategy. Figure 12.8 provides an example of this for a region within Ontario showing the linkage among planning goals, strategy, and plan objectives.

Plan Development Phase

The final phase of the tourism planning process is the development of the plan itself. The plan details the actions needed to achieve the objectives, implement the strategy, and satisfy the planning goals. A comprehensive plan deals with the five subjects of development, marketing, industry organization, awareness, and support services. It takes each of the plan objectives and specifies the following for each of them:

The programs and actions required to achieve each plan objective
The roles and responsibilities of the public and private sector in carrying on these programs and actions

FIGURE 12.7

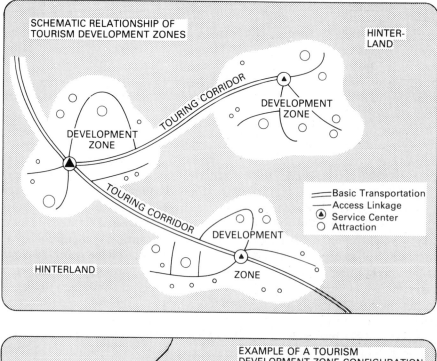

SCHEMATIC RELATIONSHIP OF
TOURISM DEVELOPMENT ZONES

HINTER-
LAND

TOURING CORRIDOR

DEVELOPMENT
ZONE

DEVELOPMENT
ZONE

TOURING CORRIDOR

DEVELOPMENT

HINTERLAND

ZONE

Basic Transportation
Access Linkage
Service Center
Attraction

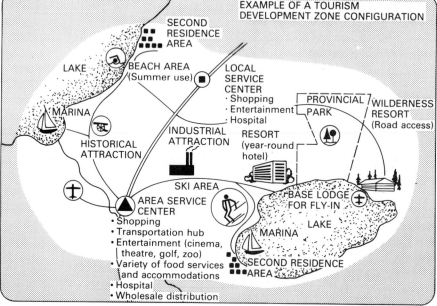

EXAMPLE OF A TOURISM
DEVELOPMENT ZONE CONFIGURATION

SECOND
RESIDENCE
AREA

LAKE

BEACH AREA
(Summer use)

LOCAL
SERVICE
CENTER
· Shopping
· Entertainment
· Hospital

PROVINCIAL
PARK

WILDERNESS
RESORT
(Road access)

MARINA

HISTORICAL
ATTRACTION

INDUSTRIAL
ATTRACTION

RESORT
(year-round
hotel)

SKI AREA

AREA SERVICE
CENTER
· Shopping
· Transportation hub
· Entertainment (cinema,
  theatre, golf, zoo)
· Variety of food services
  and accommodations
· Hospital
· Wholesale distribution

BASE LODGE
FOR FLY-IN

LAKE

MARINA

SECOND RESIDENCE
AREA

SOURCE: *Tourism Development in Ontario: A Framework for Opportunity* (Waterloo, Ontario, Balmer, Crapo & Associates, Inc., 1977).

310

FIGURE 12.8

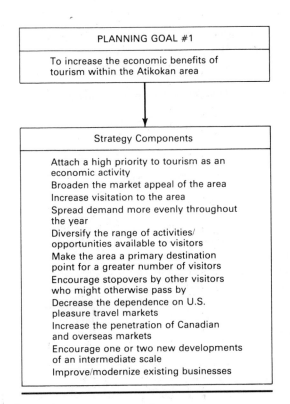

PLANNING GOAL #1

To increase the economic benefits of tourism within the Atikokan area

Strategy Components

Attach a high priority to tourism as an economic activity
Broaden the market appeal of the area
Increase visitation to the area
Spread demand more evenly throughout the year
Diversify the range of activities/opportunities available to visitors
Make the area a primary destination point for a greater number of visitors
Encourage stopovers by other visitors who might otherwise pass by
Decrease the dependence on U.S. pleasure travel markets
Increase the penetration of Canadian and overseas markets
Encourage one or two new developments of an intermediate scale
Improve/modernize existing businesses

PLAN OBJECTIVES RELATED TO GOAL 1

1.1   To create new images of what the Atikokan area has to offer to visitors, that is, much more than fishing and hunting

1.2   To develop and promote new attractions, facilities, and events that appeal to a broad range of interests

1.3   To develop and promote new travel/recreational opportunities associated with the major activities of destination and pass-through visitors

1.4   To increase the visitor market's awareness of the area's facilities, services, activities, attractions, and events

1.5   To increase awareness of the activities/opportunities afforded by the Atikokan area, with emphasis on those occurring in the winter, spring, and fall seasons

1.6   To develop means of communication to stimulate visitors already within the area to take advantage of its tourism/recreational opportunities

1.7   To increase per capita visitor expenditures by capturing those segments of the visitor market that have higher-than-average expenditures on vacation travel, by increasing average lengths of stay and by providing more "spending opportunities"

FIGURE 12.8 *(cont.)*

1.8 To improve the quality of existing tourism facilities/services in order to increase repeat patronage and to enhance positive word-of-mouth advertising

1.9 To develop facilities and services that can be used during the winter and other off-peak periods

1.10 To develop vacation packages that can be sold year-round or during a specific season

1.11 To associate Atikokan as much as is possible and advisable with Quetico Provincial Park

1.12 To develop a series of interpretive/rest areas along Highway 11

SOURCE: Balmer, Crapo & Associates, Inc., *A Strategy and Action Plan for Tourism in the Atitokan Area,* 1979, p. 66.

The specific development and marketing concepts and opportunities that will help achieve certain objectives
The funds required to carry out specific programs and actions
The sources of these funds
The timetable for carrying out specific programs and actions within the plan
The method for monitoring the success of the plan on a periodic basis during its term

Once it has been laid out in this detail, the tourism plan is then written up in formal reports, either by a private tourism consulting firm or by public sector tourism officials. The tourism plan reports are often presented in two parts—the first being a summary report containing the plan itself, the second being a larger and more detailed technical report providing all of the research, findings, and conclusions produced during the planning process. The reports are usually prepared in draft and are reviewed and revised by public and private sector representatives prior to being finalized for publication.

Summary

Every destination area interested in tourism should be involved in the tourism planning process. Although tourism planning can be arduous, time consuming, costly, and hard to sell, it is an essential activity in today's rapidly changing business environments. The absence of tourism planning in a destination can eventually lead to irreversible economic, social/cultural, and environmental damage and to loss of market share. There are many barriers to tourism planning in every destination area, but the rewards resulting from an effective tourism planning process far outweigh the efforts needed to surmount these. Empirical evidence throughout the world clearly shows that the "model" destinations for successful tourism are those that have embraced the tourism planning concept.

REFERENCES

BALMER, CRAPO & ASSOCIATES, INC., *A Strategy and Action Plan for Tourism in the Atikokan Area* (Waterloo, Ontario, Township of Atikokan, 1979), p. 66.

BALMER, CRAPO & ASSOCIATES, INC., *Tourism Development in Ontario: A Framework for Opportunity* (Waterloo, Ontario, Ontario Ministry of Tourism and Recreation, 1977).

BOSSELMAN, FRED P., *In the Wake of the Tourist Managing Special Places in Eight Countries* (Washington, DC, The Conservation Foundation, 1978).

GUNN, CLARE A., *Tourism Planning*, (New York, Crane Russak, 1979), p. 23.

MARSHALL MACKLIN, MONOGHAN, *Tourism Development Strategy: Collingwood-Midland-Orillia Zone* (Toronto, Ontario, Ontario Ministry of Tourism and Recreation, 1980).

MORRISON, ALASTAIR M., *The Planning and Development of Tourism in a Large Rural Area Regional Tourism Planning in Auvergne-Limousin* (East Lansing, MI, 1973), pp. 32–33.

POLLOCK, ANN M./B.C. RESEARCH, *A Framework for Tourism Development Planning* (Victoria, British Columbia, Tourism British Columbia, 1977), p. 22.

These figures are adapted from a seminar entitled *Tourism in Northwestern Ontario: What is the Municipal Role?* and presented by Alastair M. Morrison and Dr. Douglas Crapo in March, 1980.

THE ECONOMIC PLANNING GROUP OF CANADA, *Tourism Development Strategy and Action Plan for the County of Bruce, Owen Sound and North Grey* (Toronto, Ontario, County of Bruce, 1983).

TURNER, LOUIS, AND JOHN ASH, *The Golden Hordes: International Tourism and the Pleasure Periphery* (London, England, Constable, 1975).

WOLMAN, FRANK AND ASSOCIATES, *Yukon Tourism Development Strategy* (Toronto, Ontario, Yukon Department of Tourism and Information, 1978), pp. xi–xiii.

YOUNG, GEORGE, *Tourism: Blessing or Blight* (Middlesex, England, Penguin Books, 1973).

13

TOURISM DEVELOPMENT:
Building a Future
for the Travel Industry

Within the context of a tourism plan, development can take place. The specifics of tourism development is the topic of this chapter.

The necessity for defining the tourism product in its widest sense is stressed. The respective roles of the private and the public sectors in tourism development are outlined.

A process for analyzing individual tourism development projects is suggested, and each step is detailed. Particular attention is paid to the analysis of the project from an economic viewpoint. Sources of financing from both the private and the public sectors are examined.

BUILDING A FUTURE FOR THE TRAVEL INDUSTRY

The Linkage between Tourism Planning and Tourism Development

The tourism planning process described in Chapter Eleven should be designed to produce goals, strategies, and objectives for the destination area related to tourism development, marketing, industry organization, and awareness, and to other support services and activities. The tourism development plan normally provides overall guidelines for development, outlines broad development concepts, and identifies individual development opportunities worthy of in-depth analysis (through feasibility studies and/or cost/benefit analyses).

When proceeding with tourism development, those in the destination area will find it necessary to first establish overall development guidelines to ensure that when development occurs it complies with the area's economic, social/cultural, and environmental policies and goals. It may also be prudent for those in the destination to draft more specific guidelines describing the basic characteristics of the scale, quality, and types of development that it wishes to encourage.

The final outcome of a tourism development plan is often that a series of individual development opportunities are identified for further investigation. For the purposes of this text, the term "tourism product" is used to describe all categories of development opportunities, both commercial and noncommercial. The economic feasibility of commercial (profit making) development opportunities is usually established at a later date using techniques similar to that outlined in this chapter. The non-commercial development opportunities can include such support facilities as travel information centers, infrastructure, and nonprofit-making attractions such as museums and other historic landmarks. The advisability of proceeding with these facilities or services cannot be measured through an economic feasibility study since they may produce little or no revenue. These opportunities are thus often the subject of a technique known as cost/benefit analysis, or else they are considered in the context of their importance to the achievement of the tourism plan's goals and objectives.

Public and Private Sector Roles in Tourism Development

Both the public and private sectors have important roles to play in tourism development in a free-enterprise system. The role of the private sector in tourism development is more limited and certainly more clear-cut. Its principal role is to provide tourism facilities and services to the traveling public while maximizing financial returns in the process. In more enlightened societies, the private sector has come to accept that it has certain social and environmental responsibilities that it must respect in achieving its profit goals.

Not all tourism development projects are identified through the tourism planning process. Many project ideas emerge from the private sector itself through sponsored research studies and assessments of supply/demand relationships. Idea generation is, therefore, a key role of the private sector.

The entrepreneurial role is at the heart of the private sector's involvement in tourism development. This role embraces idea generation, development project implementation, financial risk taking and investment, and the management of operations. The private sector also provides the specialized technical skills required in the development process through tourism consultants, market research firms, economists, architects, engineers, designers, lawyers, project managers, and builders.

The private sector, through its financial institutions, other corporate lenders, and individual citizens, provides a large proportion of the capital funds for the investment in tourism projects.

Nonprofit private organizations also play an important role in tourism development in most destinations. These organizations include chambers of commerce, travel associations, foundations, historical and cultural societies, recreation and sports associations/clubs, service clubs, community associations, religious groups, and so on. The roles played by these groups vary from destination to destination, but typically the groups are involved in operating attractions (such as pioneer villages, historic buildings, museums, and art galleries), creating and running events and special meals, providing travel information services, and financing the development of community-oriented facilities (such as recreation and community halls, historical/cultural centers, and trail systems).

In North America and the majority of Western Europe, the most widely accepted function of government in tourism development is to act as a catalyst and to complement the efforts of the private sector, including nonprofit organizations. The World Tourism Organization points out that as a general principle, a government should not seek to do itself what the private sector is able and willing to do. Although this can be said to be a generally accepted principle in North America, there are still numerous instances of overlapping activities and conflict between the public and private sectors. In both the United States and Canada, the federal, state/provincial, and local governments are heavily involved in the operation of parks, most of which include camping facilities. Many private campground operators feel that the government-operated facilities offer unfair competition and that the government should not be in the campground business. Another area of contention often found is in the provision of boat-docking facilities where both the private sector and government agencies sometimes operate competitive facilities. A further area of direct competition is that of state-owned airlines versus private air carriers.

There can be several valid reasons behind the reversal in the public and private sector roles in tourism development. The most important of these is that it is not always reasonable to expect tourism to develop along the lines and at the speed desired by the government in its tourism program if left entirely to the operations of the private sector. Government agencies often find themselves with a more direct role in tourism development for the following reasons:

The private sector is unwilling to finance the development of a project because of its limited profit potential; the government may however have given this project a high priority due to its regional economic contributions or its pivotal role in stimulating tourism activity.

An existing tourism facility is bankrupt and cannot be sold on the market; for reasons similar to those mentioned in the first point, the government feels obliged to acquire the facility.

The government may wish to provide low-cost vacation opportunities for disadvantaged groups within its population, such as the poor, the sick, and the aged; this is often called "social tourism."

The government may wish to encourage private sector development by pioneering new types of developments through "demonstration" or "pilot" projects.

Due to one or both of the first two reasons listed above, several provinces within Canada and several states in the United States are directly involved in the resort business. These include Kentucky, Ontario, Manitoba, Quebec, New Brunswick, Prince Edward Island, and Nova Scotia. In these areas, the resorts are owned by the respective governments and are either operated directly by the government or by the private sector through a management contract. The social tourism function is not yet prevalent in North America, but is a widely accepted phenomenon in many countries in Western Europe. For example, France has established a network of "village de vacances" (family-oriented resorts) and "gites familiaux" (family homes in resort settings) for its disadvantaged citizens As an example of the last point listed above, Tourism Canada sponsored the design of four styles of low-cost accommodation units for use in areas with particularly short operating seasons. It subsequently provided assistance to a private developer in constructing some of these units.

THE ANALYSIS OF INDIVIDUAL TOURISM DEVELOPMENT PROJECTS

Individual development opportunities in tourism are either generated through the tourism planning process or by the private sector (entrepreneurial role) independent of this process. In destinations without tourism plans, those in the public sector may also be involved in identifying development opportunities for private-sector investment.

Although these development opportunities can have the potential of satisfying tourism planning goals and can have considerable initial appeal to those in the private sector, they may be undesirable due to financial, environmental, social, or other reasons. All individual tourism development opportunities must therefore be carefully researched and analyzed prior to the reaching of a decision to proceed with their construction.

Before this process of research and analysis is described, it is important to realize some fundamental differences in the range of potential tourism development projects. The first difference between projects is their capability to generate financial profits. Some projects, such as hotels and commercial attractions, are inherent profit generators, while others, such as travel information centers and infrastructure facilities, are usually not. Although the latter facilities may not generate any direct revenues or may only break even in a financial sense, they are nevertheless often essential components of the destination area's tourism product. Profit-generating projects are generally investigated by means of economic feasibility studies, and the remaining projects are the subject of cost/benefit analyses or other types of "contribution analysis" exercises.

Tourism development encompasses many elements. Some of these include projects that involve building construction (such as a superstructure); others require only human resources and equipment (such as guided canoe trips, under the category of programming and events). Despite these major differences in the tourism project ingredients of the eight product elements, individual projects can be analyzed by using similar techniques.

A government agency involved in providing financial incentives and technical or other assistance to individual tourism projects should as a first step establish a set of project selection criteria. These criteria will assist the agency in identifying those projects that merit its assistance and in screening out others that are not as desirable. Typically, criteria fall into the following nine categories:

1. *ECONOMIC CONTRIBUTIONS:* That the project creates a significant level of income and employment benefits.

2. *ENVIRONMENTAL IMPACT:* That the project is developed in compliance with existing legislation and regulations governing the conservation and protection of the environment.
3. *SOCIAL-CULTURAL IMPACT:* That the project does not jeopardize the social well-being of citizens.
4. *COMPETITIVE IMPACT:* That the project complements, rather than competes with, existing tourism businesses, and that it does not seriously jeopardize the financial viability of any individual enterprise.
5. *TOURISM IMPACT:* That the project adds to the destination's tourism potential by creating an attraction, by improving the area's capacity to receive and cater to visitors, or by being beneficial to the tourism industry in some other fashion.
6. *DEVELOPER AND OPERATOR CAPABILITIES:* That the developer and operators of the project must be capable of developing and operating the business successfully.
7. *COMPLIANCE WITH POLICIES, PLANS, AND PROGRAMS:* That the project complies with the destination's tourism policies, plans, and programs.
8. *EQUITY CONTRIBUTIONS:* Where the project is profit-generating, that the investors have sufficient equity to inject into the venture.
9. *FEASIBILITY:* Where the project is profit-generating, that it be economically feasible.

Figure 13.1 visually displays a tourism project evaluation and analysis system. It shows that there are at least seven important decision points in project analysis in which further consideration of the project may be terminated. These are as follows:

> A prefeasibility study produces negative results
> The site for the project is found not to be suitable, and no alternative site is available
> The market analysis indicates that the potential market is not large enough to support the project as envisioned
> The project is not found to be economically feasible
> The results of a cost/benefit analysis are negative
> The government decides that the project does not warrant financial incentives and is not feasible without these incentives
> Sufficient financing from private sources cannot be obtained

The remainder of this chapter is devoted to a description of the key steps in the tourism project evaluation and analysis system.

Prefeasibility Study

A prefeasibility study is an analysis that determines whether a more detailed economic feasibility study of a project is justified and which subjects the detailed study should address. Because detailed economic feasibility studies are costly and time-consuming, this type of preliminary project assessment can be extremely valuable to the developer. The four principal objectives of a prefeasibility study are to determine whether:

1. The available information is adequately detailed to indicate that the project will not be viable or will not be attractive to investors/lenders
2. The available information indicates that the project is so promising that an investment decision can be made on the basis of the prefeasibility study itself; that is, a detailed study is not needed
3. Certain aspects of the project are so critical to its viability that they must be analyzed as part of the detailed economic feasibility study
4. The availability of certain factors critical to the viability of the project (such as the availability of a specific site location) must be confirmed prior to a detailed economic feasibility study being initiated

Prefeasibility studies can be completed by the private developers themselves, by a government agency considering financing projects, or by private consulting organizations on behalf of the developers and/or a government agency. In some cases, the tourism development plan component of the tourism planning process produces prefeasibility analyses of key tourism project opportunities.

Detailed Economic Feasibility Study

If a project survives the prefeasibility screening process, then it normally becomes the subject of a detailed economic feasibility study. In North America, the majority of tourism-project economic feasibility studies are carried out by private consulting organizations on behalf of private developers/investors, or government agencies, or a combination of the two. Although many successful tourism projects have been developed without detailed economic feasibility studies, as have many that have not proven successful, these analyses are vitally important to a variety of participants involved in the development process. Such participants include developers, investors (if they are different from the developers), and potential lenders. Other players involved in the process can include management companies interested in operating the projects on behalf of the developers/investors. Also, the potential lenders may often fall into two groups—those providing the construction ("interim") financing, and those providing the long-term ("permanent") financing.

An economic feasibility study is a study that determines the economic feasibility of a tourism project. A project is economically feasible if it provides a rate of return that is acceptable to the investors in the project. A market study is one component of an economic feasibility study dealing with the project's market potential. Sometimes the term "economic feasibility study" is abbreviated to just "feasibility study." Because of the need to acquire an unbiased opinion on a project's viability, economic feasibility studies are usually prepared by an independent third party and

FIGURE 13.1 Conceptual Model of a Tourism Project Evaluation and Analysis System

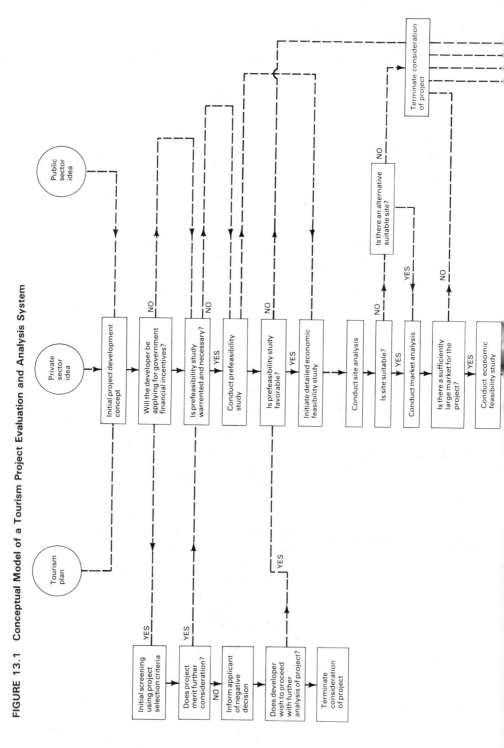

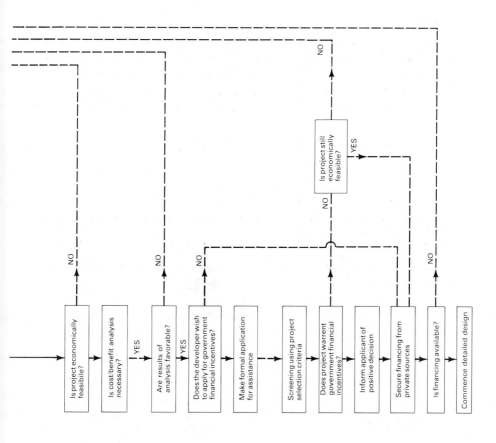

not by the developers/investors or the potential lenders. Many lenders, including both private financial institutions and government agencies providing financial incentive programs, require that these independent studies be completed before they will seriously consider projects.

An economic feasibility study is designed to answer the following questions that are of concern to the various participants in the development process:

DEVELOPERS AND INVESTORS

Which of several alternative site locations is the most appropriate for the project?

Is a specific project site appropriate for the development?

If not, is there another site available that would be suitable?

Is there a market of sufficient size available to support the project?

What are the optimum scale and components of the project?

What style of operation and quality levels should be provided?

What revenues and expenses will the project earn and incur?

What will the capital costs of the project be?

Will the project produce a satisfactory return on investment?

Should the developers/investors proceed with further analysis of the project?

LENDERS

All of the above questions should also be of concern to the lenders.

How much money will have to be loaned to the developers/investors?

Do the developers/investors have a sufficient amount of equity to invest in the project, given the financing required?

Will the project produce sufficient operating profits and cash flow to cover the interest and principal payments when they become due?

The economic feasibility study has another important use for the developers. It produces recommendations on the scale, sizes, facility types, and quality levels of operation. These recommendations are based upon the size and expectations of the market as dictated by the findings of the market study. At a later date in the development process, these will be used as the basis for the architect's preliminary drawings.

Site Analysis

Although not all tourism-related projects require physical site locations, a very large proportion do. An economic feasibility study can either specify a site (site specific), if a specific site location has been chosen for the project, or determine if an appropriate site exists within a given geographic area.

A tourism project site normally requires certain specific characteristics for it to be successful. This is not true of all industry sectors in an economy, as there are many "footloose" enterprises that are not location dependent. In tourism, location has an extremely important bearing upon financial viability.

The characteristics or criteria for site selection and evaluation vary according to the type of tourism project under consideration. For example, a proposed new alpine ski area is highly dependent on the snow conditions and slope characteristics in a given location, while an urban hotel requires proximity to a concentration of industry and commerce. Similarly, a motor hotel requires ease of access and proximity to highways, while the placement of tennis courts is dictated by the wind and sun conditions at the site. The first step in the site analysis must, therefore, be to identify the criteria that are crucial to the project being considered.

Tourism project site criteria or characteristics can be divided into three categories:

1. Market-related site criteria
2. Criteria related to the physical characteristics of sites
3. Other criteria

Typically, the market-related site criteria encompass the site's proximity to potential markets, transportation facilities/routes, essential support facilities (such as accommodation, restaurants, and shopping centers), and competitive facilities. Figure 13.2 provides a master list of individual criteria within each of the categories. The selection from this list of characteristics most crucial to a given project requires both a knowledge of the particular business type, experience with it, and a broad knowledge of construction/site engineering. Ideally, therefore, a multidisciplined team consisting of a specialized tourism consultant, engineer, landscape architect, and architect should be utilized for this purpose.

FIGURE 13.2 Master List of Tourism Site Selection Criteria

---

1. MARKET-RELATED SITE CRITERIA

Proximity of site to potential markets
Proximity and ease of accessibility to transportation facilities and modes:
Highways and roads
Airports
Railroad services
Marina and harbor facilities
Trail systems (hiking, cross-country/Alpine skiing, snowmobiling, bicycling, etc.)
Bus services
Ferry services

Proximity of site to essential support services (such as accommodation, restaurants, and shopping centers)
Proximity of site to other major tourism demand generators
Visibility of site to passing vehicular traffic
Proximity to major competitive facilities

Continued

FIGURE 13.2 *(cont.)*

2. CRITERIA RELATED TO THE PHYSICAL CHARACTERISTICS OF SITES

Aesthetics of adjoining lands and land uses
Natural conditions
  Climate and microclimate
    Temperature
    Precipitation
    Sunshine and clouds
    Humidity
    Winds
    Seasons
    Purity of air
  Water supply
    Natural springs
    Waterfalls and cascades
    Rivers and streams
    Lakes and seas
    Drainage patterns
    Flooding problems
  Geology and geomorphology
    Bedrock type
    Water-table level, well depths,
      quality
    Geologic history
  Soils and topography
    Soil types
    Slopes
    Depths

Site aesthetics
  Scale
  Views
  Focal points
  Variety (feature, form, color)
  Noise
  Smells
  Vegetation
    Tree types
    Ground cover type
    Visual and physical condition
    Clearing problems
Wildlife and fish
  Species and type
  Effects of development on these
Available infrastructure
  Sources of energy
  Water supply
  Sewer system and waste disposal
    services
  Transportation facilities
  Other needed services
Other site characteristics
  Dimensions and shape
  Existing rights of way and easements
  Length of shoreline available
  Height above sea level
  Geographical orientation
  Ability of land to support various types
    of recreation activities

3. OTHER CRITERIA

Manpower availability
Availability of staff accommodation
Availability of suitable quality of land
  for project
Cost of land
Zoning laws and other legal regulations

Social and economic characteristics of
  host area
Sources and types of financial assistance
  in host area
Labor laws and labor relations history

SOURCES: *Checklist of Factors Determining the Selection of Sites for Tourism Development* (Madrid, Spain, World Tourism Organization, undated), pp. 1-16.

Manual for the Preparation of Industrial Feasibility Studies (New York, United Nations, 1978), pp. 94-97.

Project Investigation/Recreation Facility Site Evaluation (Wisconsin Department of Local Affairs and Developlment: Bureau of Recreation, undated), pp. 4.2-4.9).

When the site analysis is not site specific, it is a common practice to first identify a "long list" of potentially suitable sites and then to rank these sites on the basis of their compatibility with the project. This is often accomplished by attaching a weighting factor to each site selection criterion/characteristic and by then giving each site under consideration a numerical score for that criterion/characteristic. The weighting factor reflects the relative importance of each individual criterion/characteristic, and the numerical score (say on a 0 to 10 basis) indicates the quality and/or quantity of that criterion/characteristic at one of the alternative sites. The multiplication of the weighting factor and the numerical score provides a final score for each criterion/characteristic at each given site. The final scores for all criteria are added to give a total score for each alternative site. The most appropriate site for the project is usually the one earning the highest total score.

A modification of this type of site ranking system is demonstrated in Figure 13.3. This recreation facility site evaluation system, developed in Wisconsin, is designed to produce numerical scores for alternative sites relative to a variety of recreation and tourism land uses. The main factors that it considers are surface water conditions, ground water conditions, land characteristics, vegetation, climate, and regional market characteristics. Figure 13.3 shows one page from among the several contained in this site evaluation matrix. Each criterion is divided into four measurable units; for instance, the distance from a metropolitan area is divided into over four hours, from one and a half to four hours, from one half to one and one half hours, and under one half hour, and each unit is given a score of between 1 and 4. Each site under consideration is assigned scores on the basis of this matrix, and the site with the highest total score for a particular project type is the most appropriate for that use.

It should be realized that the evaluation of sites for some forms of recreational and tourism projects requires a high degree of specific technical expertise. Generally, these cases occur when the project is highly dependent for its ultimate success on the characteristics of the natural resource base and when also the construction costs are high. Examples of such projects include alpine skiing areas and large full-service marina projects. Private organizations specializing in site evaluations for these types of projects have been formed and are normally engaged to perform these analyses.

An economic feasibility study may be terminated during or after the site analysis if an essential site characteristic is missing or if some insurmountable legal/zoning restriction or other barrier to development is uncovered. The study will move on to an analysis of potential market demand if this is not the case.

Market Analysis

The market analysis phase of an economic feasibility study is often the most costly and time-consuming element of the entire study process. The costs and time required are directly dependent on the mix of primary

All are important considerations — ▨
Not a major consideration — ■
Major consideration (4) most desirable — □ (number shows most desirable value)

	Beach	Marina	Fishing resort	Yachting resort	Summer resort	Water trail	Ski slope	Winter resort	Picnic ground	Campground	Golf course	Hunting resort	Wilderness resort	Dude ranch	Vacation farm	Summer trail	Vacation home	Youth camp	Day camp	Group camp	Winter trade	Resort
	WATER ORIENTED						LAND ORIENTED										COMBINATION					
CLIMATE																						
Mean January temperature — (1) Under 12° (2) 12-16° (3) 16-20° (4) over 20°	■	■	■	■	■	■	■	2	2	■	■	■	■	2	■	■	2	■	■	■	■	2
Mean July temperature — (1) Under 65° (2) 75+ (3) 65-70° (4) 70-75°	4	▨	▨	▨	3	▨	■	■	3	3	3	■	▨	▨	▨	▨	4	3	3	■	■	■
Annual precipitation — (1) −29″ (2) 30-31″ (3) 32-33″ (4) 34″ & over	▨	▨	■	■	▨	▨	■	■	■	▨	▨	■	▨	■	▨	▨	▨	▨	▨	▨	▨	▨
Snowfall — (1) under 40″ (2) 40″-80″ (3) 80″-120″ (4) 120″ & over	■	■	■	■	■	■	2	2	■	■	■	■	▨	■	▨	▨	■	■	▨	■	3	2
REGIONAL																						
Distance from metro. areas — (1) over 4 hr. (2) 1½-4 hrs. (3) ½-1½ hr. (4) under ½ hr.	3	3	3	3	3	▨	3	3	4	3	3	3	3	▨	▨	▨	3	3	4	4	3	
Distance to shopping area — (1) 30+ Min. (2) 20-30 Min. (3) 10-20 Min. (4) 10 minutes	■	■	4	■	3	3	3	3	4	4	■	■	3	3	3	3	3	3	4	3	3	3
Distance from major highways — (1) 30+ Min. (2) 10-30 Min. (3) 10 Minutes (4) Nearby	3	3	2	2	3	2	3	2	4	2	3	2	▨	2	2	▨	3	2	3	3	3	2
Road access to site — (1) None Yet (2) Sand or Dirt (3) Gravel (4) Paved	3	3	3	3	4	3	3	3	3	3	4	3	2	3	3	3	4	3	4	4	4	3
Transportation — (1) Car (2) Car, Bus (3) Air, Bus (4) Air, Bus, Rail	▨	▨	▨	▨	▨	▨	▨	▨	▨	▨	▨	▨	▨	▨	▨	▨	▨	▨	▨	▨	▨	▨
Recreational developments — (1) None (2) Light (3) Scattered (4) Heavy Concentration	3	3	▨	3	3	▨	3	3	3	3	3	3	2	▨	3	3	▨	3	3	2	3	3

(original) and secondary research utilized. Secondary research involves an analysis of readily available, published sources of information and is far less expensive than original research. Market surveys aimed at producing new information and conclusions specific to the subject project are classified as being original or primary research. Although prefeasibility studies can be based solely on secondary research, detailed economic feasibility studies must contain a mixture of both secondary and original research.

The market analysis usually commences with the collection and review of secondary sources of information since this provides a clearer focus upon the type and scope of original market research needed. With the growing attention being given to tourism on a worldwide basis, the amount of tourism-related research that has been carried out to date is enormous and it grows rapidly from year to year. An analysis of secondary sources in tourism can therefore be both time-consuming and exhausting, unless the researcher is familiar with the major tourism-related bibliographies and the institutions at which the major tourism library sources are located.

Once the review of secondary sources of information is completed, a plan of original research is drawn up and implemented. This generally involves carrying out a variety of surveys, and it requires that the researchers have a thorough understanding of marketing research techniques. Although it is not appropriate to provide an exhaustive description of these techniques in an introductory tourism text, a brief overview of the most commonly used methods can be given. These methods include the following:

1. Questionnaire method
   Personal interview
   Telephone
   Mail
2. Focus group or delphi methods

The questionnaire method in its various forms of communications is certainly the most frequently used technique in tourism project feasibility studies. Researchers direct their questions to potential users of the project and/or to the owners/managers of competitive or similar enterprises. In the latter case, the questions are normally aimed at gathering information on the facilities and services offered, and on the existing market volumes and characteristics through such competitive performance statistics as room occupancy rates, attendance figures, and so on. The common factor in all forms of the questionnaire is that they require verbal responses (written or oral) to questions (written or oral). The three major advantages of the questionnaire method are its versatility, its speed, and its cost. Questionnaires are said to be versatile because almost every

FIGURE 13.3 Recreation Facility Site Evaluation

SOURCE: *Project Investigation/Recreation Facility Site Evaluation* (Wisconsin Department of Local Affairs and Develoment: Bureau of Recreation, undated), pp. 4-8.

research problem can be addressed by using this method, including the respondent's knowledge, opinions, motivations, and intentions. The use of questionnaires is usually faster and cheaper than an observational method of research. An observational method is a process of observing and studying the behavior of people, objects, and occurrences rather than of questioning for the same information.

The questionnaire method also has recognized disadvantages. The first is that respondents may be unwilling to provide information. They may either refuse to be interviewed or may refuse to answer specific questions. Mail questionnaire surveys typically have low response rates with sometimes as many as 90 percent of the questionnaires not being returned. Skilled and experienced researchers can usually bring the response rate up to 50 percent. Personal and telephone questionnaire surveys generally have higher response rates. A second disadvantage of the questionnaire method is that a respondent may be willing to cooperate but at the same time may be unable to provide accurate answers to some of the questions. For example, the respondents may not have thought through their basic motivations for particular purchases or activities. A third limitation of the questionnaire method is that the respondent may intentionally supply incorrect or inaccurate information. Some respondents may give the types of answers that they think the researchers are looking for, or they may deliberately give misleading information. Others may answer in a particular way so as not to be embarrassed or to have their egos damaged. Respondents may also wrongly interpret the semantic meanings of particular questions and may give less-than-satisfactory answers because of this.

Broad-scale questionnaire surveys, although relatively inexpensive when compared to other market research techniques, can be very expensive to mount if they are carried out at the individual householder level. This is particularly true if the potential users reside in countries or regions far distant from the destination area. Unlike consumer product research, market research using broad-scale questionnaires may often encounter difficulties in determining the exact geographical origins of potential users of a tourism project and their relative proportions. Because there are these problems in defining the statistical universe, it is also extremely difficult to accurately state what the size and structure of a respective sample should be.

Due to these rather unique difficulties in carrying out market surveys of individual potential users of proposed tourism projects, it is a common practice to also survey persons active in the channels of distribution (such as travel agents, tour wholesalers, and tour operators) and other group/individual travel decision makers (such as convention-meeting planners, corporate travel departments, and club executives) or to utilize the focus group and/or delphi methods as a supplement to questionnaire surveys.

The focus-group method involves bringing together a small group of persons (normally five to twenty) in one place and causing these persons to focus upon the particular research subject. The research team supplies an experienced focus group leader. The objectives of these sessions are to get the group to reach a consensus on questions or statements posed by the leader. The focus group can be drawn from householders in general, or each participant may have some common affinity, such as being convention-meeting planners, travel agents, tour operators, tour wholesalers, or club executives. Because focus group participants tend to interact with one another and because there is a greater opportunity to explore individual preferences and attitudes, this method overcomes some of the principal drawbacks of the questionnaire approach. It is a common practice to prescreen focus-group participants prior to their being invited to the sessions.

The delphi method is another research technique that has broad application. It is most often associated with forecasting and futures exercises in tourism, but it can also be applied to an individual tourism project. It could also be called the "knowledgeable panel" method since it involves assembling a team of experts in a particular field and using this team as a sounding board on alternative approaches, ideas, or concepts. The delphi group need never physically meet, but individual participants are required to give their responses to a variety of written propositions prepared by the researchers, such as What probability do you attach to this resort succeeding at this location? (Provide a probability percentage between 0 percent and 100 percent.)

Another type of research that has been used for some tourism projects can be termed "analogy research." This does not involve any surveying of potential users; rather it is composed of detailed research into the performance of comparable (or analogous) businesses. By studying how comparable projects have fared, conclusions are drawn on the likely performance levels of the proposed project. Because there are a multitude of variables that contribute to a business's success, this particular research method must be utilized with great caution.

In economic feasibility studies and evaluations of noncommercial projects, it is often necessary to forecast demand for either the project itself or for the destination area in general, or for both. There are many forecasting techniques available to the researcher. These include:

1. Extrapolation

    Linear
    Exponential
    Cyclical

2. Covariation
3. Correlation
4. Summation
5. Tests

6. Calculating Methods

> Calculation by indices
> Calculation by sales potential
> Calculation by unit sales
> Calculation by elasticity coefficient
> Calculation by models

7. Guesstimate

> Individual
> Group
>> Committee
>> Delphi process

Forecasts are generally divided into time spans that are considered to be accurate. There is general agreement that there are four basic forecasting horizons—short-term (one day to two years), medium-term (between two and five years), long-term (between five and fifteen years), and futurism (over fifteen years). Figure 13.4 provides basic definitions of the forecasting methods listed earlier and indicates for which of the time spans they are considered to be most accurate. For example, the extrapolation method is thought only to be useful for short-term forecasts, while correlation techniques are considered to be good for short-, medium-, and long-term forecasting.

Returning again to the individual tourism project and the evaluation of its economic feasibility, the forecasting of potential market demand usually covers the medium-term to long-term forecasts, that is, the initial five to fifteen years of operation. This seems quite appropriate since the critical financial years of a purely commercial project are its first one to ten years. Most commercial tourism projects are expected to reach their full financial and operating potential within their first five years of operation and to pay back their investor's equity within ten years. Also, as will be seen later, the present value concept dictates that the earlier the financial returns are received from a project the greater will be their contribution to economic feasibility.

The actual forecasting of potential demand levels for an individual project can be approached in several different ways, including the following:

1. The Market Share or Market Penetration Approach

> Using information obtained from competitive facilities, historic demand growth rates, and anticipated future occurrences, or other forecasting techniques, total market demand is calculated and the subject project's share of total demand is estimated.

FIGURE 13.4 A Sample of Techniques Available for Preparing Tourism Forecasts

| Forecasting Method | Suggested Forecasting Horizon for Use | | | Potential Users of Methods* | | | Definition of Methods | Types | Caveats |
| | Short-term | Medium-term | Long-term | National Tourist Offices | | Commercial Tourist Enterprises | | | |
				National Tourism	International Tourism				
1. Extrapolation	✓	–	–	X	X	–	Process whereby a statistical series is extended by adding new terms to the known terms, following the same law as the series; or by graphically determining the ordinate point situated on the extension of the curve, proving its equation.	Linear (uniform series) Exponential (accelerating series) Cyclical Time series analysis	It should be used for short-term forecasts only and only when more accurate methods are not available.
2. Covariation	✓	✓	–	XX	XX	X	A relation between the variations in time of two or more magnitudes or statistical series, any increase or decrease in the one being accompanied by an increase or decrease in the other or others.	–	There are no "stock" models of covariation. Every destination should establish its own.
3. Correlation	✓	✓	✓	XXX	XXX	XX	Coefficients of correlations are calculated to measure the relationship between variables. There is a correlation between two factors when they are related in such a way that their values always vary in the same or contrary sense.	Simple correlation Multiple correlation Partial correlation Linear regression models	It should be used only where experience and reasoning suggest that there is some basis for correlation.

Continued

333

FIGURE 13.4 (*cont.*)

Forecasting Method	Suggested Forecasting Horizon for Use			Potential Users of Methods*			Definition of Methods	Types	Caveats
	Short-term	Medium-term	Long-term	National Tourist Offices		Commercial Tourist Enterprises			
				National Tourism	International Tourism				
4. Summation	✓	✓	–	XXX	XXX	XXX	Adding together and, where necessary, incorporating weighting factors into a number of separately established forecasts.	–	It is only as good as the individual forecasts upon which it is based.
5. Tests	–	✓	✓	XXX	XXX	XX	An experimental process in which the objective is to look for a section of the market that reacts in advance of the others.	–	It is a method that is not entirely mathematical and therefore is difficult to translate into figures.
6.1 Calculation by Indices	–	✓	–	X	X	X	An index can be defined as a unit of measurement defining a ratio between one tourist movement and others or between a tourist movement and the general situation.	–	It is a rather simple exercise since the relationships between variables are often very complex.

Method						Description	Related models	Disadvantages
6.2 Calculation by Sales Potential	✓	—	—	—	XXX	A method in which sales are calculated by multiplying the number of points of sale (such as hotels and travel agencies) by the average sales volume per point of sale.	—	It requires experienced judgment and specific research.
6.3 Calculation by Unit Sales	✓	—	—	—	XXX	A method in which sales are calculated by multiplying average expenditures per tourist.	—	It requires experienced judgment and specific research.
6.4 Calculation by Elasticity Coefficient	✓	✓	XXX	XX	X	A method in which travel volumes are related to elasticity coefficients that display the relationships of price levels to demand levels.	—	It is extremely difficult to find and develop reliable elasticity coefficients.
6.5 Calculation by Models	—	✓	X	—	—	A variety of mathematical and statistical models that attempt to simulate the relationships of various factors affecting travel.	Econometric models Gravitational models Computer systems simulation models	It does not eliminate the need for value judgments and is often very expensive to develop and use.
Economic and Planning Factors	✓	✓	XXX	XX	XX	Means using general economic forecasts and plans for places of visitor origin in preparing travel forecasts for the destination.	—	They are only as good as the individual forecasts on which they are based.

NOTE: * The number of X's shown indicates the author's opinion of the degree of desirability of applying the methods in various circumstances. (–) meant not to be used while XXX is a most desirable application.

SOURCE: Adapted from *Guidelines on Methodology Applicable for Making Annual and Medium-Term Forecasts (Relating to Tourism Development and Promotional Plans) for Members*, World Tourism Organization, p. 73.

2. The Calculation Methods

> As shown in Figure 13.4 these methods use known "rules-of-thumb" (industry averages) or consumer expenditure and behavior patterns to project potential demand.

3. The Survey and Potential Demand Quantification Approach

> Using the results from questionnaire and other survey methods, total potential demand is quantified by "grossing up" from the sample size taken.

4. The Alternate Scenario Approach

> Uses either or both of the above approaches and produces optimistic, realistic, and pessimistic scenarios of potential demand levels.

5. The Analogy Approach

> Assumes that the subject property will achieve certain demand levels based upon the known performances and penetration levels of similar facilities elsewhere.

As a general rule, it is advisable to use two or more of these approaches independently and then to cross-check and rationalize the results of each. Once a technically acceptable potential market demand forecast has been developed, an initial judgment can be made as to whether the market is of sufficient size with the appropriate characteristics to support the project. To make such a judgment at this stage requires considerable experience with the business type under consideration, and it has to be very clear that the potential demand levels will obviously not render the project viable, that is, if a hotel requires an annual occupancy percentage of 70 percent to be viable, and the potential demand will generate an occupancy of only 30 percent in the project's fifth year of operation. In many instances this judgment will not be as clear-cut, and the analysis will have to proceed further to determine if the demand levels justify the investment.

Economic Feasibility Analysis

The economic feasibility analysis determines whether the project is capable of producing a satisfactory financial return for its investors. Using the forecast demand levels and other pertinent market analysis data as a base, this step is composed of the following seven distinct steps:

1. Description of components, scale and sizes, and quality levels required to capture the potential market demand
2. Specification of unit prices and rates
3. Estimation of revenues (market demand levels × unit prices and rates)
4. Estimation of operating expenses and profits
5. Preparation of a capital budget

6. Estimation of capital expenses, net income, and cash flow
7. Calculation of rate of return on investment

The forecasts of potential market demand and the expressed desires and expectations of persons interviewed provide the key inputs in describing a detailed project concept. This project concept will describe the components, scale, sizes, and quality levels of facilities and services needed to satisfy the potential demand discovered. Again, based upon expressed market expectations, together with a review of competitive price levels and proposed market positioning, unit prices and rates are then prepared.

The next two steps are commonly referred to as the production of pro forma (or forecast) income statements that indicate the estimated revenues, operating expenses, and operating profits for the project. When estimating revenues, the total potential demand must be broken down into segments, and the applicable unit prices and rates must be multiplied against the resulting volumes in each segment. The operating expenses include those costs incurred directly in operating the project, such as the cost of food and other merchandise for resale, the cost of labor, the cost of marketing, the cost of energy, and the cost of repairs and maintenance. Publications containing industry average performance statistics can be helpful in estimating these operating costs. In North America such publications are readily available for hotels/motels, resorts, and alpine ski areas. Greater individual accuracy occurs when the forecaster is familiar with the type of business under consideration, and when detailed staffing schedules and other operating standards are developed for the project at this stage.

There are other ongoing expenses that the project will encounter, and these all relate to the capital investment in the development. To estimate the expenses requires that a capital budget be prepared first. A capital budget is a detailed, itemized forecast of the capital investment required by the project. For a tourism project, these items will normally include building construction costs; professional fees; infrastructure costs; recreational facility costs; furniture, fixtures, and equipment costs; interim financing costs; contingencies; and miscellaneous other costs. The most realistic capital budgets are usually produced by a multidisciplined team consisting of specialized tourism consultants, civil engineers, quantity surveyors, interior designers, architects, and landscape architects. The capital budget is prepared by first identifying all of the capital costs that will be encountered, and then pricing out each item. A contingency factor, normally between 10 and 20 percent, is added to the other items to cover unforeseen cost overruns or items overlooked. Once the capital budget has been completed, the capital-related expenses for the project can be calculated. These expenses include financing charges on long-term debt, depreciation, municipal taxes, and insurance premiums on fixed assets.

When these expenses have in turn been estimated, they are deducted from the forecast operating profit levels to give net income figures (after tax profit) and cash flow forecasts. The net income and cash flow projections generally cover the useful life of the project, which for most tourism enterprises, does not usually exceed fifteen to twenty years of operation.

As the final step in this process, one or more financial analysis techniques are used to measure the rate of return produced by these forecast net income and cash flow levels.

Most experts in the field favor the time-value yardsticks, especially the net-present-value and internal-rate-of-return techniques. These two methods are based on the present value concept that implies that money has a time value. Thus, a dollar received today is worth more than a dollar received a year from now, since the dollar received today can be reinvested to produce a higher overall return. It follows that under the present value methods the dollars received in profits in the earlier years are more valuable than those earned in later years. Both the net-present-value and internal-rate-of-return techniques use cash flow figures as a basis for their projections and discount the value of future cash flows at certain assumed rates of return.

Based upon the rates of return predicted through the use of one or more of these financial analysis techniques, a decision is made as to whether the project under consideration is economically feasible. If the rate is less than that which investors require, the project is normally considered not to be economically feasible, and vice-versa.

It should be realized that to date the positive impact of government financial incentives upon a project's economic feasibility has not been discussed. Later in this chapter the role of these incentives in tourism development is reviewed in detail. At this point, it should be realized that many projects that have not been economically feasible with private sector financing alone have been developed because of an injection of financial assistance from those in the public sector. By reducing the interest burden on projects or by reducing financing costs in some other way, these incentives have the effect of increasing the rates of return that the investors earn. In many instances, the increases are great enough to change an infeasible project into a feasible one. However, if a project has been found to be infeasible and if there is no possibility of receiving government financial assistance, it will probably be terminated at this point.

Cost/benefit Analysis

Commercially oriented projects that have been found to be economically feasible may or may not have to be further analyzed using cost/benefit analysis techniques. Cost/benefit analyses are also useful for evaluating noncommercial tourism projects that either generate no direct revenues or that have, at best, operating revenues equalling operating expenses. Cost/benefit analyses are generally carried out by or on behalf of government agencies. They help these agencies measure and weigh all of the costs and benefits of alternative projects. In so doing, the agencies are able to determine which project will produce the largest net benefit for their economies and for their society as a whole.

Economic feasibility analyses are just one aspect of cost/benefit analysis. There are several financial analyses or capital budgeting techniques available that will permit comparisons between alternative projects. In purely financial terms, the project that creates the highest rate of return for its investors is usually the best alternative for them. However, from a government agency's viewpoint, the size of the return on private investors' capital cannot be the sole criterion for support. A government agency has broad-scale economic, environmental, and social/cultural responsibilities that have to be considered prior to giving financial incentives or other support/approvals to a project. For example, a proposed casino may generate spectacular returns for the investors, but a government agency may feel that such a project will undermine the social well-being of its destination area. If a government agency makes financial incentives available for tourism development projects, it usually can only satisfy a small proportion of those who apply because of budgetary limitations. The agency must therefore have some means and criteria available to it to rank projects against each other and to support those that earn the highest rankings. Earlier in this chapter, the following criteria were suggested for government project screening purposes:

1. Economic contributions
2. Environmental impact
3. Social/cultural impact
4. Competitive impact
5. Tourism impact
6. Developer and operator capabilities
7. Compliance with policies, plans, and programs
8. Equity contributions
9. Feasibility

Some of the factors related to certain of the above criteria can be measured quantitatively; others cannot. For example, as should be clear from the material presented in Chapter Nine, the economic contributions of a project can be forecast in a numerical way; the social/cultural impacts, however, cannot be reduced to numbers.

A cost/benefit analysis, therefore, should attempt to weigh the quantifiable and unquantifiable costs and benefits of a tourism project against each other. Some subjectivity and judgment has to enter into this because there can be no single measurement or set of measurements of a project's overall worth to a destination area.

Assuming that the cost/benefit analysis results have proven positive, the project can progress to the next level of evaluation. Some project developers may wish to apply for government financial incentives, while others may go ahead without such assistance.

Role of Government Financial Incentives in Tourism Development

One of the major hurdles that all tourism projects face before they are realized is that of securing the financing needed for their development. Many tourism projects have been proven to be economically feasible but have not been developed because their promoters have been unable to attract the right amount or types of financing. The number of government agencies providing specific financial incentives for tourism projects has increased rapidly in recent years on a worldwide basis. In this respect, these agencies are playing their dual roles as "stimulators" and "entrepreneurs."

In Canada, for example, almost all of its provinces and territories have financial assistance programs specifically tailored for tourism development projects. The federal government has played an active role in this process by sharing the costs of some of these programs with individual provinces. For example, in October 1978, the federal government entered into a jointly sponsored, $50 million program with the province of British Columbia. The program, entitled the Canada-British Columbia Subsidiary Agreement on Travel Industry Development, provided $13 million for upgrading accommodation facilities, $15 million for tourism attraction projects and events, and $16 million for the development of alpine skiing and skiing-related facilities. The federal government contributed $25 million to the program, as did the province of British Columbia. In December 1978, the government of Canada signed a similar agreement with the province of Manitoba. The Canada-Manitoba Subsidiary Agreement received a federal contribution of $12 million with the province of Manitoba providing the balance of the funds equalling $8 million. A high proportion of the funds within the Manitoba program were earmarked as incentives to stimulate the development of individual tourism projects.

Government financial incentives for tourism projects can be classified into two broad categories. Fiscal incentives are special allowances for income tax or other tax purposes. Direct and indirect incentives constitute the second main category, and include a wide variety of programs aimed at easing the financing requirements of projects. The basic objective of most of these incentive programs is to help businesses carry out tourism development projects that, without assistance, may have been completely abandoned or seriously delayed. On a global basis, all levels of governments get involved in providing these types of incentive programs. The following is a list of some of the types of financial incentive programs provided by government agencies to tourism projects:

DIRECT AND INDIRECT INCENTIVES

Nonrefundable grants—reduce a project's capital budget

Low-interest loans—reduce the amount of interest that the project must pay during its operating life

Interest rebates—the government agency rebates a portion of the project's interest costs during its operating life

Forgiveable loans—the government agency loans funds to the project and then "forgives" all or part of these over an agreed-upon time period; this acts like a phased nonrefundable grant

Loan guarantees—the government agency guarantees a loan or loans given to a project by a private financial institution

Working capital loans—the government agency loans funds to meet the working capital needs of a project

Equity participation—the government agency purchases some of the available shares in the project, and it therefore becomes an equity investor

Training grants—the government agency provides a nonrefundable grant to the project for staff training purposes

Infrastructure assistance—the government agency assumes the costs of some or all of the infrastructure required for the project

Leasebacks—the government agency purchases land, buildings, or equipment and then leases them to the project

Land donations—the government agency donates land free of charge to the project

FISCAL INCENTIVES

Tax holidays or deferrals—the government agency defers the payment of income taxes or other taxes for a predetermined time period

Remission of tariffs—the government agency relaxes or removes import duties on goods and services required by the project

Tax reductions—the government agency lowers the normal tax rates that would be paid by the project

Because most government departments providing these financial incentives generally receive more applications for assistance than their budgets can handle, it is inevitable that not all projects that request monetary help receive it. In certain cases, this results in these projects not proceeding any further.

Private Sector Financing for Tourism Development

Although governments continue to play a greater role in providing financing to tourism projects, it is the private sector that generally supplies the majority of the financing. These private sources range from individual citizens to major institutional lenders such as banks, trust companies, credit unions, insurance companies, and other commercial finance companies. Typically, a private financing source requires that the following five points be satisfied before lending money to a tourism project:

1. Previous management experience in tourism and an established credit record within the management development team
2. Proof of economic feasibility via an independent economic feasibility study
3. Adequate collateral or security for the funds to be borrowed
4. Adequate equity capital to be invested by the owners of the project
5. Proof of stability in the tourism industry in which the project will function

Tourism projects require equity as well as borrowed capital from owners and investors. These individuals are the true "risk takers" in the development, and they are rewarded with profits from a return on their investments.

Not all projects are able to secure the types and amounts of private financing that they require, although they may have successfully survived all of the earlier screening mechanisms.

Detailed Design and Construction

In the final stages of realizing a tourism development project, various levels of architectural designs and drawings are prepared. Normally this procedure includes the following:

1. Preparation of preliminary architectural concepts
2. Preparation of preliminary architectural design
3. Preparation of final architectural design
4. Construction

At each of the first three stages, the drawings become increasingly more detailed and exact. When the final drawings have been approved, the project moves into construction.

Summary

The tourism development strategy or plan for a destination area provides overall guidelines for development, outlines broad development concepts, and identifies individual development opportunities thought to be worthy of more in-depth analysis through economic feasibility studies and/or cost/benefit analyses. Obviously the public sector has a key role to play in ensuring that developers abide by the overall guidelines and that broad development concepts are realized. The public sector is also playing an ever-increasing role in stimulating the development of individual project opportunities through many types of financial incentive schemes.

Probably only a small proportion of tourism project ideas actually reach the construction stage, as most are unable to meet certain criteria or to secure the necessary financing. Many are screened out by tourism project evaluation and analysis systems similar to the one described in this chapter.

REFERENCES

BALMER, CRAPO & ASSOCIATES, INC., *Tourism Development and Marketing Strategies for the Northwest Territories* (Calgary, Alberta, Northwest Territories Department of Economic Development and Tourism, 1979), p. 30.

BAR-ON, RAPHAEL RAYMOND V., "Forecasting Tourism—Theory and Practice," in a *Decade for Achievement* (The Tenth Annual Conference Proceedings of the Travel Research Association, Salt Lake City, Utah, 1979), p. 27.

BERGERON, PIERRE G., *Capital Expenditure Planning for Growth and Profit* (The Canadian Institute of Chartered Accountants, Toronto, Ontario, 1977), p. 60.

BOYD, HARPER W., AND RALPH WESTFALL, *Marketing Research: Text and Cases* (Homewood, IL, Richard D. Irwin, Inc., 1972), pp. 131–36.

CCH CANADA LIMITED, *Industrial Assistance Programs in Canada, 1979* (Don Mills, Ontario, 1979), p. 1.

GUNN, CLARE A., *Tourism Planning* (New York, Crane Russak, 1979), p. 318.

MORRISON, ALASTAIR M., *The Planning and Development of Tourism in a Large Rural Area: Regional Tourism Planning in Auvergne-Limousin* (East Lansing, MI, 1973), pp. 35, 76.

NAIR A., *The Role of the State in the Field of Tourism* (Madrid, Spain, World Tourism Organization/CIEST, 1970), p. 20.

ONTARIO MINISTRY OF TOURISM AND RECREATION, *Framework for Opportunity: A Guide for Tourism Development in Ontario/Canada* (Toronto, Ontario, undated), p. 10.

ORGANIZATION FOR ECONOMIC CO-OPERATION AND DEVELOPMENT, *Tourism Development and Economic Growth* (Paris, France, 1966), p. 23.

SCHUMACHER, E. F., *Small is Beautiful: A Study of Economics As If People Mattered* (New York, Harper & Row, 1973), p. 38.

UNITED NATIONS, *Manual for the Preparation of Industrial Feasibility Studies* (New York, 1978), p. 11.

WORLD TOURISM ORGANIZATION, *Guidelines on the Methodology Applicable for Making Annual and Medium-Term Forecasts (Relating to Tourism Development and Promotional Plans) For Members* (Madrid, Spain, undated), pp. 57–72).

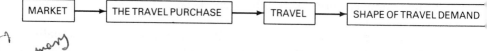

| MARKET | → | THE TRAVEL PURCHASE | → | TRAVEL | → | SHAPE OF TRAVEL DEMAND |

Summary

In order to reach the marketplace in an attempt to induce the traveler to move from origin to destination area, those at the destination area engage in a variety of marketing activities.

If one takes into account overall development objectives discussed in the previous section, a market plan can be produced (Chapter Fourteen). The marketing mix of product, price (Chapter Fourteen), promotion (Chapter Fifteen), and place or distribution (Chapter Sixteen) is put together in such a way that potential travelers in the market will be induced to travel.

The specifics of putting the promotional plan into effect are considered in detail. In order to reach the marketplace, many intermediaries are used by those at the destination area. The roles and activities of those who interact with both the destination area and the marketplace are examined.

This last part of *The Tourism System*, if it is successful, will result in you being able to induce potential travelers in a market to make a travel purchase; they will travel to the destination that, it is hoped, will have developed attractions and facilities in such a way as to satisfy the travelers while resulting in maximum gain to the destination.

READINGS

This paper is based upon a speech given by S. Gordon Phillips at a symposium at Michigan State University in September 1981. The original paper was published as part of the proceedings (*Michigan Tourism: How Can Research Help?*) by Michigan State University's Agricultural Experiment Station in 1982.

The paper was revised by S. Gordon Phillips and Robert L. Brock for inclusion in this text. The authors express their gratitude to S. Gordon Phillips, Robert L. Brock, and the Ministry of Tourism and Recreation for their assistance in this regard.

Organizing a Tourism System:
The Ontario Example

S. Gordon Phillips, Vice-President
The Economic Planning Group of Canada
Toronto, Ontario
Canada

Introduction

The province of Ontario provides an interesting model of a research-based tourism development and marketing effort supported by government. In fact, Ontario's programs are generally considered to be among the most innovative and aggressive in North America.

The tourism system elements of most interest in the context of this paper are those relating to research, and to programs designed to enhance the pace and quality of industry development. For the most part, these activities are centered in the government in Ontario, so the major focus of this paper will be on government programs and initiatives.

Before we get into the details of Ontario's tourism programs, the province's tourism industry has to be put into perspective.

Tourism in Ontario

In 1981, tourism in Ontario accounted for $8.76 billion, or approximately 7 percent of the province's gross provincial product. It is the second largest industry in Ontario, second only to automobile manufacturing. Some 541,000 man years of employment are involved in the industry annually.

The best market for the industry is the province's own citizens, who account for 70 percent of the tourism expenditure in the province. The United States market accounts for 14 percent. Other provinces, primarily Manitoba and Quebec, account for 10 percent, while the overseas market accounts for 6 percent. The overseas market is the most rapidly growing source of visitors, while the U.S. market has declined in importance since 1973 as a result of the energy situation. With the low value of the Canadian dollar relative to European currencies, Canada has become a bargain for Europeans. Ontario dominates the Canadian tourism scene, accounting for almost one-half of all tourism expenditures in Canada.

Challenges and Opportunities

Ontario's tourism industry faces a number of challenges and opportunities. Among the challenges is the energy price and supply situation. As energy prices climb, fewer dollars are available for tourism, and the pattern of tourism activity will shift away from long-haul travel toward stay-at-home and single destination holidays. Ontario's tourism plant is not very well equipped to respond to this shift in travel patterns. Changing travel preferences, life-styles, and demographics are reducing the demand for some traditional activities and expanding the demand for a variety of others.

Increasing competition is being felt from other destination areas within Canada and elsewhere.

Recognizing these and other trends, the government of Ontario has devised a four-pronged development strategy for the province. Its elements include:

1. Development of high caliber, year-round destination resorts in the province.
2. Development of a full range of attractions and events catering to the new price and income constraints, as well as the new preferences of travelers.
3. Accessibility to the tourism product must be improved, including improvements in promotion, information services, reservations, and travel modes.
4. The product must be packaged and sold in a sophisticated and aggressive manner.

We will now examine in some greater details the key activities and programs in Ontario that have been designed to pursue this strategy. We will do so in three categories:

1. Planning and development
2. Industry organization and improvement
3. Marketing

The provincial Ministry of Tourism and Recreation is Ontario's primary agency for tourism, although other ministries and the federal government have roles to play as well. We will be looking at the various roles very briefly.

I. PLANNING AND DEVELOPMENT

Role of the Tourism Development Branch

The Tourism Development Branch of the Ministry of Tourism and Recreation is the key agency for tourism planning and development in the province. The activities of the branch include:

1. Planning—The primary activities here are the "Framework for Opportunity" study and a variety of tourism zone studies which will be considered below. The branch has also been active in negotiating various federal/provincial development agreements which provide for a variety of planning activities.
2. Financial assistance—The branch advises on private sector applications for government grants and subsidized loans.
3. Studies assistance—Cost sharing is provided to assist investors and municipalities to prepare feasibility studies on various projects.
4. Grading—The branch was active in assisting in the development of a grading system for tourism establishments, which will be discussed later in this paper.
5. Tourism/parks—This relates to an advisory role to other branch and ministries regarding tourism development.
6. Consulting—The branch advises developers and others, and receives about ninety inquiries each month.
7. Advocacy—They assist developers and others in obtaining approvals from other government departments.

Framework for Opportunity

The province's first major initiative in long-term development planning came with the "Framework for Opportunity" study in 1977. This project represented an effort to advance a comprehensive development strategy for the province, so that future development efforts could be co-ordinated and directed to the right geographic areas and the right priorities. The study consisted of:

1. An inventory of resources affecting present and future tourism opportunities
2. A detailed demand analysis, focused on origins and destinations of visitors, as well as their activities and spending patterns
3. A review of tourism development guidelines and the roles of various agencies and departments in tourism development
4. The identification of seventeen tourism development zones, with suggested themes, activities, and development opportunities for each zone

The seventeen tourism development zones each contained a sufficient concentration of attractions, services, and transportation modes to create a separate identity for itself, and each had potential for further tourism development.

The seventeen zones presently account for 75 to 80 percent of total tourism spending in the province.

The second focus of the study was on "touring corridors." These are areas that link the tourism development zones with each other and with the main entry points and transportation routes. They are defined as scenic, convenient, and efficient routes, and include rail, air, waterway, and road transport modes.

All the other parts of the province are defined as "tourism hinterland." Development in these areas should be directed toward services for "off-the-beaten track" tourists and commercial travelers, and toward services for specialized activities, such as fly-in fishing.

The study was accepted as the policy and direction for tourism development in the province. Since 1977, five tourism development zones have been studied in detail. Each of these zone studies contains a detailed definition of opportunities and a strategy for development.

Preliminary feasibility analyses were made of prime development proposals. The government has since been giving precedence to supporting entrepreneurs who are prepared to develop projects in line with the zone study recommendations. Money is being made available for specific project feasibility studies.

In 1982–83, the Ministry of Tourism and Recreation introduced a new tourism planning program known as the "Municipal Tourism Development Planning Program." This program was a logical extension to the "Framework for Opportunity" zone studies, being aimed at encouraging the orderly growth of tourism in areas of high development potential. The products resulting from the new program are as follows:

1. An inventory of tourism attractions, resources, and facilities within the study area

2. An analysis of available information on the study area's existing visitor markets including the origins of visitors, seasonal visitation patterns, travel purpose, recent trends in visitation, expenditure patterns, and satisfaction levels

3. An analysis of the economic and other impacts associated with tourism within the study area

4. An analysis of the problems, opportunities, strengths, and weaknesses of the tourist industry in the study area

5. A review of future visitor markets including an examination of the overall trends affecting vacation travel in the area

6. Identification of goals for tourism in the study area and the translation of these goals into specific objectives

7. An overall strategy and action plan for tourism in the study area. This plan would include the following:

   a. Identification of new development or upgrading opportunities for the tourism plant, including attractions and events, with such matters or-

dered as to priority, scale, and type. The development opportunities identified in the report by the consultant should include a preliminary estimation of:
   market potential
   development costs
Potential developers/operators/investors should be identified where possible, and the method of approaching same recommended.
   b. A marketing plan for the study area, including definition of target markets and the proposed means of penetrating them
   c. A program to increase the awareness of tourism and its benefits in the area
   d. An organization plan defining the roles and responsibilities of existing and proposed tourism organizations in the area
   e. An implementation plan for the program/projects recommended

During 1982, the first three planning studies were initiated under the "Municipal Tourism Development Planning Program." Ontario's provincial tourism development strategy was a "first of its kind" in Canada, and several other provinces have since followed suit. These subsequent projects have been funded, in part, by the federal government. The Ontario studies and those of the other provinces have all been prepared by private tourism consulting firms working in teams.

Federal/Provincial Development Agreements

One of the key factors contributing to the recent attention to development planning in Canada is the establishment by the federal government of a large grant program through the Department of Regional Industrial Expansion (DRIE). Hundreds of millions of dollars have been made available to the provinces to assist in provincial strategy planning, project feasibility studies, infrastructure development, and for projects themselves. Each province has a separate agreement with the federal government, in keeping with its own defined objectives.

In Ontario, two regional development agreements are now in place, covering the northern and eastern areas of the province, and a third province-wide agreement is presently being negotiated. The Northern Ontario agreement provides $3 million for upgrading and improvement and for planning and development. The Eastern Ontario agreement provides $4 million for feasibility studies, infrastructure services, historic restoration, and for events.

The province-wide agreement is expected to amount to $60 to $100 million and the proposed areas for assistance include:

1. Product development

   destination resorts
   travel generators (attractions)

2. Visitor services

3. Information base and systems
    regional information centers
    reservation centers
4. Marketing
5. Administration and publicity
6. Evaluation of results of the program

The province has already designated a number of major projects that are to receive grants under the program.

Ontario Development Corporations

The province of Ontario has three development corporations, one for each of the northern, eastern, and southern zones of the province. These are crown (government-owned) corporations that provide financing on preferred terms to tourism businesses, as well as other industries in the province. For the tourism industry, term loans and guarantees are made available to tourist accommodation facilities, commercial attractions, marinas, tourist restaurants, and to commercial amusement and recreation services.

Term loans are for amounts of up to $500,000 and at a rate of 10 ½ percent (March 1983). The money must be used for new development, expansion, or for upgrading. A subsidized loan guarantee program called the Tourism Redevelopment Incentive Program (TRIP) is also available, in which the Ontario Development Corporations provide a guarantee for 90 percent of the principal amount of the loan and an interest subsidy of up to 5 percentage points. A third program, called the Ontario Business Incentives Program, provides reduced rate or no-interest loans to attractions benefitting local resort operators. Interest and principal repayment deferrals can be given under this program. Finally, the government introduced another reduced interest financing plan to assist tourist operators with upgrading their premises in line with recommendations made by Tourism Ontario grading inspectors.

Board of Industrial Leadership and Development (BILD)

In January 1981, the Ontario government announced a new program of direct grants for industrial development, including tourism development. The program is called BILD (Board of Industrial Leadership and Development). It provides large grants for selected, key projects that are expected to provide major stimulus to selected areas of the province. In tourism, the objective is to expand commercial, cultural, and infrastructure facilities.

The province has, to date, designated the following projects to receive grants under the program:

1. Convention centers in Toronto, Ottawa, and Hamilton
2. The grading program
3. An expanded marketing program
4. Resort and theme park development

> King Mountain
> Timbertown
> Infrastructure in Collingwood—a prime ski area
> Central Canada Exhibition in Ottawa (study)
> Canadian National exhibition in Toronto (study)

5. An electronic reservations system
6. A waterfront development program, including new marinas at Orillia, Peterborough, Sarnia and marina expansions at Midland and Erieau.

Other Development Programs of Government

Several government departments other than the Ministry of Tourism and Recreation are involved directly or indirectly in tourism development in Ontario.

The Ministry of Natural Resources administers the 133 provincial parks in Ontario, as well as various fish and wildlife management programs. The ministry is currently initiating a series of studies into the feasibility of developing resorts and other commercial tourism facilities in selected parks in the province. The Ministry of Northern Affairs coordinates government programs and services in the northern area of the province. Funds have been made available on a shared basis for various studies and tourism projects in the north. The Ministry of Citizenship and Culture provides funds and assistance for heritage restoration projects, community centers, and museums. The Ministry of Revenue administers the Small Business Development Corporations' program, which provides tax grants toward equity investment in tourism accommodation facilities.

The provincial government has, on occasion, directly sponsored projects in the tourism industry. Ontario Place in Toronto is one example. This is a major themed recreation area in downtown Toronto. Another example is the "Timbertown" theme park proposed for a site northwest of Ottawa. The federal government operates various programs in addition to the grants provided through the Department of Regional Industrial Expansion. They provide major grants to cities in support of the development of new convention centers.

II. INDUSTRY ORGANIZATION AND IMPROVEMENT

The Ministry of Tourism and Recreation has an Operations Branch which administers seventeen field offices throughout Ontario. The tourism consultants employed in these offices provide counseling services to tourist operators, municipalities, and tourism associations. Their activities and services include:

1. Consulting assistance to tourism operators on operations, management, marketing, expansion, and financing
2. Information and assistance to potential developers of tourism facilities
3. Tourism loan and grant approvals for the Ontario Development Corporations and the federal/provincial DRIE grant programs
4. Policy input to government departments and regulatory agencies on the local impact of programs and regulations
5. Advice to municipalities on by-laws and local regulations affecting tourism
6. Direct assistance to tourism industry associations (grants, programs, speakers, seminars, etc.)
7. Operation of seminars and training programs, such as the "We Treat You Royally" seminars for tourist operators. These seminars are designed to improve the quality of hospitality and attitudes of industry employees toward tourists.
8. Administration of the tourism act, involving the physical inspection and licensing of tourist organizations

The ministry was responsible in large part for the formation of Tourism Ontario, an association of most of the other tourism-related associations in the province. Tourism Ontario presents a single, united voice to government on tourism issues. The members of Tourism Ontario include:

1. Ontario Hotel and Motel Association
2. Ontario Motel Association
3. Northern Ontario Tourist Outfitters Association
4. Resorts Ontario
5. Ontario Ski Resorts Association
6. Ontario Restaurant Association
7. Ontario Marine Operators Association
8. Ontario Private Campground Operators Association . . . and others.

Tourism Ontario has been generally successful in getting a better "deal" for the industry, and for drawing the government's attention to industry problems and concerns.

Tourism Ontario administers the accommodation grading program which was developed with the support of the government. In 1982, 672 accommodation establishments were inspected by Tourism Ontario, and 602 were awarded grades. The Ministry of Tourism and Recreation's annual accommodation directory shows all the province's establishments but highlights those which are graded by Tourism Ontario. The government and the industry have high hopes for the success of the relatively new grading program in facilitating and improving the buying decisions of tourists.

As mentioned earlier, the government has introduced a subsidized loan program for operators who wish to upgrade their premises in line with the recommendations of the grading inspectors.

The Ministry of Tourism and Recreation was largely responsible for the "Ontario Travel Association Program," the formation of twelve regional associations of tourist operators. Funds are provided by the ministry for administration and area promotion activities of each of these regional associations.

III. MARKETING

Finally, we turn to the activities of the government in supporting the marketing of tourist facilities in the province. The Ministry of Tourism and Recreation's marketing program is the most sophisticated in Canada, and perhaps in North America. A major consumer research program is maintained in support of these marketing programs. The prime target markets of the program, in order of priority, are:

1. Ontario
2. United States
3. Overseas
4. Manitoba and Quebec

The elements of the marketing mix employed by the Ministry include:

1. *Advertising.* Print, radio, TV, and magazine media are all used in varying combinations in the key markets of Ontario, the United States, Quebec, Manitoba, and overseas. The "Yours to Discover" promotion has achieved a high awareness level among target audiences, and has resulted in a marked increase in customer inquiries.
2. *Publicity and Promotion.* Numerous tourism publications designed to meet the information needs of the traveling public are produced by the ministry and distributed widely both within and without the province. They include the Travelers Encyclopedia, Accommodation Guide, Events, Ontario Official Road Map, etc. A variety of merchandising materials is also produced. Other promotional activities include familiarization tours for media, editorial support programs, films, PR services, and participation in sports and travel shows.
3. *Customer Sales and Service.* The government operates forty-one travel information centers in the province, to provide travel counseling services on request.
4. *Travel Trade and Convention Services.* The ministry maintains travel trade offices in New York, Los Angeles, Chicago, and Toronto as well as overseas offices in London, Frankfurt, Paris, and Tokyo. These offices endeavor to

convince key elements of the travel trade that Ontario represents a salable travel experience.

5. *Research.* In support of its varied marketing programs, research is conducted in each of the following areas:

> Activities of competing provinces and states
> Evaluation of "state of trade" conditions
> Inventory of Ontario's travel product
> Potential for increased travel from existing and new markets
> Changing market conditions
> Trends in demographics and purchasing behavior

The ministry is developing a computerized data base for its product inventory.

Conclusion

In conclusion, the government plays a very active and key role in Ontario's "Tourism System." Many of the province's development and marketing initiatives are unique and represent "state of the art" technology in these fields. Canada has a well-established tradition of very active government involvement in the economy and, in spite of recent trends in the United States, this major role of government in the Canadian tourism scene is unlikely to diminish. In fact, it is more likely to grow.

14

TOURISM
MARKETING

This chapter is concerned with the marketing of the tourism product. The factors that make tourism marketing different from marketing of other goods and services are pointed out, and a definition of tourism marketing is developed. The definition stresses the need for a marketing orientation, market segmentation, and the concept of the product life cycle.

A model for market planning is suggested. The model takes forces external to the destination, overall development objectives, and the analysis of market, product, and competitor into account in producing marketing objectives. Target markets are selected, and an appropriate marketing mix for each target market is determined. Two parts of the marketing mix — product and price — are examined.

THE TOURISM SYSTEM

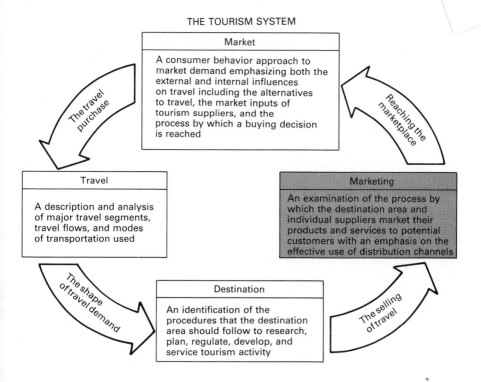

TOURISM MARKETING

Marketing Uniqueness

The problems of marketing in tourism are somewhat different from the problems of traditional product marketing. The differences are the result of the characteristics of tourism supply and demand. Tourism, first of all, is a service. An intangible experience is being sold, not a physical good that can be inspected prior to purchase. Because it is a service, production and consumption take place at the same time. In manufacturing, goods are produced, stored, and sold. The inventory process serves as a way of linking these stages of production and consumption. Tourism supply cannot be stored. Unlike a can of food which, if it is not sold one day can be sold the next, airline seats, hotel rooms, or restaurant seats not sold today lose that particular sale forever. Although the inventory cannot be stored and adjusted to changes in demand, the capacity to produce these tourism services must be developed ahead of time. This puts a great deal of pressure on producers to effectively plan the proper amounts of facilities and, having developed those facilities, to keep them as fully used as possible. This in itself creates another kind of problem, for tourism supply is relatively fixed. The resources and infrastructure of a destination cannot change as quickly as can tourist demand.

A second important factor that makes tourism different from other industries is that the service provided—a vacation—is in fact an amalgam of several products and services. A vacation has a transportation component, a lodging component, a food and beverage component, an attractions component, an activities component, and so on. These components are usually offered by different firms, and they may be marketed directly to the tourist or combined into a package in which they are offered as one vacation but the services are supplied by different firms. This lack of control over the entire vacation means that a great deal of interdependence results. A satisfied tourist results from many independent businesses, each providing a satisfying part of the total vacation. The marketing efforts of each of the parts are thus affected by the efforts of the others providing a part of the vacation. The satisfaction provided is also a function of the human element providing the service. This also is very difficult to control in terms of the consistent quality of service provided.

A third factor that makes tourism different from other industries concerns the role of travel intermediaries. Because most tourist services are located at distances far from their potential customers, specialized intermediaries—organizations that operate between the producer and the tourist—are often necessary to bridge the gap. Also, the fact that many tourism producers are relatively small means that they cannot afford to set up their own retail outlets. Thus, while in most industries, the producer exerts much control over every stage in the development and delivery of the product, in tourism the travel intermediaries can influence if not determine which services should be offered, to whom, when, and at what price.

The last factor that makes tourism different from other industries relates to demand. Tourism demand is highly elastic, seasonal in nature, and subject to subjective factors such as taste and fashion as well as the more objective factors of demand such as price. In many cases, the "product" sought can be satisfied by any number of destinations, with particular emphasis on no one in particular.

DEFINITION

"Marketing is a management philosophy which, in light of tourist demand, makes it possible through research, forecasting and selection to place tourism products on the market most in line with the organization's purpose for the greatest benefit."[1] This definition suggests several things.

---

[1]"Testing the Effectiveness of Promotional Campaigns in International Travel Marketing," World Tourism Organization Seminar, Ottawa, 1975, p. 3.

First, it indicates that marketing is a way of thinking about a situation that balances the needs of the tourist (as indicated through tourist demand) with the needs of the organization or destination. This can be explained by an examination of the development of an appropriate orientation. Second, the definition stresses tourist research that culminates in the selection of tourist demand. The concept of market segmentation is useful here. Third, the concepts of the product life cycle and positioning are useful to underscore the proper placement of tourism products on the market and to suggest the appropriate marketing policy and strategies resulting from that decision.

Orientation

Before embarking on a program to market tourism in general or a specific tourism product or service in particular, it is necessary to develop a philosophy or orientation that will guide one's marketing efforts. Such a philosophy will set the tone for every subsequent decision made as part of the overall marketing effort. Although several different orientations are possible, experience has shown that they are not all equally effective.

Some destination areas have marketing efforts that are guided by a product orientation. A product orientation suggests that the emphasis be placed upon the products or services available. A destination area has many physical, historical, and cultural resources, for example. The extent to which "our" resources are better than those of the competition will determine how many tourists visit our destination. This orientation has been used by the local authorities of a town on the south coast of England who decided in the late 1960s to print brochures only in English. When it was pointed out that a major potential market was the French residents across the English Channel, the reply was given that if the French wanted to visit, then they would be interested enough to learn to read English in order to understand what was available. Although it cannot be denied that the quality of resources is important, a total emphasis on tourism supply fails to take the wishes of the potential tourist into account. A product orientation may, in fact, be successful if there is a surplus of demand over supply. In this case, the destination or company that offers the best product will get the tourist. The old adage that reflected this said "build a better mousetrap, and the world will beat a path to your door."

When there is more supply than demand, however, the problems becomes "How can I sell all these mousetraps?" The number of destinations actively seeking tourism has increased as has the number of places throughout the world with easy accessibility. The entry into the marketplace of more professional tour packagers has increased competition for the tourist dollar and has meant that destination areas can no longer sit back and wait for tourists to come to them. It has become increasingly necessary to sell tourists on the benefits of visiting a particular destination or of purchasing a particular product or service. The orientation for many has moved from one of emphasizing product to one of emphasizing selling. The accent has been placed on promotion of what is available for sale. Yet, this selling orientation focusses on the needs of the seller—to sell the product—rather than the needs of the buyer—What will satisfy me? The attempt here is to convince the potential tourist that what is available will please.

A further development in orientation is one in which the needs and wants of the tourist are placed foremost in the mind of the marketer. This is a marketing orientation philosophy that begins with the needs and wants of the tourist and seeks to provide a product or service that will satisfy those needs and wants. It involves being open when the tourist wants us to be; serving breakfast when the tourist wants it rather than when it is convenient for management; providing the kind of experiences that tourists want rather than what we feel they "should" want. It is realizing that, from the example used above, an individual does not want to buy a mousetrap; rather she wants to kill mice. If and when a better way is developed *of satisfying a need,* people will use it. This philosophy is evident at the beginning of this book when an emphasis was placed on the satisfaction of needs and wants.

The uniqueness of tourism suggests that a philosophy that concentrates solely on the needs of the market is not the best orientation, even for the market itself. Tourism supply is oriented toward the resources of a community. To become totally marketing oriented, all aspects of the community would have to be oriented toward satisfying the needs and wants of the tourist. The risk for the community as well as for the tourist ultimately is that by orienting strictly and totally for the tourist's needs, the needs and integrity of the community may be abused. Consider the situations explored in earlier chapters of tourist destination areas that have adapted to the needs of the tourist and have, in the process, lost their uniqueness, their heritage, and their natural resources while getting a relatively poor economic return on their investment. Destination areas that have attempted to adapt their resources to satisfy tourist needs may have lost the very thing that has made them attractive and unique in the first place. The tourist is the ultimate loser, as more and more destinations take on an increasingly similar and familiar appearance.

A solution to the problem is to develop a marketing approach that focusses on the satisfaction of tourist needs and wants while respecting the long-term interests of the community. This orientation is often referred to as a societal marketing approach. Such a philosophy will provide for planning, development, and marketing activities that will focus on the needs of the tourist, but it will also enable one to equally consider the effects of such action on the long-term interests of the community before the action is taken.

All marketing activities will be guided by the philosophy of those responsible for the marketing campaign. It is essential that any marketing effort have an agreed-upon philosophy to guide the further development and marketing efforts of any property, company, or destination.

Segmentation

The second aspect of our definition of marketing refers to selection of tourism demand. Market segmentation is a recognized and universally accepted way of analyzing demand. Market segmentation refers to the process by which people with similar needs and wants are grouped together for the purpose of better focussing on and serving the market.

Segmentation is based on four assumptions. First, the market for a product or service, for example a vacation, is made up of particular segments the members of which have distinctive needs and preferences relative to the product or service being marketed. Second, these potential tourists can be grouped into segments the members of which each have similar and identifiable characteristics. Third, a single product offering, such as a Caribbean cruise, will appeal to some segments of the market more than others. Fourth, firms and organizations can improve their overall marketing effort by developing specific product offerings to reach specific segments of the market. A cruise package will be suitable for one part of the market, but an historical tour may be more suitable for another.

The process of segmenting a market can lead to many strategic management decisions. Market segmentation can be more than a statistical technique used to analyze demand. It can be utilized as a management tool that leads to specific marketing decisions. The development of such a strategy begins with the identification of profiles of segments of the market. At one extreme, a firm or destination may maximize its marketing orientation by developing a unique product offering for every potential tourist. Limitations of time and money prevent this. At the other extreme, the firm or destination may save time and money by offering one basic option to everyone. Although that one option will undoubtedly appeal to some potential tourists, it will not to others. The compromise is to assemble potential tourists into segments, each segment having similar preference characteristics, and produce offerings geared to the needs of these segments.

To determine the compromise point between developing a product for everyone and offering one product for all, it is necessary to examine the criteria a segment must meet to determine its viability. A segment must be:

1. *Measurable.* Can we determine how many potential tourists are in this segment?
2. *Accessible.* Can these tourists be reached through promotion and through existing or potential methods of distribution? How easy will this be?
3. *Substantial.* Are there sufficient numbers of tourists in this segment to support a marketing effort aimed specifically at them?
4. *Defensible.* Are the tourist characteristics unique enough to justify a separate program targeted at them? Is such a program immune to the mass marketing approach of competitors?
5. *Durable.* As the market develops, will this segment maintain its differences, or will these differences disappear?
6. *Competitive.* Do we have a relative advantage over the competition in our attempts to serve this market segment?

Many criteria have been developed by which a market segment can be constructed. Four general categories have been developed: (1) socioeconomic, (2) product-related, (3) psychographic, and (4) geographic. (See Table 14.1.)

SOCIOECONOMIC OR DEMOGRAPHIC SEGMENTATION. Early segmentation studies used socioeconomic criteria as the basis for forming market segments. These criteria remain the most commonly used today. This is probably due to the relative ease of collecting data, the comparability of such information through census as well as media data, and the fact that such data is easy to understand and apply. Age and income have, in fact, been very successful predictors of recreation participation. However, the use of only socioeconomic criteria to segment markets has come under attack. It has been argued that the rapidly changing nature of society makes it impossible to rely solely on demographic data as a means of plotting marketing strategy. Just because a segment of people are within a particular age or income group does not necessarily mean they will have similar vacation preferences. Also, socioeconomic information does not give the marketer sufficient information about likes and dislikes to properly position the product in the marketplace. Positioning refers to the decision to serve a particular segment of the market with a product offering that is specifically aimed at satisfying its needs and wants.

Greater success has been found in using demographic criteria that are multivariate. Status, for example, includes dimensions of income, education, and occupation, and family life cycle is a composite of marital status, age, and the numbers and ages of children at home. Life-cycle segmentation has proven to be an effective way of segmenting in a number of tourism and recreation cases.

It is unlikely that segmentation on the basis of socioeconomic criteria will cease to be used. Although other segmentation methods provide substantial information useful for strategic decisions on what to offer, it is still necessary to reach the market segment so described. For all its

TABLE 14.1   Recreation and Tourism Market Segmentation Bases

SOCIOECONOMIC AND DEMOGRAPHIC VARIABLES

Age
Education
Sex
Income
Family size
Family life cycle
Social class
Home ownership
Second home ownership
Race or ethnic group
Occupation

PRODUCT-RELATED VARIABLES

Recreation activity
Equipment type
Volume usage
Brand loyalty
Benefit expectations
Length of stay
Transportation mode
Experience preferences
Participation patterns

PSYCHOGRAPHIC VARIABLES

Personality traits
Life-style
Attitudes, interests, opinions
Motivations

GEOGRAPHIC VARIABLES

Region
Market area
Urban, suburban, rural
City size
Population density

SOURCE: Daniel J. Stynes, "Market Segmentation in Recreation and Tourism" (Michigan State University Agricultural Experiment Station project NE-137, unpublished paper); adapted from William M. Pride and O. C. Ferrell, *Marketing, Basic Concepts and Decisions,* 2nd ed. (Boston, Houghton Mifflin, 1980).

shortcomings, demographic segmentation offers the best way to determine the accessibility of the market.

PRODUCT-RELATED SEGMENTATION. A major advantage of segmenting by means of product-related criteria is that the information gained is directly related to the particular product in question. Indeed, a major flaw in some studies is that information is sought from the potential tourist that deals with general benefits sought or, in the case of psychographic segmentation, general attitudes about types of products/services rather than with specific products and services. Some attempts have been made in recreation and tourism to use heavy-half segmentation. Heavy-half segmentation refers to the idea of segmenting a market on the basis of quantity purchased or consumed. As with other types of products, however, heavy-half segmentation has been found lacking. A major problem is that, in many cases, the characteristics of the heavy half (the major purchasers) have been found to be similar to those of the light half. In a study of downhill skiers, it has been found that preferences and use patterns of both heavy and light skiers are similar except for such volume-related characteristics as level of skill, incidence of ski vacations, ownership of equipment, and quality of slopes.[2] Similar difficulties have been found when one tries to segment on the basis of brand loyalty.

Benefit or attribute segmentation is fast becoming a very popular segmentation method to use in recreation and tourism. This method involves segmenting a market according to the relative importance assigned to benefits that consumers expect to realize after purchasing the product. The method entails determining the relative importance of specific product benefits to prospective consumers. Clusters are then formed of people who attach a similar degree of importance to the same product benefits. Although results can have important ramifications for the development of new products and the determination of advertising messages, it is necessary to develop demographic profiles of those identified in the clusters in order to reach the market segments.

PSYCHOGRAPHIC SEGMENTATION. Much has been made of this relatively new tool. This technique of segmentation, although expensive to use and difficult to carry out, has been useful for describing segments. It can probably be best used in highly specialized and extensively developed markets to supplement the information gained from simpler analyses. Demographic data may be likened to the bones of a skeleton, and psychographic data may be likened to the flesh. The bones form the basis of the structure, but it is only by covering the form with flesh that the features

[2]Daniel J. Stynes and Edward M. Mahoney, "Michigan Downhill Ski Marketing Study: Segmenting Active Skiers" (Michigan State University Agricultural Experiment Station Research Report 391, 1980).

become recognizable. Information about an individual's attitudes, interests, and opinions give a much closer picture of the segment being described.

GEOGRAPHIC SEGMENTATION. Geographic considerations are very important to tourism. Much of the attractiveness of a tourist destination is based on contrast—contrasting cultures, climates, or scenery, for example. This implies there being a certain distance between origin and destination. Also, we have already seen the crucial role that accessibility of tourists to a destination plays in tourism. To date, destinations have used geographically based studies solely to identify primary, secondary, and in some cases, tertiary markets. State and national tourist offices tend to use geographic segmentation for the purposes of determining the extent of their promotional efforts.

Once market segments have been identified and profiles drawn up, it is necessary to select which segment(s) the firm or destination will seek to attract and serve. This decision can be made only in light of an analysis of which market segments will bring most benefit to the firm or destination. Such an analysis involves four concerns:

Sales potential: What is the current and future potential for revenue from this segment? Revenue is a combination of the number of current and potential tourists and their current and potential per-person spending.

Competition: To what extent does competition exist for the segment(s) in question? How strong is our advantage compared to the competitors?

Cost: How much investment is required to develop products to attract this segment?

Serviceability: Do we have the financial and managerial capability to design, promote, and distribute the appropriate products and satisfactorily serve the market segments attracted by the products produced?

The segments chosen become the target market. The process of selection and the corresponding decisions to develop a marketing program suitable to meet the needs of those segments is known as "positioning."

The concept of the product life cycle is useful to the marketer at this stage as an additional guide to appropriate strategies to use in choosing, attracting, and serving target markets.

Product Life Cycle

The concept of the product life cycle suggests that a product, service, or destination moves through distinct stages. In Chapter Twelve the various stages were described from a planning perspective.

The stage of development in which a product or destination finds itself has profound marketing implications.

Thus, within the context of the earlier definition of marketing, it is necessary for the benefit of the organization or destination to adopt a marketing outlook, to segment the market by appropriate means, and, taking the stage in the product life cycle into account, to position effectively the product or destination within the marketplace. This decision is operationalized by developing specific marketing strategies on price, product, promotion, and distribution within the context of a market planning approach.

MARKET PLANNING

Market planning implies a future orientation. It involves identifying suitable marketing objectives as well as determining appropriate marketing strategies to achieve those objectives. A model of the planning process is suggested in Figure 14.1.

External Forces

Marketing objectives can be set only after an analysis of the interaction of five factors—product, market, competition, overall development of objectives of the firm or destination, and the external forces within which the destination or firm in question must act.

Planning must be accomplished within the framework of the external environment over which the marketing manager may have little or no control. The first of these factors concerns the legal environment. Certain countries in the past have placed legal restrictions on their residents that have hampered the flow of tourism. Residents may be restricted from

FIGURE 14.1 Market Planning Process

traveling, or they may be unable to take more than a certain sum of money out of the country. Political factors must also be considered. Tensions or hostilities between country of origin and a country of destination will affect the marketing function. On the cultural level, it is important to consider the educational background of the countries being considered for tourism purposes. More international travel is generated from countries exhibiting higher educational standards, from societies regarded as more cultured, and from countries having a higher degree of industrialization. An important factor is the technical consideration. The destination must be accessible to tourists from the generating countries being considered. A final factor is economic. It is obviously important that there exist in a country of origin sufficient numbers of people that can afford to travel.

Development Objectives

The marketing plan should be part of the overall business goal of the firm or the development plan of the destination. Tourism is one, and only one, strategy for development. As it was noted in previous chapters, tourism can be used as a political, social, and economic force. Yet, other alternatives are available. The overall plan for tourism must be consistent with the overall plan for the destination area.

Market/Product/Competitor Analysis

The overall objective of the market/product/competitor analysis is to determine where our product presently stands compared to the competition in the eyes of the market. Competition is defined as any firm or destination seeking to serve the same market as ourselves. This objective is accomplished by analyzing product, market, and competition. The product and competitor analysis consists of a comparative evaluation of the following factors:

1. *Natural tourist resources*
   such as climate and topography
2. *Cultural and historical resources*
   such as historical monuments, museums, traditional events, ways of life
3. *Infrastructure*
   such as fresh water supply, road network, and communications
4. *Means of access and internal transportation facilities*
   such as airports, railroads, and bus companies
5. *Attractions and facilities*
   such as sporting events, hotels, and restaurants

The culmination of such a comparison between a product and its major competitors is a determination of comparative strengths and weaknesses. What do we have that is better than our competition? This information is important by itself, but in keeping with the marketing orientation stated above, it is necessary to place such intelligence in the context of the existing and potential market. Although marketing is not a science and has no scientific laws to guide its actions, there are several useful principles that guide its actions. For a firm or destination developing a marketing plan for the first time, one such principle may be: Attract people similar to those you already serve. This implies defining our existing market and seeking to develop more people with characteristics similar to those already attracted. An analysis of people in the market seeks to answer:

Who are they? How many of them are there? What are their socio-economic and psychographic characteristics?

Where do they come from and travel to?

How do they make plans, travel to and within the destination?

When do they vacation and for how long? When is the decision made?

Why do they vacation? What are their important motivations?

The crucial task is to determine a picture of the actual tourist, then project that picture into the future by considering trends in the country of origin. A second task is to discover potential markets by compiling a picture of the present tourist and seeking to find other markets that meet that profile. For example, if most people in the existing market come from within a 500-mile radius, potential markets may be discovered from areas within 500 miles from which visitors do not yet come.

Objectives

From a consideration of the above five elements, a picture will emerge of problem areas and areas of opportunity. This will enable planners to set marketing objectives, to determine where they are, where they want to be. If one recognizes the guidelines of overall business or development objectives, is aware of the constraints of the external environment, and is cognizant of the strengths and weaknesses of product compared to competition in light of market demand, objectives can be set. Objectives may relate to:

Type of image—elite or mass market
Type of tourist—low spending or high spending, repeat or new business, historical buff, and so on

Type of spending—foreign exchange generation or domestic

Type of product—high class hotels or small, locally owned facilities or foreign-owned ones

Remember that objectives can only come from an analysis of the elements discussed previously. The next step in the planning process, target market selection, can only come after objectives have been defined.

Target Market Selection

The concepts, discussed earlier, of product life cycle and market segmentation are extremely useful when selecting target markets. The tourism producer can, in fact, select a target segment. Once the target segment is selected, a marketing mix is developed that will meet the needs of the target. Yet, the very provision of the marketing mix will help ensure that the segment selected is attracted. For example, if a high-income, high-status target segment is selected, products will be developed to appeal to high-income, high-status tourists. Prices will be set high, and promotional messages may show pictures of tourists in tuxedos at dinner or older couples dancing cheek to cheek. Thus, the provision of the elements of the marketing mix means that only high-income, high-status tourists can afford to visit. The elements of the marketing mix are the way we "tell" the market what kinds of tourists we want.

Target segments will be defined in demographic, product-related, psychographic, or geographic terms. Which of these segments are actually chosen depends upon the size of the market and its position. The size of the market can be measured in terms of the number of tourists, the number of tourist nights, or the amount of tourist expenditures. Market segments that are large offer less of a risk than ones that are relatively small. The position of the destination relative to the market refers to the extent to which the market has been penetrated. If a destination area has managed to obtain a significant share of the market of a particular segment, efforts should be made to break into a new, unexplored market.

MARKET POTENTIAL INDEX. The following example of how the United States Travel and Tourism Administration selects market segments also shows how one destination area combines the analysis elements discussed above. The selection of target markets is done through a market potential index. The index consists of three parts. The first part shows the number of individuals in each country that have the financial means for a visit to the United States. In Table 14.2 it can be seen that on the sole basis of income, Canada is ranked number one. The first six countries listed account for 57 percent of the market potential. The second part of the index shows some qualitative market factors that are used to modify the first set of figures. The nine qualitative factors and their importance are

TABLE 14.2   Market Potential Index—Step 1

BASE POTENTIAL FOR TRAVEL TO THE U.S.		
COUNTRY OF RESIDENCE	NUMBER OF INDIVIDUALS WITH THE FINANCIAL MEANS FOR TRAVEL TO THE U.S.	
	Millions of Individuals	Rank
CANADA	12	1
MEXICO	11	2
WEST GERMANY	9	3
JAPAN	9	4
UNITED KINGDOM	8	5
FRANCE	8	6
SUBTOTAL 6 PRIMARY MARKETS (United States Travel Service)	57 (57%)	—
ITALY	5	7
BRAZIL	4	8
AUSTRALIA	2	9
NETHERLANDS	2	8
SPAIN	2	9
SWEDEN	2	9
ARGENTINA	1	13
BELGIUM	1	13
SWITZERLAND	1	13
VENEZUELA	1	13
COLOMBIA	1	13
IRAN	1	13
SUBTOTAL OTHER MARKETS	23 (23%)	—
OTHER AREAS	20 (20%)	—
TOTAL WORLD	100 (100%)	—

SOURCE: Beverly Shipka, "Practical Application of Travel Research in Marketing," in *Using Travel Research for Planning and Profits* (The Travel Research Association, Ninth Annual Conference Proceedings, June 1978), p. 99.

shown in Table 14.3. The regulatory factors as a whole are equally as important as marketing factors. The regulatory factors are essentially cost oriented and refer to restrictions placed on potential tourists in the country of origin as well as on the costs of traveling to and spending within the United States. The relative weights of these factors should also be noted. These weightings, as with the others, are subjective and based upon the experience of those making the selection of the segments.

In the marketing factors, competition refers to the amount of competition the United States would face from other countries in attempting

TABLE 14.3   Qualitative Market Profile

REGULATORY FACTORS	MARKETING FACTORS

Currency restrictions (25%)
Government restrictions (25%)
Cost impediments (50%)
------------------------------ 	
Total weighted ratings of
   regulatory factors (100%)
	Competition (15%)
	Attitude toward the United
	   States (25%)
	Trade structure (25%)
	Buying habits (10%)
	Language (5%)
	Product awareness (20%)
	------------------------------ 	
	Total weighted ratings of
	   marketing factors (100%)

Combined weighted ratings for regulatory and marketing factors produces qualitative index

SOURCE: Shipka, p. 101.

to attract visitors from a particular country. The greater the competition, the more difficult the marketing task and the less attractive that segment. The attitude of potential tourists to the United States as a tourist destination and to the American people as a whole is regarded as an important item, being weighed at 25 percent of the total marketing factors. Trade structure refers to the role of wholesalers and travel agents in selling travel as well as in shaping and influencing tourist decisions. It is easier to reach the tourist in Japan, where a few wholesalers control a great deal of international travel. Closely related to trade structure is the factor of buying habits, which is an indication of whether tourists tend to buy travel on their own, as they do in France and Mexico, or whether they buy packages developed by wholesalers. The latter will obviously receive higher ratings in the matrix. Being able to communicate in English is given a surprisingly low rating of 5 percent. Product awareness is a measure of the extent to which potential tourists are aware of the United States as a travel destination.

The effect of applying these factors to the previous figures is to reduce the number of potential tourists. An estimate is developed that reflects the unique marketing situation of each potential market relative to the United States. An examination of Table 14.4 indicates that the top six countries now account for almost three-quarters of the potential market numbers. Note that Australia and Venezuela have moved up in rank (due to concentrated trade structures, favorable attitudes toward the United States, and relatively good product awareness). Brazil, on the other hand, has moved down sharply from eighth to seventeenth place, because of government-imposed restrictions on travel.

The third part of the index involves applying per capita spending

TABLE 14.4   Market Potential Index—Step 2

Country of Residence	BASE POTENTIAL FOR TRAVEL TO THE U.S. — Number of Individuals with the Financial Means for Travel to the U.S. — Millions of Individuals	Rank	EFFECT OF REFINING FACTORS ON BASE POTENTIAL — Market Potential — Millions of Individuals	Rank
CANADA	12	1	11.5	1
MEXICO	11	2	9.6	2
WEST GERMANY	9	3	5.9	4
JAPAN	9	4	7.8	3
UNITED KINGDOM	8	5	5.8	5
FRANCE	8	6	5.0	6
SUBTOTAL 6 PRIMARY MARKETS (United States Travel Service)	57 (57%)	–	45.6 (74%)	–
ITALY	5	7	2.0	7
BRAZIL	4	8	.5	17
AUSTRALIA	2	9	1.5	8
NETHERLANDS	2	9	1.4	9
SPAIN	2	9	.8	11
SWEDEN	2	9	.9	10
ARGENTINA	1	13	.6	14
BELGIUM	1	13	.6	14
SWITZERLAND	1	13	.7	13
VENEZUELA	1	13	.8	11
COLOMBIA	1	13	.6	14
IRAN	1	13	.4	18
SUBTOTAL OTHER MARKETS	23 (23%)	–	10.8 (18%)	–
OTHER AREAS	20 (20%)	–	5.0 (8%)	–
TOTAL WORLD	100 (100%)	–	61.4 (100%)	–

SOURCE: Shipka, p. 103.

figures to the second part. Because Australian and Latin American tourists spend more than other tourists in the United States, their relative rank increases. The final ranking is shown in Table 14.5. In the year that these figures were developed, actual arrivals from the six primary geographic markets accounted for 86 percent of all arrivals. This type of occurrence is not uncommon. In many cases a large percentage of the business comes from a relatively small number of sources. Obviously, the figures presented in this example will change from year to year. Over several years rankings will also change. The important consideration is

TABLE 14.5   Market Potential Index—Step 3

Country of Residence	*BASE POTENTIAL FOR TRAVEL TO THE U.S.* Number of Individuals with the Financial Means for Travel to the U.S. Millions of Individuals	Rank	*EFFECT OF REFINING FACTORS ON BASE POTENTIAL* Market Potential Millions of Individuals	Rank	*ADDITION OF PER CAPITA RECEIPTS INDEX* Spending Index	Rank
CANADA	12	1	11.5	1	1.5	1
MEXICO	11	2	9.6	2	4.3	2
WEST GERMANY	9	3	5.9	4	2.6	4
JAPAN	9	4	7.8	3	4.0	3
UNITED KINGDOM	8	5	5.8	5	1.9	5
FRANCE	8	6	5.0	6	2.5	7
SUBTOTAL 6 PRIMARY MARKETS (United States Travel Service)	57 (57%)	–	45.6 (74%)	–		
ITALY	5	7	2.0	7	2.4	10
BRAZIL	4	8	.5	17	4.5	9
AUSTRALIA	2	9	1.5	8	3.5	6
NETHERLANDS	2	9	1.4	9	2.5	13
SPAIN	2	9	.8	11	2.4	16
SWEDEN	2	9	.9	10	2.5	15
ARGENTINA	1	13	.6	14	3.8	11
BELGIUM	1	13	.6	14	2.5	17
SWITZERLAND	1	13	.7	13	2.6	14
VENEZUELA	1	13	.8	11	4.5	7
COLOMBIA	1	13	.6	14	4.0	11
IRAN	1	13	.4	18	2.8	18
SUBTOTAL OTHER MARKETS	23 (23%)	–	10.8 (18%)	–		
OTHER AREAS	20 (20%)	–	5.0 (8%)	–		
TOTAL WORLD	100 (100%)	–	61.4 (100%)	–		

SOURCE: Shipka, p. 103.

the method used—one resulting from product, market, competitive, and external forces in line with the overall objective of using tourism to improve the balance of payments situation.

Marketing Mix

Once the target markets of a property or destination have been determined, an appropriate marketing mix can be developed. The marketing mix is comprised of four elements—product, price, promotion, and distribution. All four elements are provided in accordance with the needs of the target markets.

PRODUCT. It has already been noted that a vacation consists of a number of different parts or products—from transportation and lodging to sightseeing and souvenirs. It is clear that a variety of providers will offer one or more of these products or services. Each provider is thus interdependent with the others to offer an attractive and satisfying overall vacation experience. The philosophy of a marketing orientation suggests that products be developed to satisfy the needs and wants of those in the market. Also, market segmentation indicates that properties or destination areas cannot possibly provide products that will satisfy everyone. It is necessary to select a target market and then provide a variety of products and services that will satisfy its needs. The balance between providing narrow customized products to appeal to a particular market segment and providing sufficient variety to appeal to a wide diversity of tastes is a difficult one for management.

Crissy has suggested several important criteria that should be met in the decision to provide a product or service.[3] First, there should be a relatively heavy demand for the product or service from at least one important market segment, with the possibility of additional business from other segments of the market. It may be that the product can expect to break even on the basis of business from the major market segment and produce profit from business from the rest of the market. There may, of course, be a period of time before sales for a new attraction or service reach the break-even point.

Second, new products and services should fit in with the general image of the property or destination area and complement existing offerings. This does not mean that a destination area must appeal to only one segment of the market and that all products must meet the needs of that market segment. A great deal obviously depends upon the size of the destination area. One part of a destination area may appeal to the jet-set, while another part may be appealing to senior citizens. Within each of these parts, however, it is important that separate products and services be oriented around the one theme and market segment.

Third, any new offerings should be proposed in keeping with the avail-

[3]W. J. E. Crissy, Robert J. Boewadt, and Dante M. Laudadio, *Marketing of Hospitality Services: Food, Lodging, Travel* (E. Lansing, MI, Educational Institute of the American Hotel and Motel Association, 1975), pp. 69-70.

able supply of manpower, money, and natural resources. Although new products and services should exploit an advantage that a property or destination area has, it is important that new offerings be within the ability of the destination area or the management to satisfactorily provide them. A destination area may have magnificent mountain terrain suitable for skiing but may lack management knowledge in ski-area operations. Experienced management may have to be hired on a permanent or temporary basis before a ski area can be proposed.

Finally, it is necessary that any product or service added contribute to the profit and/or growth of the entire property or destination. In some cases the new offering may bring in no profit itself, but its provision may contribute to growth. The hotel pool, for example, may cost the operation money while bringing in no direct revenue from admission for swimming. However, the provision of a pool may bring in additional room business, and its elimination may drive existing room business elsewhere. Similarly, a destination may institute its own airline, not as a revenue-producing venture but as a necessary means to bring visitors in to spend money.

PRICE. Several factors influence the pricing policy set as part of the marketing mix. The price charged in any situation is unique to that situation and is affected by the combination of the factors to be discussed. Nevertheless, some guidelines can be suggested to assist in the pricing decision.

In purely economic terms, price is a result of supply and demand. When supply exceeds demand, price will tend to decrease. The reverse is true also. Of greater importance is the extent to which demand changes (as measured by the amount purchased) as price changes. This refers to the elasticity involved. A 5 percent reduction in price may result in a corresponding 10 percent increase in the number of buyers and a subsequent increase in total sales revenue. Demand in this case is elastic. General products aimed at the luxury end of the customer scale are less susceptible to changes in price and consequently tend to be price inelastic. For destinations or properties that are open only part of the year, supply is limited and prices will have to be correspondingly higher (everything else being equal) than destinations open year round. Because demand is not often uniform throughout the year, it is common to charge higher prices during the peak season and lower prices when demand slackens. The expected length of and the product's place in the previously discussed product life cycle is also relevant here. A "fad" item with an expected short life cycle will have to charge sufficiently high prices to recoup the investment in a relatively short period of time. A product that expects a long life can be priced lower.

The price charged is influenced by the competition. If our offerings are essentially the same as those of our competitors, our prices must be similar to theirs. The extent to which we are unique reflects the extent to which we can charge more than the competition. Related to the influence of competition is the management policy regarding market share. If a decision is made to increase market share, prices will probably be lower than if a decision to skim a small number of tourists from several market segments is made.

Pricing policy is obviously related to the needs of the market segment that is served. If a destination or property is seen as serving the needs and wants of the market and if those needs and wants are perceived as being important to the members of the market segment, those members will be willing to pay a higher price for the destination or property. The price charged must also be perceived by the market as less than or at least equal to the value received. In certain situations the influence of the market seems to go against economic principles. With certain luxury items, demand may increase as price increases. This phenomenon reflects a certain amount of snobbishness on the part of the market. The feeling may be that the higher the price the greater the perceived value and the greater the demand. But the actual value in the minds of the buyers must still equal or exceed the price paid.

The effect of each of these variables cannot be determined exactly in quantitative terms. The effect of their interaction is more difficult to determine. However, the general guidelines stated above can give guidance on pricing decisions for particular destinations or properties.

The remaining two elements of the marketing mix—promotion and distribution—will be dealt with in the next two chapters.

REFERENCES

BIGGADIKE, E. RALPH, "The Contribution of Marketing to Strategic Management," *Academy of Management Review*, vol. 6, no. 4, 1981, pp. 621–32.

DHALIA, NARIMAN K., and SONIA YUSPEH, "Forget the Product Life Cycle Concept," *Harvard Business Review*, January-February 1976, p. 104.

HOWARD, DENNIS R., and JOHN L. CROMPTON, *Financing, Managing and Marketing Recreation and Park Resources*, (Dubuque, IA, William C. Brown, 1980), ch. 1, p. 314.

MAHONEY, EDWARD MICHAEL, "Two Alternative Approaches to Segmenting Michigan's Downhill Ski Market" (Ph.D. dissertation, Michigan State University, 1979), Appendix A.

PLOG, STANLEY, "Why Destination Areas Rise and Fall in Popularity," *Cornell Hotel and Restaurant Administration Quarterly*, vol. 12, no. 1, November 1973, pp. 13–16.

REIME, MAT, and CAMERON, HAWKINS, "Planning and Developing Hospitality Facilities That Increase Tourism Demand," in *Tourism Marketing and Man-*

agement Issues, eds. Hawkins, Shafer, and Rovelstad (George Washington University, 1980), pp. 239-48.

SCHMOLL, G. A., "The Planning of Marketing Campaigns in Tourism," in *Managerial Aspects of Tourism: Products, Markets and Plans* (Proceedings of an International Seminar, ed. Salah Wahab, Alexandria, Egypt, 1975), pp. 262-65.

SCHMOLL, G. A., *Tourism Promotion* (London, Tourism International Press), pp. 19-21.

STYNES, DANIEL J., "Market Segmentation in Recreation and Tourism" (Michigan State University Agricultural Experiment Station Project NE-137, unpublished paper), p. 11.

WAHAB, SALAH, L. J. CRAMPON, and L. M. ROTHFIELD, *Tourism Marketing* (London, Tourism International Press, 1976), pp. 22-23.

15

TOURISM'S PROMOTION MIX: The Uses, Advantages, and Disadvantages of the Parts

The process of promotion is essentially the process of communication — communication between seller and buyer.

This chapter deals with the promotion mix. A link is established between the objectives of promotion and the tourist's buying process described in Chapter Four. Appropriate types of promotion are suggested relative to where the tourist is in the buying process.

The process of communication is laid out in detail. Objectives must be established and a target audience identified. Once a budget sufficient to reach the objectives has been drawn up, the content and form of the message can be agreed upon. The actual promotional mix is determined at this stage and the appropriate media to use are selected. At each step of the way it is necessary to set up controls to ensure that the campaign is on track.

Promotional efforts at the federal and state levels are described in some detail to give the reader a picture of what is actually being done to promote tourism destinations.

PROMOTION = COMMUNICATION

Developing the promotional mix is essentially an exercise in communication. As suppliers of a tourism product or as intermediaries in the distribution channel, our task is to communicate our message to the potential tourist. Through explicit communication, language is used in an attempt to promote a common understanding between the sender and the receiver of a message. Communication may also be implicit through nonverbal means such as gestures and facial expressions. For communication to take place a common understanding must be present or must be developed between the message sender and the message receiver.

The end goal of promotion is behavior modification. The task is to initiate a purchase where none has been made before; initiate a change in purchase behavior by having the tourist "buy" a different destination, package, and so on; or reinforce existing behavior by having the tourist continue to purchase the brand being promoted. This end result is accomplished through messages that seek to inform, persuade, or remind the receiving public. Informative promotion is more important during the early stages of the product life cycle when, for example, a new destination is entering the marketplace. Little is known about the destination, and potential visitors must have sufficient knowledge of it before they can be expected to buy. Persuasive promotion seeks to get a tourist to buy. This becomes the primary objective of promotion when the growth stage of the life cycle is entered. During the maturity stage of the product life cycle, reminder promotion becomes important. The public has bought the product or service. Reminder messages serve to jog the memory and keep the product in the public's mind.

Promotion and the Buying Process

The relationship between the goals of promotion and the buying process of the traveler discussed in Chapter Four is explained in Figure 15.1. To meet the goal of behavior modification the three types of promotion described above are used. Informative advertising is important to the tourist at the attention and comprehension stages of the buying process. Persuasive advertising seeks to change attitudes, to develop intentions to buy, and then to initiate the purchase. Reminder promotion comes into play after a purchase has been made.

The Communication Process

The communication process is illustrated in Figure 15.2. Objectives from the sender are set in terms of the target market audience. Once a budget is developed, the content and form of the message are determined and the appropriate promotional mix and medium are selected and

FIGURE 15.1   Goals of Promotion and the Traveler's Buying Process

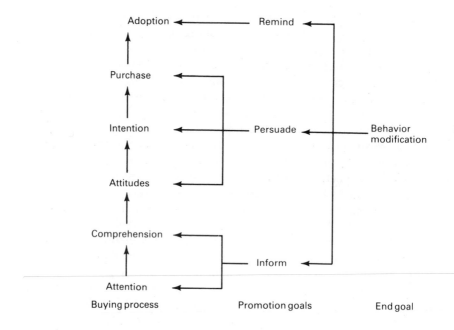

planned. The response from the receiver can then be compared with the objectives of the sender to determine the overall effectiveness of the campaign. This effectiveness control is insufficient, however. If the response does not match the objectives, much of the time and money will have been wasted. In addition, this final comparison will not indicate where the problem lies. Were the objectives set too high? Was the message appropriate but for the wrong target audience? Were the right media used to project a message that said the wrong things? To find out where the problem lies and to find out quickly enough so that a minimum of time and money is wasted, it is necessary to control the communications process at each step of the way. The steps in this process will be explored in fuller detail.

OBJECTIVES. The objectives of a campaign must be established before anything else takes place. To be effective, objectives must be specific, quantifiable, measurable, realistically attainable, and have a time frame. In order to place potential tourists at the appropriate stage in the buying process, we need to know how much is known or unknown about our product before setting appropriate objectives. If those in the target market are at the intention stage in the buying process, then informative messages to reach them will be an unwise use of time and money. Similarly, the promotion of a new package will not be effective if it is assumed that the

FIGURE 15.2 Tourism's Communication Process

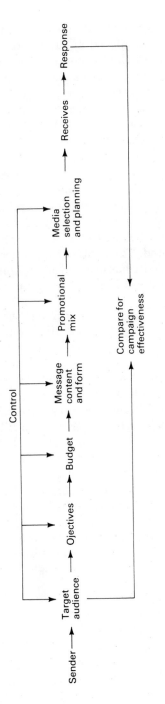

intention to buy already exists. By means of a knowledge and awareness study the market can be placed in the buying process and appropriate objectives can be set. At the beginning stage, for example, an objective may be to expose the message to a specified number of members of the target-market within a specific time period. At the intention stage, the objective will be oriented toward increasing purchases. The control at this stage determines that the target audience has been correctly placed in the buying process and that objectives have met the criteria noted above.

TARGET AUDIENCE. Through basic market data and research results from such things as focus groups the target audience can be identified. The target audience should be defined demographically and psychographically and should consist of definable segments of the population having members with similar attributes who are the best prospects for purchasing what is being promoted. The control aspect seeks to determine whether or not the correct audience has been selected. This process of target market selection has been covered in detail in the previous chapter.

BUDGET. Unfortunately, no scientific system exists to determine the appropriate budget to complete a specific promotion job. It is important, however, that objectives be developed before a budget is constructed. Only by knowing what is to be done can a determination be made of how much it may cost. All too often a sum of money is obtained, then objectives are set based upon how much one has to spend. Certainly businesses and destinations are faced with economic constraints. It must be recognized, however, that setting objectives after the sum of money has been budgeted will probably mean that the necessary goal will not be reached. In a practical sense, the formulation of a budget should be a combination of several factors. It should be developed in accordance with previously set objectives while taking into account the ability of the business or destination to financially support that kind of effort. Also, the amount of money being spent by the competition has to be taken into account. The budget should be flexible enough to allow for changes due to changing market conditions or competitive actions. According to Schmoll, the following promotion budgets as a percentage of net sales are typical:[1]

Tour operator—10 to 20 percent
Travel agency—5 percent
Hotel—2.5 to 5 percent
Airline—3 to 7 percent
National tourist office—50 percent
= 75 percent of the total operating budget

---

[1]G. A. Schmoll, *Tourism Promotion* (London, Tourism International Press, 1977), p. 108.

MESSAGE CONTENT. Through such things as nondirective interviews, the motives of the target audience can be measured in an attempt to determine what to say. Alternative message concepts can be formulated and shown to a sample of the target audience. Based on its ratings of the various themes, the most effective message concept can be chosen. The control objective at this stage is to develop the appeal that is best suited for the target audience.

MESSAGE FORM. After determining what to say, the best form of the message is explored—*how* to say it. The objective is to develop messages that are understandable, distinctive, and believable. This can be accomplished in a number of ways. Various messages can be shown to sample members of the target audience and their reactions to the various messages can be compared. Surveys of the target market can be taken after exposure to the message to determine what has been remembered as a test of the message's memorability.

PROMOTIONAL MIX. Many promotional tools exist to convey the message to the audience. The major parts of the promotional mix are:[2]

> *Advertising*—Any paid form of nonpersonal presentation and promotion of ideas, goods, or services by an identified sponsor
>
> *Personal selling*—Oral face-to-face presentation in a conversation with one or more prospective purchasers for the purpose of making sales
>
> *Sales promotion*—Those marketing activities, other than personal selling, advertising, and publicity, that stimulate consumer purchasing and dealer effectiveness, such as displays, shows/exhibitions, demonstrations, and nonrecurrent selling efforts not in the ordinary routine
>
> *Publicity*—Nonpersonal stimulation of demand for a product, service, or business unit by planting commercially significant news about it in a published medium or obtaining favorable presentation of it upon radio, television, or stage that is not paid for by the sponsor

The emphasis on the many parts of the promotional mix will vary with the characteristics of the market, the type of product, and the amount of funds available. The more expensive and complicated the product being sold, the greater the need for some form of personal selling. Although only an advertisement may induce a couple to spend a weekend at a resort, an individual planning a convention for fifty people or a couple thinking of a cruise will tend to require some form of personal selling to solidify the purchase. Within the tourism industry there are actually two markets. Promotional efforts must be directed to the potential tourist as well as to the travel trade intermediaries, including the media. The tools used will

---

[2]*Marketing Definitions: A Glossary of Marketing Terms* (Chicago, American Marketing Association, Committee on Definitions, 1960).

be dependent, in part, upon the audience. Sales workshops are very important to the travel trade; advertising is important to the potential tourist. Obviously, the mix is constrained by the amount of money available. A four-color advertisement in a national magazine may cost half of the annual salary of a sales representative. Schmoll has distinguished between the many targets as follows:[3]

PROMOTIONAL ACTIVITIES AND COMMUNICATIONS CHANNELS

Target: Potential customers	Target: Travel trade
General media advertising (press, television, radio, cinema) Outdoor advertising (posters) Direct mail distribution of catalogs, etc. Showing of travel films Special offers (rebates, etc.) Joint promotion with trade Point-of-sale advertising Participation in travel exhibitions and travel fairs Enquiry and information service	Trade press advertising Newsletters and releases Distribution of publicity materials (catalogs, brochures, audiovisual shows) Information and servicing manuals Schedules and price lists Seminars, workshops for sales staff Familiarization visits Sales contests and premiums

Target: Visitors/actual customers	Target: General and trade media
Welcoming and reception service Local travel information service Visitor surveys Visitor assistance	Press conferences, press releases Editorial material Familiarization visits

---

To the limited extent that it is possible to generalize about promotional activities, the following conclusions can be made:[4]

Advertising, especially in newspapers and magazines, accounts for more than half of all promotion expenditures.

Consumer literature is the basis of sales support; most is published by tour operators.

Most budgets combine all elements of the promotion mix.

The percentages allocated to the many elements are relatively stable from year to year.

MEDIA SELECTION AND PLANNING. In this part of the process the objective is to identify the appropriate media to get the message across to the audience. The media used in the travel and tourism industry are news-

---

[3]G. A. Schmoll, *Tourism Promotion*, p. 121.

[4]G. A. Schmoll, *Tourism Promotion*, p. 125.

papers, magazines, television, radio, and outdoor billboards. Airlines spend more than twice what any other tourism and travel supplier spends on advertising. Almost half of their advertising dollars is spent on newspaper advertising; about one-quarter is spent on television. Radio is the next most favored medium, followed by magazines, with outdoor receiving a very small percentage of the total. Hotels, motels, and resorts account for about one-fifth of total industry advertising outlay, approximately the same as is spent by travel services such as travelers' checks companies. Other segments of the industry each account for less than 5 percent of the total media expenditures.

The crucial part of media selection is choosing those which will be seen, read, or heard by the intended audience. Television and radio stations and newspaper and magazine offices will often have market research available on the characteristics of their viewers, listeners, and readers. Also, there are general criteria against which the other media can be compared to determine the most appropriate vehicle for the message. The following criteria are very useful:

Cost per contact
Total cost
Market selectivity
Geographic selectivity
Source credibility
Visual quality
Noise level
Life span
Pass-along rate
Timing flexibility

Although the cost per contact (cost of reaching one member of the audience) is low for television, the total cost is very high. To a moderate extent, it is possible to select the market we desire by a careful selection of the shows in which we choose to advertise. To a greater extent, it is possible to be geographically selective. Television suffers from a rather low level of credibility or trust among consumers. The visual quality, however, is very high. Noise level refers to the amount of stimuli competing for the viewer's attention. Because of the tendency to watch television with other people, the noise level tends to be higher than average. Also, because advertising schedules often have to be decided far in advance the timing flexibility for television is below average.

Radio offers a medium that is low in total cost and cost per contact. Like television, radio is selective for broad market groups and has a high geographic selectivity. The credibility and noise level are similar to that of television. However, the timing flexibility is far greater.

Newspapers also offer a low total cost and cost per contact. Market selectivity is low, and geographic selectivity is average. It is possible to zero-in on particular cities and towns, for example. The trust factor appears to be low, and the visual quality is less than average. To compensate for a high noise level, low life span, and pass-along rate, newspapers offer a great deal of flexibility in the timing of advertisements.

Magazines have a much higher cost per contact and total cost than do newspapers. Because of the specialized nature of magazines, the market selectivity is above-average; regional editions offer some geographic selectivity. The visual quality is much higher than newspapers, and the noise level is lower. Both the life span and pass-along rate are above-average, but the timing flexibility is low.

Although the total cost of a direct mail campaign tends to be rather high, the cost per contact varies widely depending upon the quality of the mailing list. Both market selectivity and geographic selectivity are the highest of all media. Source credibility seems to be below average, as is the life span of a direct mail piece. The visual quality can be very high, but the noise level is low. This can make for a high degree of impact. Timing flexibility, however, is rather low due to the need for production lead times.

Although newspapers will continue to dominate as the most used advertising medium for travel and tourism, their efficiency has been eroding. The travel sections of newspapers tend to be read only after the decision to travel has been made. Because of this, those who do read these sections are highly motivated readers. In order to expand the travel market, the use of other media such as radio and television may be appropriate.

RECEIVER RESPONSE. The response to a communication is based upon the way the message is perceived by a receiver (see Chapter Two). It has already been noted that one stimulus can be perceived differently by different people. The problem should be minimized if, in fact, the campaign is controlled and its effectiveness tested at each stage of the way. This, however, appears to be something that is sorely lacking. Many reports indicate that less than half of the organizations from travel agents to national tourist offices that have been surveyed measure the effectiveness of their promotional campaigns.

National Tourist Offices—Uses of Promotion

A national tourist office is the organization officially responsible for the development and marketing of tourism for a country. When the organization is such that the development and marketing functions are split, the body responsible for marketing is usually designated the national tourist office. The range and importance of the many promotional activities can be seen in Table 15.1. Approximately 14 percent of the total budget is spent on media advertising, with an additional 10 percent being spent on sales promotion and personal selling directed toward the trade. A major amount of the budget goes toward the establishment of offices overseas. Less than 10 percent of the budget is spent on public relations and head office research and administration. Almost a quarter of the budget is spent on producing sales support literature and audiovisuals.

The promotional activities of a national tourist office can be divided into those aimed at the travel trade and those aimed at the consumer.

TRAVEL TRADE

In order to inform the travel trade about and familiarize it with the tourist product(s) of its country, a national tourist office will organize educational tours for selected wholesalers and retailers, who can then sell the country as a tourist destination more easily. During these tours, the foreign travel wholesalers and retailers inspect the country's tourist facilities, visit its tourist attractions, and generally have contacts with the local travel trade, which acts as their partner in channeling tourist traffic to the country. Such tours may be conducted in small groups, especially for retailers, or individually, especially for wholesalers.

TABLE 15.1 Typical Budget of a National Tourist Office

Direct Market Costs		
Media advertising	14%	
Trade seminars and promotions	5	
Regional promotional cooperation	5	24%
Foreign representation:		
Overseas offices	40	
Overseas exhibitions	2	
Subtotal		42
Head Office Costs on Supporting Promotion		
Research and administration	9	
Promotional literature	10	
Publications	4	
Photographs and slides	1	
Films	3	
Public relations	7	
Subtotal		34%
Total		100%

SOURCE: Salah Wahab, L. J. Crampon, and L. M. Rothfield, *Tourism Marketing* (London, Tourism International Press, 1976), p. 200.

Tourist workshops are normally organized and staged in the market itself and are intended to bring together in both the generating and the receiving country all the main components of the tourist industry, such as hotels, travel agents, airlines, and providers of tourist services. The main objectives of such workshops are, first, to promote the tourist product mix of the receiving country to the travel trade and other principals of the generating country and, second, to provide a suitable opportunity for the travel principals of the receiving and generating countries to establish working relationships.

Like educational tours and tourist workshops, sales seminars are organized by a national tourist office in order to familiarize the travel trade with the tourist product and the latest developments in the tourist industry of its country and to motivate it to increase sales of tours and to encourage travel there.

Within the framework of a national tourist office's activities aimed at servicing the travel trade, sales calls are made by its staff to travel agents and other retail outlets. The aim of such calls is to assist the travel retailers in selling the country in question by providing them with information, advice, and promotional material.

To keep the travel trade well-stocked with promotional material on the country, a national tourist office carries out regular direct mailing shots of tourist literature. The travel trade is, thus, itself in a better position to more adequately service inquiries from its clients and to actually promote and sell the country.

As part of the regular supply of information within the framework of its promotional efforts, the national tourist office normally establishes a permanent channel of communication with the travel trade through the regular issue and distribution of newsletters or bulletins. Through such newsletters or bulletins a national tourist office informs the travel trade about all relevant developments concerning the tourist product and the tourist industry of its country. At the same time, it also attempts to promote sales of its product.

In order to increase sales, a national tourist office may provide incentives or bonuses, usually in the form of free holidays or material gifts. These incentives may or may not be linked with so-called retail agents' competitions. Incentives and bonuses are invariably offered in conjunction with the main tourism principals of the country, that is, hotel and airline companies.

Promotional evenings may be organized exclusively for members of the travel trade and are basically good-will exercises. They are usually staged in hotels or similar establishments and combine food, drink, and entertainment, often imported from the country concerned.

CONSUMER

Servicing of inquiries from the public can be either in writing, by telephone, or made in person. Tourist literature and other promotional material are used for the servicing of inquiries from the public, but not all inquiries originate from potential or prospective holiday makers. A small proportion of inquiries received by a national tourist office originates from returning tourists and concerns the widest possible range of subjects, including complaints and praise. Thus, a national tourist office abroad has to carry out a kind of "customer relations" or "after-sales service" function.

National tourist offices abroad offer different kinds of incentives to consumers. These range from free holidays given as prizes to gas coupons, and special discounts or concessions for children or family groups.

Participation in tourism fairs and exhibitions is done with suitably decorated stands that present the tourist attractions of the country. Here, a tourist office aims at contacting large numbers of potential tourists in order to inform them about the tourist attractions of its country and to persuade them to travel there. In doing so, the tourist office distributes relatively large quantities of tourist literature to interested people.

Window display campaigns are specially designed and exhibited in travel agencies and other retail outlets. They give promotional exposure to the product, conveniently enough, at its points of sale.

Many kinds of promotional events may be organized and staged by a national tourist office abroad, the aims of which are to convert potential consumer demand into real consumer demand, to create good-will toward the product, and to improve its image. Such events are often as much public relations exercises as they are sales promotional activities. Some of the most common events of this kind are: promotional evenings, exhibitions of arts and handicrafts, and "national" weeks that are held in department stores and hotels.

OVERSEAS OFFICES.[5]   As was seen earlier, a national tourist office typically spends approximately 40 percent of its budget for overseas representation. There are several hundred national tourist offices abroad. Can or should the expenditure be justified? An overseas marketing campaign can certainly be administered from the head office of the destination. The results are unlikely to be effective, however. The effort will probably be more expensive because of the need to hire outside specialists for the marketing effort. Also, the costs of distribution are higher. The effectiveness of a home-based campaign will be affected by the difficulty in establishing suitable communications channels and in getting enough quality feedback to monitor the campaign.

In an attempt to reduce the costs of marketing, overseas countries have in the past used their own embassies and consulates to house those involved in the marketing effort. By and large, this strategy has not worked. The functions of both the political and marketing groups seem to be too dissimilar. The necessary expertise for tourism marketing is lacking in the embassy group, and the necessary contacts in the trade press are different for both the marketing and political groups. It also appears that the trade press in an overseas market prefers to deal with a professionally staffed marketing office. A final point is that embassies, located in a nation's capital, may not necessarily be optimally located for maximizing potential tourist contact. Such would be the case in West Germany (Bonn), Australia (Canberra) and the United States (Washington). Tourist offices would be better placed in larger population centers.

The role of a tourist office abroad has changed in many ways over the past several decades. First, in the past, a major function of a national tourist office was to distribute literature to potential tourists. The increase in potential tourist destinations has meant an increase in national tourist offices promoting these destinations. This increase in competition has meant that NTOs have been forced to adopt a more professional marketing approach rather than be a passive distributor of information. Second, a factor that has caused the NTOs to change has been the growth of package or inclusive tours. As tour operators have grown in size and power and vertically integrated systems of distribution have been set up, tourist destinations have grown increasingly dependent on organized flows of tourists. This growing dependence on the travel trade has forced tourist offices to shift their marketing emphasis from appealing to the independent traveler to promoting to and in cooperation with the travel trade. Third, as both intermediaries and tourist consumers have become more sophisticated and experienced, the NTOs have been forced to adopt a much more professional attitude in their approach to tourism marketing.

---

[5]"The Role and Functions of a National Tourist Office Abroad," *International Tourism Quarterly*, no. 3, 1976, pp. 39–58. This section is an abbreviated form of this excellent article.

Basically, the objectives of a national tourist office abroad can be identified as follows:

To increase the availability of the tourist product(s) of its country by help-ing to increase the number of tour operators' programs and the capacity of existing ones, or to maintain at targeted levels the number and capacity of such programs

To secure maximum promotional exposure for the product mix of its country

To promote a favorable image of its country as a tourist destination, and to maintain or enhance such an image

To stimulate and increase demand for the tourist product(s) of its country

To familiarize the travel distribution channels with its tourist product mix and stimulate them in order to facilitate and increase sales

To increase and make more effective the supply of information on the tour-ist product mix of its country

To carry out these objectives, the aforementioned functions are car-ried out. Although advertising is very important, it is also very costly. Because few, if any, offices have enough funds to carry out the kind of advertising campaign necessary to do the job, public relations has become the most important marketing function. An effective campaign aimed at either the travel trade or the ultimate consumer requires the effective utili-zation of the media. Establishing good relationships with the press is a crucial step toward successfully reaching the ultimate object of the public relations campaign.

A large amount of literature is produced to support the market ef-fort. Literature tends to be either general (it may be brief and compre-hensive pieces on the destination with information of interest to all potential tourists) or specialized (it may be detailed information on a par-ticular area or theme of interest to fewer people). A general piece may ask potential visitors to write for more information on some specialized topics. Because of the large quantity of information requested, and because of rising costs of paper, printing, and postage, NTOs tend to concentrate on producing smaller, standardized folders. Others may include adver-tising or charge the consumer for the promotional literature.

NTOs will locate where the potential market is. The number of of-fices set up will depend upon how important the market is to the destina-tion and how large and decentralized the market country is. It is doubtful that the United States could be covered by one office, for example. NTOs traditionally have relied upon street-level offices in prestigious locations. The rationale has been that such locations expose the destination to as many people as possible. This assumption has been questioned since the change from consumer relations to trade relations and with the rising cost of prime site rents. In light of this, many offices are moving to less ex-pensive locations in the central business district. The preferred location also depends upon the structure of the distribution system. In West Germany, where tourists are mainly independent travelers, there is a greater need for consumer access than in the United States, where much travel is done in organized tours. In the latter case, contact with the trade is more important.

It is better to staff an NTO with citizens of the country that is being marketed. This strategy allows destinations to train their staff overseas and, upon transfer, to utilize their firsthand knowledge. It also appears that those in the trade prefer dealing with a citizen of the country that is being marketed. In reality, most offices are managed by a citizen of the destination but assisted by a locally recruited staff.

It is difficult, if not impossible, to determine the effectiveness of a national tourist office abroad. The number of arrivals from a particular country cannot be directly attributed to the efforts of an NTO. The marketing cost per arrival or per dollar of gross earnings is equally unsatisfying due to the difficulty of determining the effect of the NTO in achieving the end product. The marketing cost per inquiry can be determined. This figure has to be determined separately for consumer, trade, and media groups, for a contact from each carries different weight. However, the real effectiveness measure is the conversion ratio of those contacts. How many of these inquiries result in sales, and how much are the sales worth? In reality, this is impossible to track. The research available indicates that a relatively small percentage of tourists seek information or assistance from national tourist offices in making their travel decision or in planning their trip. This should not, however, be used as a condemnation of national tourist offices. As noted above, the NTO role has changed to involve less contact with consumers and more with the travel trade. It is likely that national tourist offices are the source of information to those who deal with the potential tourist.

U.S. TRAVEL AND TOURISM ADMINISTRATION

The mission of the U.S. Travel and Tourism Administration (formerly called the U.S. Travel Service) is to "develop travel to the U.S. from abroad as a stimulus to economic stability and to the growth of the U.S. travel industry, to reduce the Nation's travel deficit and to promote friendly understanding and appreciation of the United States."[6] Within that mission, the USTTA has five major responsibilities:

---

[6]*25th Program Report of the United States Travel Service, 1980*, U.S. Department of Commerce, p. 6.

Stimulating travel to the United States
Encouraging low-cost tours and visitor services
Cooperating with local, state, and foreign governments
Reducing barriers to travel
Collecting and exchanging tourism statistics

Stimulating Travel to the United States

The many methods used by the USTTA to stimulate travel can be influenced by such external factors as changes in foreign government travel regulations or fluctuations in economic patterns. Thus, it is important that programs be individually tailored to each particular market and constantly refined and updated. Working through regional offices in Toronto, Mexico City, London, Paris, Frankfurt, and Tokyo, the USTTA aims at providing technical assistance to tour operators and travel wholesalers, increasing the knowledge and sales effectiveness of foreign retail travel agents and other travel counselors that deal with the public, and motivating consumers to select the United States as a travel destination.

As marketing budgets have been eroded, there has been little or no money for advertising. The emphasis has been on conducting educational workshops and organizing familiarization visits for those in the travel trade. This is encouraged in several ways. Mobile seminars are conducted in overseas markets. Members of U.S. travel companies and destinations, in conjunction with USTTA staffers, may travel to several population centers for workshops with invited retail and wholesale agents. If a retail agent is willing to designate someone in his or her office as a U.S. specialist, he or she is furnished with extra promotional literature and, often, sales leads. Consumers are reached indirectly through journalist familiarization visits. By encouraging foreign journalists to tour the country the hope is that articles extolling the virtues of the United States will appear in media read by a target market. Both trade and consumer requests for information are handled by staff.

Business travel is promoted through foreign tour operators. A listing of U.S. trade shows of potential interest to foreign businesses is produced and distributed to encourage the development of special travel-related package tours featuring these trade shows. Also, trade show organizers can be counseled by USTTA staff members about making their events more attractive to international attendees. Technical assistance is also provided to convention and visitor bureaus in the United States to assist them in developing international convention business. International assocation executives are also brought to the United States to inspect convention facilities.

Encouraging Low-Cost Tours and Visitor Services

A crucial part of bringing volume tourism to a destination is establishing packaged tours. Packaged arrangements preclude travelers making their own travel arrangements and allow the prospective visitor to cost-compare destinations because most parts of the vacation are included in the package. Because the development and promotion of a tour involves substantial investment of risk capital in advance of sales, tour operators tend to be reluctant to introduce "new" destinations. Until recent years most tour operators in the major travel-generating markets of Europe and Asia considered the United States to be a "new" destination. Consequently, few package tours to the United States were available to foreign travel consumers.

By providing not only educational workshops and familiarization tours but also seed money, wholesalers were encouraged to risk their own capital in setting up U.S. tour packages. Seed money was provided to help produce and distribute brochures, catalogs, and promotional materials, to assist in defraying advertising costs, and to help train retail travel agents. As more tour packages have been developed, the emphasis has shifted towards providing information about the available offerings.

Cooperating With Local, State, and Foreign Governments

Guidance is offered to state and local government officials in developing and marketing tourism programs for foreign visitors. This may involve assisting in the development of effective marketing strategies and forming travel missions abroad to develop foreign language sales promotion materials and select promotional themes and advertising media in specific international markets.

At the international level, the USTTA is an involved member of the World Tourism Organization.

Reducing Barriers to Travel

In an attempt to simplify the movement of people and things across and through international borders, the USTTA has been involved in many activities. One program has involved the introduction of a uniformed corps of multilingual receptionists at U.S. airports to provide interpreter service to arriving tourists. To overcome the problem of converting foreign currency into U.S. dollars or of cashing foreign-currency-denominated travelers checks, an educational program abroad has advised travelers of the advantages of purchasing U.S. dollar–denominated travelers checks before leaving for the United States. Discussions have also been sponsored between Amtrak and the National Railways of Mexico to institute various methods of facilitating bilateral rail travel.

Collecting and Exchanging Tourism Statistics

In order to measure the economic and demographic impact of international tourism while meeting the demand for marketing intelligence, the USTTA serves as a conduit for tourism statistics. Basic data on international tourism arrivals and receipts compared to worldwide figures determine whether the United States' share of the world market is stable, growing, or shrinking. Also, a number of market research reports are prepared annually that deal with an analysis of existing travelers in the United States from a foreign country and of travel interests and plans of the major U.S. target markets.

STATE TRAVEL OFFICES[7]

Several states, expecting an increase in domestic travel after World War II, established travel offices at the beginning of the 1940s. By the end of the war, half of the states had established some mechanism to promote tourism. At present, every state but Maine, which has a private nonprofit organization to handle that role, has a state travel office. Because of the promotion of tourism for reasons of economic development, almost three-quarters of the travel offices are divisions of agencies that deal in some way with economic development. The remainder are housed in state highway departments or parks and recreation agencies or are in separate offices reporting to commissions or directly to the governor.

Advertising

All offices have an individual within the department who is responsible for the development of a travel advertising program. In approximately 90 percent of the offices an outside advertising agency is retained. In well over eight out of ten states, various groups outside of state government—such as convention and visitor bureaus and regional travel organizations—cooperate in advertising programs. Over half of the states have a matching funds program, usually on a 50–50 basis, with various groups stimulating the promotional effort.

Most of the states direct their advertising toward stimulating inquiries. Over 80 percent of the states claim to evaluate the effectiveness of their advertising effort.

Budgets

The states have assumed a more important role than the federal government in promoting tourism. The total federal budget for tourism

---

[7]*Survey of State Travel Offices*, U.S. Travel Data Center, annual since 1973.

is a small percentage of the combined total spent by the states. Although state government travel office expenditure averages less than 2 percent of visitor expenditures, the total budget has been increasing faster than growth in travel industry receipts.

In eight out of ten states the entire travel office is funded by state general revenue. In a very few cases funding may be obtained by gasoline taxes.

More than 25 percent of the budget is spent on advertising, generally in magazines and newspapers. Printing is by far the largest component in the promotional budget. Travel shows are an important marketing activity for many states. Most states participate in travel shows, although the number attended ranges from one to almost forty. An interesting budget item is that approximately half of the offices advertise and promote to foreign countries, primarily Canada. Canadian promotion comes from border states and southern states appealing to Canadians during the winter.

General Promotion

Every state has a special travel promotion theme or slogan. Approximately one in six of the states direct different themes or slogans to different target markets. Out-of-state information centers are operated by less than one-third of the states; they are mainly located in New York City. About the same number of states operate information centers outside of the United States, the most popular location being Brussels, Belgium. Almost half of the states have full-time or part-time employees in the travel office assigned to encourage travel-related investment. This number has been steadily increasing over the past few years.

About two-thirds of the states hold annual state travel conferences. An equal number have private statewide tourism associations within their states. Only 20 percent of the states have a toll-free telephone number for travel information inquiries.

Package Tours

Approximately 90 percent of state travel offices have programs devoted to developing package tours. Less than one-third of the states, however, publish and distribute state package-tour catalogs. About two-thirds of the states have a staff member whose task is tour packaging. A similar number of states host familiarization tours for tour operators, retail travel agents, or travel writers.

Press and Public Relations

Fewer than 10 percent of the states do not have a staff member specifically assigned as a public relations or press information officer. In the vast majority of states this person is employed by the state travel office and directs most of the publicity programs to out-of-state audiences.

Research

Just over half of the state offices assign a staff member to research. In many cases, research is conducted on behalf of the state by university or college faculties or by members of another agency of state government. Almost every state has a continuing travel data–gathering program involving either visitors at welcome centers or motor vehicle counts.

Welcome Centers

Most states operate welcome centers or highway information centers. There are between 300 and 400 such centers in the United States. Over 90 percent of these are permanent facilities, and almost two-thirds are open year-round.

Marketing Strategies

The variation in state travel office budgeted activities can be explained by different travel marketing activities. Three specific strategies can be defined:[8]

At-home marketing
Impulse marketing
Enroute marketing

Whichever strategy is chosen will define the way the budget is spent. The strategy chosen is, in turn, dependent on the market position of the state.

States that can be classified as destination attractions will make heavy use of an at-home marketing strategy. This strategy aims at encouraging the tourist to visit a state before the tourist leaves home. Promotional programs concentrate on creating a positive image, and they rely heavily on out-of-state advertising to stimulate inquiries for more information. The effectiveness of such a strategy can be determined by the proportion of people that have requested information as a result of advertising who subsequently visit the state. The advertising cost per inquiry and the tourism revenue per inquiry have also been used to evaluate the effort.

Impulse marketing strategy aims to persuade the tourist to make

---

[8]Thomas R. Doering, "Geographical Aspects of State Travel Marketing in the U.S.A.," *Annals of Tourism Research*, July/September 1979, pp. 314–16.

unplanned side trips while traveling. The automobile vacationer is particularly susceptible to such messages. For the transit or pass-through state, a strategy emphasizing impulse buying may be appropriate. An emphasis will be placed on in-state outdoor advertising and highway information centers at entrances to the state to capture this market. A basic difference between the two strategies is that the impulse marketing strategy is aimed at the actual visitor rather than the potential visitor to the state. The effectiveness of such a strategy, although difficult to measure, is a reflection of how many in-state visits are influenced.

Enroute marketing strategy is somewhat of a combination of the previous two strategies. The campaign is mostly aimed out-of-state and is directed at the traveler who has already embarked on a trip. Out-of-state radio and outdoor advertising seeks to have the tourist plan in advance but plan enroute rather than at home. As before, the effectiveness is difficult to measure in terms of the number of visits or extra days that have been influenced.

In short, the market positioning of the state will determine which strategy should best be employed. The strategy chosen will largely determine how the budget is allocated.

REFERENCES

McDANIEL, JR., CARL, *Marketing: An Integrated Approach,* (New York, Harper & Row, 1979), pp. 377–79.

O'DRISCOLL, TIMOTHY J., "The Impact and Importance of Travel Marketing," in *Testing the Effectiveness of Promotional Campaigns in International Travel Marketing* (World Tourism Organization, 1975).

SCHULBERG, ROBERT, "The ARMS II Study and Its Significance for Travel Researchers & Marketers," in *The 80's: Its Impact on Travel and Tourism Marketing* (The Travel Research Association, Eighth Annual Conference Proceedings, June 1977), p. 167.

WILLIAMS, DONALD F., "Appropriating Advertising Allocations for Print Media Promoting the Small to Medium Sized Travel Agency" (Ph.D. dissertation, University of Northern Colorado, 1975).

16

TOURISM DISTRIBUTION CHANNELS:
Getting the Message to the Market

The final link in *The Tourism System* involves getting the message to the market. This is accomplished through the distribution system, which is the subject of this chapter.

The purpose of the tourism channel of distribution is actually twofold: To get sufficient information to the right people at the right time and in the right place to allow a purchase decision to be made, and to provide a mechanism whereby the consumer can make and pay for the necessary purchase.

Distribution is described as an integral part of the marketing mix. As such, it must fit in with the overall marketing effort. The different types of distribution channels are discussed, and guidelines are given to assist in the degree of vertical integration appropriate within the channel for tourism products.

The roles of the wholesaler and retailer within the channel are described in depth. The characteristics of both types of business are outlined and so are their functions.

The chapter concludes with a view toward the future. An ongoing CAB marketing case is summarized, and the implications to distribution of changing consumer markets and advances in electronic information systems are pointed out.

INTRODUCTION

The purpose of distribution is to establish a link between supply and demand, producer and consumer. It is the system of distribution that makes the product available. In the case of tourism, the task is somewhat different than it is in traditional manufacturing systems. Unlike manufacturing products the tourism "product" cannot be packaged and shipped to the consumer, nor can it be held in inventory. While eliminating the functions and problems of transportation and warehousing, additional pressures are felt. The hotel room, airline seat, or lift ticket must be sold each and every day, flight, or trip. The sale lost now is lost forever. More than in other industries, sales intermediaries—individuals or businesses that operate between the producer and consumer—are the rule rather than the exception. A major task of the intermediaries is the "packaging" of a number of complementary travel products to achieve a vacation experience for the consumer. A retail travel agent may book an airline seat, a hotel room, sightseeing excursions, and a rented car and offer this vacation to the tourist. A tour operator may assemble the above components into a tour to be promoted in a brochure and sold through retail travel agents. The system thus aims to get the necessary information to the consumer to make a sale and allow for the sale to be made and confirmed.

Distribution Channel

McIntosh defines the tourism channel of distribution as "an operating structure, system or linkages of various combinations of travel organizations through which a producer of travel products describes and confirms travel arrangements to the buyer."[1] This implies a twofold purpose—ensuring that potential travelers can obtain the information they need to make a vacation or trip choice and, having made that choice, that they can make the necessary reservations. Distribution may be direct or indirect. Direct distribution occurs when the producer sells directly to the consumer; indirect distribution when the sale to the consumer is made through an intermediary. This is diagrammed in Figure 16.1.

Intermediaries

WHOLESALERS. A tour wholesaler is a "business entity which consolidates the services of airlines or other transportation carriers and ground service suppliers into a tour which is sold through a sales channel to the public."[2] The term "wholesaler" is often used to describe a tour operator who strictly handles the operation of a tour. The wholesaler, on the other

---

[1]Robert W. McIntosh, *Definitions*, unpublished, 1979.

[2]*Tour Wholesaler Industry Study*, Touche Ross & Co., 1976, p. 68.

FIGURE 16.1   Tourism Distribution System

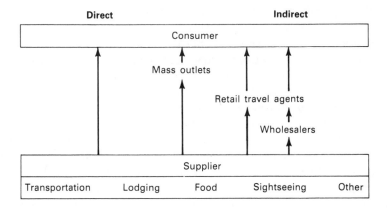

Adapted from: Salah Wahab, L. J. Crampon, and L. M. Rothfield, *Tourism Marketing* (London, Tourism International Press, 1976), p. 101.

hand, is involved with planning, preparing, marketing, reserving, and possibly operating. The wholesaler does not sell directly to the public but through such outlets as retail travel agents or airline sales offices.

RETAIL TRAVEL AGENTS.   Retail travel agents are the businesses or people who handle the actual sale of tours, air tickets, and other travel services to the consumer. There are currently approximately 20,000 retail travel agencies in the United States alone, over 35,000 worldwide. The retail agent is compensated by the supplier or wholesaler for sales made. The consumer pays no fee for the services of the agent. Although there is some talk that the retailer will eventually charge a fee to the traveler for the advice and assistance given, it will be many years, if ever, before this happens on a regular basis. The value of a retail agent to the traveler is that the agent as an impartial and independent businessperson can recommend the best offering for the traveler. For suppliers and wholesalers, the retailer represents an outlet for their products or offerings. It would be expensive, if not impossible, to establish a company system of distribution nationwide.

MASS OUTLETS.   In North America, travel is not yet sold through supermarkets and television/computer systems. There is some use of mass outlets such as lottery kiosks, supermarkets, and trade union offices in West Germany. Technology is such that systems to allow travelers to make a travel purchase in their own home through a television or computer are available and their use will grow.

MARKETING MIX—DISTRIBUTION

It should be recalled that the system of distribution is part of the marketing mix. Any decision regarding the type of distribution system chosen must be made in light of the fact that distribution is an integrated part of the overall marketing effort. Once marketing objectives and appropriate targets have been established, an appropriate marketing mix is determined. The marketing mix chosen is one that will reach the specified target segments and fulfill its stated objectives. The system of distribution chosen will affect parts of the marketing mix. The product offered may be modified. If airline seats are distributed through a tour operator, the schedules and perhaps even the seating configuration may have to be adapted to meet the needs of the intermediary.

The promotion strategy may also change. Because a retail travel agent carries no inventory, there is little or no incentive for the agent to promote a specific destination. The burden will fall to the supplier. A wholesaler, however, does carry an inventory of airline seats and hotel beds. The wholesaler thus has an investment (in terms of reservations) in the destination and will share in promoting the destination in order to sell tours to make a profit. For the supplier, the promotional burden is shared. Joint or cooperative advertising may be appropriate.

The pricing policy of a supplier will also change depending upon the decision to distribute directly or indirectly. When a tour wholesaler buys in bulk—such as 100 rooms per night for three months—a lower rate per room will be demanded and received.

CHANNEL CLASSIFICATION

Distribution channels can be classified in terms of control into four types:

Consensus channels

Vertically integrated channels commanded by intermediaries/retail travel
   agents

Vertically integrated channels commanded by producers/tour operators

Vertically coordinated channels led by producers/tour operators

Consensus Channels

In a consensus channel, no one part of the channel exercises control over the system. The many participants in the system work together because they see it in their mutual interest to do so. Distribution channels in North America and the United Kingdom tend to be of this type.

Vertically Integrated Channels

Vertically integrated channels are those in which the functions of production and retail distribution are owned and/or commanded by a single enterprise. Because tour operators have historically emerged from the retail travel agency business, vertically integrated channels commanded by retail travel agents are commonly found in the United Kingdom (Thomas Cook), West Germany (Deutsches Reiseburo), and North America (American Express).

A tour operator may exert control over the entire channel activity through retail outlet ownership and organization of the channel. This system is commonly found in West Germany where tour wholesalers control not only their own chain of retail outlets, which deal exclusively with the products of the one wholesaler, but also their own system of direct mail distribution.

Vertically Coordinated Channels

A vertically coordinated channel led by tour operators is one in which the tour operator's power of control over the channel comes from contractual or financial commitments with retail travel agents. Franchising is an obvious example of such a system. In West Germany, franchising is a large part of travel distribution. The franchisor of a particular company agrees to retail only through certain retail outlets and to promote no other methods of distribution. The retail franchisee benefits from the marketing activities of the franchisor.

Degree of Vertical Integration

Within the constraints of the legal environment each entity within the channel of distribution wants potential tourists to get maximum exposure to information (such information may be written messages and/or personal sales messages) so buying decisions can be made and so reservations and payments can be made to complete the purchase. The more control a supplier or intermediary has over distribution of the product (vertical integration) the easier it is to ensure that information on the product will be available and that reservations and payments will be easily made. The task is to derive a system that is the most effective. Several factors must be considered.

MARKET COVERAGE. If a tour wholesaler or supplier shuns the existing retail channel system, an alternative will have to be developed. It appears that the existing network of retail travel agents offers a substantial network capable of effectively reaching the marketplace.

COST. The cost of setting up one's own distribution channel is essentially fixed. Salaries must be paid and offices must be maintained irrespective of the sales volume generated. Although a sales staff may, to some extent, be paid on commission, the cost of an individual distribution effort is a fixed cost. Working through intermediaries involves a variable cost. A payment or commission is made only after a sale has been made. Overhead is thus reduced.

IMAGE. The choice of distribution channel must be consistent with the image that the supplier is seeking for the travel product. The marketing of a quality product or destination to an up-scale segment of the market must be made through quality intermediaries.

MOTIVATION. Each entity within the channel is looking for different things to satisfy its own needs and wants. This is outlined in Figure 16.2. The client is seeking a variety of products from which to choose in a convenient way in order to have a satisfying vacation experience. The retailer also wants a constant variety of products to offer to clients, but a variety that will produce a high margin of profit. The wholesaler seeks high volume and high margins but is concerned about developing products that will motivate retailers as well as offer the wholesaler little risk. The producer wishes to minimize distribution costs while encouraging maximum atten-

FIGURE 16.2 Wants and Needs in the Channel

Tourism Producer	Wholesaler
Sales volume	Sales volume
Loyal repeat business	High margins
High return on investment	Producer reliability
Low-cost channels of distribution	Low risk, little novelty
Maximum channel attention to his or her products	Products that motivate retailers

Retailer	Client
Sales volume	Anticipation-creating stimulus
High margins	Product knowledge
Image	Product variety
Regular innovation in products	New products
Good producer service	Help in evaluating product alternatives and coming to a decision
Maximum range of products for his or her attention	Minimum waste of time (including moving from counter to counter or returning to the point of sale)
	Minimum form filling
	Competent staff
	Pleasant service
	Individual identification

SOURCE: Salah Wahab, L. J. Crampon, and L. M. Rothfield, *Tourism Marketing* (London, Tourism International Press, 1976), p. 102.

tion to particular products to produce high volumes of traffic that will become repeat business. The more integration within the channel the more employees will be motivated to sell particular products at the expense of others.

In the absence of direct ownership, suppliers seek to increase the motivation of intermediaries by offering larger commissions for volume business, familiarization trips to increase product knowledge, and different types of sales support ranging from toll-free numbers to adequate amounts of literature.

Strategies

Two of the factors (market coverage and cost) would suggest the use of intermediaries, but two (image and motivation) would argue for a vertically integrated system. The strategy chosen will be one of intensive distribution, exclusive distribution, or selective distribution.

An intensive distribution strategy involves maximizing the exposure of the travel product by distributing through all available intermediaries. Exclusive distribution occurs when a supplier or wholesaler limits the channels and outlets for the products. The producer attempts to have intermediaries sell only specific products and not those of the competition. This can be done through franchising or ownership. In selective distribution a strategy between intensive and exclusive distribution is pursued. More than one but less than all available outlets are used.

PRODUCT CHARACTERISTICS. The characteristics of the product can suggest the appropriate distribution strategy. Selective or exclusive distribution is favored for products that have a high unit price, that are purchased infrequently, and that have a price that is not subject to price cutting. When the customer perceives the product as being distinctive and when personal selling is involved, selective or exclusive distribution is appropriate.

ECONOMIC CONCENTRATION. A further consideration in the strategy chosen is related to the power exerted within the channel. The amount of channel power depends upon the degree of concentration. The fewer the tour wholesalers a destination works through, the greater the power those few wholesalers have over the destination and the more demands they can make on that destination. Also, the more wholesalers that are used, the higher will be the cost of selling to and servicing them.

West Germany is an example of a country in which travel is exclusively distributed through vertically integrated channels, but in the United Kingdom and North America there has been a movement away from intensive distribution to selective distribution. Suppliers seek sales volume. For tour wholesalers volume is even more critical. Although this should imply a policy of intensive distribution, many suppliers now realize that, given the kind of product being sold and notwithstanding the risk involved in dealing with a smaller number of intermediaries, the cost involved in dealing with all intermediaries is too great. It is a truism that a small percentage of intermediaries produces most of the business for any one supplier. By concentrating on cultivating those in the channel that produce most of the sales, an effective system of distribution can be established.

TOUR WHOLESALER

Introduction

Although tour wholesaling began in the mid-nineteenth century it was not until the 1960s that the packaging of tours increased dramatically. The increase came about due to the development of larger aircraft capable of flying greater distances. Increased capacity led to lower prices by the airlines that stimulated demand for low-cost vacations. Although it is true that demand stimulates supply, it is also possible for supply to stimulate demand. To meet this demand, tour wholesalers came into the marketplace to put together low-cost vacation packages.

Scope

The function of a tour wholesaler is to combine both transportation and ground services into a tour to be sold through a sales channel to the public.

This function is handled primarily by independent tour wholesalers who make up about three-quarters of all wholesalers. Also, tour wholesaling is performed by several other types of companies. Retail travel agents may prepare individual and group tours for retail through their own business. Many airlines have wholesaling divisions that put together tours. This movement has been slow because of legal restrictions and the possibility of a negative reaction from the travel trade that might view an airline's entry into the tour business as competition. Companies specializing in incentive travel, steamship companies, travel clubs, and various nonprofit organizations also organize tours.

Tour wholesalers may specialize their operation by market, destination, or transportation used. A wholesaler may decide to cater to a specific segment of the market (ethnic or sporting groups, for example) or may sell to the mass market promoting to popular destinations. Other wholesalers will specialize in developing tours to specific regions of the world. Wholesalers may also decide to specialize in one type of transportation. Well over 90 percent of the tours marketed by independent tour wholesalers involve air travel.

The independent tour wholesaling business is very concentrated, with a small number of companies accounting for a large percentage of total revenue generated and passengers carried.

Three types of tours tend to be offered:

Escorted tours—A type of organized tour that includes the services of a tour escort who accompanies an individual or group throughout the tour

Hosted tours—A type of organized tour that includes the services of a tour host who meets an individual or group at each destination to make local arrangements, but does not accompany the tour

Package tours—A type of organized tour, individual or group, that includes airfare and some ground arrangements, but does not necessarily include the services of anyone meeting the individual or group at the destination

Economics

The tour wholesaling industry is characterized by relative ease of entry, high velocity of cash flow, low return on sales, and the potential for high return on equity invested.

EASE OF ENTRY. Although independent tour wholesalers are not licensed by any governmental agencies their activities are constrained by various regulations. To be considered a tour a vacation offering must meet established guidelines. It must be of a certain minimum duration and priced at a certain minimum, and it may have to include a minimum number of travelers. To be commissionable to travel agents the air transportation element must conform to standards of the Air Traffic Conference or the International Air Traffic Association for a domestic or international air tour, respectively. To sell a charter the tour wholesaler must meet regulations on pricing, advertising, and bonding. In general, however, it is relatively easy to become a tour wholesaler.

CASH FLOW. Cash flow is particularly crucial to a tour wholesaler. The wholesaler contracts for bulk quantities of transportation and ground services. Deposits have to be made for these services. By contracting in bulk for ground services a discount on the regular rate is given. A wholesaler may, for example, contract for 200 rooms in a hotel every night for three months. The ground portion of a tour, which comprises about half the cost of an average tour, is then marked up by the wholesaler to show a profit, then combined with the transportation segment of the tour to arrive at a selling price. The transportation segment of the tour cannot be marked up. All commissions from the transportation segment of the tour usually flow directly to the retailer. Cash flow or float is generated because both a deposit and final payment for the tour are received prior to the departure of the tourist while the suppliers are not paid until after they have serviced the tour. The resultant cash flow can be used to pay the operating expenses of the business. The difficulty arises when the float from one tour is used to finance the production of another. If demand slows, then even a large operation, having little in the way of assets to shield it, can have a cash loss.

RETURN ON SALES. The average return on sales for an independent tour wholesaler is approximately 3 percent. Sales volume is the key to profitability for the wholesaler. Usually just under half of total tour revenue is generated from the transportation part of the tour, and over 90 percent of that, on an industrywide basis, goes to the airlines. The wholesaler does not receive any of the airfare revenue. It passes directly to the airline. Just over half of the cost of an average tour is comprised of revenue from ground services, with hotel and meals accounting for almost 60 percent of it. The wholesaler is left with approximately 50 percent of total revenue from which to pay costs.

Costs are either direct or indirect. Direct costs represent about 85 percent of total costs and consist of payments made directly to suppliers of tour services as well as to retail travel agent commissions. The retailer receives a commission directly from both the airline for selling the transportation part of an air tour and from the wholesaler for selling the ground part of the tour.

Indirect costs are all operating costs that do not involve direct payments to suppliers or retail commissions. About half of all in direct costs are accounted for by employee wages. The major functional areas of indirect costs are:

Reservations, record keeping, and accounting	25%
Tour preparation	22%
Literature production and printing	15%
Promotion	12%

The economics of a tour is illustrated in Figure 16.3. Although these figures may not reflect the exact pricing structure of any one tour, they are indicative of an industry average.

Because of the importance on sales volume, a relatively small change in the number of tours sold can mean the difference between a large profit and a large loss. The gross profit is, on the average, 10 percent of the total revenue generated. From this must be paid the fixed or indirect costs of running the operation. Thus, each 1,000-dollar tour contributes 100 dollars toward payment of the indirect costs. Once these costs have been paid, the contribution goes toward generating net profit.

RETURN ON EQUITY. Because the capital requirements for entering the business are so low, the opportunity is available for a substantial return

FIGURE 16.3   Economics of a Tour

	Revenue	minus	Direct Costs	equals	Gross Profit
Transportation					
Air	$ 480		$480		
Ground					
Hotels and meals	$ 305		$222		
Sightseeing	65		60		
Car rentals	35		30		
Travel agent commission	78		78		
Miscellaneous	37		30		
Selling price	$1000		$900		$100
Indirect Costs					
Salaries and wages			$35		
Promotion			14		
Telephone and telegraph			8		
Rent			4		
Miscellaneous			9		
Total			$ 70		
Net profit					$30

on equity. The opportunity for a high return on equity (net profit divided by owner's equity) comes about because the equity invested is small, not because the net profit is high.

Business Functions

A single tour program consists of three parts (see Figure 16.4):

Tour preparation
Tour marketing
Tour administration

TOUR PREPARATION. The preparation of a tour begins with market research. By using the results of research organizations, by analyzing tourist movements, and by surveying retailers and past and potential tourists the wholesaler gets an indication as to which tours will sell. This information is combined with past operating results as to which tours have sold well and have made a profit. The policies and tour destinations of competitors are also considered.

When preparing the development of a new destination it is likely that

FIGURE 16.4 The Tour Wholesaler Operating Cycle* Single Season Tour Program

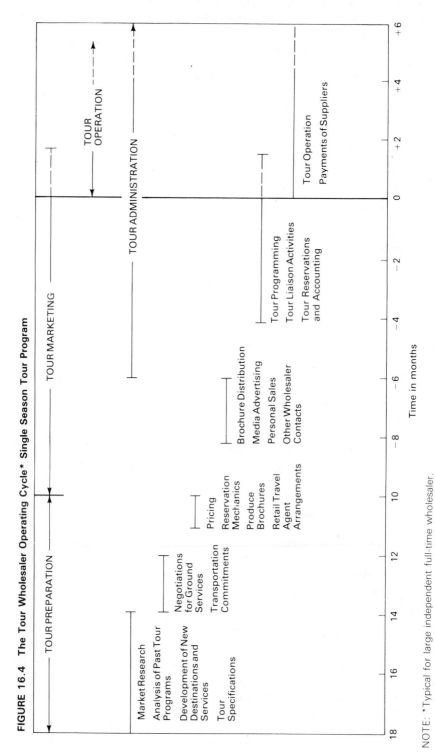

NOTE: *Typical for large independent full-time wholesaler.

SOURCE: *Tour Wholesaler Industry Study,* Touche Ross & Co., 1976, p. 48.

the wholesaler will participate in a familiarization visit to determine the tour potential, to evaluate ground services, and to solicit government support for tour business.

At this point, detailed tour specifications are prepared on such items as departure dates, length of the tour, and types of transportation and ground services that will be used. These activities may take place fourteen to eighteen months before the tour is scheduled to take place.

Usually from twelve to fourteen months prior to the tour, ground services are negotiated and often signed, and transportation commitments are made. At this point the tour program can be finalized. The tour price is reached by taking the negotiated cost figures and adding on the ground service markup, in light of the expected number of travelers, sufficient to cover overhead and profit.

A checklist for pricing a tour is illustrated in Figure 16.5. It should be noted that tour costs (cost to the wholesaler) are either fixed or variable. A cost is fixed if it is paid irrespective of the number of passengers taking the tour. If a bus is chartered or a tour director engaged, the cost to the wholesaler is the same whether five or twenty-five people take the tour. A variable cost is one charged on the basis of the number of passengers on the tour. Airfare (unless for a charter flight), hotel rooms, or admissions are examples of variable costs.

The three columns in Figure 16.5 indicate cost computations for three different group sizes. The first would be the minimum size necessary. This would be based upon the price given the wholesalers by suppliers who expect a certain minimum number of people. In some cases the type of airfare used may necessitate a minimum number of people. The third column might contain costs based upon the maximum number of people the wholesaler could handle while the middle column would be an estimate of the likely number of tour participants.

The markup may be expressed as either a percentage of net costs or as a dollar figure. It should be realistic yet also reflect the time and effort involved in organizing the tour. Airfare is added to total costs and markup to arrive at the selling price to the retailer. (Earlier in the section dealing with variable costs the basis for the airfare, but not the amount of airfare, was noted. It was mentioned that airfares are not discounted.) The selling price to the public will be determined by adding in the amount of commission to be paid the retailer.

The mechanics of handling reservations and payment are made and brochure production begun. This expensive function is often shared by the transportation company involved in the tour. At this point, appropriate commission rates and volume incentives are also negotiated with retail travel agents.

At this point, there are typically ten months left before the tour takes place.

FIGURE 16.5 Price Structure Sheet

Tour _____   Tour Dates _____

Compiled _____   Cancellation Date _____

Revised _____   Gateway _____

Variable Costs (per person)

1. Air Fare Basis ...... _____	7. State/VAT taxes .... _____	13. Package .... _____
2. Surcharges .... _____	8. Service Charges .... _____	based on ( )
3. Airport Taxes ..... _____	9. Meals .... _____	14. Insurance .... _____
4. Transfers .... _____	10. Meal Taxes & Tips .. _____	15. Publications/
5. Baggage Tips ...... _____	11. Sightseeing .... _____	Postage ...... _____
6. Hotel Rooms ...... _____	12 Admissions .... _____	16. Miscellaneous ..... _____

Single Room Supplement _____   Total .... _____

Fixed Costs (Tour Director)   Include only costs not complimented

1. Transportation ..... _____	7. Sightseeing/ ...... _____	12. Passports/Visas .... _____
(home/gateway/home	Admissions	13. Vaccinations ...... _____
2. Transportation ..... _____	8. Baggage Tips ..... _____	14. Currency Conversion _____
(on tour)	9. Insurance .... _____	15. Miscellaneous ..... _____
3. Airport Taxes ...... _____	10. Meals/Hotels ...... _____	16. Salary .... _____
4. Hotel Rooms ...... _____	(Day before/	(days @)
5. Meals, Taxes, Tips .. _____	Day after tour)	
6. Transfers .... _____	11. Travelers Checks ... _____	Total .... _____

Fixed Costs (Group)

1. Chartered Vehicles .. _____	7. Programs .... _____	13. Administrative ..... _____
2. Tolls/Ferries .... _____	8. Speaker Fee .... _____	14. Miscellaneous ..... _____
3. Sightseeing .... _____	9. Driver Tips .... _____	15. Orientation .... _____
4. Admissions ...... _____	10. Brochures .... _____	16. Fund Raising ...... _____
5. Local Guides ...... _____	11. Promotion .... _____	
6. Transfers .... _____	12. Communications ... _____	Total .... _____

Grand Total of all Fixed Costs

Computations Group Size .... _____   _____   _____

Land Costs

A. Total Variable Costs .... _____   _____   _____

B. Grand Total of Fixed Costs
(Divided by Size of Group) .. _____   _____   _____

C. Sum of A and B .... _____   _____   _____

D. Dollar Markup (%) .... _____   _____   _____

E. Air Fare .... _____   _____   _____

F. Sum of C, D, and E .... _____   _____   _____

Selling Price .... _____   _____   _____

Minimum number of paying pas-   Markup on Land (D) _____
sengers. _____   Air Commission _____
Maximum number of paying pas-   Gross Net _____
sengers. _____   (Per Person)

SOURCE: Rosa Mae Howe, "Analyzing The Trip: Checklist of Steps," The 1980 Travel Agency Guide to Business and Group Travel, *Travel Weekly*, April 1980, p. 110.

412

TOUR MARKETING. The marketing of a tour is the aspect most crucial to its success. The marketing program will depend upon the size of the wholesaler and the market segments being targeted. All marketing programs, however, involve brochure distribution, media advertising, personal selling, and contact with other wholesalers.

Brochures are usually distributed to all retail outlets. Emphasis may, however, be given to retailers who have worked with the wholesaler before or whose customers have exhibited the characteristics of the target market. Tours are often consolidated into brochures of the airline providing transportation and distributed by the airline. The reverse is also true.

Media advertising consists of advertising to the trade as well as to potential tourists. The messages are, of necessity, different. Advertisements in trade publications describe the tour and give retailers information on how to book the tour. A coupon is often included to allow retailers to order tour brochures, posters, and other sales aids. Consumer advertising tends to be more glamorous and oriented toward creating interest in the tour. By completing a coupon, consumers may send for a tour brochure with the suggestion to book the tour through a retail travel agent.

Wholesalers will also employ sales representatives who concentrate on personally selling the wholesaler's offerings to those retailers regarded as the best prospects for selling the tours.

Because of the high cost of distribution, tour wholesalers from one part of the country may use wholesalers from another part of the country to distribute their tours in that region for a fee.

Marketing may begin up to ten months prior to departure and continue until a few days beforehand. Reservations, deposits, and payments are requested from one to two months in advance of the departure. If insufficient advance bookings are made, tours may be consolidated or promotion increased.

TOUR ADMINISTRATION. The administration of a tour tends to begin six months prior to the tour departure. Detailed schedules or worksheets are prepared describing the tour program, and a reservation system sufficient to detail the documentation and payment status of each passenger is set up. Liaison procedures have to be established between the reservation system and the ground services providers at each destination for each trip.

Reservations are usually received by telephone from different retail outlets. They must be confirmed, recorded, and filed. Deposits and payments are processed and documentation sent to the retailer for distribution to the traveler. Upon completion of the tour the suppliers are paid.

The tour operation part of the administration of the tour may be handled by the tour wholesaler or by ground service operators at the many destinations.

Operating Cycle

The tour wholesaling business is a seasonal one. At any one time the staff may be preparing the following year's program while marketing and operating the existing year's offering. The operating cycle of a wholesaler is illustrated in Figure 16.6.

RETAIL TRAVEL AGENTS[3]

Introduction

Thomas Cook is credited with developing the concept of a travel agent in 1841 when he chartered a train to carry people from Leicester to Loughborough, a distance of twenty-two miles, to attend a temperance convention. In the United States in the early 1900s rail travel was the primary mode of transportation for the business traveler. Little pleasure travel existed. The travel agent of the day was the hotel porter, who would make reservations for the businessman staying at the hotel. The porter received a commission from the railroad and would add a delivery charge for going to the railroad station to purchase the ticket. The airlines, which first purchased planes with seats for passengers in the late 1920s, saw the railroads as their major competitor for the business market. (The pleasure market would not become significant for another ten years.) The airlines approached the hotel porters, equipped them with ticket stock, and offered a 5 percent commission for making the sale. Little expertise was required as most carriers had only one route and the tickets already contained information about fare origin and destination of the flight. The feeling of the carriers was that the porters were providing a ticketing service for business that was already there rather than creating new business. Thus, from the beginning hotel porters and then travel agents were seen as distributors of tickets and entitled to a small commission.

As carriers opened their own offices in hotels that provided large enough traffic volume to justify the expense, porters were forced out of business. Also, the carriers restricted the new breed of travel agent from opening an office where it would compete with the airline sales office.

After World War II two trends resulted in the growth of travel agent business. These were the growth in personal or pleasure travel and the growth in international travel. The airlines continued to exert considerable influence over the birth of an agency. Prior to 1959, when the so-called need clause was abolished by the Civil Aeronautics Board, a travel agency could be opened only if it was sponsored by an airline and its opening approved by two-thirds of the carriers represented. The sponsoring airline

---

[3]Since 1970 *Travel Weekly* has sponsored a biannual survey, conduced by Louis Harris & Associates, of travel agency operations. This section is largely taken from the results of those studies.

FIGURE 16.6 Independent Tour Wholesaler Two-Year Operating Cycle

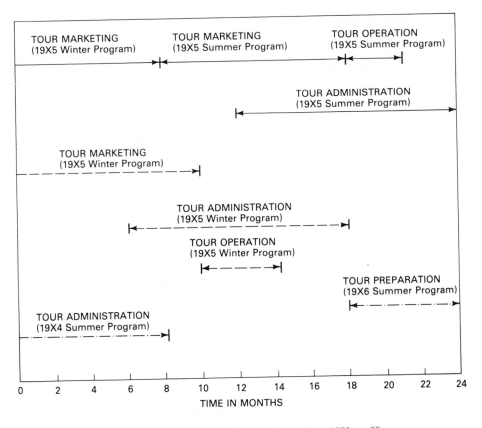

SOURCE: *Tour Wholesaler Industry Study*, Touche Ross & Co., 1976, p. 55.

was responsible for checking that the agency was sound from a financial viewpoint, had an acceptable location, and had a staff with sufficient experience. It is now necessary for the agency to be appointed by the appropriate conference to sell tickets and receive commissions. Virtually all agencies have appointments by the Air Traffic Conference and the International Air Transport Association to sell domestic and international air tickets. About two-thirds of all agencies have the necessary appointments from the International Passenger Ship Association and just over half from the Pacific Cruise Conference to sell cruises. These percentages have declined over the years. In 1971, for example, 90 percent of all agencies had the equivalent of IPSA appointments. The percentage of agencies holding Amtrak appointments has also decreased from 64 percent in 1970 to 51 percent in 1981. It should be noted, however, that the number of agencies in that period increased by almost 200 percent.

Organization

Almost two-thirds of all agencies are organized as incorporated businesses. One in five is a sole proprietorship, and approximately 10 percent are partnerships or operate as branch offices. Virtually no agencies are operated as franchises. However over one-third of all agencies are affiliated with a travel agency cooperative or similar group. This number has increased dramatically in recent years and the trend seems likely to continue.

Although six out of ten agencies are located at the "traditional" ground floor street-level location, almost one in six is at the second floor or higher in a building, and approximately 10 percent are located either on the ground floor in a lobby or in a shopping mall or arcade.

Size and Volume

The number of retail travel agencies has grown an average of 10 percent annually since 1970. The resulting fivefold increase in dollar volume places travel agents within the top ten retail segments of the country. Agencies tend to be small businesses in terms of employees. The average agency employs about seven people, a number that has remained approximately the same over the past ten years.

The overall geographic concentration of agencies has not changed very much. The south and west have grown a little in both numbers and share of the market. Eastern agencies account for less than one-third of all dollar volume, a share that has been declining since 1970. There has also been a slow erosion of the share of the market from center city locations in favor of the suburbs.

The most significant trend, however, has been in the distribution of travel agency sales by size of agency. Those agencies producing less than $1 million in bookings have shown a consistent decline in market share while those producing more than $1 million in bookings have shown a corresponding increase. The small agency is declining rapidly. The larger the agency the more productive the employees. The sales volume per employee increases as the size of the agency increases.

A 1978 survey by Touche Ross & Co. indicated that although certain product lines were profitable for retailers, others resulted in a loss.[4] When product line profitability is considered as a percentage of travel agency revenue (commissions), several interesting facts emerge. Domestic point-to-point air travel incurred an estimated 31 percent loss, and both domestic promotional fares and domestic air tours resulted in profits. All international air travel was profitable for the agency. Besides scheduled air travel, charters broke even and hotels represented a loss for agencies. All other product line studies produced a profit.

---

[4]This study was extensively reported in *Travel Weekly*, June 5, 8, 12, 15, 19, 1978 editions.

Type of Business

Over three-quarters of the U.S. travel agents handle a retail business only. The percentage of agents who handled both retail and wholesale business had increased dramatically in the early seventies, had remained constant during the middle part of the decade, then tumbled as the eighties approached. More than two-thirds of the travel agency volume comes from domestic rather than international volume. Domestic volume has increased over the decade when it represented just over half of total business volume. This has been largely due to the increase in both commercial accounts and business travel bookings since 1970. Commercial accounts are more important to the larger agencies and those located in the central city district.

The vast majority of sales volume comes from individuals or families, not to groups. This segment of the market prefers an independent itinerary. Less than one-third of them utilize package tours, a ratio that has not increased much over recent years. Packages are purchased more by international travelers, but even here by only slightly over half of all such customers. Larger agencies account for more than a proportionate share of group business, made up of equal amounts of special interest and business meetings and conventions and a smaller percentage of incentive travel.

The most common type of travel arrangement is air transportation, both domestic and international. Just under two-thirds of total dollar volume comes from the sale of air travel, a figure that has increased very slightly since 1970. The one area that has increased in popularity is that of air/sea packages. The combination of air transportation and a cruise accounts for 20 percent of total dollar volume, more than double the volume in 1970.

Automation

The end of the 1970s was marked by a growing increase in the number of retail agencies that automated. By the early 1980s four out of five agencies were able to offer computerized booking and other services to their clients. Those agencies that are computerized handle proportionately more volume than those that are not. Slightly more domestic and air travel is handled by automated agencies. As might be expected, a greater proportion of automated agencies handle corporate accounts, and the number of individual accounts handled is, on average, over three times as many as with nonautomated ones. The biggest differentiating factor, however, is size. The smaller agencies are less likely to be automated. Additionally, a larger proportion of agencies in the west and midwest are automated compared to those in the south and east.

It appears likely that automation will continue. For those agencies that automate report not only gross volume increases as a result but also individual significant employee productivity gains.

Corporate Travel

The increase in the importance of corporate accounts to retail travel agencies was brought about by a number of factors. First, deregulation resulted in the growth of inplants—branch offices or additional authorized agency locations of approved agents located at the firm's place of business—as well as more liberal commission policies. Second, as computerization added to the agent's capacity the agents sought to increase corporate accounts to make full use of their capacity. Last, the combination of deregulation and an increase in agency computerization produced a situation in which airfares were constantly changing and agents were seen as being able to provide the kind of dependable service required.

Although the major services to corporate accounts are the planning and booking of business trips, ticketing, and the provision of itineraries, approximately three-quarters of the agencies that handle corporate accounts also offer billing and accounting services. Over two-thirds of the agencies provide maps and brochures, while slightly less than that plan group travel for meetings and conferences or offer arrangements for credit. Half of the agencies offer special services, such as the provision of limousine service to the airport.

Corporate business tends to come as the result of a recommendation of an individual client affiliated with the corporation. However, about two-thirds of the agencies indicate that they also make formal presentations in person to potential accounts. Slightly more than one-third of the agencies solicit corporate business by direct mail or over the telephone.

Vacation/Pleasure Travel

As noted earlier, the proportion of personal/pleasure travel compared to business travel booked by retail agents has declined over the past decade. The role of the agent in determining and influencing vacation plans seems to be increasing. The predominant feeling is that clients—just over 40 percent of them—usually have only a general idea as to where they want to go. They may have decided on a region of the world, but they need and seek guidance on which destination to visit. Over the past ten years the percentage of travelers who fall into this category has increased considerably. An almost equal but opposite movement has occurred in the percentage of clients who have a destination firmly in mind. Whereas a decade ago six out of every ten clients had a destination firmly fixed in their minds when coming to an agent, less than four out of ten presently fall into that category.

After choosing the destination, the client in fewer cases seeks the travel agent's advice and guidance with the choice of a carrier, though this is still done more than half the time. A large majority of clients seek agent advice and guidance in the selection of other parts of the vacation, from side trips, sightseeing, and car rental choices to the selection of basic tours, packages, and hotel. It appears that the retail travel agent has the ability to heavily influence the decision as to what vacation pieces are eventually chosen. The business traveler has an itinerary that is considerably more fixed than that of the pleasure traveler. However, well over one-third of the time on business trips, advice and guidance is sought from a retail travel agent on the choice of carrier, hotel, destination, itinerary, and car rental.

Customer Services

Most retail travel agents accept credit cards, although the percentage of clients who use credit cards to finance their trip is less than 50 percent, despite a large increase in this percentage in recent years. The ratio of agencies that check with their customers on the quality of service received on the trip has been increasing, although it is more commonly done for international clients rather than for domestic ones. Almost every agency offers advice on passports, visas, and shots, while an overwhelming majority of them advise on clothing, customs, currency, travel reading, and supply travel insurance. A relatively small number of agencies offer guides on shopping and eating or, for businesses, on secretarial service at the destination.

Channel Relationships

A large majority of agents consider familiarization trips as being very important factors in influencing their recommendations of a particular destination to a client. A majority of agents are also concerned with the attractiveness of the price.

In dealing with tour wholesalers, the critical factor is the quality of service received—the dependability, promptness, and efficiency. This is far more important to agents than even prices and customer feedback. Client feedback, however, is important to agents in their selection of package tours for clients. Most agents prefer certain packages over others. The major factor in their selection of a particular package is the reliability and efficiency of the tour operator.

Channel Power

As we noted earlier, the alliance among those in the channel of distribution is often an uneasy one. The motivations of the different distribution "partners" are different. Although people at a destination seek tourists, they do not pay a commission to those who produce them. Wholesalers contract for inventory in destinations that they believe will sell, and because of this commitment they actively push the sale of the destination through retail outlets. Retailers carry no inventory and are interested in selling a product that will result in satisfied clients (unhappy clients will probably blame the retailer) while ensuring sufficiently high commission payments.

Who has the power in such a system? Many have thought that control is exerted by the tour wholesalers who can elect whether or not to put a destination on the tourist map.

A tour wholesaler may have the power in the early stages of destination development. At this point, destinations and other suppliers may be more willing to make concessions to a wholesaler who will take an active role in marketing a new destination to a mass market. Once the destination gains in popularity, however, wholesalers' influence is reduced and they may even be excluded from the market. Such was the case in London when, with the assistance of tour wholesalers, London became an attractive destination for U.S. travelers. As hotel space became tighter, the balance of power moved to the hotel companies. Tour wholesalers who had helped promote the demand were faced with increased room rates, demands for prepayments, and in some cases, cancellations. The balance of power is very much a balance of supply and demand.

FUTURE

As the shape of tourism changes, the system of distribution is expected to change. Some changes will occur as tourism continues to develop from a luxury item to a mass-market product. Other changes will be forced upon the distribution system by external forces such as governmental agencies.

CAB Marketing Case

In order to sell airline tickets as an agent of a domestic or international carrier that is a member of the respective conferences, an agency must be accredited by a conference and appointed by the member carriers. The intercarrier agreements have been granted immunity from the antitrust laws.

In 1979 the Civil Aeronautics Board ordered an investigation to weigh the anticompetitive nature of the Air Traffic Conference and International Air Traffic Association travel agency programs against the benefits to the public. The impetus came from the 1978 Airline Deregulation Act that prevented the board from approving immunity from antitrust unless it could be shown that important public benefits were being provided by that immunity. The final decision has not yet been made by the CAB. However, the major recommendations of the CAB law judge are as follows:

The joint agency agreement should be kept with some modification and given antitrust immunity.

Agency exclusivity, which prevents conference carriers from appointing nonaccredited agencies, should be kept.

Marketing exclusivity, which prohibits carriers from paying commissions to nonagent distributors, should be dropped. (IATA has no such rule.)

JOINT AGENCY AGREEMENTS. The original purpose of the ATC and IATA travel agency programs was to protect the public from unprofessional abuses that had crept into the system. It was ruled that the existing system did not substantially reduce intercarrier competition. It was felt that individual agents were very competitive with each other since under another provision of the ruling price rebating on tickets would be allowed. (In reality, rebating is officially discouraged by the airlines.) It was also felt that the barriers to entry of the existing system were lower than if systems of entry were to be established by each individual carrier.

EXCLUSIVITY. Exclusivity has two aspects to it—agency and marketing. Agency exclusivity refers to the fact that carriers cannot appoint agencies to sell tickets for them unless they have been accredited by the respective conference. It was felt that this provision should be kept (though there are indications that it will eventually be changed). Much of air transportation involves the sale of a joint product to the public. A ticket may involve transportation on more than one carrier. Also, since a carrier may accept a ticket for transportation by and paid to another carrier there has to be some system for ensuring that each carrier receives the appropriate payment for the travel carried. Under the present system, carriers are assured that tickets have been sold and issued correctly, that monies are collected, and that they will receive their appropriate payment. The present accreditation system, it has been felt, is necessary to provide security to the carrier. Abolishing the system might mean that carriers will be reluctant to accept sales made by agents of another airline. If this were to happen, travel would be more complicated for the public.

Marketing exclusivity refers to the fact that ATC rules prohibit the payment of commission or sales remuneration to any person other than accredited agents. This provision was disapproved in large part because IATA has no such rule. This opens the way for marketing through nonagent ticket holders.

Changing Markets

As tourism shifts from a luxury item to a mass consumer product there are those who feel that suppliers will exert more control on distribution. Vertical integration, in which transportation and ground suppliers merge and try to control the entire distribution channel, is expected to increase. New selling methods, such as through mail order, department stores, and bookshops, are predicted.

Others feel that the retail agent will continue to be the primary distribution intermediary for future travel services. They cite three reasons for this:[5]

1. The industry is growing in terms of agencies and sales volume.
2. Agents will be difficult to replace as they account for a large percentage of bookings.
3. The system works, and it will be too expensive to replace agents with other methods.

There are some indications, however, that the cost of distributing through agents is approaching the point in which carriers are questioning its cost effectiveness. At present, the average commission rate paid to agents domestically is just under 10 percent, and it is approaching the point at which its cost effectiveness can be studied closely.

Electronic Information Systems

Present telecommunication methods are not advanced far enough in the United States to represent a threat to the distribution system. In other countries videotex systems that allow two-way communications on a television screen are in different stages of development. These systems, called Prestel in Great Britain, Antiope in France, and Telidon in Canada, offer exciting possibilities.

Prestel is the world's first electronic system to be offered on a national scale. It combines television with the telephone and allows a subscriber to call up required information on the telephone and have it displayed on the television screen. The beauty of the system is that information stored in the computer can be continuously updated and that the system is available twenty-four hours a day without busy signals to the subscriber. The updating allows suppliers to pass changes in prices and schedules along instantly. When a particular tour may not be sold out as the departure date approaches, reductions in price can be made and communicated to potential buyers at once.

[5]Mary J. Bitner and Bernard H. Booms, "Trends in Travel and Tourism Marketing: The Changing Structure of Distribution Channels," *Journal of Travel Research*, Spring 1982, pp. 39–44.

Such a system can also cost less for agents who are spending increasing time and money on telephone calls to suppliers. Videotex systems do not have busy signals.

The fear of agents is that such a system might bypass them altogether. Eventually, suppliers and wholesalers will be able to beam their messages directly to the consumer who will be able to make a choice, book a tour, and pay for it in his or her own home. It is unlikely, however, that such a system will soon displace retail agents. There are two reasons for this. First, the cost of such a system will mean that many will not be able to afford it. Much of the so-called mass market will only be able to access such information through an intermediary. Second, some time will pass before anything but the simplest vacations will be sold from a television set. Only if and when wholesalers establish a brand image reputation of quality such that travelers feel secure in buying a package from them will such sales be made.

REFERENCES

DAVIS, BOB, "How It All Began," in *Sales Management for Travel Agents* (Institute of Certified Travel Agents, 1974), pp. 1–3.

FRIEDHEIM, ERIC, "Who Dominates the Tour Trade?" *The Travel Agent*, September 3, 1979, p. 54

RUBIN, KAREN, "How's Business?" *The Travel Agent*, August 3, 1981, pp. 60–61.

RUBIN, KAREN, "How's Business?" *The Travel Agent*, September 6, 1982, pp. 22–23.

SCHMOLL, G. A., *Tourism Promotion* (London, Tourism International Press, 1977), p. 32.

SIMS, J. TAYLOR, J. ROBERT FOSTER, and ARCH G. WOODSIDE, *Marketing Channels: Systems and Strategies* (New York, Harper & Row, 1977), pp. 138–40.

Tour Wholesaler Industry Study (New York, Touche Ross & Co., 1976), pp. 6, 47.

YACOUMIS, JOHN, *Air Inclusive Tour Marketing: The Retail Distribution Channels in the U.K. and West Germany* (International Tourism Quarterly Special Report No. 2, November 1975), pp. 35–37, 43.

READINGS

The inclusion of this final reading is intended to give readers an idea of how the marketing process is actually operationalized.

An annual marketing report from the province of Ontario demonstrates how at the provincial level destinations use both direct and indirect methods of distribution to get their messages out.

Tourism Marketing Plan, 1982-83: Ontario—Yours to Discover

*Ontario Ministry of Tourism
and Recreation*

Objectives

The ministry's overall marketing objective is to maintain the upward trend of tourism in the province in terms of an increase in both expenditures and person-trips from markets exhibiting the highest growth potential.

Within this framework, the ministry will strive to stimulate and expand sales of Ontario tours, packages and facilities by the travel trade; to increase the use of Ontario convention and meeting facilities; to provide a counselling and information service second to none; and to stimulate more direct investment in both the existing plant and new areas of opportunity.

For 1982 we have developed a program that will expand on the recreational opportunities available in the province and re-emphasize the excitement of our ongoing campaign. Finely tuned and geared for response, the new program is designed to compete in today's aggressive market conditions.

Strategy

The Ministry's marketing objectives will be met within the context of the far-reaching "Ontario—yours to discover!" campaign which encompasses all aspects of the province's tourism marketing activity including advertising, sales promotion, merchandising, publicity, sales and counselling services.

THE ONTARIO MARKET

Broadcast

Four new television commercials will kick off the new campaign, highlighting a number of major attractions and featuring a variety of recreational activities. These are designed to reinforce the image of Ontario as a destination offering every member of the family a variety of things to do within an environment of fun and excitement.

Newspaper

Research confirms that Ontario's residents want detailed information to plan their vacations—suggested regional itineraries, sites and attractions, specifics and particulars. In 1982, newspaper will be used to satisfy this demand.

In May of this year, a forty-eight page full-colour roto supplement will be delivered to almost 3 million Ontario households. Patterned after its two successful precursors, this magazine will outline the highlights in each of the province's twelve travel regions, provide introductory information on a number of individual activities unique to Ontario, and indicate as well, the range of highly specific support publications available through our TOLL FREE telephone service or at Travel Information Centres. One week prior to its publication a hard hitting radio campaign will announce the imminent arrival of this very successful vacation guide to the consuming public. The same principle will be employed, and pattern repeated, in January of 1983 when the winter insert will be distributed, again preceded by a week-long radio blitz.

A series of 1,000 line spotcolour newspaper ads will be used year round to stimulate and sustain interest in in-province travel.

GO WILD! details particular features of outpost camps, rustic lodges, outfitters and wilderness retreats.

GREAT ESCAPES an invitation to unwind at Ontario's country inns and lakeside resorts.

LIVING LEGENDS chronicles the delights of Ontario's many historic sites, forts, stockades, pioneer villages and museums.

TONS OF FUN an outline of some of Ontario's more spectacular parks and playgrounds, and family amusement centres.

UP TOWN describes the cultural and recreational attractions and the cosmopolitan delights of our showcase urban scene—the city of Toronto.

REEL REWARDS   lures the sybaritic fisherman to a civilized approach to sports fishing.

GO WITH THE FLOW   suggests a number of regional tour itineraries in the Niagara region, ideal for day trips, weekends, or extended excursions.

CAPITAL STUFF   Parliament Hill, and the particular pleasures of our nation's heritage, in the nation's capital, Ottawa.

MAKE WAVES   the scenic splendours of Ontario's many boat tours, from the "Maid of the Mist" to the "Island Queen."

FRESH, DAILY   explains in detail the facilities and amenities which can be found at the province's many private campgrounds.

SHARE THE HARVEST   a seasonal reminder to tour the autumn countryside, savour the flavours of farm-fresh produce and catch the colour change.

WINTER DELIGHTS   a whole new season for fun in our cities, from harness-racing on ice, to ballet, opera, theatre, and show openings.

SNOW WONDER   ice fishing, ice-sailing, snowmobiling, and a number of recreational opportunities to our winter scene.

MAKE TRACKS   a regional outline of cross-country skiing facilities.

SKIING IS BELIEVING   and it's downhill all the way. Highpoints on our principal Alpine areas.

JULY 1st JUBILATIONS   an events calendar listing the fairs, festivals and celebrations by community that mark our country's national day.

"Stoplights"

Bus-shelter display advertising will again be used in Metro Toronto to highlight special events throughout the spring/summer season. This medium is comparatively new, highly visible, and both graphic and informative.

Posters

A series of new travel posters has been developed, to carry the "Ontario—yours to discover!" message to travel agents and the travel trade and the travelling public. Subjects include Toronto, Niagara Falls, Fort William and fishing.

PROMOTION AND PUBLICITY

The promotion program will again support the advertising campaign by continuing to build awareness for the "Ontario—yours to discover!" logo and theme.

In 1982, the "yours to discover!" logo will appear on buttons, decals, postcards, plastic tote-bags, T-shirt transfers as well as T-shirts, and on specialized stationery items used at Ministry promotional and travel trade functions.

Ontario will again sponsor a special "yours to discover!" float in parades associated with regionally significant events.

The Visit Ontario Program, designed to acquaint print and broadcast journalists in Canada, the United States and Overseas with the province's attractions and facilities will continue. They will be selected on the basis of market and media importance.

Our editorial support program will take advantage of increased opportunities to have the media carry editorial features highlighting Ontario's attractions and facilities. Feature stories and photos will be distributed to key media on a regular basis.

In 1982 we will have five new films completed, featuring Toronto, Ottawa, Winter Activities, Fishing in Northern Ontario and Ontario Resorts. These films will be placed in distribution in Canada, U.S. and overseas.

The Ministry is participating in sport and travel shows in seven markets in the U.S., two in Ontario as well as the World Travel Market in London, England, and I.T.B. in Berlin.

The Ontario Tourism News will continue as an important bi-monthly information vehicle to members of the Tourism industry.

The major photographic program will continue to provide updated photography for all seasons across the province. It is being planned to meet specifically identified photographic requirements.

The program to inform Ontario and border state auto clubs of the desirability of Ontario as a tourism destination will continue. This involves familiarization tours, seminars and mailings.

THE MANITOBA CAMPAIGN

A combination of newspaper and radio advertising will be used to bring the "yours to discover!" invitation to Manitoba.

Advertising will focus on the immediately adjacent vacation areas of Ontario's Northwest, featuring fishing, camping and out-of-doors activities in the summer, fishing again in the fall, and skiing in the winter months.

THE QUEBEC MARKET

In 1980, a new campaign, geared to the theme of discovery, was launched in the Quebec market—and enthusiastically received. In 1981, and again in 1982, newspaper and radio will be used to highlight the availability of new French-language travel publications and an enlarged travel counselling service.

THE U.S. CAMPAIGN

Magazines

National editions of selected U.S. Magazines will be used to reach the better-educated up-scale audience which research has shown is most likely to make extended trips to Ontario.

Ad subjects include a wide range of wilderness activities, an introduction to Ontario's natural wonders, the many amenities and diversions of the resort experience, and the civilized appeals and foreign flavour of our major urban centres.

Outdoor Magazines

Magazine advertising will also be directed to U.S. (and Canadian) sport fishermen through a number of special-interest outdoor publications.

The messages highlight the services of our Northern resorts and fly-in fishing camps, as well as the special exhilaration of fishing on ice.

U.S. Newspaper

Within the radius of a day's drive from the Ontario border, newspaper and radio advertising are used to extend a warm and varied invitation to prospective U.S. visitors. And concurrent this year with the publication of the roto insert in Ontario, 7 major markets in these U.S. cities will receive a total of 4 million copies of the Ontario Yours to Discover tabloid insert.

A total of 15 newspaper ads will be placed, covering urban appeals, family attractions, tour possibilities, the pleasures of our resorts and wilderness, fall colour tours and winter recreational opportunities. Twelve of the fifteen ads will closely parallel domestic topics, with added 'incentive' information about the U.S. dollar premium.

Two ads have been created specifically for the U.S. market.

SAVE! SAVE! outlines in detail the great vacation values now available to American visitors, including the U.S. currency advantage and sales tax rebates.

C'MON OVER suggests a number of regional tour itineraries just across the border, ideal for day trips, weekends, or extended excursions.

U.S. Fall and Winter Newsprint

One Fall and four Winter newspaper ads will extend the invitation to sample our appeals all the year 'round.

U.S. Radio

Radio for 1982 will feature the newspaper insert to be distributed in early May, and again in January of 1983. This method was employed very successfully in Ontario and increases the effectiveness of the insert.

SPORT AND TRAVEL SHOWS

Newspaper ads are scheduled to run in selected North American cities hosting major sports and travel shows, listing Northern Ontario operators and outfitters participating in the shows.

In addition, the province's participation in international travel exhibitions will be highlighted beforehand in the Travel Trade press.

MEDIA 1982/83

A Media-mix of Television, Radio, Newspapers, Magazines and outdoor has been selected to achieve approximately 90% reach of all Adults 18+ in Ontario and designated areas in Manitoba, Quebec and the U.S.

Television offers the highest penetration of the target audience (95%) and because of the medium's intrusive characteristics, provides dramatic audio and visual exposure to the creative message. Variety in programs provides the opportunity for the selection of shows with a suitable environment.

Newspapers as a supporting medium, in addition to increasing the awareness of the television message, provide the outlet to supply more detailed information to motivate the traveller.

Radio, perceived as a personalized medium, offers a degree of control in audience selection according to time periods (e.g. 4:00–7:00 p.m.–Men; 10:00–3:00 p.m.–Women), and is an excellent retail device to generate interest in our newspaper insert.

Magazines offer excellent colour fidelity, long life after publication and the opportunity to schedule advertising opposite complementary editorial. A national magazine campaign reaches the affluent, upscale audience in markets where no other carrier vehicle is utilized.

MEDIA 1982/83 DOMESTIC & U.S. MEDIA				
Television	Newspapers	Radio	Magazines	Outdoor
Ontario U.S.	Ontario U.S. Quebec Manitoba	Ontario U.S. Quebec Manitoba	Ontario U.S.	Ontario

Outdoor (Stoplights) provides the opportunity to position the creative message in full colour at eye-level in the desired geographical location.

CUSTOMER SERVICE

A comprehensive consumer publication program ensures that information pertaining to vacation opportunities in the province is readily available to the prospective traveller.

Ministry Tourism publications are distributed to visitors through the Ministry's Travel Information Centres, recognized travel centres and travel associations within the province. They are also mailed in response to inquiries directed to Tourism Information at Queen's Park. Outside Ontario, they are available through offices of the Tourism Canada, auto clubs, and travel agencies.

TRAVELLER'S ENCYCLOPAEDIA is the basic travel information publication which describes in detail the 12 travel regions of Ontario, points of interest, attractions, events and suggested sightseeing routes to help travellers enjoy their trip to the fullest.

ACCOMMODATIONS provides information on facilities such as location, prices, pools, pets, etc. so that the traveller will have a wide variety of accommodation choices to suit his/her individual needs. A listing of Ontario Farm Vacations is also provided. 1982 marks the introduction of a comprehensive grading system. Properties graded will be identified and their grading noted.

CAMPING provides information on all the facilities at private and provincial campsites throughout the province. In addition, information is available on canoe trips and canoe packages as well as hiking, back-packing and camper rental facilities.

BOATING contains information on marina facilities with maps of specific water routes throughout the province and details of the things to see and do along these routes.

WINTER describes the location and facilities available for downhill skiing, cross-country skiing, ice-fishing, snowmobiling and winter camping.

EVENTS outlines, in four seasonal books, by event and date, a thousand things to see and do in Ontario.

ONTARIO OFFICIAL ROAD MAP themed to the "Yours to Discover!" promotion.

In 1982, to improve service, a system of TOLL FREE telephone numbers was introduced. Direct access to our Travel Counsellors from Continental North America is as simple as picking up the phone and dialing, at no expense to the customer. The numbers are: for calls originating from within Canada and outside the Toronto area, 1-800-268-3735; calls originating from within Continental U.S.A., excluding New York State, 1-800-828-8585; and calls originating from within New York State, 1-800-462-8404.

The network of Travel Counselling Centres will be expanded by the addition in June of a new Centre at Ontario Place. Located at the Centre Entrance approximately 75% of the entering traffic will have direct access to our counsellors.

The first out-of-province Travel Centre established in the U.K. continues to provide an ever increasing number of U.K. residents with travel information to Ontario.

Established in November of 1981, a radio Tourism Advisory service began beaming tourism information in the Sarnia area and across the border into Michigan. It is the first low frequency AM station of its kind located at 1150 on the radio dial. A continuous, 24 hour a day service, the station beams a taped message of highway regulations, differences between miles per hour and kilometres per hour, customs information and locates the local Travel Centre. Interspersed at regular intervals in the taped portion are live local segments with up to the minute road and weather conditions and events.

TELEGUIDE FOR TOURISTS

In 1982, the Ontario Tourism campaign will be adding a new feature, Teleguide, which makes Ontario even more accessible. An innovative Canadian development, offered free to the public in the Toronto area, Teleguide is a system of transmitting tourist information to publicly located video terminals from a central computer. The computer holds 50,000 pages of information covering every area of possible interest to tourists. Teleguide will become a major force in bringing knowledge of Ontario's many attractions to both tourists and residents alike.

TRAVEL TRADE

An entirely new four-colour campaign will be directed at North American Travel Agents and group travel planners themed in the vein of "Ontario—yours to discover!"

The Trade campaign, directed to Travel Agents in particular, will highlight the availability of the Travel Trade Manual, and describe in detail the wide range of vacation packages and touring possibilities now available. Individual ads will focus on urban visitor facilities and wilderness travel experiences, unique to Ontario, and now packaged for profit.

In 1981, the Travel Trade Division of the Ministry of Industry & Tourism substantially enlarged its promotional efforts geared to the growing mass travel modes.

Tourism officers, dealing directly with the trade, are stationed in the Ministry's seven offices, in the major international markets of Asia, Europe and the U.S. And to give them higher visibility and greater accessibility, advertisements for these markets will feature these people, their offices and phone numbers.

Backing the trade, consumer vacation planners have been produced in Dutch, English, French, German and Japanese.

In 1982, this expanded effort continues.

Our flagship publications to the Travel Agents (Travel Trade Manual) and to convention planners (Convention & Meeting Guide) have been redesigned and updated with new offerings.

The Convention and Meeting Campaign outlines the advantages of meeting in our larger urban centres, our smaller cities and towns, and the particular pleasures of a get-together in a resort setting.

Pehaps the most exciting developments for 1982 lie overseas, where new four-colour trade advertising, developed in close consultation with the Ministry's on-the-ground personnel, will be placed in England, Holland, West Germany and Japan.

The individual messages have been tailored to the widely varied interests of the individual markets—and cover natural wonders, the lure of the wide open spaces, the sophisticated entertainments of our major urban centres, and a range of vacation experiences found only in Ontario.

A spot-colour trade campaign has been developed for the French market. A vacation of contrasts with accessible natural experiences and the urban appeals of our cities, Ontario makes a unique alternative to this market of varied interests.

OVERSEAS CONSUMER CAMPAIGN

Consumer ad campaigns for '82 will be launched in selected publications in the United Kingdom and West Germany.

These ads will invite prospective travellers to find out more about the large and growing number of package plans, fly-drive itineraries, and the houseboat and motorhome vacations.

The West German and United Kingdom ads again will feature write-in coupons for comprehensive information on all available package tours.

INDEX

Air New England, 165
Air Traffic Conference, 415,
420-21
Air Transport Association, U.S.,
166, 275
Air Transport Committee,
Canadian, 279
Alaska, 166
Algarve, 178
Algeria, 243
Algoma Central Railway, 156
Alhambra, the, 193
Allocentrics, 265
Alma Highland Games, 209
American Airlines, 165
American Express, 403
Amsterdam, 192, 193
Amtrak, 155, 167, 394, 415
Analogy research, 331
Angkor Wat, Cambodia, 195
Antiope, 422
Architectural impacts of
tourism, 233
Argentina, 185
Arizona, 138, 209
Arkansas, 209
Arlington Cemetery,
Washington, 208
Aruba, 115
Asia, 290, 394
Aspen, 204
Assemblies (*see* Meetings,
conventions, congresses)
Association convention market
(*see* Institutional
meetings, conventions
and congresses)
Association of American
Geographers, 174
Athens, 192
Atlantic City, 115, 177
Atlantic Provinces, 137, 158
Attractions:

accessibility, 209-10
climate, 206-7
culture, 207
development and design,
210-11
ethnicity, 209
events, 211
historical attractions, 191-95
historical resources, 207-9
natural resources, 205-6
theme parks, 116, 197, 211
typology of attractions (*table*),
203
Auschwitz, 195
Australia, 73, 127, 187-88, 371,
390, 372
Goldcoast, 181
Austria, 33, 120, 185, 208
Automation in travel agency
business, 417-8
Automobile travel, 20-21, 137,
140, 146, 158-62, 169, 170
attractive attributes, 159-60
automobile-based travel
system era, 149 (*see also*
Energy crisis)
Auvergne, 299
Awareness:
community awareness
programs, 219-20

Bahamas, 115, 131
rain insurance, 31
Balearic Islands, 178
Baltic Sea, 177
Banaras, 195
Banff, Canada, 278
Bankok, 194
Bangladesh, 195
Barbados, 131

12 8 13